遗 传 学

Genetics

[加] Michael K. Deyholos　王傲雪　[加] Jian Zhang　编著

科 学 出 版 社
北 京

内 容 简 介

遗传学是生物学专业，以及农、林、医、师范类院校相关专业的核心课程之一。本书中英文对照，语言精练，通俗易懂，并配有大量经典图片，具有很强的针对性和可读性。全书既反映遗传学的基本原理、兼顾该学科的最新进展，同时又考虑到以遗传学作为基础课程的相关专业本科生的中英文阅读能力和理解能力，在知识体系上按照单基因、两个基因、多基因及分子遗传，以及基因调控的前后顺序，逐步进行遗传分析和讲解，并在各章后配有小结、关键术语和综合性思考题，便于学生整体掌握内容和增强对内容的理解，提高学生的创新性和逻辑性思维能力。书中彩图可扫描对应二维码显示。

本书可作为生物学相关专业，特别是以遗传学作为基础课程的农、林、医类院校和师范院校相关专业本科生和研究生的遗传学双语教材，也可作为从事遗传学教学的教师、科研人员和对生命科学感兴趣的读者的参考用书。

图书在版编目(CIP)数据

遗传学= Genetics：英汉对照/ (加) 戴豪勒斯 (Deyholos, M. K.)，王傲雪，(加)张健编著. —北京：科学出版社，2013

ISBN 978-7-03-038343-3

Ⅰ. ①遗… Ⅱ. ①戴… ②王… ③张… Ⅲ.①遗传学-双语教学-高等学校-教材-英、汉 Ⅳ. ①Q3

中国版本图书馆 CIP 数据核字(2013)第 191615 号

责任编辑：席 慧 / 责任校对：宣 慧

责任印制：张 伟 / 封面设计：迷底书装

科 学 出 版 社 出版

北京东黄城根北街 16 号

邮政编码：100717

http://www.sciencep.com

北京凌奇印刷有限责任公司 印刷

科学出版社发行 各地新华书店经销

*

2013 年 9 月第 一 版 开本：787×1092 1/16

2023 年 7 月第六次印刷 印张：14 1/4

字数：374 000

定价：59.80 元

（如有印装质量问题，我社负责调换）

前言（PREFACE）

进入新千年以来，随着新技术、新方法、新学科的发展，遗传学进入了新的发展阶段。每每通过科研和阅读文献材料感受遗传学上的新发现、新进展时，都不禁惊叹于遗传基因的奥秘和生命的精彩。然而，很多时候专业人士由于语言的限制，不能领略到国际上的最新进展，或者因为专业术语不熟，阅读英文文章较为吃力，从而影响对遗传、基因和生命相关文献的理解。随着科学研究和生物学及相关产业的国际化程度越来越高，对生物学及相关专业本科生的语言能力要求也越来越高。怎样提高本科生的专业外语水平是我们目前亟待解决的问题。原版教材阅读起来相对难度大，在一定程度上影响了本科的教学质量。而且，遗传学是生物学及农、林、医学的核心和重要的基础课程之一。为了更好地适应遗传学双语教学的需求，达到既掌握英语专业术语，培养学生的语言习惯，同时又能系统和全面地掌握遗传学原理和知识的目的，我们编写了本书。本书的编写源于我们和 Alberta 大学 Deyholos 教授、Alberta 研究院 Jian Zhang 研究员多年来在遗传学教学和科研上的合作与交流。全书力图反映遗传学的基本原理，并且兼顾该学科的最新进展，同时又考虑了本科生，特别是农、林、医、师范类院校以遗传学作为基础课程的相关专业学生的阅读能力和理解能力。书中英文由以英语为母语的加拿大教授编写，采用了通俗易懂的语言进行简明而又系统地论述，既利于专业知识的传授又便于英语专业术语的掌握。

本书紧紧以经典遗传学为主线，进行了遗传学知识的讲述和分析。具体来说，主要有以下几个特点：①注重遗传学基本原理的讲述，这是遗传学的精髓和基础；②注重遗传学与实际生活中例子的结合，增强学生的学习兴趣；③注重从实验到科学理论及科学理论指导实验的研究实践过程，提高学生分析问题的能力；④注重通过遗传分析培养学生解决问题的能力；⑤内容尽量避免与基因工程、生物化学、分子生物学等课程重复的部分，但保留遗传学的完整性和系统性；⑥注重英语与汉语的对称结构和表达习惯的结合，实现学生迅速掌握英语术语的目的；⑦教学体系上注重从一个位点到两个位点再到多个位点及分子水平上调控，以及系统遗传分析的理念的过程，使整个教材由浅入深，由简入繁，让学生逐渐深入其中，构建遗传学的知识体系。

全书内容共分 12 章，包括概论，染色体、有丝分裂与减数分裂，一个位点的遗传学分析，突变与变异，系谱与群体，两个位点的遗传学分析，连锁与作图，分子生物学技术，分子标记与数量性状，基因组学与系统生物学，基因表达调控，癌症遗传学等。

本书可作为综合性院校，农、林、医类院校和师范院校生物学相关专业，特别是以遗传学作为基础课程的本科生的遗传学双语教材，也可作为从事遗传学教学的教师及相关科研人员、研究生的参考用书。

本书在编写过程中参考了国内外相关教材和研究成果，同时在出版过程中得到了科学出版社的大力支持，在此一并表示感谢。由于时间关系和水平有限，书中疏漏之处在所难免，敬请读者在使用过程中提出批评和意见，以便再版时完善。

编　者

2013 年 7 月

CONTENTS

目 录

Chapter 1

INTRODUCTION 概论

Bears' offspring look like their parents (see the cover)
熊的子代与亲代相似（见封面）

Why do offspring look like their parents? Even ancient people were aware that the characteristics of an individual plant or animal could be passed between generations. They also knew that some heritable characteristics (such as the

为什么子女们看起来像他们的父母？甚至古人也意识到一个植物或动物个体的特征会在世代之间传递。他们还知道一些遗传特征（如果实的

size of fruit) varied between individuals, and that they could select for the most favorable traits while breeding crops and animals. The once prevalent (but now discredited) concept of **blending inheritance** proposed that some undefined essence, in its entirety, contained all of the heritable information for an individual. Much like the mixing of two colors of paint, it was thought that mating combined the essences from each parent. Once blended together, the individual characteristics of the parents could not be separated again.

大小）在个体之间会有所变化，并且他们在培育农作物和动物时会选择最有利的性状。曾经流行的**融合遗传**概念（但是现在证实是错误的）提出一个不明确的本质，该本质全面地包括一个个体所有的可遗传的信息。该概念认为交配将父母的本质结合了，就像将两种颜色的染料混合。一旦融合，父母的个体特征不可能再被分开。

GENES ARE UNITS OF INHERITANCE 基因是遗传的单位

Mendel was one of the first to take a scientific approach to the study of heredity (Figure 1.1). He started with well-characterized materials, repeated his experiments many times, and kept careful records of his observations. Working with peas, Mendel showed that white-flowered plants could be produced by crossing two purple-flowered plants, but only if the purple-flowered plants themselves had at least one white-flowered parent (Figure 1.2). This was evidence that the genetic factor that produced white-flowers had *not* blended irreversibly with the factor for purple-flowers. Mendel's observations helped to disprove blending inheritance, in favor of an alternative concept called **particulate inheritance**, in which heredity is the

孟德尔是早期采用科学的方法研究遗传的人（图 1.1）。他以特征很清晰的材料开始研究，多次重复试验，仔细记录他所观察到的结果。例如，以豌豆作为材料，孟德尔证明了两个紫花植株杂交能产生白花植株，但是只有在紫花植株本身至少有一个白花作为父母本的情况下才能得到这样的结果（图 1.2）。证据表明，产生白花的遗传因子没有不可逆转地与紫花的遗传因子融合。孟德尔的观察推翻了融合遗传，取而代之的是被称为**颗粒遗传**的概念，遗传

Figure 1.1 Gregor Mendel
图 1.1 格雷戈尔 · 孟德尔

product of discrete factors that control independent traits. Each hereditary factor could exist in one or more different versions, or **alleles**.

是控制独立性状的离散因子的产物。每个遗传因子能够以一个或多个不同的形式或者**等位基因**存在。

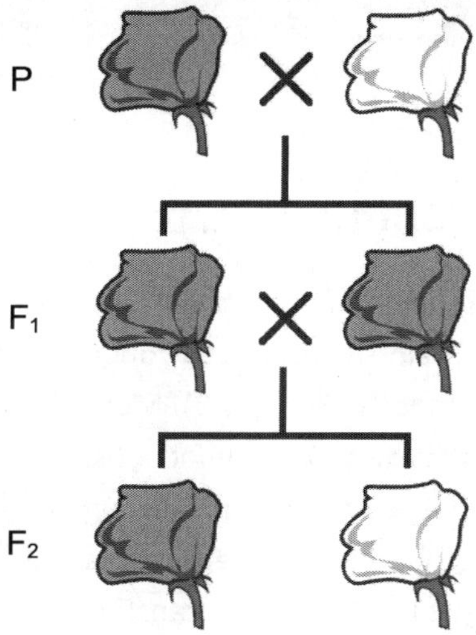

Figure 1.2 Inheritance of flower color in peas. Mendel observed that a cross between pure breeding,white and purple peas (generation P) (grayish color stands for purple color) produced only progeny (generation F_1) with purple flowers. However, white flowered plant reappeared among the F_2 generation progeny of a mating between two F_1 plants. The symbols P, F_1 and F_2 are abbreviations for parental, first filial, and second filial generations, respectively

图 1.2 豌豆花色的遗传。孟德尔观察纯育系之间的一个杂交，白花豌豆和紫花豌豆（P 世代）（图中浅灰色代表紫色）只会产生紫花的后代。然而，白花植株在两个 F_1 植株杂交产生的 F_2 世代中又重新出现了。符号 P、F_1 和 F_2 分别是亲本、子一代和子二代的缩写

Mendel's discrete factors of heredity later became known as **genes**. In its narrowest definition, a gene is an abstract concept: a unit of inheritance. The connection between genes and substances like DNA and chromosomes was established largely through the experiments described in the remainder of this chapter. However, it is worth noting that Mendel and many researchers who followed him were able to provide great insights into biology, simply by observing the inheritance of specific traits.

孟德尔的离散遗传因子后来被称为**基因**。狭义上讲，基因是抽象的概念：遗传的单位。基因与 DNA 和染色体等物质之间的联系，主要是通过在本章其他部分描述的实验建立起来的。然而，值得关注的是，孟德尔和追随他的许多研究人员仅仅通过观察特殊性状的遗传就能够深入地洞察生物学理论。

DNA IS THE GENETIC MATERIAL DNA 是遗传物质

By the early 1900's, biochemists had isolated hundreds of

到了 20 世纪早期，生物化学学家已

different chemicals from living cells. Which of these was the genetic material? Proteins seemed like promising candidates, since they were abundant and complex molecules. However, a few key experiments helped to prove that DNA, rather than protein, is the genetic material.

经从活体细胞中分离出数百种不同的化学物质。这些物质中到底哪一种才是遗传物质呢？蛋白质看起来很像，因为它们不仅数量庞大而且是很复杂的分子。然而，一些关键性的实验证实了 DNA 是遗传物质，而非蛋白质。

Griffith's experiment　Griffith 的试验

Microbiologists identified two strains of the bacterium *Streptococcus pneumoniae*. One strain (R) produced rough colonies, while the other (S) was smooth (Figure 1.3). More importantly, the S-type bacteria caused fatal infections, while the R-type did not. **Griffith** noticed that simply mixing the strains together could transform some R-type bacteria into smooth, pathogenic strains (Figure 1.4). This transformation occurred even when the S-type strains were first killed by heat. Thus, some component of the S-type strains contained genetic information that could be transferred to the R-type strains.

微生物学家已经确定了细菌性肺炎链球菌的两个株系。一个株系（R 型）产生粗糙型的菌落，而另外一个株系（S 型）产生光滑型的菌落（图 1.3）。更重要的是，S 型的细菌感染是致命的，R 型则不会。**Griffith** 注意到通过将菌株混合在一起会将一些 R 型的细菌转化成光滑型的致病菌株（图 1.4），甚至当 S 型的菌株预先通过加热被杀死后也会发生这种转化。因此，S 型菌株中有一些成分包含能够被转移到 R 型菌株的遗传信息。

Figure 1.3　Colonies of Rough (top) and Smooth (bottom) strains of *S. pneumoniae*

图 1.3　粗糙型（上图）和光滑型（下图）肺炎链球菌的菌落

Avery, MacLeod and McCarty's experiment

Avery、MacLeod 和 McCarty 的试验

What kind of molecule from within the S-type cells was responsible for the transformation? To answer this, researchers named **Avery, MacLeod** and **McCarty** separated the S-type cells into various components, such as proteins,

在 S 型细胞内什么类型的分子对转化起作用？为了回答该问题，研究人员 **Avery**、**MacLeod** 和 **McCarty** 从 S 型细胞分离出多种成分，如蛋

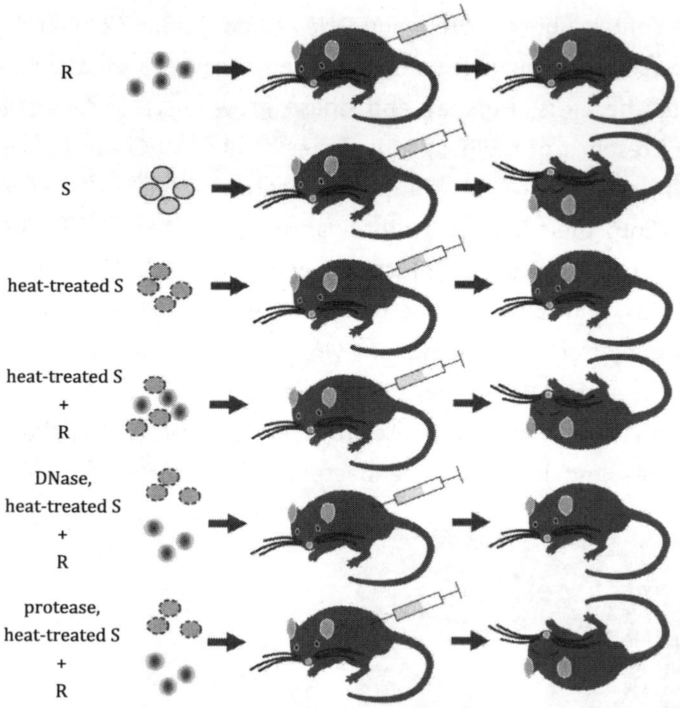

Figure 1.4 Experiments of Griffith and of Avery , MacLeod and McCarty. R strains of *S. pneumoniae* do not cause lethality. However, DNA-containing extracts from pathogenic S strains are sufficient to make R strains pathogenic

图 1.4 Griffith 和 Avery 及 MacLeod 和 McCarty 的试验。肺炎链球菌 R 型菌株不会致病。然而，S 型致病菌株的 DNA 提取物使得 R 型菌株具有致病性

polysaccharides, lipids, and nucleic acids. Only the nucleic acids from S-type cells were able to make the R-strains smooth and fatal. Furthermore, when cellular extracts of S-type cells were treated with DNase (an enzyme that digests DNA), the transformation ability was lost. The researchers therefore concluded that DNA was the genetic material, which in this case controlled the appearance and pathogenicity of the bacteria.

白质、多糖、脂质和核酸等。只有 S 型细胞里的核酸能使 R 型菌落变得光滑并且能够致命。而且，当 S 型细胞的细胞提取物用 DNA 酶处理（消化 DNA 的酶）后，转化能力就丧失了。研究人员因此推断出 DNA 是遗传物质，在这个试验中 DNA 控制了细菌的表观特征和致病性。

Hershey and Chase's experiment

Hershey 和 Chase 的试验

Further evidence that DNA is the genetic material came from experiments conducted by **Hershey** and **Chase**. These researchers studied the transmission of genetic information from a virus called the T2 bacteriophage to its host bacterium, *Escherichia coli* (Figure 1.5). Like all viruses, T2 hijacks the cellular machinery of its host to manufacture more vi-

进一步证明DNA是遗传物质的证据来自 **Hershey 和 Chase** 的实验。他们研究了叫做 T2 噬菌体的病毒对宿主大肠杆菌遗传信息的转移（图 1.5）。同所有病毒一样，T2 劫持其宿主的细胞机器来制造更多的病

ruses. The T2 phage contains both protein and DNA. To determine which of these types of molecules contained the genetic blueprint for the virus, Hershey and Chase grew viral cultures in the presence of radioactive isotopes of either phosphorus (^{32}P) or sulphur (^{35}S). The phage incorporated these isotopes into their DNA and proteins, respectively (Figure 1.6). The researchers then infected *E. coli* with the radiolabeled viruses, and looked to see whether ^{32}P or ^{35}S entered the bacteria. After ensuring that any viruses had been removed from the surface of the cells, the researchers observed that infection with ^{32}P labeled viruses (but not the ^{35}S labeled viruses) resulted in radioactive bacteria. This

毒。T2 噬菌体含有蛋白质和 DNA。为了确定这些分子类型中哪种分子包含病毒的全部遗传信息，Hershey 和 Chase 在放射性同位素磷（^{32}P）或硫（^{35}S）存在的条件下培养病毒，让这些放射性同位素分别标记病毒的 DNA 和蛋白质（图 1.6）。然后，研究人员用有放射标记的病毒感染大肠杆菌，看是否有 ^{32}P 或者 ^{35}S 进入了细菌。在确保任何病毒已经从细菌细胞表面移除后，研究人员观察到仅仅被 ^{32}P 标记的病毒（而

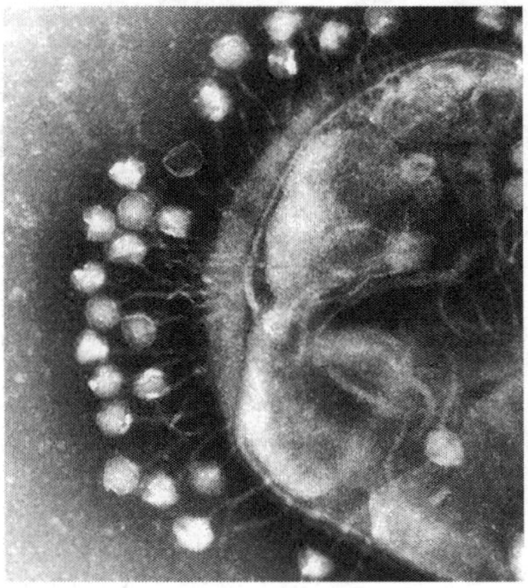

Figure 1.5 Electron micrograph of T2 bacteriophage on surface of *E. coli*

图 1.5 大肠杆菌表面 T2 噬菌体的电镜显微照片

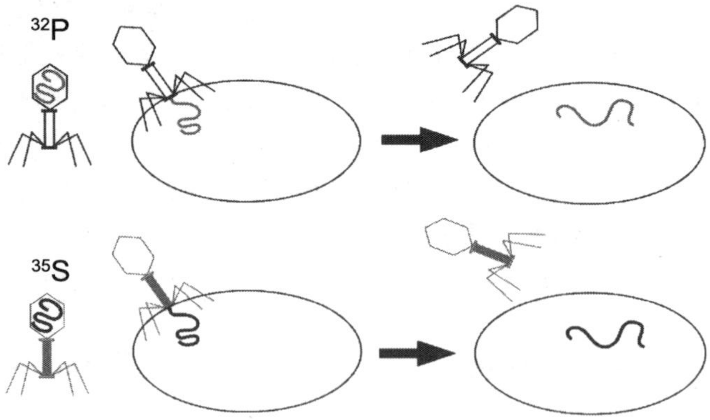

Figure 1.6 When ^{32}P-labeled phage infects *E. coli*, radioactivity is found only in the bacteria, after the phage are removed by agitation and centrifugation. In contrast, after infection with ^{35}S-labeled phage, radioactivity is found only in the supernatant that remains after the bacteria are removed

图 1.6 当标记有 ^{32}P 的噬菌体侵染大肠杆菌后，通过搅动和离心，噬菌体被移除后能在细菌中发现放射性。相反，当标记有 ^{35}S 的噬菌体侵染后，在细菌被移除后，残留的上清液中发现了放射性

demonstrated that DNA was the material that contained genetic instructions.

不是 ^{35}S 标记的病毒）感染的细菌中产生了放射性细菌。这个试验再一次证明了 DNA 是遗传物质。

THE FUNCTION OF GENES 基因的功能

Beadle and Tatum's Experiment Beadle 和 Tatum 的试验

Life depends on metabolism to supply energy and to produce the molecules that make cells. In 1941, **Beadle** and **Tatum** demonstrated the connection between genes and metabolic pathways. Their results led to the "**one gene, one protein**" principle, which states that each of the enzymes that acts in a biochemical pathway is encoded by a different gene. Although we now know of many exceptions to this model, it is generally true that each gene produces a protein that has a particular catalytic, regulatory, or structural function. Beadle and Tatum's experiments are important because of this conceptual advance and also because they demonstrate the utility of **mutant screening**.

生命依靠代谢供给能量和产生构成细胞的分子。1941 年，**Beadle** 和 **Tatum** 证实了基因与代谢途径的联系。他们的试验结果提出了“**一个基因一个蛋白质**”原理，即在生物化学途径中起作用的酶由不同的基因编码。虽然现在我们知道有很多例外的情况，但一般来讲，一个基因能够产生一种有特定催化活性、调控或结构功能的蛋白质。Beadle 和 Tatum 的试验是非常重要的，不仅因为它发展了这个概念，还因为他们论证了**突变体筛选**的作用。

Beadle and Tatum and their colleagues Srb and Horowitz were interested in the metabolic pathways that produce amino acids. They used the fungus ***Neurospora crassa*** (a mold) for their studies because it had practical advantages as a laboratory subject. The researchers knew that *Neurospora* was **prototrophic** for most amino acids, meaning that it could synthesize amino acids from minimal medium, which lacked most nutrients except for simple sugars and a few vitamins and minerals. They also knew that by exposing *Neurospora* to X-rays, they could randomly damage its DNA. Each spore that was exposed to X-rays potentially contained a mutation in a different gene. Some mutations changed *Neurospora* into an **auxotroph**, which would no longer grow on minimal medium, but which did grow on complete medium supplemented with all of the amino acids (Figure 1.7). Importantly, the researchers tested the ability of individual

Beadle 和 Tatum 及他们的同事 Srb 和 Horowitz 对产生氨基酸的代谢途径感兴趣。他们用真菌**粗糙链孢霉**（一种霉菌）做研究，因为这种霉菌有作为实验材料的优势。研究者知道链孢霉对于大多数氨基酸是**原养型**的，即它能够在缺乏大多数营养成分而在只包括简单的糖和少量维生素及矿物质的基本培养基上自己合成氨基酸。他们还知道把链孢霉暴露在 X 射线下能够随机地破坏它的 DNA。被暴露在 X 射线下的每个孢子潜在地包含不同基因的突变。一些突变把链孢霉变成了**营养缺陷型**，不能在基本培养基上生长，但是能够在添加所有氨基酸的完全

amino acids to rescue the auxotrophs: they added one of each of the amino acids to minimal medium and recorded which of these restored growth to independent mutants. For example, if the progeny of a mutagenized spore could grow on minimal medium only when it was supplemented with arginine (Arg), then the auxotroph must bear a mutation in the Arg biosynthetic pathway.

培养基上生长（图 1.7）。重要的是，研究者检测了单个氨基酸恢复营养缺陷型生长的能力：他们分别加了各种氨基酸的一种到基本培养基上，记录恢复独立突变体生长的培养基。例如，如果突变孢子后代能够在仅仅添加精氨酸的基本培养基上生长，该营养缺陷型必然在精氨酸生物合成途径中发生了突变。

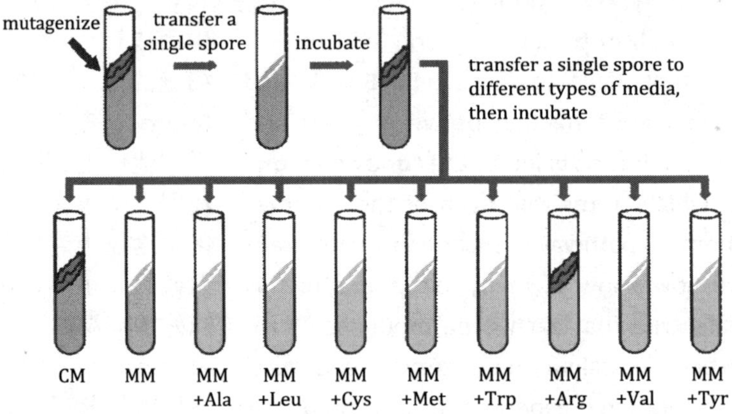

Figure 1.7　A single mutagenized spore is used to establish a colony of genetically identical fungi, from which spores are tested for their ability to grow on different types of media. Because spores of this particular colony are able to grown only on complete medium (CM), or on miminal medium supplemented with arginine (MM+Arg), they are considered Arg auxotrophs and we infer that they have a mutation in a gene in the Arg biosynthetic pathway. This type of screen has been repeated many times to identify other mutants in the Arg pathway and in other pathways

图 1.7　一个单个突变的孢子被用来建立一个遗传上一致的真菌菌落，菌落中的孢子被验证它们具有在不同类型培养基生长的能力。因为特定菌落的孢子仅能够在完全培养基（CM）上或在添加精氨酸的基本培养基（MM）上生长，这些孢子被认为是精氨酸营养缺陷型，并且我们推断它们在精氨酸合成途径中有一个基因发生了突变。这种类型的筛选已经被开展了很多次，用来鉴定精氨酸途径和其他途径中的突变体

Synthesis of even a relatively simple molecule such as Arg requires many different enzymes. Each enzyme works sequentially on a different intermediate in the pathway (Figure 1.8). For Arg, two of the intermediates are called ornithine (Orn) and citrulline (Cit). In theory, mutation of any one of the enzymes in this pathway could turn *Neurospora* into an Arg auxotroph. The researchers extended their analysis by testing the ability of intermediates of amino acid biosynthesis to restore growth of mutants (Figure 1.9). They found that some of the Arg auxotrophs could be rescued

即使一个相对简单的分子（如精氨酸）也需要许多不同酶的作用。每一种酶在途径中对不同的中间产物依次作用（图 1.8）。对于精氨酸来说，两个中间产物分别是鸟氨酸（Orn）和瓜氨酸（Cit）。理论上，这个途径中的任何一个酶的突变都能把链孢霉变成精氨酸营养缺陷型。研究者把他们的分析用于验证氨基酸生物合成的中间产物恢复突

only by Arg, others could be rescued by either Arg or Cit, and still other mutants could be rescued by Arg, Cit, or Orn (Table 1.1). Based on these results, they could deduce the location of each mutation in the Arg biochemical pathway, i.e. which gene was responsible for the metabolism of which intermediate.

变体生长的能力上（图 1.9）。他们发现一些精氨酸营养缺陷型仅仅能被精氨酸恢复生长，其他一些突变体能被精氨酸或鸟氨酸恢复生长，另外一些突变体能够被精氨酸、鸟氨酸或瓜氨酸恢复生长（表 1.1）。基于这些结果，他们能推断出在精氨酸生化途径中每个突变的位置，即哪个基因用于哪个中间产物的代谢。

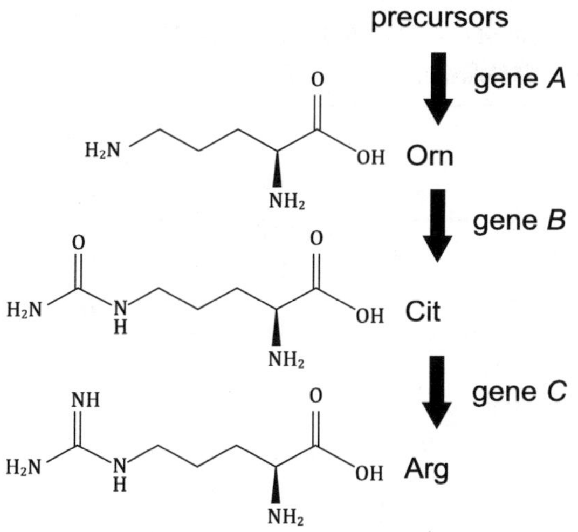

Figure 1.8 A simplified version of the Arg biosynthetic pathway, showing citrulline (Cit) and ornithine (Orn) as intermediates in Arg metabolism. These chemical reactions depend on enzymes represented here as the products of three different genes

图 1.8 一个精氨酸合成的简化途径，显示瓜氨酸（Cit）和鸟氨酸（Orn）作为精氨酸代谢的中间产物。这些化学反应依赖于 3 个不同基因产生的酶

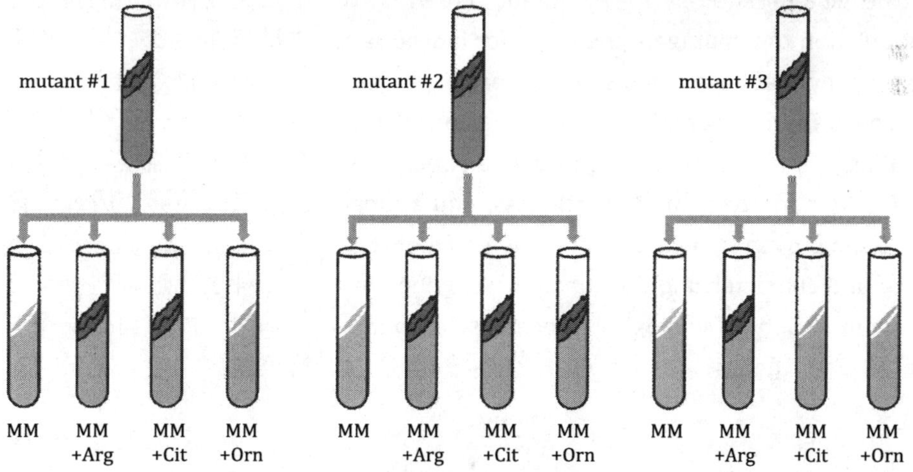

Figure 1.9 Testing different Arg auxotrophs for their ability to grow on media supplemented with intermediates in the Arg biosynthetic pathway

图 1.9 在培养基中加入精氨酸合成途径中的中间产物，以检测中间产物对不同精氨酸缺陷株的生长能力的影响

Table 1.1 Ability of auxotrophic mutants of each of the three enzymes of the Arg biosynthetic pathways to grow on minimal medium (MM) supplemented with Arg or either of its precursors, Orn and Cit. Gene names refer to the labels used in Figure 1.8

mutant	MM + Orn	MM + Cit	MM + Arg
gene A	**Yes**	**Yes**	**Yes**
gene B	No	**Yes**	**Yes**
gene C mutants	No	No	**Yes**

表 1.1 精氨酸生物合成途径中 3 种酶营养缺陷型突变体在分别添加精氨酸、前体瓜氨酸和鸟氨酸的基本培养基上生长的能力。基因名称参照图 1.8 用的标识

突变体	MM + Orn	MM + Cit	MM + Arg
基因 *A*	**能**	**能**	**能**
基因 *B*	不能	**能**	**能**
基因 *C* 突变体	不能	不能	**能**

Mutant screening helps characterize genes

突变体筛选有助于描述基因特征

Beadle and Tatum's experiments paved the way for the genetic dissection of many biochemical and developmental pathways. The general strategy for a mutant screen is to expose a population to a mutagen, then look for individuals among the progeny that have defects in a biological process of interest. There are many details that must be considered when designing a mutant screen (e.g. how can recessive alleles be made homozygous). Nevertheless, mutational analysis has been proven to be a powerful and efficient tool in identifying and characterizing the functions of genes related to a wide variety of biological processes, including many disease-related genes.

Beadle 和 Tatum 的试验为许多生化和发育途径的遗传解析铺平了道路。突变体筛选的策略是把一个群体暴露在突变剂下，然后寻找在感兴趣的生物过程中有缺陷的后代个体。当设计一个突变体筛选试验时有许多细节需要考虑（如隐性等位基因怎么能够变成纯合体）。然而，突变分析已经被证实在鉴定和阐明与多种生物过程包括许多疾病相关的基因功能方面是一个强大而有效的工具。

THE STRUCTURE OF DNA　DNA 的结构

The experiments outlined in the previous sections proved that DNA was the genetic material, but very little was known about its structure.

前面讲述的试验证明了 DNA 是遗传物质，但是对它的结构知之甚少。

Chargaff's rules Chargaff 规则

When **Watson** and **Crick** set out in the 1940's to determine the structure of DNA, it was already known that DNA is made up of four different types of molecules, called bases or nucleotides: adenine (A), cytosine (C), thymine (T), guanine (G). Watson and Crick also knew of **Chargaff's Rules**, which were a set of observations about the relative amount of each nucleotide that was present in almost any extract of DNA. Chargaff had observed that for any given species, the abundance of A was the same as T, and G was the same as C. Using metal models of the individual nucleotides, Watson and Crick were able to deduce a structure for DNA that was consistent with Chargaff's Rules and with X-ray crystallography data that was obtained (with some controversy) from another researcher, Rosalind Franklin.

当沃森和克里克在 20 世纪 40 年代开始研究 DNA 的结构时，他们知道 DNA 是由 4 种不同类型的分子组成的，被称为碱基或核苷酸：腺嘌呤 (A)、胞嘧啶 (C)、胸腺嘧啶 (T)、鸟嘌呤 (G)。他们也知道 **Chargaff 规则**，通过对几乎任何 DNA 的每种核苷酸相对数量的大量观察，Chargaff 观察到碱基 A 同 T 的含量相等，G 同 C 的含量相等。通过使用个体核苷酸的金属模型，沃森和克里克能够推断出与 Chargaff 规则和从另一个研究者罗莎琳德•富兰克林获得的 X 射线结晶照片数据（有一些争议）相一致的 DNA 结构。

The double helix 双螺旋结构

In Watson and Crick's famous double helix, each of the two strands contains DNA bases connected through covalent bonds to a sugar-phosphate backbone (Figure 1.10, Figure 1.11). Because one side of each sugar molecule is always connected to the opposite side of the next sugar molecule, each strand of DNA has polarity: these are called the 5' (5-prime) end and the 3' (3-prime) end, in accordance with the nomenclature of the carbons in the sugars. The two strands of the double helix run in anti-parallel (i.e. opposite) directions, with the 5' end of one strand adjacent to the 3' end of the other strand. The double helix has a **right-handed** twist, (rather than the left-handed twist that is often represented in popular media). The DNA bases extend from the backbone towards the center of the helix, with a pair of bases from each strand forming hydrogen bonds that help to hold the two strands together. Under most conditions, the two strands are slightly offset, which creates a major groove on one face of the double helix, and a minor groove on the other. Because of the structure of the bases, A can only form hydrogen bonds with T, and G

在沃森和克里克的著名双螺旋结构中，两条链中的每一条链的 DNA 碱基是通过共价键连接到磷酸糖骨架上的（图 1.10，图 1.11）。因为每个糖分子的一侧总是连到下一个糖分子的反侧，所以 DNA 的每条链是有极性的：这些极性末端被称为 5'端（5-prime）和 3'端（3-prime），与在糖中的碳的命名法一致。双螺旋的两条链反向平行（即相反），一条链的 5'端与另一条链的 3'端毗邻。双螺旋**右向**旋转（而不是经常所说的左向旋转）。DNA 碱基从骨架延长到螺旋的中心，两条链中相对应的碱基形成氢键使得两条链连接在一起。在大多数情况下，两条链轻微的弯转，在双螺旋的一面形成一个大沟，在另一面形成一个小沟。由于碱基的结构，A 只能与 T 形成氢键，G 只能与 C 形成氢键（Chargaff

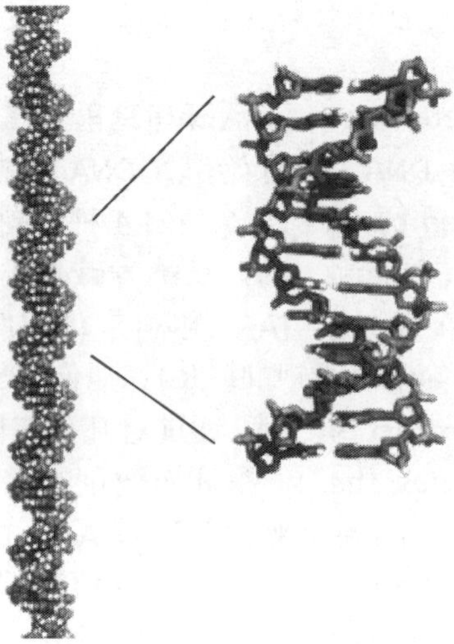

Figure 1.10 DNA structure

图 1.10 DNA 结构

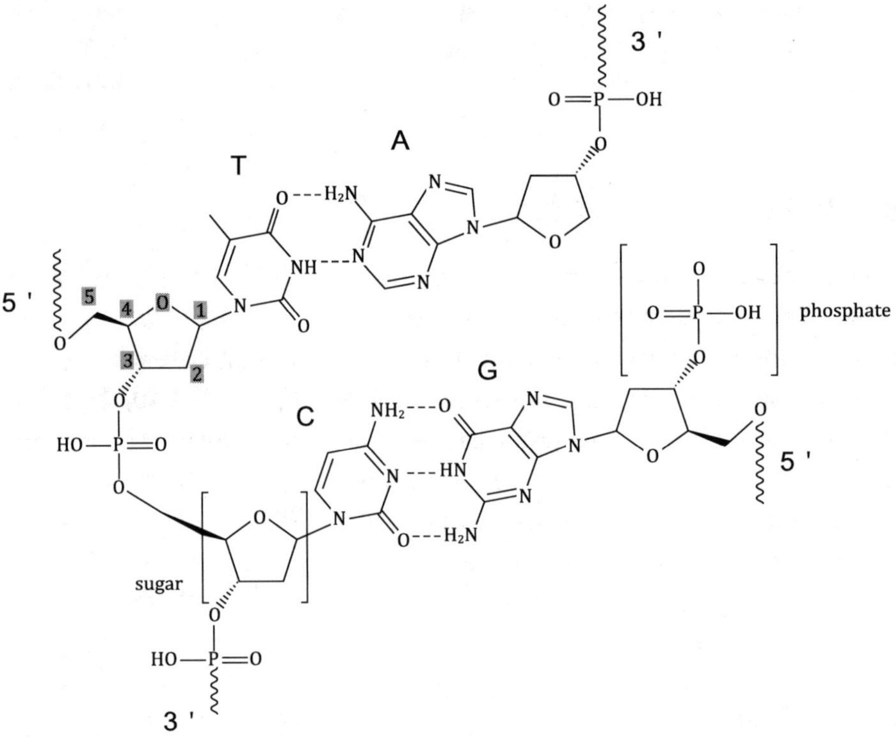

Figure 1.11 Chemical structure of two pairs of nucleotides in a fragment of double-stranded DNA. Sugar, phosphate, and bases A,C,G,T are labeled. Hydrogen bonds between bases on opposite strands are shown by dashed lines. Note that the G-C pair has more hydrogen bonds than A-T. The numbering of carbons within sugars is indicated by shaded numbers. Based on this numbering the polarity of each strand is indicated by the labels 5′and 3′

图 1.11 一个双链 DNA 片段中两对核苷酸的化学结构。图中标注了糖、磷酸和 A、C、G、T 碱基。反向链碱基之间的氢键以虚线显示。注意 G-C 对比 A-T 对有更多的氢键。糖中碳的编号用加阴影数字显示出来。根据编号每条链的极性通过标注 5′和 3′表示

can only form hydrogen bonds with C (hence, Chargaff's Rules). Each strand is therefore said to be complementary to the other, and each strand also contains enough information to replace the other. This redundancy is important in repairing DNA, and also in its replication.

规则）。因此每条链与另一条链互补，并且每条链也包含替代另一条链的足够信息。这种冗余在 DNA 修复和复制中是很重要的。

The Central Dogma 中 心 法 则

How does the structure of DNA relate to inheritance of biological traits such as the flower color of Mendel's peas? The answer to this lies in what has become known as molecular biology's **Central Dogma**(Figure 1.12), which states that each gene is encoded in DNA, and then as needed, this genetic information is transcribed into RNA and then translated into protein. In certain circumstances, RNA may also be converted to DNA through a process called reverse transcription. The order of bases in DNA directly controls the order of amino acids that make up a protein. Proteins do most of the work in a cell, and catalyze the formation and breakdown of almost all of the molecules within an organism. By dictating the structure of each protein, DNA affects the function of that protein, and can thereby affect the entire organism. In the case of Mendel's peas, purple-flowered plants have a gene that encodes an enzyme that produces a purple pigment molecule. In the white-flowered plants, the DNA for this gene has been changed so that it no longer encodes a functional protein. This is an example of a natural mutation in a biochemical pathway.

DNA 结构是怎样与生物性状（如孟德尔豌豆的花色）遗传相关的呢？对这个问题的回答在于分子生物学中著名的**中心法则**（图 1.12），它指出每个基因在 DNA 中编码，当有需要时，遗传信息转录成 RNA，然后翻译成蛋白质。在某种情况下，RNA 也会通过逆转录过程转化成 DNA。DNA 中碱基的顺序直接控制着组成蛋白质的氨基酸顺序。蛋白质在细胞中做了大部分的工作，催化生物体中几乎所有分子的合成与分解。通过指挥每个蛋白质的结构，DNA 影响蛋白质的功能从而影响整个生物体。在孟德尔豌豆实验中，紫花植株有编码产生紫色色素分子酶的一个基因。在白花植株中，这个基因的 DNA 已经被改变了，因此它不再编码功能性蛋白质。这是一个生化途径中自然突变的例子。

Figure 1.12 Central Dogma of molecular biology

图 1.12 分子生物学的中心法则

THE GENOME 基 因 组

The complete set of DNA within the nucleus of any organism is called its genome (Table 1.2). Organelles such as mitochondria and chloroplasts also have their own genomes.

任何生物体细胞核中的全套 DNA 被称为基因组（表 1.2）。细胞器，如线粒体和叶绿体也有它们的基因

There is surprisingly little correlation between the nuclear DNA content of a genome (i.e. the ***C*-value**) and the physical size or complexity of an organism. For example, a single copy of the human genome contains approximately 3×10^9 DNA bases, while a single wheat genome contains 17×10^9 DNA bases. This apparent paradox (called the *C*-value paradox) can be explained by the fact that not all DNA encodes genes. In fact, in many organisms, genes are separated from each other by long stretches of DNA that do not code for a protein. Some of this "non-coding" DNA may be transposable elements, which are an interesting class of self-replicating DNA elements discussed in more detail in a subsequent chapter.

组。令人惊讶的是，一个基因组的核 DNA 含量（即 ***C*** **值**）和一个生物体的实际大小或者复杂性几乎没有关系。例如，单拷贝人类基因组大约包含 3×10^9 个 DNA 碱基，而一个小麦单拷贝基因组包含 17×10^9 个 DNA 碱基。这个明显的悖论被称为 *C* 值悖论，能够解释悖论的事实就是，不是所有的 DNA 都能编码基因。事实上，在许多生物体中，基因通过不编码蛋白质的长链DNA彼此分开。这种"不编码"的 DNA 也许是转座元件，在以后的章节中将会详细叙述这类有趣的、自我复制的 DNA 元件。

Table 1.2 Measures of genome size in selected organisms. The DNA content (1*C*) is shown in millions of basepairs (Mb). Average gene density is the mean number of non-coding bases (in bp) between genes in the genome. For eukaryotes, the chromosome number is the chromosomes counted in a gamete (1*N*) from each organism

organism	DNA content (Mb, 1*C*)	estimated gene number	average gene density	chromosome number(1*N*)
Homo sapiens	3 200	25 000	100 000	23
Mus musculus	2 600	25 000	100 000	20
Drosophila melanogaster	140	13 000	9 000	4
Arabidopsis thaliana	130	25 000	4 000	5
Caenorhabditis elegans	100	19 000	5 000	6
Saccharomyces cerevisiae	12	6 000	2 000	16
Escherichia coli	5	3 200	1 400	1

表 1.2　一些生物体的基因组大小。DNA 含量（1*C*）以数百万计的碱基对（Mb）显示。平均基因密度是基因组中基因之间不编码的碱基的平均数。对真核生物而言，染色体数目是每种生物体一个配子（1*N*）中的染色体数目

生物体	DNA 含量(Mb, 1*C*)	估计基因数	平均基因密度	染色体数目(1*N*)
人	3 200	25 000	100 000	23
小鼠	2 600	25 000	100 000	20
果蝇	140	13 000	9 000	4
拟南芥	130	25 000	4 000	5
线虫	100	19 000	5 000	6
酿酒酵母	12	6 000	2 000	16
大肠杆菌	5	3 200	1 400	1

MODEL ORGANISMS 模式生物

We have seen already that many of the great advances in genetics were made using species that are not especially important from a medical, economic, or even ecological perspective. Geneticists, from Mendel onwards, have used model organisms for their experiments. Today, a small number of species are widely used as model genetic organisms. All of these species have characteristics that make them easy to grow in large numbers in laboratories: they are small, have a short generation time and produce lots of progeny from matings that can be easily controlled. Genetic model organisms also usually have small genomes (small *C*-value), and are diploid (i.e. chromosomes are present in pairs). Yeast (***Saccharomyces cerevisiae***) is a good general model for the basic functions of eukaryotic cells. The roundworm, ***Caenorhabditis elegans*** is a useful model for the development of multicellular organisms, in part because it is transparent throughout its life cycle, and its cells undergo a well-characterized series of divisions to produce the adult body. The fruit fly (***Drosophila melanogaster***) has been studied longer, and probably in more detail, than any of the other genetic model organisms still in use, and is a useful model for studying development as well as physiology and even behaviour (Figure 1.13). As a mammal, mouse (***Mus musculus***) is the model organism most closely related to humans. However, some of the practical difficulties of working with mice led researchers more recently to develop zebrafish (***Danio rerio***) as a genetic model for vertebrates. Unlike mice, zebrafish embryos develop externally to their mothers and are transparent, making it easier to study their development. Finally, a small weed, ***Arabidopsis thaliana***, is the most widely studied plant genetic model organism.

我们可以看到，许多在医学、经济甚至生态视角上都不是非常重要的物种在遗传学上取得了巨大进步。从孟德尔开始，遗传学家已经在他们的实验中使用模式生物。目前，一些物种被广泛用作模式遗传生物。所有这些生物都具备易于在实验室大量生长的特性：它们很小并且世代短，而且可以通过容易控制的交配产生大量后代。遗传模式生物也通常有小的基因组（小 *C* 值），并且是二倍体（即染色体是成对出现的）。酿酒酵母（***S. cerevisiae***）是研究真核细胞基本功能的一个好的通用模型。一种线虫，秀丽隐杆线虫（***C.elegans***）是研究多细胞生物形成的一个有用的模型，部分是因为在整个生命周期内它是透明的，并且它的细胞进行一系列易于描述的分裂来形成成体。黑腹果蝇（***D.melanogaster***）被研究的时间更长，比任何其他还在使用的遗传模式生物研究得更为详细，是研究进化和生理甚至行为的一个用处很大的模式生物（图 1.13）。作为一个哺乳动物，老鼠（***M.musculus***）是最接近人类的模式生物，然而研究老鼠遇到的一些实际困难使研究人员将斑马鱼（***D.rerio***）作为脊椎动物的一个遗传模型。与老鼠不同的是，斑马鱼胚胎在母体外形成并且是透明的，使得研究它们的发育变得更加容易。最后，一种小杂草，拟南芥（***A.thaliana***）是被研究得最为广泛的遗传模式生物。

（彩图）

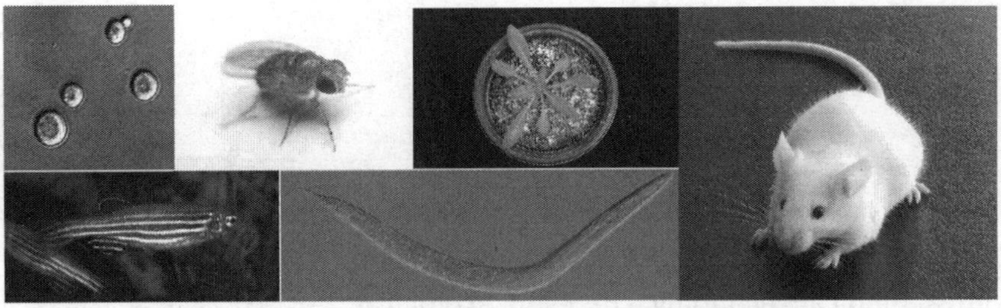

Figure 1.13 Some of the most important genetic model organisms in use today. Clockwise from top left: yeast, fruit fly, arabidopsis, mouse, roundworm, zebrafish

图 1.13 今天使用的一些最重要的遗传模式生物。顺时针方向从左上角：酵母、果蝇、拟南芥、老鼠、线虫、斑马鱼

The study of genetic model organisms has greatly increased our knowledge of genetics, and biology in general. Model organisms also have important implications in medical research. For example, at least 75% of the approximately 1,000 genes that have been associated with specific human diseases have highly similar sequences in both humans and ***D. melanogaster***. Information learned from model organisms about particular biochemical pathways can usually be applied to other species, since the main features of many biochemical pathways tend to be shared between species.

遗传模式生物的研究极大增强了我们整体上对遗传学和生物学的认识。模式生物在医学研究上也有重大的意义。例如，与特定人类疾病有关的约 1000 个基因中，至少 75% 在人类和果蝇中有高度相似序列。从模式生物中了解到的关于某种生化途径的信息也通常被应用于其他物种，因为许多生化途径的主要特征在物种中是共享的。

It is also possible, and sometimes necessary, to study biological processes in non-model organisms. Humans, for example, have none of the characteristics of a model organism, and there are some diseases or other traits for which no clear analog exists in other organisms. Some of the tools of genetic analysis can be applied to non-model organisms, especially with the development of new types of genetic mapping and whole genome sequencing.

在非模式生物中研究生物过程也是可能的，并且有时是必要的。例如，人类就具备模式生物没有的特征，有一些疾病或者其他性状在其他生物中不存在明显的可模拟性。尤其随着新型遗传图谱和整个基因组测序的发展，遗传分析的一些工具也能被应用于非模式生物上。

Summary

- Mendel demonstrated that heredity involved discrete, heritable factors that affected specific traits.

- 孟德尔论证了遗传包括影响特定性状的离散的遗传的因子。

- A gene can be defined abstractly as unit of inheritance; many genetic experiments can be conducted without knowledge of DNA.

- 一个基因能被抽象地定义为遗传的单位；没有 DNA 的知识也能进行很多遗传试验。

- The ability of DNA from bacteria and viruses to transfer genetic information into bacteria helped prove that DNA is the genetic material.
- 细菌和病毒的 DNA 将遗传信息转移到细菌的能力辅证了 DNA 是遗传物质。
- DNA is a double helix made of two anti-parallel strands of bases on a sugar-phosphate backbone.
- DNA 是以磷酸糖为骨架、由两条反向平行的碱基链组成的双螺旋结构。
- Specific bases on opposite strands pair through hydrogen bonding, ensuring complementarity of the strands.
- 相对应的两条链上特定碱基通过氢键配对，确保链的互补。
- Genes encode proteins. Usually one structural, regulatory, or catalytic function is encoded in each protein.
- 基因编码蛋白质。通常每个蛋白质负责一个结构、调控或者催化功能。
- Genes and biochemical pathways can be studied by mutation.
- 基因和生化途径可以通过突变来进行研究。
- The Central Dogma explains how DNA affects heritable traits.
- 中心法则解释了 DNA 是怎样影响遗传性状的。
- Not all of the DNA in an organism contains genes.
- 在生物体中不是所有的 DNA 都包含基因。
- Model organisms accelerate the use of genetics in basic and applied research in biology, agriculture and medicine.
- 在生物、农业和医学的基础和应用研究上，模式生物加快了遗传学的应用。

Key Terms

blending inheritance 融合遗传
particulate inheritance 颗粒遗传
Mendel 孟德尔
gene 基因
allele 等位基因
trait 性状
P, F_1, F_2 亲本、子一代和子二代
Griffith 格里菲斯
Avery, MacLeod, McCarty 埃弗里，麦克劳德，麦克卡提
Hershey, Chase 赫什，蔡斯
DNase DNA 酶
proteinase 蛋白酶
^{35}S
^{32}P
sugar-phosphate backbone 磷酸糖骨架
anti-parallel 反向平行
complementary 互补
hydrogen bond 氢键
minor groove 小沟
major groove 大沟
adenine 腺嘌呤
cytosine 胞嘧啶
thymine 胸腺嘧啶
guanine 鸟嘌呤
Central Dogma 中心法则
transcription 转录
translation 翻译
RNA
genome 基因组

bacteriophage 噬菌体
Beadle, Tatum 比德尔，塔图姆
auxotroph 营养缺陷型
prototroph 原养型
metabolic pathway 代谢途径
Neurospora 链孢霉属
Chargaff's Rules Chargaff 规则
Watson and Crick 沃森和克里克
DNA bases DNA 碱基
C-value paradox *C* 值悖论
model organism 模式生物
Saccharomyces cerevisiae 酿酒酵母
Caenorhabditis elegans 秀丽隐杆线虫
Drosophila melanogaster 黑腹果蝇
Mus musculus 小家鼠
Danio rerio 斑马鱼
Arabidopsis thaliana 拟南芥
Escherichia coli 大肠杆菌

Study Questions

1.1 How would the results of the cross in Figure 1.2 have been different if heredity worked through blending inheritance rather than particulate inheritance?

1.1 如果遗传通过融合遗传而非颗粒遗传，图 1.2 中的杂交结果会有怎样的不同？

1.2 Imagine that astronauts provide you with living samples of multicellular organisms discovered on another planet. These organisms reproduce with a short generation time, but nothing else is known about their genetics.

a) How could you define laws of heredity for these organisms?

b) How could you determine what molecules within these organisms contained genetic information?

c) Would the mechanisms of genetic inheritance likely be similar for all organisms from this planet?

d) Would the mechanisms of genetic inheritance likely be similar to organisms from earth?

1.2 假设宇航员提供给你在另外星球上发现的多细胞生物的活体样本。这些生物繁殖的时间很短，但是对于它们的遗传一无所知。

a) 你怎样确定这些生物的遗传法则？

b) 你怎样确定这些生物中什么分子包含遗传信息？

c) 在这个星球上所有生物的遗传机制都可能是相似的吗？

d) 它们有可能与地球上生物的遗传机制相似吗？

1.3 It is relatively easy to extract DNA and protein from cells; biochemists had been doing this since at least the 1800's. Why then did Hershey and Chase need to use radioactivity to label DNA and proteins in their experiments?

1.3 从细胞中提取 DNA 和蛋白质是相当容易的；生物化学家们自从 19 世纪就已经开始了。为什么 Hershey 和 Chase 需要在他们的试验中用放射性标记 DNA 和蛋白质？

1.4 Compare Watson and Crick's discovery with Avery, MacLeod and McCarty's discovery.

a) What did each discover, and what was the impact of these discoveries on biology?

b) How did Watson and Crick's approach generally differ from Avery, MacLeod and McCarty's?

1.4 比较 Watson、Crick 与 Avery、MacLeod、McCarty 的发现。

a) 每个发现是什么，并且这些发现对生物学的影响是什么？

b) Watson、Crick 与 Avery、MacLeod、McCarty 的方法大体上有怎样的不同？

c) Briefly research Rosalind Franklin on the internet. Why is her contribution to the structure of DNA controversial?

c) 在网络上简单调查一下 Rosalind Franklin。为什么她对 DNA 结构的贡献是有争议的？

1.5 Starting with mice and R and S strains of *S. pneumoniae*, what experiments in additional to those shown in Figure 1.4 to demonstrate that DNA is the genetic material?

1.5 从老鼠和肺炎链球菌的 R 和 S 菌株试验开始，在图 1.4 中需要增加什么试验来证明 DNA 是遗传物质？

1.6 List the information that Watson and Crick used to deduce the structure of DNA.

1.6 列出 Watson 和 Crick 用来推导 DNA 结构的信息。

1.7 Refer to Watson and Crick'

a) List the defining characteristics of the structure of a DNA molecule.

b) Which of these characteristics are most important to replication?

c) Which characteristics are most important to the Central Dogma?

1.7 参照 Watson 和 Crick 的成果

a) 列出一个 DNA 分子的结构的确切特征。

b) 这些特征中的哪些是对复制最重要的？

c) 哪些特征对中心法则最重要？

1.8 Compare Figure 1.9 and Table 1.1. Which of the mutants (#1, #2, #3) shown in Figure 1.9 matches each of the phenotypes expected for mutations in genes A, B,C?

1.8 比较图 1.9 和表 1.1，图 1.9 中的突变（#1、#2、#3）是如何分别与基因 A、B、C 相对应的？

1.9 Refer to Table 1.2

a) What is the relationship between DNA content of a genome, number of genes, gene density, and chromosome number?

b) What feature of genomes explains the *C* value paradox?

c) Do any of the numbers in Table 1.2 show a correlation with organismal complexity?

1.9 参照表 1.2

a）一个基因组的 DNA 含量、基因数目、基因密度和染色体数目之间的关系是什么？

b）基因组的什么特征能够解释 *C* 值悖论？

c）表 1.2 中哪些数字显示出与生物复杂性相关？

1.10

a) List the characteristics of an ideal model organism.

b) Which model organism can be used most efficiently to identify genes related to:

i) eye development

ii) skeletal development

iii) photosynthesis

iv) cell division

v) cell differentiation

1.10

a）列出一个理想模式生物的特征。

b）哪种模式生物能够被用来高效地确定与下列性状有关的基因：

i）眼睛的发育

ii）骨骼的发育

iii）光合作用

iv）细胞分裂

v）细胞分化

vi) cancer

vi）癌症

1.11 Refer to Figure 1.6

a) Identify the part of the DNA molecule that would be radioactively labeled in the manner used by Hershey & Chase.

b) DNA helices that are rich in G-C base pairs are harder to separate (e.g. by heating) that A-T rich helices. Why?

1.11 参看图 1.6

a）识别 Hershey 和 Chase 用放射性标记的 DNA 分子的部分。

b）富含 G-C 碱基的 DNA 双螺旋比富含 A-T 的双螺旋更难分开（如通过加热），为什么？

Chapter 2

CHROMOSOMES, MITOSIS, AND MEIOSIS
染色体、有丝分裂与减数分裂

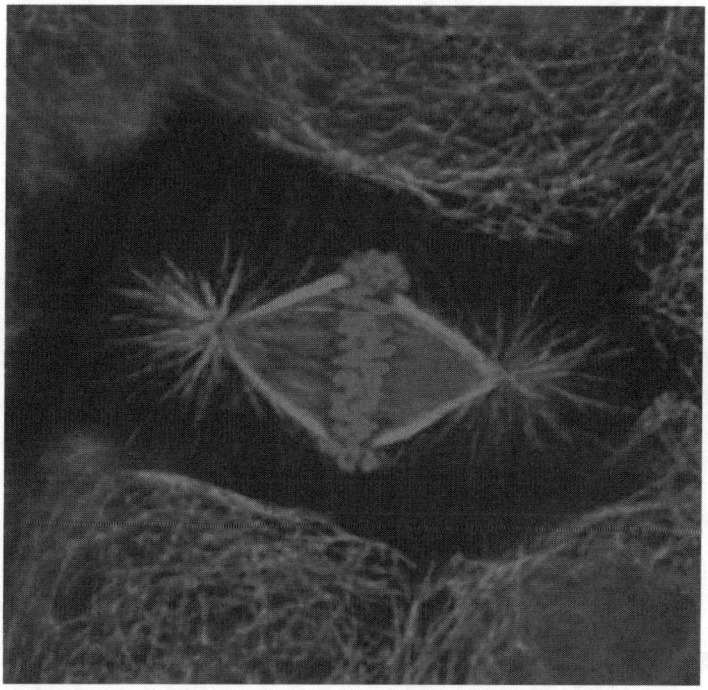

(彩图)

Human metaphase chromosomes. DNA is labeled with a blue fluorescent dye, and microtubules are labeled green

人的细胞分裂中期染色体。用蓝色荧光染料标记的为 DNA，绿色荧光染料标记的为微管

Chromosomes contain genetic information. We often take this fact for granted, but just over a century ago, even the best biologists in the world were uncertain of the function of these rod-shaped structures. We now know that most chromosomes contain a single molecule of double-stranded DNA that is complexed with proteins. This arrangement allows very long DNA molecules to be compacted into a small volume that can more easily be moved during mitosis and mei-

染色体包含着遗传信息。我们经常认为这个事实是理所当然的，但是就在一个世纪以前，即便是世界上最著名的生物学家，也不能确定这些棒状结构的功能。我们现在知道大多数染色体都包含一条 DNA 双螺旋分子，且与蛋白质组成复合结构。这种结构使得很长的 DNA 分

osis. The compact structure also makes it easier for pairs of chromosomes to align with each other during meiosis. Finally, we shall see that chromosomal structure can affect whether genes are active or silent.

子压缩到一个很小的体积，以便在有丝分裂和减数分裂过程中容易移动。这种致密的压缩结构使染色体在减数分裂过程中更容易与其同源染色体对齐。最后，我们还将知道染色体的结构能够影响基因的表达或沉默。

CHROMOSOMES MAY BE LOOSE OR COMPACT
染色体的疏松和致密结构

If stretched to its full length, the DNA molecule of the largest human chromosome would be 85mm. Yet during mitosis and meiosis, this DNA molecule is compacted into a chromosome approximately 5μm long. Although this compaction makes it easier to transport DNA within a dividing cell, it also makes DNA less accessible for other cellular functions such as DNA synthesis and transcription. Thus, chromosomes vary in how tightly DNA is packaged, depending on the stage of the cell cycle and also depending on the level of gene activity required in any particular region of the chromosome.

如果将DNA分子伸展到其全长，人类最大的染色体DNA分子是85mm。但在有丝分裂和减数分裂过程中，这个DNA分子被压缩到大约只有5μm长的染色体中。尽管这种压缩使得DNA分子在分裂细胞内更加容易转运，但是这也降低了DNA对其他细胞功能的可执行性，如DNA的合成和转录。因此，染色体上DNA的包装致密程度是变化的，这取决于细胞周期的不同阶段，也取决于染色体的某些特殊区域对基因活性水平的要求。

There are several different levels of structural organization in eukaryotic chromosomes, with each successive level contributing to the further compaction of DNA (Figure 2.1). For more loosely compacted DNA, only the first few levels of organization may apply. Each level involves a specific set of proteins that associate with the DNA to compact it. First, proteins called the **core histones** act as spool around which DNA is coiled twice to form a structure called the **nucleosome**. Nucleosomes are formed at regular intervals along the DNA strand, giving the molecule the appearance of "beads on a string". At the next level of organization, **histone H1** helps to compact the DNA strand and its nucleosomes into a **30nm fibre**. Subsequent levels of organization involve the

真核生物的染色体中，随着连续不同程度地对 DNA 逐步压缩，会形成几个不同层次的结构形态（图2.1）。更为疏松的压缩 DNA 只需压缩到前几个组装层次。每个组装阶段都包含一套特殊的蛋白质，与 DNA 连接在一起压缩 DNA。首先，**核心组蛋白**充当线轴，DNA 分子盘绕线轴两圈，形成**核小体**。沿着 DNA 链每隔一定距离会有规律地形成核小体，在微观下呈“串珠状”结构。紧接着，**组蛋白 H1** 协助将 DNA 链与核小体一起压缩成 **30nm**

addition of **scaffold proteins** that wind the 30nm fibre into coils, which are in turn wound around other scaffold proteins.

的纤丝。然后，30nm 的纤丝与**支架蛋白**一起缠绕成线圈，接着继续缠绕其他支架蛋白。

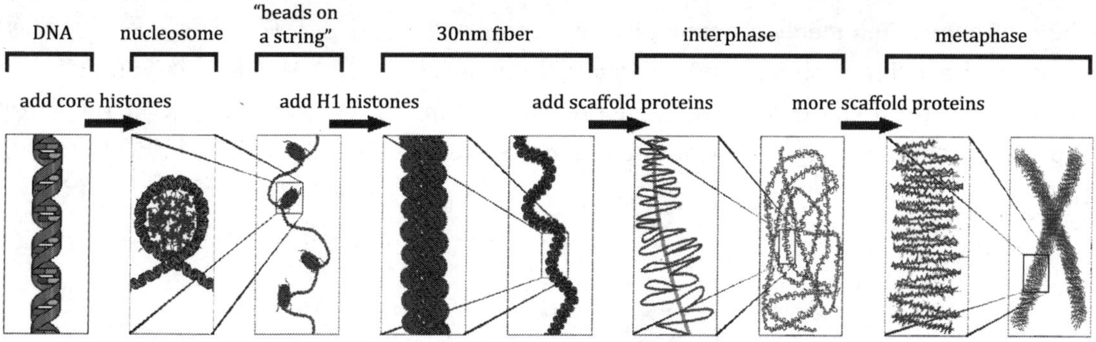

Figure 2.1 Successive stages of chromosome compaction depend on the introduction of additional proteins

图 2.1 通过引入不同蛋白质对 DNA 进行逐级压缩形成染色体

（彩图）

Chromosomes stain very intensely with some types of dyes, which is how they got their name (chromosome means "colored body"). Certain dyes stain some regions within a chromosome more intensely that others, giving some chromosomes a banded appearance. The material that makes up chromosomes, which we now know to be proteins and DNA, is called **chromatin**. There are two general types of chromatin. **Euchromatin** is more loosely packed, and tends to contain more genes that are being transcribed, as compared to the more densely compacted **heterochromatin** which is rich in short, repetitive sequences called **microsatellites**.

染色体易被一些染料染上颜色，这也是取名为染色体的原因（染色体意为"被染色的物体"）。一些染料在染色体的某些区域着色更深，会显现出一些条带。染色体主要由蛋白质和 DNA 组成，而染色体的初始形态叫做**染色质**，一般有两种类型：**常染色质**和**异染色质**。常染色质是指染色质折叠压缩程度低并且包含较多正在转录的基因的染色质；而异染色质是指染色质折叠压缩程度高且富含短的重复序列（叫**微卫星序列**）的染色质。

Chromosomes also contain other distinctive features such as centromeres and telomeres. Both of these are heterochromatic. In most cases, each chromosome contains one **centromere**. These sequences are bound by centromeric proteins that link the centromere to microtubules that transport chromosomes during cell division. Under the microscope, centromeres can sometimes appear as constrictions in the body of the chromosome (Figure 2.2). If a centromere is located near the middle of a chromosome, it is said to be **met-**

染色体也包含一些独特的结构，如着丝粒和端粒，两者都是异染色质。在大多数情况下，每个染色体只含有一个**着丝粒**，此处的 DNA 序列与着丝粒蛋白结合，并且将着丝粒与微管相连接，以便在细胞分裂过程中转运染色体。在显微镜下，着丝粒有时以缢痕的形式显现在染色体上（图 2.2）。如果着丝粒

acentric, while an **acrocentric** centromere is closer to one end of a chromosome, and a **telocentric** chromsome is at the very end. More rarely, in a **holocentric** centromere, no single centromere can be defined and the entire chromsome acts as the centromere. **Telomeres** are repetitive sequences near the ends of linear chromosomes, and are important in maintaining the length of the chromosomes during replication, and protecting the ends of the chromosomes from alterations.

位于染色体的中部或近中部，称其为**中着丝粒**。**近端着丝粒**则靠近染色体的末端，**端着丝粒**在染色体的末端。更罕见的是**全着丝粒**染色体，它没有一个独立的着丝粒而整个染色体扮演着丝粒的角色。**端粒**是线性染色体近末端的重复序列，其在 DNA 复制过程中对于保持染色体长度是重要的，并且保护染色体末端使其免受改变。

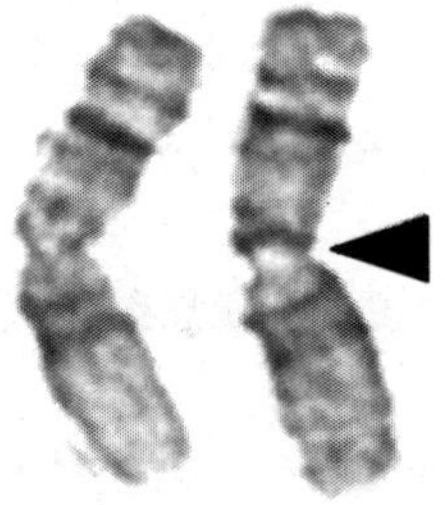

Figure 2.2 A pair of metacentric chromosomes. The arrow shows a centromeric region

图 2.2 一对中着丝粒染色体。箭头指着丝粒区域

It is useful to describe the similarity between chromosomes using appropriate terminology (Figure 2.3). **Homologous** chromosomes are typically pairs of similar, but non-identical, chromosomes in which one member of the pair comes from the male parent, and the other comes from the female parent. Homologs contain the same genes but not necessarily the same alleles. **Non-homo-logous** chromosomes contain different sets of genes, and may or may not be distinguishable based on cytological features such as length and centromere position. Within a chromosomes that has undergone replication, there are **sister chromatids,** which are physically connected to each other at the centromere and remain joined until cell division. Because a pair of sister chromatids is produced by the replication of a single DNA molecule, their sequences are essentially identical. On the other hand, **non-sister chromatids** come from two separate, but homologous chromosomes, and therefore usually contain the same genes in the same order, but do not necessarily have identical DNA sequences.

用恰当的专业术语对染色体的相似性进行描述是很有必要的（图 2.3）。**同源**染色体是一对典型的相似染色体，但又是不完全相同的，一条来自父本，另外一条来自母本。并且同源染色体所含的基因相同，但不一定都是同一等位基因。**非同源**染色体所含的基因不同，且有些可以通过细胞学特征加以区别，如染色体长度、着丝粒位置等。在复制的染色体中由两条姐妹染色单体构成，这两条姐妹染色单体通过着丝粒相连接，直到细胞分裂时它们才分开。因为一对姐妹染色单体是通过单个 DNA 分子复制而来的，因此它们所含的 DNA 序列本质上是完全相同的。另外，**非姐妹染色单体**来自两条独立的同源染色体，因此在同样的顺序上含有相同的基因，但是 DNA 序列未必完全相同。

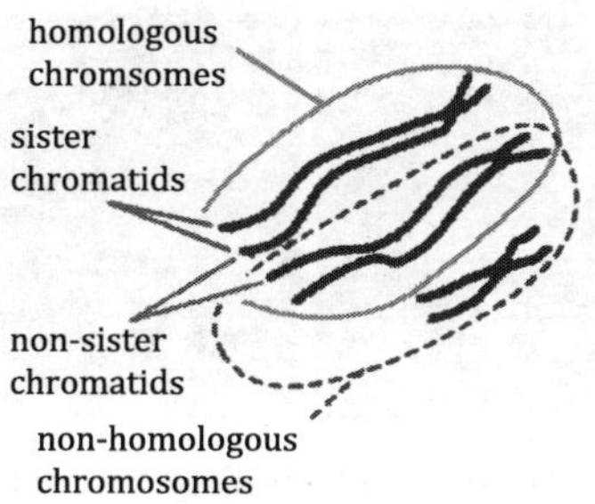

Figure 2.3 Relationships between chromosomes and chromatids

图 2.3 染色体和染色单体之间的关系

MITOSIS 有丝分裂

Cell division is essential to asexual reproduction and the development of multicellular organisms. Accordingly, the primary function of mitosis is to ensure that each daughter cell inherits identical genetic material, i.e. exactly one copy of each chromosome. To make this happen, replicated chromosomes condense (**prophase**), and are positioned near the middle of the dividing cell (**metaphase**), and then one sister chromatid from each chromosome migrates towards opposite poles of the dividing cell (**anaphase**), until the identical sets of chromosomes are completely separated from each other within the newly formed nuclei of each daughter cell (**telophase**) (see Figures 2.4~2.6 for diagrams of the process). This is followed by the completion of the division of the cytoplasm (**cytokinesis**). The movement of chromosomes is aided by microtubules that attach to the chromosomes at centromere.

细胞分裂对无性繁殖和多细胞生物的发育都是必不可少的。因此，有丝分裂的主要功能就是确保每个子细胞继承相同的遗传物质，即对每条染色体进行精确的拷贝。要实现这一目的，就要经历复制的染色体浓缩（**前期**），所有染色体排列到细胞分裂的赤道面上（**中期**），然后两条姐妹染色单体彼此分离，并分别向两极运动（**后期**），直到相同的一套染色体彼此完全分开，并在各自的子细胞中形成新的细胞核（末期）（图 2.4～图 2.6 的过程图解）。这一过程中伴随着细胞质的分裂（**胞质分裂**）。附着在染色体着丝粒的微管协助了染色体的移动。

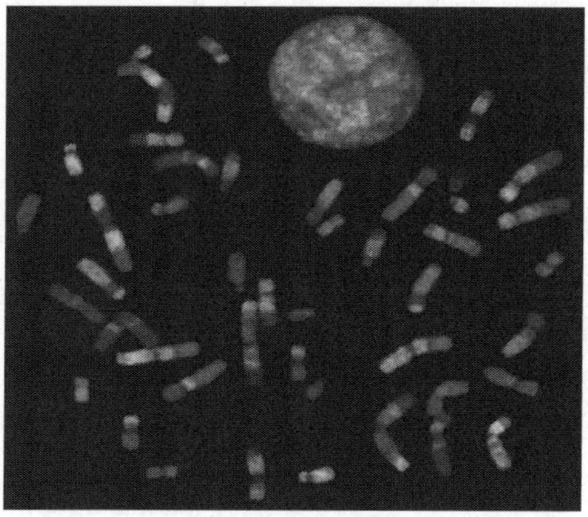

Figure 2.4 Human metaphase chromosomes that have been labeled with sequence-specific fluorescent probes to distinguish chromosomes. The circular object is an interphase nucleus labeled with the same fluorescent probes, and shows the complex spatial distribution of chromosomes during interphase (see the color figure)

图 2.4 用序列特异性荧光探针对人类细胞分裂中期染色体进行标记加以区别，圆形物体是用同样的荧光探针进行标记的处于细胞间期的细胞核，显示了间期染色体的复杂空间分布（见彩版）

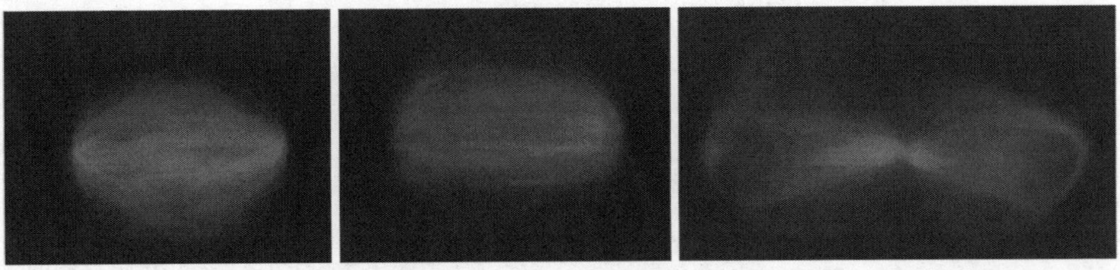

Figure 2.5 Mitosis in *Arabidopsis* showing fluorescently labeled chromosomes (blue) and microtubules (green) at metaphase, anaphase and telophase (from left to right) (see the color figure)

图 2.5 在拟南芥有丝分裂中期、后期和末期（从左向右）中用荧光染料标记的染色体（蓝色）和微管（绿色）（见彩版）

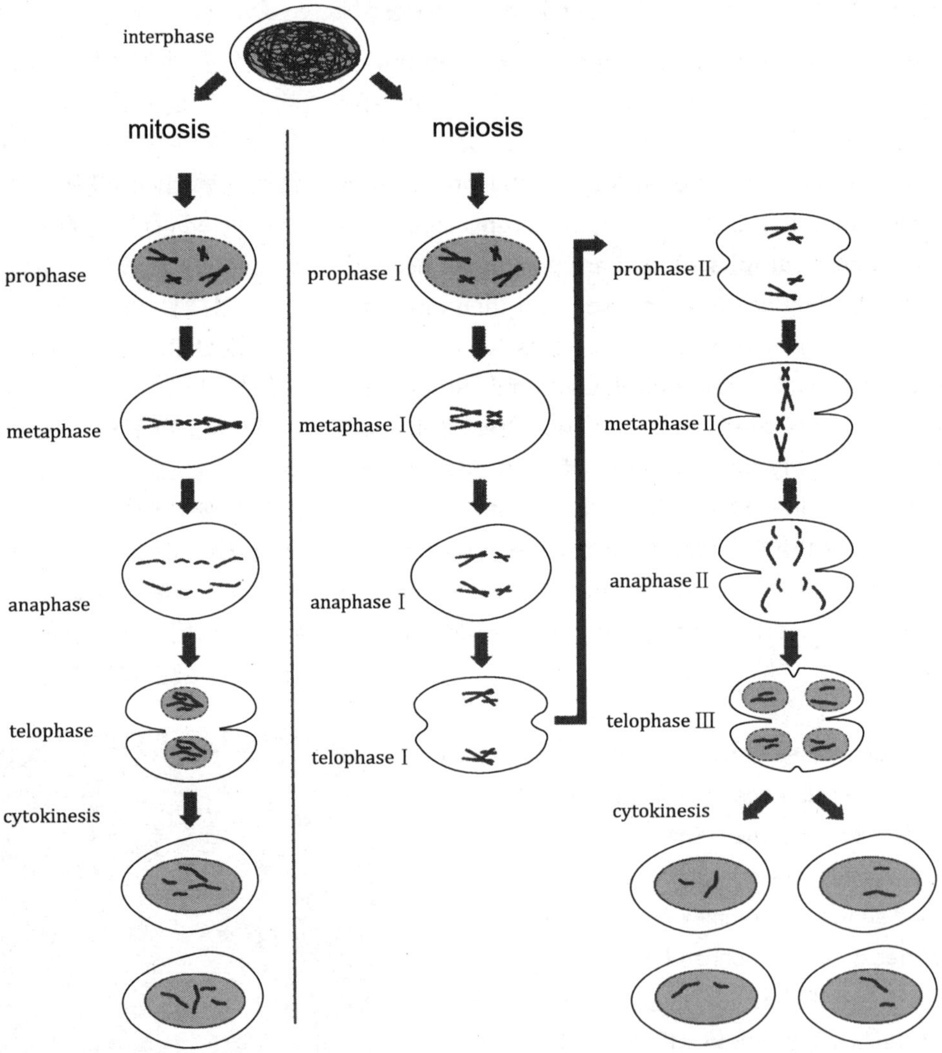

Figure 2.6 Mitosis and meiosis. Note the similarities and differences between metaphase in mitosis and metaphase Ⅰ and Ⅱ of meiosis

图 2.6 有丝分裂和减数分裂。注意在有丝分裂中期和减数分裂中期Ⅰ、Ⅱ之间的相似点和不同点

MEIOSIS 减数分裂

Meiosis, like mitosis, is also a necessary part of cell division. However, in meiosis not only do sister chromatids separate from each other, homologous chromosomes also separate from each other. This extra, reductional step of meiosis is essential to sexual reproduction. Without meiosis, the chromosome number would double in each generation of a species and would quickly become too large to be viable.

减数分裂和有丝分裂一样也是细胞分裂必不可少的一部分。然而，在减数分裂过程中不仅有姐妹染色单体的彼此分离，而且还包含着同源染色体的彼此分离。减数分裂中染色体数目减半这一“额外”的阶段对有性生殖是必要的。如果没有减数分裂，染色体数目会在每个物种各自的子代中加倍并且很快会使基因组变得过大而无法存活。

Meiosis is divided into two stages designated by the roman numerals Ⅰ and Ⅱ. Meiosis Ⅰ is called a **reductional** division, because it reduces the number of chromosomes inherited by each of the daughter cells. Meiosis Ⅰ is further divided into Prophase Ⅰ, Metaphase Ⅰ, Anaphase Ⅰ, and Telophase Ⅰ, which are roughly similar to the corresponding stages of mitosis, except that in Prophase Ⅰ and Metaphase Ⅰ, homologous chromosomes pair with each other in transient structures called **bivalents** (Figures. 2.6, 2.7). This is an important difference between mitosis and meiosis, because it affects the segregation of alleles, and also allows for recombination to occur through crossing-over, as described later in the course. During Anaphase Ⅰ, one member of each pair of homologous chromosomes migrates into a daughter cell. Meiosis Ⅱ is essentially the same as mitosis, with one sister chromatid from each chromosome separating to produce two identical cells. Because Meiosis Ⅱ, like mitosis, results in products that contain identical sequences, Meiosis Ⅱ is called an **equational** division.

减数分裂被人为分成两个阶段，分别用罗马数字Ⅰ和Ⅱ表示。减数分裂Ⅰ是**染色体减半**的阶段，因为与母细胞相比子细胞继承的染色体数目减半了。减数分裂Ⅰ又可进一步划分为前期Ⅰ、中期Ⅰ、后期Ⅰ和末期Ⅰ，这和体细胞有丝分裂的相应阶段有许多相似之处。但前期Ⅰ和中期Ⅰ这两个阶段除外，这两个阶段同源染色体彼此配对，形成暂时的结构，称为**二价体**（图 2.6，图 2.7）。这是减数分裂和有丝分裂的一个主要区别，因为它影响了等位基因的分离和交换重组，后面内容会对此过程进行描述。在后期Ⅰ，同源染色体彼此分离并向两极移动进入子细胞。减数分裂Ⅱ本质上和有丝分裂是一致的，也是两条姐妹染色单体彼此分离，最终产生两个完全相同的子细胞。因为减数分裂Ⅱ与有丝分裂相似，都是产生包含完全相同 DNA 序列的子细胞，因此减数分裂Ⅱ也被称为**均等分裂**。

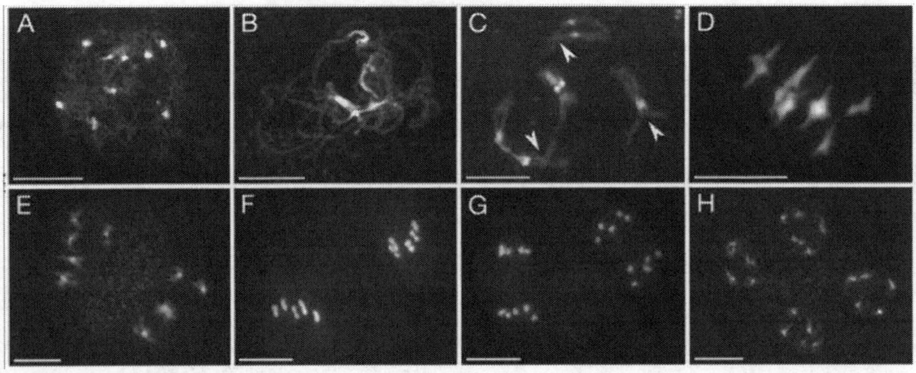

Figure 2.7 Meiosis in *Arabidopsis* (n=5). Panels A~C show different stages of prophase Ⅰ, each with an increasing degree of chromosome condensation. Subsequent phases are shown: metaphase Ⅰ (D), telophase Ⅰ (E), metaphase Ⅱ (F), anaphase Ⅱ (G), and telophase Ⅱ (H)

图 2.7 拟南芥的减数分裂（n=5）。图片中的 A~C 表示前期Ⅰ的不同阶段，每个阶段伴随着染色体浓缩程度的增加。后面的图片显示的阶段是：中期Ⅰ(D)、末期Ⅰ(E)、中期Ⅱ(F)、后期Ⅱ(G)和末期Ⅱ(H)

THE CELL CYCLE AND CHANGES IN DNA CONTENT
细胞周期和 DNA 含量的改变

The life cycle of an eukaryotic cell can generally be divided into at least four stages (Figure 2.8). When a cell is produced through fertilization or cell division, there is usually a lag before it undergoes DNA synthesis. This lag period is called Gap 1 (**G_1**), and ends with the onset of the DNA synthesis (**S**) phase, during which each chromosome is replicated. Following replication, there may be another lag, called Gap 2 (**G_2**), before mitosis (**M**). Cells undergoing meiosis do not usually have a G_2 phase. Interphase is as term used to describe all phases of the cell cycle excluding mitosis or meiosis. A typical cell cycle is shown in Figure 2.8. My variants of this generalized cell cycle also exist. Some cells never leave G_1 phase, and are said to enter a permanent, non-dividing stage called **G_0**. On the other hand, some cells undergo many rounds of DNA synthesis (S) without any mitosis or cell division. These endoreduplicated cells are described later in this chapter. Understanding the control of the cell cycle is an active area of research, particularly because of the relationship between cell division and cancer.

一个真核细胞的生活周期至少可以人为地划分为 4 个阶段（图 2.8）。某细胞通过受精或细胞分裂产生之后，在 DNA 开始合成之前通常会有一个延缓期，该延缓期称为间期 1（**G_1**）。紧接着开始进入 DNA 合成期（**S**），在这个时期染色体彼此进行复制。复制完成之后和在细胞有丝分裂（**M**）之前，或许存在另一个延缓期，称为间期 2（**G_2**）。细胞进行减数分裂时一般不会有 G_2 期。分裂间期指的是细胞周期中除了有丝分裂和减数分裂以外的其他所有阶段。一个标准的细胞周期如图 2.8 所示，但也存在不符合普遍现象的细胞。有些细胞会停在 G_1 期，并停留在这一阶段，不进行细胞分裂，称其为 G_0 期。另外，有些细胞会进行多轮的 DNA

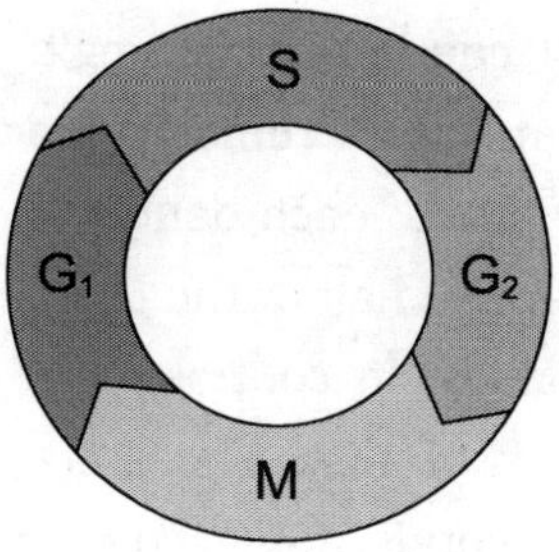

Figure 2.8 A typical eukaryotic cell cycle
图 2.8 一个标准的真核细胞周期

合成（S 期）而不进行有丝分裂或细胞分裂。这些 DNA 核内复制的细胞将在本章后面介绍。对细胞周期调控的理解是一个活跃的研究领域，特别是因为细胞分裂与癌症之间存在一定关系。

The amount of DNA within a cell changes following each of the following events: fertilization, DNA synthesis, mitosis, and meiosis (Figure 2.9). We use "***c***" to represent the DNA content in a cell, and "***n***" to represent the number of complete sets of chromosomes. In a gamete (i.e. sperm or egg), the amount of DNA is 1*c*, and the number of chromosomes is 1*n*. Upon fertilization, both the DNA content and the number of chromosomes doubles to 2*c* and 2*n*, respectively. Following DNA synthesis, the DNA content doubles again to 4*c*, but

一个细胞中 DNA 的总量会随着下列事件而发生改变：受精、DNA 合成、有丝分裂和减数分裂（图 2.9）。我们用 "***c***" 表示一个细胞中 DNA 的含量，用 "***n***" 表示一个细胞中整套染色体的数目。在一个配子（如精子或卵子）中，DNA 总量是 1*c*，染色体的数目是 1*n*。一旦受精，DNA 含量和染色体数

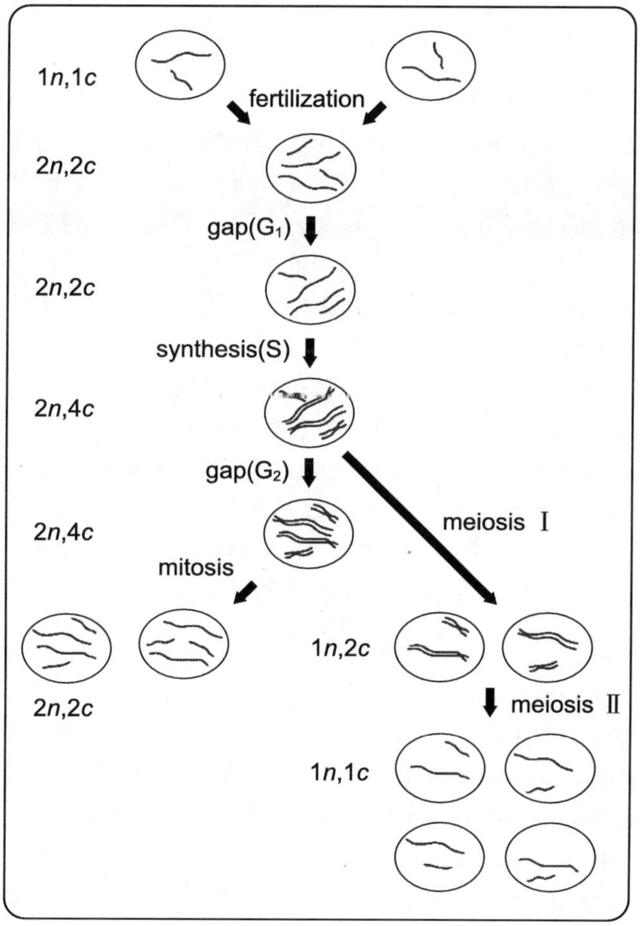

Figure 2.9 Changes in DNA and chromosome content during the cell cycle. For simplicity, nuclear membranes are not shown, and all chromosomes are represented in a similar stage of condensation
图 2.9 在细胞周期中 DNA 含量和染色体数目的改变。为简单起见，核膜没显示在图中，且所有的染色体都用同一个类似的浓缩阶段代替

each pair of sister chromatids is still counted as a single chromosome, so the number of chromosomes remains unchanged at 2*n*. If the cell undergoes mitosis, each daughter cell will be 2*c* and 2*n*, because it will receive half of the DNA, and one of each pair of sister chromatids. In contrast, the cells that are produced from the meiosis of a 2*n*, 4*c* cell are 1*c* and 1*n*, since each pair of sister chromatids, and each pair of homologous chromosomes divides during meiosis.

目就会加倍，分别为 2*c* 和 2*n*。随后进入 DNA 合成阶段，DNA 含量会再次加倍成 4*c*，但是每对姐妹染色单体仍然是一条染色体，因此染色体的数目还是 2*n* 未变。如果细胞进行有丝分裂，每个子细胞的 DNA 含量和染色体数目将会是 2*c* 和 2*n*，因为每个子细胞获得了一半的 DNA 和每对姐妹染色单体的其中之一。相反，一个 4*c*、2*n* 的细胞进行减数分裂时会因同源染色体的彼此分离和姐妹染色单体的彼此分离产生 1*c*、1*n* 的子细胞。

KARYOTYPES SHOW CHROMOSOME NUMBER AND STRUCTURE
核型显示染色体数目和结构

Each eukaryotic species has its total nuclear genome divided among a number of chromosomes that is characteristic of that species. For example, a haploid human nucleus (i.e. sperm or egg) normally has 23 chromosomes (*n*=23), and a diploid human nucleus has 23 pairs of chromosomes (2*n*=46). Various stains and fluorescent dyes produce characteristic banding patterns on some chromosomes. This can make it easier to identify specific chromosomes. The number of chromosomes varies between species (see Table 1.2), but there appears to be very little correlation between chromosome number and either the complexity of an organism or its total amount genomic DNA.

每个真核生物种的核基因组分布在它的代表物种特征的若干染色体上。例如，一个人的单倍体细胞核（如精子或卵子）正常有 23 条染色体（*n*=23），一个人的二倍体细胞核正常有 23 对染色体（2*n*=46）。用不同的染色剂和荧光染料会在一些染色体上获得特征性带型，这样会更加容易地去鉴别特殊的染色体。染色体的数目在物种之间是不同的（表 1.2），但是染色体数目似乎与一个生物体的复杂性或基因组 DNA 的总量之间没有太大的关系。

A **karyotype** shows the complete set of chromosomes of an individual (Figure 2.10). Analysis of karyotypes can identify of chromosomal abnormalities, including **aneuploidy**, which is the addition or subtraction of a chromosome from a pair of homologs. More specifically, the absence of one member of a pair of homologous chromosomes is called **monosomy**. On the other hand, in a **trisomy**, there are three, rather than

核型显示的是某个个体的一整套染色体（图 2.10）。核型分析能够鉴定染色体的畸变，包括由于同源染色体的某条染色体增加或缺失而引起的**非整倍体**现象。更具体地说，一对同源染色体的一条染色体丢失就称为**单体**。另外，有一对同

two homologs of a particular chromosome. Different types of aneuploidy are sometimes represented symbolically; if **2*n*** symbolizes the normal number of chromosomes in a cell, then **2*n*–1** indicates monosomy and **2*n*+1** represents trisomy.

源染色体是3条而不是2条的称为三体。不同类型的非整倍体一般用不同的符号表示：**2*n*** 表示细胞中的染色体数目正常，**2*n*–1** 表示单体，**2*n*+1** 表示三体。

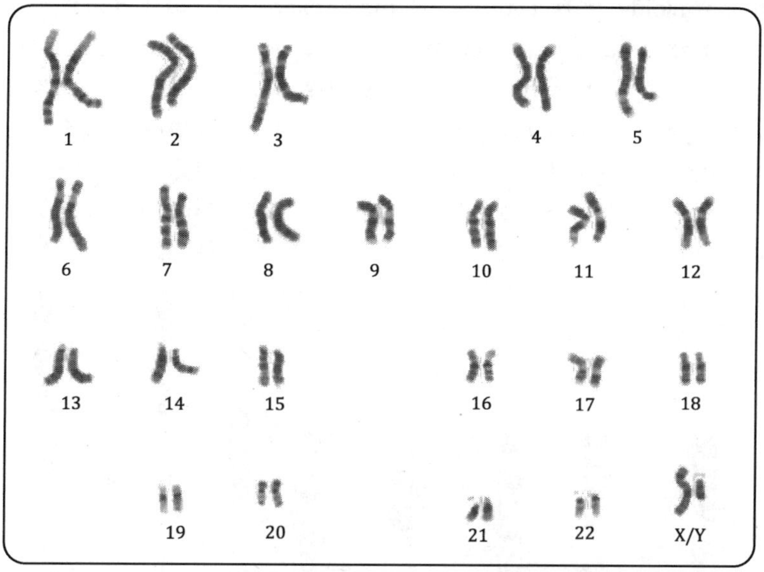

Figure 2.10 Karyotype of a normal human male

图 2.10 一个正常男性的核型图

The most familiar human aneuploidy is trisomy-21 (i.e. three copies of chromosome 21), which is one cause of **Down's syndrome**. Most (but not all) other human aneuploidies are lethal at an early stage of embryonic development. Note that aneuploidy usually affects only one set of homologs within a karyotype, and is therefore distinct from **polyploidy**, in which the entire karyotype is duplicated (see below). Aneuploidy is almost always deleterious, whereas polyploidy appears to be beneficial in some organisms, particularly some species of plants.

人最常见的非整倍体是 21 号染色体三体（即多了一条第 21 号染色体），这也是得**唐氏综合征**的病因。人的其他大多数（但不是全部）非整倍体在胚胎发育的早期是致死的。既然非整倍体一般只会影响核型中的一组同源染色体，那么它会与**多倍体**形成明显区别，因为多倍体是对完整的核型进行加倍（见下文）。非整倍体几乎总是有害的，但是多倍体在某些生物中是有利的，特别是一些植物物种中。

Structural defects in chromosomes are another type of abnormality that can be detected in karyotypes (Figure 2.11). These defects include **deletions, duplications**, and **inversions**, which all involve changes in a segment of a single

染色体结构缺陷是可以在核型中检测到的另一类畸变（图 2.11）。这些缺陷有**缺失**、**重复**和**倒位**，它们都是单条染色体片段的改变。**插**

chromosome. **Insertions** and **translocations** involve two non-homologous chromosomes. In an insertion, DNA from one chromosome is unidirectional, while in translocation, the transfer of chromosomal segments is bidirectional. Structural defects affect only part of a chromosome, and so tend to be less harmful than aneuploidy. In fact, there are many examples of ancient chromosomal rearrangements in the genomes of species including our own. Duplications of some small chromosomal segments, in particular, may have some evolutionary advantage by providing extra copies of some genes, which can then evolve in new ways.

入和**易位**发生在两条非同源染色体之间，但是插入是一条染色体DNA 片段的单向移动，而易位是染色体片段的双向转移。染色体结构缺陷只是影响染色体的一部分，因此其危害性会比非整倍体的小。事实上，在生物物种的基因组中有许多关于古老染色体重排的例子，包括我们人类自己。尤其是一些小的染色体片段的重复会产生一些基因的额外拷贝，这或许对进化是有利的，使其以一种新的方式进化。

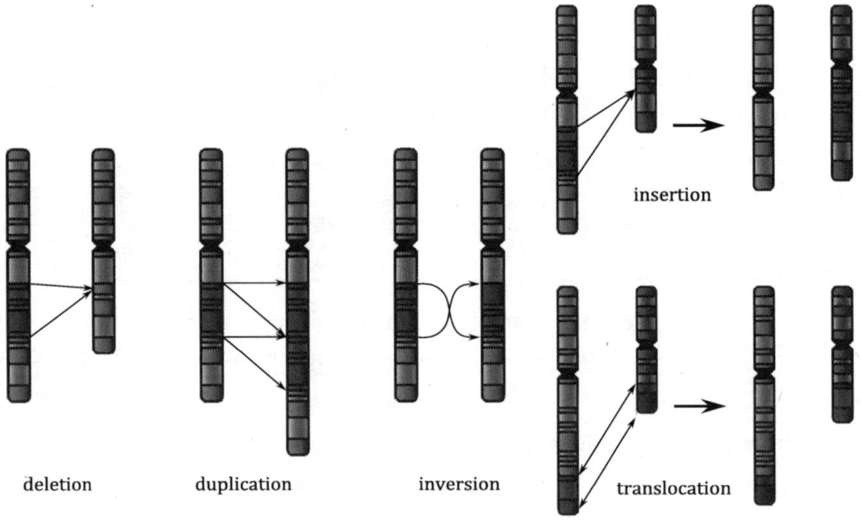

Figure 2.11 Structural abberations in chromosomes

图 2.11 染色体结构畸变

Chromosomal abnormalities arise in many different ways. Many of these can be traced to rare errors in natural cellular processes. **Non-disjunction** is the failure of at least one pair of chromosomes or chromatids to separate during mitosis or meiosis. **Chromosome breakage** also occurs infrequently as the result of physical damage (such as radiation), movement of some types of transposons, and other factors. During the repair of a broken chromosome, deletions, insertions, translocations and even inversions can be introduced.

染色体畸变由许多不同的产生方式。这些畸变大多可以追溯到自然的细胞过程造成的罕见错误。**染色体不分离**是指至少一对染色单体或染色体在有丝分裂或减数分裂过程中不分开。由于物理伤害（如辐射）、一些转座子的活动和其他因素，也会在少数情况下发生**染色体断裂**。对一个损坏了的染色体，生物体会采用删除、插入、易位，甚至是倒位等方法进行修复。

POLYPLOIDY 多倍体

Humans, like most animals and all of the eukaryotic genetic model organisms in wide use, are diploid. This means that most of their cells have two homologous copies of each chromosome. In contrast, many plant species and even a few animal species are **polyploids**. This means there are more than two homologs of each chromosome in each cell.

与大多数动物和所有被广泛应用的真核遗传模式生物一样，人类也是二倍体。这就意味着在这些生物的大多数细胞中，每条染色体都含有两个同源拷贝。但不同的是，许多植物甚至一些动物却是**多倍体**，即在每个细胞中每组同源染色体都多于两条。

When describing polyploids, we use the letter "***x***" to define the level of ploidy. A diploid is 2*x*, because there are two basic sets of chromosomes, and a tetraploid is 4*x*, because it contains four copies of each chromosome. For clarity when discussing polyploids, geneticists will often combine the "*x*" notation with the "*n*" notation already defined previously in this chapter. Thus for both diploids and polyploids, "*n*" is the number of chromosomes in a gamete, and "2*n*" is the number of chromosomes following fertilization. For a diploid, therefore, *n*=*x*, and 2*n*=2*x*. For a tetraploid, *n*=2*x*, and 2*n*=4*x*.

在描述多倍体时，我们用字母"***x***"表示倍性。由于一个二倍体具有两套染色体，所以用 2*x* 表示；一个四倍体具有四套染色体，所以用 4*x* 表示。为了更加清楚地讨论多倍体，遗传学者经常将"*x*"和本章前面定义的"*n*"联系起来。那么对于二倍体和多倍体而言，"*n*"表示一个配子的染色体数目，"2*n*"表示受精之后染色体的数目。因此一个二倍体中，*n*=*x*，2*n*=2*x*；四倍体中，*n*=2*x*，2*n*=4*x*。

Like diploids (2*n*=2*x*), stable polyploids generally have an even number of copies of each chromosome: tetraploid (2*n*=4*x*), hexaploid (2*n*=6*x*), and so on. The reason for this is clear from a consideration of meiosis. Remembering that the purpose of meiosis is to reduce the sum of the genetic material by half, meiosis can equally divide an even number of chromosome sets, but not an odd number. Thus, polyploids with an uneven number of chromosomes (e.g. triploids, 2*n*=3*x*) tend to be sterile, even if they are otherwise healthy. The mechanism of meiosis in stable polyploids is essentially the same as in diploids: during metaphase Ⅰ, homologous chromosomes pair with each other. Depending on the species, all of the homologs may be aligned together at metaphase, or in multiple separate pairs. For example, in a tetra-

像二倍体（2*n*=2*x*）一样，遗传稳定的多倍体一般每个染色体具有偶数个拷贝：四倍体（2*n*=4*x*）、六倍体（2*n*=6*x*）等。要搞清楚这些需要从减数分裂开始考虑。减数分裂的目的是使遗传物质的总数减半，那么减数分裂就能将偶数的染色体组平均分开，而不是奇数的染色体组。因此，具有奇数染色体组的多倍体（如三倍体，2*n*=3*x*）即使它们在其他方面是正常的，但往往还是不育的。对于遗传稳定的多倍体，其减数分裂的机制在本质上和二倍体的一样：在中期Ⅰ，同源

ploid, some species may form **tetravalents** in which the four homologs from each chromosome align together, or alternatively, two pairs of homologs may form two bivalents. Note that because that mitosis does not involve any pairing of homologous chromosomes, mitosis is equally effective in diploids, even-number polyploids, and odd-number polyploids.

染色体彼此配对。根据物种的不同，所有的同源染色体在中期或许彼此联合在一起，亦或成为多个独立的染色体对。例如，在一个四倍体中，一些物种或许每 4 个同源染色体彼此聚集在一起，形成**四价体**，或许两两配对形成两个二价体。注意，因为有丝分裂不涉及任何同源染色体的配对，所以在二倍体、偶数染色体组的多倍体和奇数染色体组的多倍体中有丝分裂是同等有效的。

Triploidy is used in the production of seedless fruits, such as watermelon, grapes and bananas(Figure 2.12). All of the tissues of these fruit are triploid. Because almost all of the cells of the plant, including its fruit, are produced through mitosis, the uneven number of chromosome sets does not affect their development. However, cells that contribute to the production of gametes are produced through meiosis, and because the triploids are unable to complete normal meioses, their gametes fail to develop, so no zygotes are formed, and the seeds (which normally contain embryos that develop from the zygotes) are aborted.

三倍体应用于生产无籽果实，如西瓜、葡萄和香蕉（图 2.12）。这些水果的全部组织都是三倍体，因为这些植物几乎所有的细胞都是通过有丝分裂产生的，包括它们的果实，并且奇数的染色体组不会影响它们的发育。然而，形成配子的细胞是通过减数分裂产生的，但因为是三倍体而不能完成正常的减数分裂，所以它们的配子是败育的，也就不会产生合子，更不会有正常的种子（正常情况下种子会包含由合子发育而来的胚）。

Figure 2.12 Part of a triploid watermelon, showing white, aborted seeds within the flesh (see the color figure)

图 2.12 三倍体无籽西瓜的截图。果肉中白色的是败育的种子（见彩版）

If triploids cannot make seeds, how do we obtain enough triploid individuals for cultivation? The answer depends on the plant species involved. In some cases, such as banana, it is possible to propagate the plant asexually; new progeny can simply be grown from cuttings from a triploid plant. On the other hand, seeds for seedless watermelon are produced sexually: a tetraploid watermelon plant is crossed with a

既然三倍体植物不能产生种子，那么我们怎么才能获得足够的三倍体植物用于栽培呢？这个问题的解决在于植物品种。例如，香蕉有时可能进行无性繁殖，只要从三倍体植株上切下一部分，就可获得新个体；而无籽西瓜的种子则是进行有性繁

diploid watermelon plant. Both the tetraploid and the diploid are fully fertile, and produce gametes with two ($1n=2x$) or one ($1n=1x$) sets of chromosomes, respectively. These gametes fuse to produce a zygote ($2n=3x$), that is able to develop normally into an adult plant through multiple rounds of mitosis, but is unable to compete normal meiosis or produce seeds.

殖而来的：一个四倍体西瓜植株和一个二倍体西瓜植株进行杂交。四倍体和二倍体都是可育的，其产生的配子分别具有两套（$1n=2x$）和一套（$1n=1x$）染色体组。这两种配子结合产生合子（$2n=3x$），它能够不断进行有丝分裂而正常发育成成体植株，但不能完成正常的减数分裂或不能产生种子。

ENDOREDUPLICATION 核内复制

Endoreduplication, also known as **endopolyploidy**, is a special type of tissue-specific genome amplification that occurs in many types of plant cells and in specialized cells of some animals including humans. Endoreduplication does not affect the germline or gametes, so species with endopolyploidy are not considered polyploids. Endopolyploidy occurs when a cell undergoes multiple rounds of DNA synthesis (S-phase) without any mitosis. This produces multiple chromatids of each chromosome. Endopolyploidy seems to be associated with cells that are metabolically very active, and produce a lot of enzymes and other proteins in a short amount of time. The highly endoreduplicated salivary gland chromosomes of *D. melanogaster* have been useful research models in genetics, since their relatively large size makes them easy to study under the microscope(Figure 2.13).

核内复制（也称为**核内多倍体**）是特异组织中基因组扩增的特殊类型，它发生在许多植物细胞中和一些动物包括人的特殊细胞中。核内复制不影响生殖细胞系和配子的产生，因此有核内复制的物种不能被认为是多倍体。当一个细胞经过多次 DNA 的合成（S 期）但不进行有丝分裂时就会产生核内多倍体。这个过程会使每条染色体具有多条染色单体。核内多倍体似乎与代谢非常活跃的细胞相关，这些细胞能够在短时间内产生许多酶和其他蛋白质。由于果蝇的相对大的个体，使它们很容易在显微镜下研究，所以这个高度核内复制的果蝇唾腺染色体也成了有用的遗传学研究模型（图 2.13）。

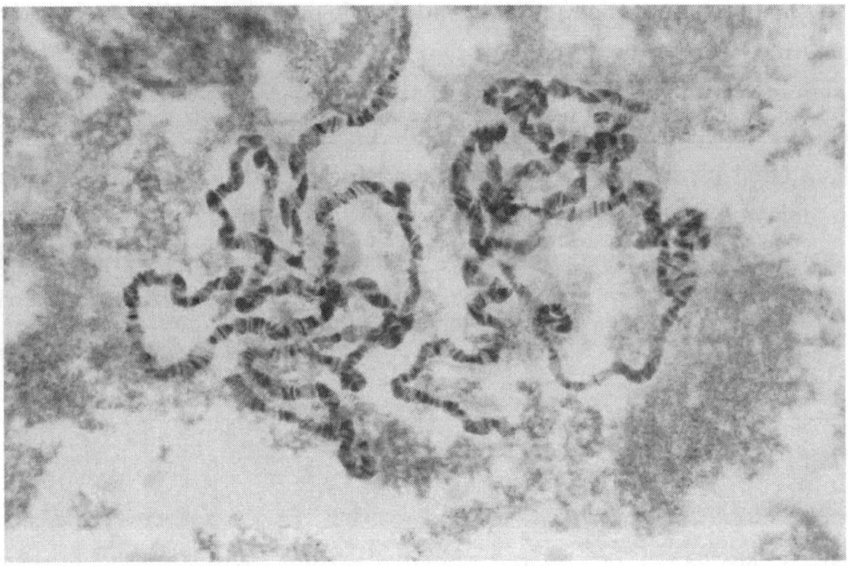

Figure 2.13 Endoreduplicated chromosomes from an insect salivary gland. The banding pattern is produced with fluorescent labels

图 2.13 昆虫唾腺的核内复制染色体，染色体带型是由荧光标记产生的

GENE BALANCE 基因平衡

Why do trisomies, duplications, and other chromosomal abnormalities that increase gene copy number sometimes have a negative effect on the normal development or physiology of an organism? This is particularly intriguing because in many species, aneuploidy is detrimental or lethal, while polyploidy is tolerated or even beneficial. The answer is probably related to the concept of **gene balance**, which can be summarized as follows: genes, and the proteins they produce, have evolved to be part of complex metabolic and regulatory networks. Some of these networks function best when certain enzymes and regulators are present in specific ratios to each other. Increasing the gene copy number for just one part of the network may throw the network out of balance, leading to increases or decreases of certain metabolites, which may be toxic in high concentrations or which may be limiting in other important processes in the cell. The activity of genes and metabolic networks is regulated in many

为什么三体、重复和其他的一些增加基因拷贝数的染色体畸变对机体的正常发育和生理功能会有负面影响？为什么在许多物种中非整倍体是有害的或是致死的，而多倍体却是可以存在甚至对物种是有益的？这是特别耐人寻味的。问题的答案可能与**基因平衡**的概念有关。对基因平衡可以做如下概述：基因和基因产生的蛋白质已进化为生物体复杂的代谢和调控网络的一部分。当某种酶和调控蛋白以一定比例出现时，这些网络功能配合可能恰到好处。而增加基因拷贝数会使调控网络失去平衡，导致某种代谢物的增加或减少，最终会导致在细胞中代谢物浓度过高而毒害细胞或限制细

different ways besides changes in gene copy number, so duplication of just a few genes will usually not be harmful. However, trisomy and large segmental duplications of chromosomes affect the dosage of so many genes that cellular networks are unable to adjust to the changes.

胞的其他重要代谢过程。基因的活性和代谢网络是以许多不同的方式进行调控的，包括基因拷贝数的改变，所以仅对几个基因的重复通常不会造成危害。然而，三体和染色体大片段的重复影响到了很多基因的剂量，以致细胞网络不能调整去适应这些改变。

ORGANELLAR GENOMES 细胞器基因组

Chromosomes also exist outside of the nucleus, within both the chloroplast and mitochondria. These organelles are likely the remnants of a prokaryotic endosymbionts that entered the cytoplasm of ancient progenitors of today's eukaryotes. These endosymbionts had their own, circular chromosomes, like most bacteria that exist today. Likewise, chloroplasts and mitochondria also have circular chromosomes that behave more like bacterial chromosomes than eukaryotic chromosomes, i.e. these organellar genomes do not undergo mitosis or meiosis. Organellar genomes are also often present in multiple copies within each organelle, and in most species are inherited maternally.

在细胞核外的叶绿体和线粒体中也存在染色体。这些细胞器可能是原核内共生体进入到现在真核生物的原始祖先细胞中的残留物，这些内共生体和现在的大多数细菌一样都有它们自己的环状染色体。同样，叶绿体和线粒体也具有环状染色体，并且与真核生物染色体相比，它们更类似于细菌染色体而非真核染色体。也就是说，这些细胞器基因组不进行有丝分裂和减数分裂。细胞器基因组也经常会出现多个拷贝，并且在多数物种中进行母系遗传。

Summary

- Chromosomes are complex and dynamic structures consisting of DNA and proteins (chromatin).

- 染色体是由 DNA 和蛋白质组成的复杂的动态结构（染色质）。

- The degree of chromatin compaction varies between heterochromatic and euchromatic regions and between stages of the cell cycle.

- 染色质的致密程度在细胞周期的不同阶段，以及在异染色质和常染色质之间是变化的。

- Some chromosomes can be distinguished cytologicaly based on their length, centromere position, and banding patterns when stained dyes or labelled with sequence-specific probes.

- 一些用染料染色的或用序列特异性探针标记的染色体，可以基于它们的长度、着丝粒位置和带型等细胞学特征对其进行区别。

- Homologous chromosomes contain the same genes, but not necessarily the same alleles. Sister chromatids usually contain the same genes and the same alleles.

- 同源染色体包含相同的基因，但未必是相同的等位基因。姐妹染色单体一般含有相同的基因且是相同的等位基因。

- Mitosis reduces the *c*-number, but not the *n*-number. Meiosis reduces both *c* and *n*.

- 有丝分裂只是降低 *c*，而 *n* 不变；减数分裂既降低 *c*，也减少 *n*。

- Homologous chromosomes associate with each other during meiosis, but not mitosis.

- 减数分裂有同源染色体的联会，但有丝分裂过程中没有。

- Several types of structural defects in chromosomes occur naturally, and can affect cellular function and even evolution.

- 自然产生的染色体结构畸变的某些类型能够影响细胞的功能甚至是进化。

- Aneuploidy results from the addition or subtraction of one or more chromosomes from a group of homologs, and is usually deleterious to the cell.

- 非整倍体来自一组同源染色体中增加或减少一条或多条染色体，且非整倍体对细胞一般是有害的。

- Polyploidy is the presence of more than two complete sets of chromosomes in a genome. Even-numbered multiple sets of chromosomes can be stably inherited in some species, especially plants.

- 多倍体是指具有两套以上完整基因组的个体。一些物种中偶数染色体组的多倍体能够稳定遗传，特别是在植物中。

- Endopolyploidy is tissue-specific type of polyploidy observed in some species, including diploids.

- 核内多倍体是指包括二倍体在内的一些物种中观察到的组织特异型多倍体。

- Both aneuploidy and structural defects such as duplications can affect gene balance.

- 非整倍体和像重复这样的畸变染色体都会影响基因平衡。

- Organelles also contain chromosomes, but these are much more like prokaryotic chromosomes than the nuclear chromosomes of eukaryotes.

- 细胞器也含有染色体，但是与真核生物的核染色体相比，它更类似于原核生物的染色体。

Key Terms

chromosome 染色体
core histones 核心组蛋白
nucleosome 核小体
30nm fiber 30nm 纤丝
histone H1 组蛋白 H1
scaffold proteins 支架蛋白
heterochromatin 异染色质
bivalent 二价体
reductional division 减数分裂
equational division 均等分裂
G_1
G_2
S
M

euchromatin 常染色质
microsatellite 微卫星
chromatid 染色单体
centromere 着丝粒
metacentric 中着丝粒的
acrocentric 近端着丝粒的
telocentric 端着丝粒的
holocentric 全着丝粒的
telomere 端粒
homolog 同源染色体
non-homologous 非同源染色体
chromatid 染色单体
sister chromatid 姐妹染色单体
non-sister chromatid 非姐妹染色单体
interphase 间期
mitosis 有丝分裂
prophase 前期
metaphase 中期
anaphase 后期
telophase 末期
meiosis 减数分裂
prophase (Ⅰ,Ⅱ) 前期(Ⅰ,Ⅱ)
metaphase (Ⅰ,Ⅱ) 中期(Ⅰ,Ⅱ)
anaphase (Ⅰ,Ⅱ) 后期(Ⅰ,Ⅱ)
telophase (Ⅰ,Ⅱ) 末期(Ⅰ,Ⅱ)
cytokinesis 胞质分裂
G_0
interphase 间期
n 整套染色体数（*n*）
c DNA 含量（*c*）
karyotype 核型
aneuploidy 非整倍体
monsomic 单体
trisomic 三体
Down's syndrome 唐氏综合征
deletion 缺失
duplication 重复
insertion 插入
inversion 倒位
translocation 易位
non-disjunction 染色体不分离
chromosome breakage 染色体断裂
polyploidy 多倍体
x 倍性（*x*）
tetravalent 四价体
endoreduplication 核内复制
endopolyploidy 核内多倍性
gene balance 基因平衡
cellular network 细胞网络
endosymbiont 内共生体
organellar chromosome 细胞器染色体

Study Questions

2.1 Define chromatin. What is the difference between DNA, chromatin and chromosomes?

2.1 定义染色质。阐述 DNA、染色质和染色体的差异。

2.2 Species A has *n*=4 chromosomes and Species B has *n*=6 chromosomes. Can you tell from this information which species has more DNA? Can you tell which species has more genes?

2.2 假定物种 A 的整套染色体数目 *n*=4，物种 B 的 *n*=6。你能根据这个信息确定这两物种哪个含有更多的 DNA，哪个含有更多的基因吗？

2.3 The answer to question 2 implies that not all DNA within a chromosome encodes genes. Can you name any examples of chromosomal regions that contain relatively few genes?

2.3 对于问题 2.2 的回答可知并非在一条染色体的所有 DNA 都编码基因。你能举例说明包含较少基因的染色体区域吗？

2.4

a) How many centromeres does a typical chromosome have?

b) What would happen if there was more than one centromere per chromosome?

c) What if a chromosome had zero centromeres?

2.4

a）一条典型的染色体有几个着丝粒？

b）如果每条染色体具有一个以上的着丝粒，将会怎样？

c）如果一条染色体没有着丝粒，又会怎样？

2.5 For a diploid with $2n$=16 chromosomes, how many chromosomes and chromatids are per cell present in the gamete, and zygote and immediately following G_1, S, G_2, mitosis, and meiosis?

2.5 对于 $2n$=16 的一个二倍体，在其配子、合子、随后的 G_1、S、G_2 期，以及有丝分裂和减数分裂过程中，每个细胞中染色体数和染色单体数各是多少？

2.6 Bread wheat (*Triticum aestivum*) is a hexaploid. Using the nomenclature presented in class, an egg cell of wheat has n=21 chromosomes. How many chromosomes in a zygote of bread wheat?

2.6 面包小麦（*T. aestivum*）是六倍体。用学过的术语来说，即小麦的卵细胞中染色体数目 n=21。那么在面包小麦的合子中有多少条染色体呢？

2.7 For a given gene:

a) What is the maximum number of alleles that can exist in a $2n$ cell of a given diploid individual?

b) What is the maximum number of alleles that can exist in a $1n$ cell of a tetraploid individual?

c) What is the maximum number of alleles that can exist in a $2n$ cell of a tetraploid individual?

d) What is the maximum number of alleles that can exist in a population?

2.7 对于给定的一个基因：

a）在二倍体的一个 $2n$ 细胞中，能够存在的最大等位基因数是多少？

b）在四倍体的一个 $1n$ 细胞中，能够存在的最大等位基因数是多少？

c）在四倍体的一个 $2n$ 细胞中，能够存在的最大等位基因数是多少？

d）在人的一个细胞中，能够存在的最大等位基因数是多少？

2.8

a) Why is aneuploidy more often lethal than polyploidy?

b) Which is more likely to disrupt gene balance: polyploidy or duplication?

2.8

a）为什么非整倍体的出现一般是致死的，而多倍体却不是？

b）对于多倍体和重复，哪个更可能破坏基因平衡？

2.9 For a diploid organism with $2n$=4 chromosomes, draw a diagram of all of the possible configurations of chromosomes during normal anaphase Ⅰ, with the maternally and paternally derived chromosomes labelled.

2.9 以一个 $2n$=4 的二倍体生物为例，画一个图表，表示出正常的后期Ⅰ染色体可能的分布排列，并标出每条染色体来自父母哪方。

2.10 For a triploid organism with $2n=3x=6$ chromosomes, draw a diagram of all of the possible configurations of chromosomes at anaphase I (it is not necessary label maternal and paternal chromosomes).

2.10 以一个 $2n=3x=6$ 的三倍体生物为例，画一个图表，表示出正常的后期 I 染色体可能的分布排列（不必标出每条染色体来自父母哪方）。

2.11 For a tetraploid organism with $2n=4x=8$ chromosomes, draw all of the possible configurations of chromosomes during a normal metaphase.

2.11 以一个 $2n=4x=8$ 的四倍体生物为例，画一个图表，表示出正常的中期染色体可能的分布排列。

Chapter 3

GENETICS OF ONE LOCUS
一个位点的遗传学分析

Pea plants were used in the discovery of some fundamental laws of genetics (see the cover)
用来探索一些基本遗传学法则的豌豆植物（见封面）

Before Mendel, the basic rules of heredity were not understood. For example, it was known that yellow-seeded pea plants occasionally produced offspring that had green seeds; but were the hereditary factors that controlled seed color somehow changing from one generation to the next, or were

孟德尔之前，人们还不理解遗传的基本规律。例如，人们都知道具有黄色种子的豌豆植物偶尔会产生具有绿色种子的后代，然而这是因为控制种子颜色的遗传因子在一

certain factors disappearing and reappearing? And did the same factors that controlled seed color also control things like plant height?

代代的过程中变化了，还是某种因子消失后又重现了？并且同一个因子既控制着种子颜色又控制着株高呢？

MENDEL'S FIRST LAW 孟德尔第一定律

Through careful study of patterns of inheritance, Mendel recognized that a single gene could exist in one or more versions, or **alleles**, even within an individual plant or animal. For example, he found two alleles of a gene for seed color: one allele gave yellow seeds, and the other gave green seeds. Mendel also observed that although different alleles could influence a single trait, they remained independent and could be inherited separately. This is the basis of **Mendel's First Law**, also called **The Law of Equal Segregation**, which states: during gamete formation, the two members of a gene pair segregate from each other; each gamete has an equal probability of containing either member of the gene pair (Figure 3.1).

通过遗传模式的认真研究，孟德尔意识到即使在一个植物或动物个体中单个基因也能以一种或多种形式或**等位基因**存在。例如，他发现两个控制种子颜色的等位基因：一个产生黄色种子，另一个产生绿色种子。孟德尔还观察到，尽管不同的等位基因能够影响单个性状，但它们还能保持独立并且能够分别遗传。这就是**孟德尔第一定律**又称为**均等分离定律**的基础。这个定律是这样陈述的：在配子形成的过程中，每对基因的两个成员彼此分离，每个配子均等地获得基因对中的任何一个成员（图 3.1）。

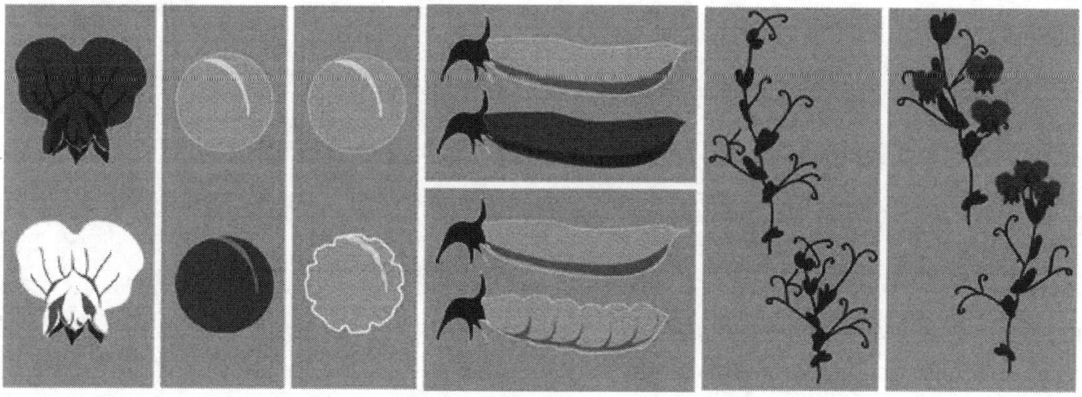

Figure 3.1 Seven traits Mendel studied in peas (see the color figure)

图 3.1 孟德尔研究豌豆的 7 个性状（见彩版）

Mendel's First Law is especially remarkable because he made his observations without knowing about the relationships

孟德尔第一定律非常卓越，因为孟德尔在不了解基因、染色体和 DNA

between genes, chromosomes, and DNA. We now know that the reason that more than one allele of a gene can be present in an individual is that most eukaryotic organisms have at least two sets of homologous chromosomes. For organisms that are predominantly diploid, such as humans or Mendel's peas, chromosomes exist in pairs, with one homolog inherited from each parent. Diploid cells can therefore hold up to two different alleles of each gene, with one allele on each member of a pair of homologous chromosomes. If both alleles of a particular gene are identical, the individual is said to be **homozygous** for that gene. On the other hand, if the alleles are different from each other, the genotype is **heterozygous**. In some cases, such as when describing genes on the sex chromosomes of a human male, we use the term **hemizygous**. This is because the cell contains only one X and one Y chromosome, so there is only one possible allele for each gene. Although a typical diploid individual can have at most two different alleles of a particular gene, more than two alleles can exist in a population of individuals. The most common allele in a natural population is called the **wild-type** allele (Figure 3.1).

之间的关系的情况下发现了这个规律。我们现在知道，一个以上的等位基因能够存在于同一个个体里的原因是大多数真核生物至少有两套同源染色体。对于那些主要是二倍体的生物来说，如人类和孟德尔所研究的豌豆，染色体成对存在，同源染色体单体分别来自于父母。因此二倍体细胞能够容纳每个基因的两个不同的等位基因，且每个等位基因位于同源染色体的每一条单体上。如果一个基因的两个等位基因是相同的，该个体就叫做这个基因的**纯合体**。相反，如果两个等位基因不同，基因型就是**杂合的**。例如，在描述人类男性性染色体上的基因时，我们常用名词：**半合子**。这是因为细胞仅包括一个 X 染色体和一个 Y 染色体，所以每个基因只有一个等位基因。虽然在典型的二倍体个体中一个特定基因最多只能有两个不同的等位基因，但是也有一定数量的个体具有两个以上的等位基因。在自然群体中最常见的等位基因被称为**野生型**等位基因（图 3.1）。

RELATIONSHIPS BETWEEN ALLELES AND PHENOTYPES
等位基因和表现型的关系

A specific position on a chromosome is called a **locus**. Most of the loci geneticists discuss are occupied by genes, and the terms locus and gene are often used interchangeably. The complete set of alleles at any loci of interest in an individual define its **genotype**. The detectable effect of these alleles on the structure or function of that individual is called its **phenotype**. The phenotype studied in any particular genetic experiment may range from simple, visible traits such as hair

染色体上的特定位置叫**位点**。遗传学家所讨论的多数位点经常用基因所代替，基因和位点之间经常通用。在个体中任何一个感兴趣位点上的整套等位基因定义为它的**基因型**。这些等位基因对个体的结构和功能所造成的可检测的效应即为个体的**表现型**。在任何一个独立

color, to more complex phenotypes including disease susceptibility or behavior.

的遗传学实验中表现型的范围可以从简单、可见的性状（如毛发颜色）到更为复杂的表现型，包括感病性或行为等。

Let us return to an example of a simple phenotype: flower color in Mendel's peas. We have already said that one allele produces purple flowers, while the other allele produces white flowers (Figure 3.2). But what does this tell us about the flower color of an individual that has one purple allele and one white allele, in other words, what is the **phenotype** of an individual whose genotype is heterozygous? We know from experimental data that individuals heterozygous for the purple and white alleles of the flower color gene have purple flowers. The allele associated with purple color is therefore said to be **dominant** to the allele that produces the white color. The other allele, whose phenotype is masked by a dominant allele in a heterozygote, is called **recessive**. Often, a dominant allele will be represented by a capital letter (e.g. *A*) while a recessive allele will be represented in lower case (e.g. *a*). However, many different systems of genetic symbols are in use (Table 3.1), so it is important to understand the different types of notation and to use them consistently.

让我们回到简单表现型的例子：孟德尔豌豆实验中的花色。我们已经提到一个等位基因产生紫花，而另外一个则产生白花（图 3.2）。但是具有一个紫花等位基因和一个白花等位基因的个体，其花色是什么样的呢？换句话说，杂合基因型的个体**表现型**是什么样的呢？我们从实验数据中可知，紫色和白色等位基因杂合体开紫花。这个和开紫花有关的等位基因对开白花的等位基因来说叫做**显性**。另外一个表现型在杂合体中被显性等位基因所覆盖的等位基因，被称为**隐性**的。显性基因常常用大写字母来表示（如 *A*），而隐性基因用小写字母来表示（如 *a*）。但是，也有很多不同种的遗传符号被使用（表 3.1），所以重要的是理解不同类型符号和使用时的一致性。

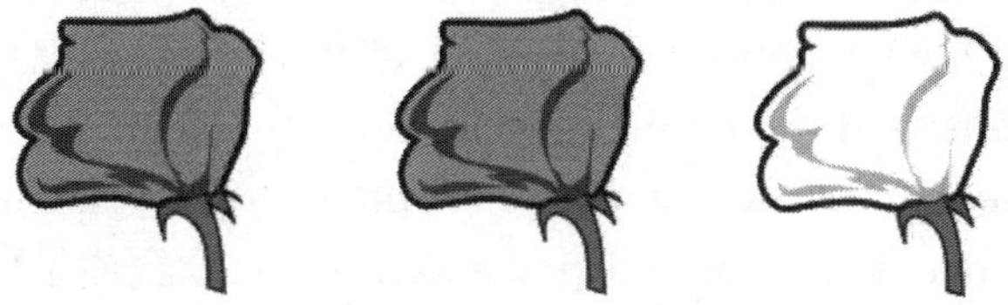

AA *Aa* *aa*

Figure3.2 Relationship between genotype and phenotype for a dominant allele (grayish color stands for purple color)

图 3.2 显性等位基因中基因型和表现型的关系（图中灰色表示紫色）

Table 3.1 Examples of symbols used to represent alleles, and their dominance relationships

examples of genotypes of heterozygotes	typical interpretation
Aa	Uppercase letter(s) most often represents dominant allele, and lowercase letter(s) indicates recessive allele
$a^{+}aw^{c2}$	Lowercase letters with + superscript represent wild-type allele, which is often dominant. A lower case letter with other superscripts (or with no superscripts) represents other alleles, which are often recessive
A_1A_2	The name of the locus is in uppercase or lower case letters, with subscripts or superscripts used to indicate different alleles. Generally, neither allele is completely dominant, or else the dominance relationships are unknown

表 3.1 用来表示等位基因及其显性关系的一些符号

杂合基因型例	典型解释
Aa	大写字母通常代表显性等位基因，小写字母表示隐性等位基因
$a^{+}aw^{c2}$	小写字母上标为加号代表野生型等位基因，通常为显性。小写字母带其他上标（或下标）代表另一个等位基因，通常为隐性
A_1A_2	位点的命名用大写或小写字母，上标或下标通常表示不同的等位基因。一般来说，没有一个等位基因是完全显性的，或者显隐性关系还不确定

Besides dominance and recessivity, other relationships can exist between alleles. In **semi-dominance** (also called **incomplete dominance,** Figure 3.3), both alleles affect the trait additively, and the phenotype of the heterozygote is intermediate between either of the homozygotes. For example, alleles of for red color in carnations and some other species exhibit semi-dominance, so that a heterozygote has pink petals, while a homozygote for one allele has red petals and the other has white petals. Thus in semi-dominance, the dosage of the alleles affects the phenotype, e.g. the phenotype of the heterozygote is approximately half as strong as the phenotype of a homozygote.

除了显隐性，在等位基因中还存在其他关系。**半显性**（或称**不完全显性**，图 3.3），是两种等位基因叠加影响性状表现，杂合体的表现型介于两种纯合体表现型中间的性状。例如，康乃馨和其他物种红色花瓣的等位基因呈现不完全显性，所以杂合体呈现粉色花瓣，而一个等位基因的纯合体呈现红色花瓣，而另一个纯合体呈现白色花瓣。所以在不完全显性中，等位基因的剂量影响着表现型。例如，杂合体的表现型大约是纯合体性状强度的一半。

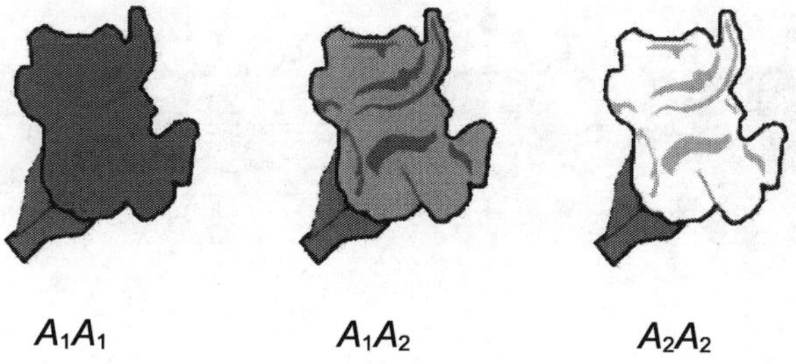

Figure 3.3 Relationship between genotype and phenotype for semi-dominant alleles (see the color figure)

图 3.3 半显性等位基因中基因型和表现型的关系（见彩版）

Co-dominance is another type of allelic relationship, in which a heterozygous individual expresses the phenotype of both alleles simultaneously. An example of co-dominance is found within the ABO blood group of humans, which is controlled by a gene called *I* (Figure 3.4). There are three possible alleles at this locus: I^A, I^B, and *i*. Homozygous individuals for I^A or I^B produce only A or B type antigens, respectively, on the surface of their blood cells, and therefore have either type A or type B blood. Heterozygous I^AI^B individuals have both A and B antigens on their cell surface, and so have type AB blood. Notice that the heterozygote expresses both alleles simultaneously, and is not some kind of novel intermediate between A and B. Co-dominance is therefore distinct from semi-dominance, although they are sometimes confused. Many types of molecular markers, which we will discuss in a later chapter, display a co-dominant relationship among alleles. It is also important to note that the third allele, *i*, does not make any antigens and is recessive to all other alleles. Homozygous recessive individuals (*ii*) have type O blood. This is a useful reminder that different types of dominance relationships can exist, even for alleles of the same gene.

共显性是另一种等位基因关系，杂合个体同时呈现两种等位基因的表现型。一个呈现共显性的例子就是 *I* 基因控制的人 ABO 血型（图 3.4）。在这个位点上有 3 个等位基因：I^A、I^B和 *i*。有 I^A或 I^B两种纯合型的个体在其血细胞表面只产生 A 型或 B 型两种抗原，所以有 A 或 B 两种血型。杂合型 I^AI^B的个体在其血细胞表面既有A型也有B型抗原，所以就有了 AB 血型。需要注意的是，杂合体同时表达两种等位基因，而且不是一种新的 A 和 B 中间过渡类型。因此，尽管共显性与半显性常常混淆，但是却有所不同。我们将在后面的章节中讨论许多能显示出等位基因间共显性关系的分子标记类型。同样值得重视的是第三个等位基因 *i*，它并不产生抗原，并对其他基因呈现隐性。纯合隐性个体（*ii*）是 O 型血。这提示我们，即使是相同基因的等位基因，也存在不同类型的显性关系。

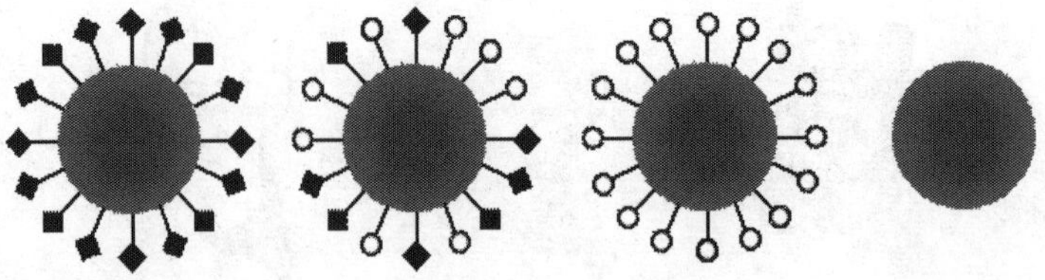

Figure 3.4 Relationship between genotype and phenotype for co-dominant alleles (I^A, I^B), and a recessive allele

图 3.4 共显性等位基因和一个隐性等位基因中基因型和表现型的关系

BIOCHEMICAL BASIS OF DOMINANCE 显性的生化基础

We cannot predict whether an allele will be dominant based simply on the phenotype of homozygotes; we must also know the phenotype of a heterozygote. What, then, causes dominance? There are many different biochemical conditions that may make one allele dominant to another, but one of the most common is **haplosufficiency**. Most genes produce more than enough protein to accomplish their normal biological function. If an allele is haplosufficient, then just one copy of that allele produces enough protein to have the same effect as the amount of protein produced by two copies of that allele. For the majority of genes studied, the normal (i.e. **wild-type**) alleles are haplosufficient, so even if a mutation causes a complete loss of function in one allele, the wild-type allele will be dominant and the normal function of the biochemical pathway will be retained. On the other hand, in some biochemical pathways, a single wild-type allele may be **haploinsufficient**, i.e. it may not produce enough protein to result in a normal phenotype if the other allele in a heterozygote is not functional. In this case, a non-func- tional allele will be dominant to a wild-type allele.

我们不能简单地从纯合体的表现型来预测一个等位基因是否是显性的；我们必须知道杂合体的表现型。那什么决定显性呢？有很多不同的生化条件使得该等位基因对另一个等位基因呈显性。最普遍的生化基础是**单倍充足性**。大多数基因产生充足的蛋白质来完成它们正常的生物功能。如果一个等位基因是单倍充足的，那么该等位基因的一个拷贝就可以产生充足的蛋白质，而且和该等位基因的两份拷贝产生的蛋白质的效果相同。对于研究的大多数基因来说，正常的（也就是**野生型**）等位基因具有单倍充足性的，所以即使一个突变导致了一个等位基因功能的完全丧失，由于野生型等位基因是显性的，也能保持该生化途径的正常功能。另外，在一些生化途径中，单个的野生型等位基因可能是**单倍不充足**的，即如果杂合体的另一个等位基因失去功能，就不能产生足够的蛋白质而形成正常的表现型。在这种情况下，一个非功能性的等位基因对于野生型等位基因呈显性。

THE PUNNETT SQUARE AND MONOHYBRID CROSSES
旁氏棋盘法和单基因杂种杂交

Geneticists, including Mendel, make use of **true breeding lines** (Figure 3.5 A). These are populations of plants or animals in which all parents and their offspring have identical phenotypes over many generations with respect to a particular trait. True breeding lines are useful, because they can be assumed to be homozygous for the alleles that affect a trait of interest. When two individuals that are homozygous for the same alleles are crossed, all of their offspring will all also be homozygous.

遗传学家，包括孟德尔，用的是**纯育系**（图 3.5A）。这些动物或植物的种群，相对于某一特定的性状，它们的亲代和子代在数代保持相同的表现型。纯育系是有用的，因为它们可以被认作是影响感兴趣性状的纯合的等位基因。当两个有相同等位基因的纯合体杂交时，它们的所有后代均为纯合体。

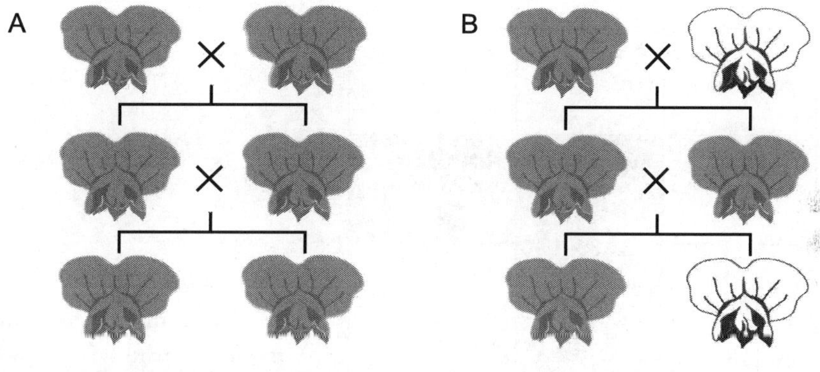

Figure 3.5 A: a true-breeding line; B: a monohybrid cross produced by mating two pure-breeding lines

图 3.5 A: 纯育系; B: 通过两个纯育系杂交产生的单基因杂种杂交

Given the genotypes of any two parents, we can predict all of the possible genotypes of the offspring. Furthermore, if we also know the dominance relationships for all of the alleles, we can predict the phenotypes of the offspring. A convenient method for calculating the expected genotypic and phenotypic ratios from a cross is the use of Punnett Square, which is a matrix in which all of the possible gametes produced by one parent are listed along one axis, and the gametes from

给出任意双亲的基因型，我们能预测出他们后代所有可能的基因型。此外，如果我们还知道所有等位基因的显隐性关系，就能够预测出所有后代的表现型。一种能够快捷地计算出预期的杂交后代基因型和表现型比率的方法是旁氏棋盘法，该方法将其中一个亲本产生的所

the other parent are listed along the other axis. Each possible combination of gametes is listed at the intersection of each row and column.

有可能的配子列在矩阵的一侧坐标轴上，另一亲本的配子列在另一坐标轴上。每一个可能的配子组合列在该行、列的交叉处。

When two heterozygotes are crossed, what genotypes are produced, and what is the expected frequency of each genotype? If we use the symbols *A* and *a* to represent each the two alleles of the heterozygote, then from the **Punnett Square** (Figure 3.6) we see that three genotypes are produced in a ratio of 1 : 2 : 1. If we know something about the phenotypes and dominance relationships of these alleles (as implied by the symbols used), we can predict the expected phenotypic ratio of the progeny from this cross is 3 : 1. A cross between two individuals that are both heterozygous at a single locus is so common in genetics that this cross is given its own name: the **monohybrid cross** (Figure 3.6).

当两个杂合子杂交时会产生出什么样的基因型，各个基因型的期望频率是多少？如果我们用 *A* 和 *a* 代表杂合子的两个等位基因，通过**旁氏棋盘法**（图 3.6）可以看到3个基因型产生的比例是1：2：1。如果我们知道这些等位基因的表现型和显隐性关系，就能预测出杂交后代的期望表现型比例是3：1。两个单一位点均为杂合的个体杂交在遗传学上十分普遍，这种杂交有自己的名称，叫做**单基因杂种杂交**（图 3.6）。

	A	***a***
A	*AA*	*Aa*
a	*Aa*	*aa*

Figure 3.6　A Punnett Square showing a monohybrid cross

图 3.6　旁氏棋盘法表示单基因杂种杂交

TEST CROSSES CAN BE USED TO DETERMINE GENOTYPES
测交确定基因型

Knowing the genotypes of an individual is usually an important part of a genetic experiment. However, genotypes cannot be observed directly; they must be inferred based on phenotypes. Because of dominance, it is often not possible to distinguish between a heterozygote and a homozgyote

了解一个个体的基因型通常是遗传学实验非常重要的一部分。但基因型并不能够被直观地观察到，必须依据表现型来推断。因为显性效应的存在，通常并不能单纯依据表

based on phenotype alone (e.g. see the purple-flowered F_2 plants in Figure 3.5B). To determine the genotype, a **test cross** can be performed, in which an individual with an ambiguous genotype is crossed with an individual that is homozygous recessive for all of the loci being tested (Figure 3.7). For example, if you were given a pea plant with purple flowers (and no other information), you would not know whether the plant was a homozygote (*AA*) or heterozygote (*Aa*). You could cross this purple-flowered plant to a white-flowered plant as a **tester**, since you know the genotype of the tester is *aa*. You will observe different ratios in the F_1 generation, depending on the genotype of the purple-flowered parent. If the purple-flowered parent was a homozgyote, all of the F_1 progeny will be purple. If the purple-flowered parent was a heterozygote, the F_1 progeny should segregate purple-flowered and white-flowered plants in a 1 : 1 ratio.

现型来判断是纯合体还是杂合体（如图 3.5B 紫花的 F_2 代植株）。为确定基因型，用基因型不确定的个体和所有位点均明确的隐性纯合个体进行**测交**（图 3.7）。例如，假如有一个开紫花的豌豆植物（没有其他信息），你不能明确这个植物是纯合体（*AA*）还是杂合体（*Aa*），就可以用这个紫花植物和用作测验种的白花植物杂交，因为已知这个白花植物的基因型是 *aa*。你可以通过观察 F_1 代紫花和白花的不同比例来判断紫花亲本的基因型。如果紫花亲本是纯合体，F_1 代全为紫花；如果紫花亲本为杂合体，那么 F_1 代就会分离，紫花和白花的比例为 1 : 1。

	A	***A***
a	*Aa*	*Aa*
a	*Aa*	*Aa*

	A	***a***
a	*Aa*	*aa*
a	*Aa*	*aa*

Figure 3.7 A Punnett Squares showing examples of test crosses

图 3.7 旁氏棋盘法显示测交试验

SEX-LINKAGE IS AN IMPORTANT EXCEPTION TO MENDEL'S FIRST LAW
伴性遗传是孟德尔第一定律中一个重要的例外现象

In mammals, *Drosophila*, and many other organisms, males have one copy of each of two different sex chromosomes (XY), while females have two copies of the same chromosome (XX) (but note that although the chromosomes have

在哺乳动物中，果蝇和其他生物体里，雄性各有两种不同的性染色体（XY），而雌性有两个相同的性染色体（XX）（值得强调的是，尽管

the same names, the mechanism of sex determination is very different in mammals and flies). The X and Y chromosomes do not carry the same loci, so some genes are present on the X, but not Y chromosomes. Such genes are said to be X-linked (there are very few examples of Y-linked genes, except those involved specifically in sexual differentiation). A cross involving an X-linked gene with a heterozygous female and a hemizygous male therefore produces progeny in phenotypic ratios very different from the 3 : 1 ratio obtained in a monohybrid cross for an **autosomal** (i.e. not sex-linked) locus. Other species with sex chromosomes may also be subject to sex-linkage, although the chromosomes may be called something other than X and Y.

染色体有着同样的命名，但性别决定机制在哺乳动物和蝇类间是极为不同的）。X 和 Y 染色体并不携带相同的基因位点，所以一些基因在 X 染色体上存在，但在 Y 染色体上却没有。这种基因被称为 X 连锁（很少有 Y 连锁基因，那些参与性别分化的基因除外）。一个涉及 X 连锁基因的杂合母本和半合子的父本杂交产生后代的表现型和**常染色体**（非伴性遗传）位点单基因杂种杂交产生的 3 : 1 比例完全不同。其他物种的性染色体可能也属于伴性遗传，尽管它们的染色体并未用 X 和 Y 来命名。

A researcher may not know beforehand whether a novel allele is sex-linked. The definitive method to test for sex-linkage (and other forms of sex-dependent inheritance) is to conduct **reciprocal crosses** (Figure 3.8). This means to cross a male and a female that have different phenotypes, and then conduct a second set of crosses, in which the phenotypes are reversed relatively to the sex of the parents in the first cross. For example, cross a white-eyed female with a red-eyed male fly, then separately cross a red-eyed female with a white-eyed male. Note how in reciprocal crosses, the phenotypes among the progeny of sex-linked genes are different from what is expected for autosomal genes (Figure 3.9).

研究人员可能不会事先知道是否一个新的等位基因是伴性连锁的。确定伴性遗传（或其他性别依赖的遗传形式）通过**正反交**来进行（图 3.8）。就是不同表现型的雄性和雌性交配，然后进行与第一次交配性别相反的双亲表现型的第二次交配。例如，白眼雌性果蝇与红眼雄性交配，然后让红眼雌性与白眼雄性交配。在正反交试验中值得注意的是，伴性遗传的后代表现型与常染色体上基因所期望的表现型并不相同（图 3.9）。

	X^{w+}	X^{w+}
X^{w}	$X^{w+}X^{w}$	$X^{w+}X^{w}$
Y	$X^{w+}Y$	$X^{w+}Y$

	X^{w}	X^{w}
X^{w+}	$X^{w}X^{w+}$	$X^{w}X^{w+}$
Y	$X^{w}Y$	$X^{w}Y$

Figure 3.8 Reciprocal crosses involving a sex-linked trait (1)

图 3.8 与伴性遗传性状有关的正反交 (1)

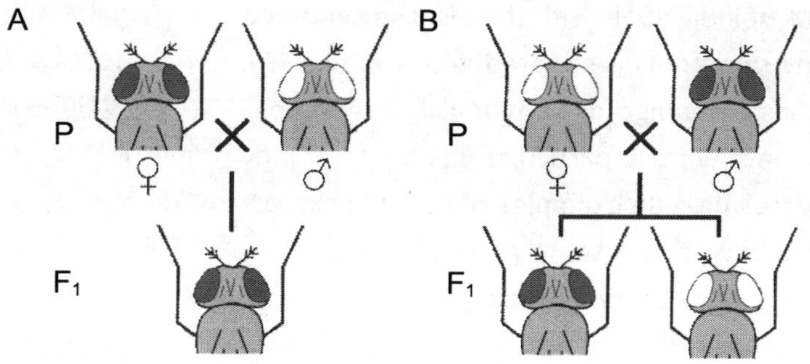

Figure 3.9 Reciprocal crosses involving a sex-linked trait (2). A: direct cross; B: back cross

图 3.9 与伴性遗传性状有关的正反交 (2)。A: 正交; B: 反交

PHENOTYPE MAY BE INFLUENCED BY OTHER FACTORS BESIDES GENOTYPE
表现型可能受基因型之外的其他因素影响

The phenotypes described in the examples used in this chapter all have nearly perfect correlation with their associated genotypes, in otherwords an individual with a particular genotype always has the expected phenotype. However. many phenotypes are not determined entirely by genetics; these are instead determined by an interaction between genotype and non-genetic, environmental factors. This **genotype-by-environment** (**G × E**) interaction is especially is especially relevant in the study of economically important phenotypes, such as human diseases or agricultural productivity. For example, a particular genotype may pre-dispose an individual to cancer, but cancer may only develop if the individual is exposed to certain DNA-damaging chemicals. Therefore, not all individuals with the particular genotype will develop the cancer phenotype.

在这一章的例子中表现型和基因型有着近乎完美的相关性，换句话说，一个有着特定基因型的个体总有着相应的预期表现型。但许多表现型并不能完全取决于遗传，而是由基因型和非遗传的环境因素互作所决定。这种**基因-环境**（**G×E**）互作现象在重要的经济性状，如人类疾病或农业生产效率研究中非常有意义。例如，一个特殊的基因型可能使一个人患上癌症，但是只有这个个体接触到易使 DNA 损伤的化学物质时才能患上癌症。所以不是所有带有这种特定基因型的个体都能发展成癌症。

The terms penetrance and expressivity are useful when describing the relationship between certain genotypes and their phenotypes. **Penetrance** is the proportion of individuals with a particular genotype that display a corresponding phenotype. Because all pea plants that are homozygous for the allele for white flowers (e.g. *aa* in Figure 3.2) actually have white flowers, this allele is 100% penetrant. In contrast, many human genetic diseases are incompletely penetrant,

外显率和表现度在描述特定基因型和其表现型的关系中起着重要作用。**外显率**就是特定基因型的个体显示相应表现型的比例。因为所有纯合白花等位基因的豌豆植物都是开白花的（如在图 3.2 的 *aa*），该等位基因就是 100%外显的。相反，许多人类遗传疾病是不完全外

since less than 100% of individuals with the disease genotype actually develop any symptoms associated with the disease. **Expressivity** describes the range of variation in phenotypes observed in individuals with a particular genotype. Many human genetic diseases provide examples of variable expressivity, since individuals with the same genotypes may vary greatly in the severity of their symptoms. Both incomplete penetrance and variable expressivity may be due to environmental or other genetic or non-genetic factors.

显的，因为有疾病基因型的个体并不会 100%表现出该疾病的相关症状。**表现度**描述了一个特定基因型个体的表现型的变化范围。许多人类的遗传性疾病提供了表现度不一致的例证，即使有着相同基因型的不同个体也可能在病症严重程度上差异很大。不完全外显和可变表现度不一致可能取决于环境或其他遗传或非遗传因素。

DEVIATIONS FROM EXPECTED RATIOS 预期比率的偏离

For a variety of reasons, the phenotypic ratios observed from real crosses rarely match the ratios expected based on a Punnett Square or other prediction techniques. There are many possible explanations for deviations from expected ratios. Sometimes these deviations are due to **sampling effects**, in other words, the random selection of a non-representative subset of individuals for observation. On the other hand, it may be that the expected ratios were calculated using incorrect assumptions. For example, a particular allele may actually be semi-dominant rather than dominant, or maybe the genotype of one parent was really heterozygous, rather than homozygous, or perhaps a gene that was assumed to be autosomal is really sex-linked.

由于各种原因，实际所观察到的表现型比率很少与基于旁氏棋盘法或其他预测技术所期待的比率能完全吻合。对于期待的比率产生的偏差有很多可能的解释。有时，偏差来自于**取样效应**，换句话说，就是随机选择了不具代表性的个体子集。此外是在不正确的假定条件下计算出的预期比率。例如，一个特定基因是不完全显性的而不是显性的，或者亲本之一的基因型是杂合的而不是纯合的，或者这个基因被假定为在常染色体上的而事实上却是伴性遗传。

A statistical procedure called the **chi-square** test (χ^2) can be used to help a geneticist decide whether the deviation between observed and expected ratios is due to sampling effects, or whether the difference is so large that some other explanation must be sought by re-examining the assumptions used to calculate the expected ratio. The procedure for performing a chi-square test is explained in some lab manuals. Essentially, the procedure calculates the difference between observed and expected frequencies of each phenotypic class, squares the difference (to remove negative values), and then

一种叫做**卡方检验**（χ^2）的统计学方法能够帮助遗传学家确定观察和预期的比率差异是否来自**取样效应**，或者这个差异是否过大，以至于我们必须通过重新检验计算该预期比率的假设找到其他原因。卡方检验的过程会在一些实验手册中有所解释。从本质上说，程序中首先计算每种表现型的观察值和预期值的差异，平方差（排除负

adjusts the scale of this difference as a proportion of the expected frequency. The chi-square statistic is the sum of all of these values, and is therefore a standardized measure of the total deviation between observed and expected phenotypic ratios; the larger the chi-square statistic, the larger the difference between observed and expected ratios.

值），然后调整这个差异的比率作为期望频率的比率。卡方统计数值就是所有这些值的总数，因此也是预期比率和表现型比率总偏差的标准值；卡方统计数值越大，观察值和期望值的差异就越大。

How do we decide whether a chi-square statistic is likely too large to be due to sampling effects alone? To do this, we compare the chi-square value for our experiment to a previously calculated probability distribution for all possible chi-square values. This distribution shows the probability of obtaining any particular chi-square value due to sampling effects. As you might expect, the distribution shows that low chi-square values are fairly common, while larger chi-square values are rare (Figure 3.10). From this distribution (or more conveniently, from a table of chi-square values), you can find the probability (or ***P*-value**) that matches the chi-square statistic calculated for your experiment. For example, a *P*-value of 0.05 means that in only one or fewer of 20 experiments will such a large difference be observed between observed

我们如何确定卡方统计数值是否大到不可能仅仅是由于取样效应导致的呢？为此，我们将试验中的卡方值与之前计算的所有可能卡方值的概率分布做了比较。分布显示了由于取样效应获得任意一个特定卡方值的概率。正像所期望的那样，这个分布显示，低卡方值非常普遍，而高卡方值很少（图3.10）。通过这个分布（或简单地从卡方分布图表上看），你会发现符合你试验计算的卡方统计数值概率（或称 ***P*** 值）。例如，如果期望值计算正确的话，0.05 的概率就

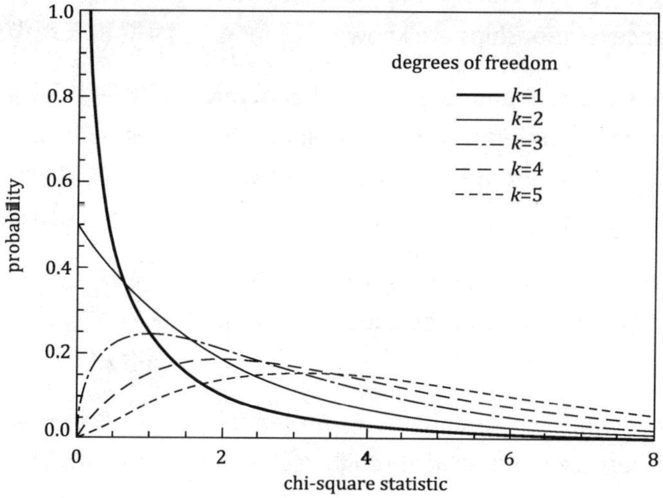

Figure 3.10 Probability distribution of the chi-square statistic for five different degrees of freedom

图 3.10 5 种自由度下的卡方统计数值的概率分布

and expected results, if the expected values were calculated accurately. As a general rule, geneticists use a *P*-value of 0.05 as a cut-off to determine whether deviations between observed and expected ratios can be attributed to sampling effects, or whether the underlying assumptions must be re-examined. Finally, it must be noted the chi-square distribution depends on the number of degrees of freedom, which is a statistical concept that in the context of genetics is usually one less than the number of phenotypic classes ($n-1$).

意味着 20 次试验中就有一次或更少试验能发现观察值和期望值的较大差异。一般来讲，遗传学家用 0.05 的 *P* 值作为确定观察值和期望值的差异是来自取样效应，还是需要重新检测基本假设正确与否的界限。最后，必须注意的是，卡方分布取决于自由度数值，自由度是统计上的概念，遗传学上取表现型数量减一（$n-1$）。

Summary

- A diploid can have up to two different alleles at a single locus. The alleles are distributed equally between gametes during meiosis.

- 一个二倍体在单一位点上有两个不同的等位基因。该等位基因在细胞减数分裂中在配子间平均分配。

- Phenotype depends on the alleles that are present, their dominance relationships, and sometimes also interactions with the environment and other factors.

- 表现型取决于等位基因的存在和显隐性关系，有时也和环境及其他因素的交互作用有关。

- The expected ratios of genotypes and phenotypes can be calculated for the progeny of any cross, if the mode of inheritance and the dominance relationships are known.

- 如果遗传模式和显隐性关系已知，就能够计算出任一杂交后代基因型和表现型的预期比率。

- Deviations between expected and observed phenotypic ratios may result from sampling effects, or from additional genetic or non-genetic factors not initially considered when calculating the expected ratios.

- 预期和观察表现型比率的差异可能来自取样效应，或来自计算预期比率前没考虑到的额外的遗传或非遗传因素。

- The chi-square test is useful when deciding whether to investigate the underlying assumptions of the expected ratios.

- 在决定是否要探讨预期比率的基本假设是否正确时，卡方测验是很有用的。

- Sex-linkage is an exception to some definitions of Mendel's First Law, and can be best demonstrated through reciprocal crosses.

- 伴性遗传是孟德尔第一定律的例外，可通过正反交得到很好的证实。

Key Terms

allele　等位基因
Mendel's First Law　孟德尔第一定律
Law of Equal Segregation　均等分离定律
haploinsufficiency　单倍不充足性
pure breeding lines　纯育系
Punnett Square　旁氏棋盘法

homozygous 纯合体
heterozygous 杂合体
hemizygous 半合子
wild-type 野生型
locus 基因位点
genotype 基因型
phenotype 表现型
dominant 显性
recessive 隐性
semi-dominance 半显性
incomplete dominance 不完全显性
co-dominance 共显性
ABO
haplosufficiency 单倍充足性
monohybrid cross 单基因杂种杂交
test cross 测交
tester 测验种
sex-linked 伴性遗传的
autosomal 常染色体
reciprocal cross 正反交
G × E
penetrance 外显率
expressivity 表现度
sampling effects 取样效应
chi-square, χ^2 卡方分布, χ^2
P-value *P* 值
degrees of freedom 自由度

Study Questions

3.1 What is the maximum number of alleles for a given locus in a normal gamete of a diploid species?

3.1 在一个正常的二倍体配子中，一个基因位点上最多有几个等位基因？

3.2 Wirey hair (*W*) is dominant to smooth hair (*w*) in dogs.

3.2 狗的卷曲毛(*W*)对光亮毛(*w*)是显性。

a) If you cross a homozygous, wirey-haired dog with a smooth-haired dog, what will be the genotype and phenotype of the F_1 generation?

b) If two dogs from the F1 generation mated, what would be the most likely ratio of hair phenotypes among their progeny?

c) When two wirey-haired *Ww* dogs actually mated, they had alitter of three puppies, which all had smooth hair. How do you explain this observation?

d) Someone left a wirey-haired dog on your doorstep. Without extracting DNA,what would be the easiest way to determine the genotype of this dog?

a）如果你将一个纯合的卷曲毛狗与光亮毛狗进行杂交，F_1代的基因型和表现型是什么？

b）如果F_1代狗杂交，在它们后代中毛表现型的最可能比率是多少？

c）当两个卷曲毛狗（*Ww*）杂交，得到的3个小狗都是光亮毛的，你怎样解释这种现象？

d）有人将一只卷曲毛狗扔在你家门前，不通过提取DNA，你能用最容易的办法来决定这个狗的基因型吗？

e) Based on the information provided in question 3.1, can you tell which, if either, of the alleles is wild-type?

e）根据问题3.1提供的信息，你能说明哪一个等位基因是野生型吗？

3.3 An important part of Mendel's experiments was the use of homozygous lines as parents for his crosses. How did he

3.3 孟德尔试验中一个重要的部分是用纯合系作为杂交的亲本，他

know they were homozygous, and why was the use of the lines important?

怎么知道它们是纯合的呢？为什么使用这些纯合系是重要的？

3.4 In the table below, match the mouse hair color phenotypes with the term from the list that best explains the observed phenotype, given the genotypes shown. In this case, the allele symbols do not imply anything about the dominance relationships between the alleles. List of terms: haplosufficiency, haploinsufficiency, pleiotropy, semi-dominance, co-dominance, incomplete penetrance, variable expressivity.

3.4 在下表中，根据给定的基因型，用列出的解释表现型的术语匹配老鼠毛发颜色的表现型。在这种情况下，等位基因符号不意味等位基因之间的任何显隐性关系。术语：单倍充足性、单倍不充足性、基因多效性、半显性、共显性、不完全外显、可变表现度。

Table for Question 3.4

	A_1A_1	A_1A_2	A_2A_2
1	all hairs black	on the same individual: 50% of hairs are all black 50% of hairs are all white	all hairs white
2	all hairs black	all hairs are the same shade of grey	all hairs white
3	all hairs black	all hairs black	50% of individuals have all white hairs 50% of individuals have all black hairs
4	all hairs black	all hairs black	mice have no hair
5	all hairs black	all hairs white	all hairs white
6	all hairs black	all hairs black	all hairs white
7	all hairs black	all hairs black	hairs are a wide range of shades of grey

问题 3.4 的表

	A_1A_1	A_1A_2	A_2A_2
1	所有毛发黑色	同一个个体上：50% 毛发是黑色的50% 毛发是白色的	所有毛发白色
2	所有毛发黑色	所有毛发呈现一样的灰色	所有毛发白色
3	所有毛发黑色	所有毛发黑色	50% 个体所有毛发白色 50%个体所有毛发黑色
4	所有毛发黑色	所有毛发黑色	没有毛发
5	所有毛发黑色	所有毛发白色	所有毛发白色
6	所有毛发黑色	所有毛发黑色	所有毛发白色
7	所有毛发黑色	所有毛发黑色	毛发呈现较大变化范围的灰色

3.5 Does equal segregation of alleles into daughter cells happen during mitosis, meiosis, or both?

3.5 等位基因都均等地分配到子细胞中去是发生在有丝分裂，还是减数分裂？还是在两个阶段中均可发生？

3.6 If your blood type is B, what are the possible genotypes of your parents at the locus that controls ABO blood types?

3.6 如果你的血型是 B 型血，在控制 ABO 血型的基因位点上你的父母可能的基因型是什么？

3.7 A rare dominant mutation causes a neurological disease that appears late in life in all people that carry the mutation. If a father has this disease, what is the probability that his daughter will also have the disease?

3.7 一个罕见的显性突变会导致一种神经性疾病，该病只在携带该突变的人群中晚年患病。如果一个父亲患该病，他的女儿患病的概率有多少？

3.8 The recessive *w* allele of the *white* gene in fruit flies produces white eyes.

a) If a heterozygous female and a white-eyed male are crossed, what are their phenotypic ratios among their F_1 progeny with respect to eye color?

b) What are the phenotypic ratios among their F_1 progeny with respect to both sex and eye color?

3.8 果蝇中 *white* 基因的隐性等位基因（*w*）呈现白眼。

a）如果一个雌性杂合体和一个白眼雄性杂交，就眼睛颜色来说，F_1 中表现型比率是多少？

b）就性别和眼睛颜色来说，F_1 中表现型比率是多少？

3.9 A particular mutant allele of the Hairy wing (*Hw*) gene is dominant and causes hairy wings, while the wild-type allele (Hw^+) is recessive.

a) How could you test whether this gene is sex-linked?

b)What would be the expected genotypic and phenotypic ratios in the F_2 generation?

3.9 一个毛翅特定的突变的等位基因是显性的，能够促进毛翅的产生，而野生型等位基因（Hw^+）是隐性的。

a）你怎样能够验证这个基因是否为伴性遗传？

b）在 F_2 代中，预期的基因型和表现型比率是多少？

3.10 Almost all of the examples of sex-linked inheritance refer to genes on the X chromosome. Imagine a gene with a non-sexual phenotype that was located exclusively on the Y chromosome. What would be inheritance pattern of this gene?

3.10 几乎所有伴性遗传的例子指的都是 X 染色体上的基因。设想一个非性别表现型的基因特定地位于 Y 染色体上，这个基因的遗传模式是什么？

3.11 Mendel's First Law (as stated in class) does not apply to alleles of most genes located on sex chromosomes. Does the law apply to the chromosomes themselves?

3.11 孟德尔第一定律（课上讲过）不适用于性染色体上的大多数基因。那么这个定律能够适用于染色体本身吗？

3.12 When can you have more confidence in your assumptions about an expected pattern of inheritance :

a) with a bigger χ^2 value or a smaller χ^2 value?

3.12 什么时候你对遗传期望模式的假设更可信:

a）一个大的卡方值或一个小的卡方值？

b) with a bigger *P*-value or a smaller *P*-value?

c) with a bigger df or a smaller df?

b）一个大的 *P* 值或一个小的 *P* 值？

c）一个大的自由度或一个小的自由度？

3.13 Determine the appropriate degrees of freedom to use when scoring progeny from each of the following crosses.

a) *Aa*×*aa*, where *A* is dominant

b) *Aa*×*Aa*, where *A* is dominant

c) *Aa*×*Aa*, where *A* is semi-dominant

3.13 对下列杂交后代评价时确定合适的自由度。

a）*Aa*×*aa*, *A* 是显性的

b）*Aa*×*Aa*, *A* 是显性的

c）*Aa*×*Aa*, *A* 是半显性的

Chapter 4

MUTATION AND VARIATION 突变与变异

The difference in appearance between blue and white peacocks is due to mutation (see the cover)
白色孔雀和蓝色孔雀之间的表现型差异源于突变（见封面）

The techniques of genetic analysis that we discussed in the previous chapters depend on the availability of two or more alleles for a gene of interest. Where do these alleles come from? The short answer is **mutation**. We have previously noted that an important property of DNA is its fidelity: most of the time it accurately passes the same information from one generation to the next. However, DNA sequences can also change. Changes in DNA sequences that we purpose-

我们在前面章节中讨论过的遗传分析技术依赖于两个或多个等位基因为目标基因的有效性。那么这些等位基因从何而来呢？简单得说就是**突变**。我们已经预先注意到了 DNA 的一个重要特性就是它的保守性：绝大多数情况下 DNA 能精确地将相同的遗传信息从亲代传递给子代。尽管如

fully induce are called **mutations**. If a mutation changes the phenotype of an individual, the individual is said to be a **mutant**. Naturally occurring, but rare, sequence variants that are clearly different from a normal, wild-type sequence are also called mutations. On the other hand, many naturally occurring variants exist for traits for which no clearly normal type can be defined; thus, we use the term **polymorphism** to refer to variants of DNA sequences (and other phenotypes) that co-exist in a population at relatively high frequencies (>1%). Polymorphisms and mutations arise through similar biochemical processes, but the use of the word "polymorphism" avoids implying that any particular allele is more normal or abnormal. For example, a change in a person's DNA sequence that leads to a disease such as cancer is appropriately called a mutation, but a difference in DNA sequence that explains whether a person has red hair rather than brown hair is an example of polymorphism. Molecular markers, which we will discuss in Chapter 9, are a particularly useful type of polymorphism for some areas of genetics research.

此，DNA 序列也会发生改变。我们把有目的地诱导 DNA 序列改变称为**突变**。一方面，如果一个突变改变了一个个体的表现型，那么这个个体被称为**突变体**。同时极少数自发产生的，但却明显不同于正常野生型的序列变异也叫做突变。另一方面，许多标准性状没有明确定义的自然发生的变异，因此我们利用**多态性**这一术语去考虑那些以相对较高的频率（>1%）共同存在于群体中的 DNA 序列变异。多态性和突变均是由相似的生物化学过程产生的，但是多态性一词的用法却避开了暗指任意特定的等位基因是正常的还是异常的。例如，导致一个人癌症发生的 DNA 序列突变被相应地称之为突变，而能解释一个人是红发而不是棕发的 DNA 序列上的差异则是多态性的一个例子。我们将在第 9 章讨论的分子标记，就是一种在一些遗传学研究领域上特别有用的多态性类型。

Humans have an interesting relationship with mutation. From our perspective, mutations can be extraordinarily useful, since mutations allow evolution to proceed. Mutation is also the basis for the domestication and improvement of almost all of our food. On the other hand, as the cause of many cancers and other diseases, mutation can be devastating to individuals. Yet, the vast majority of mutations probably go undetected. In this section, we will examine some of the causes and effects of mutations.

人类与基因突变有着有趣的关系，从人类的角度上来说，基因突变可能是非常有用的，因为突变推动了进化过程。同时突变也是几乎所有粮食作物驯化和改良的基础。此外，作为许多癌症和其他疾病的起因，基因突变对于个体来说可能是毁灭性的。然而，大部分的基因突变可能还未被发现。在这一章中我们将探讨突变产生的原因和其产生的影响。

ORIGINS OF MUTATIONS 基因突变的来源

Mutation may involve the **insertion** or **deletion** of one or

基因突变包括一个或多个碱基的**插**

more bases, or else the **substitution** of one DNA sequence with another DNA sequence of equal length. These changes in DNA sequence can arise in many ways, some of which arise spontaneously from natural sources and some of which are induced intentionally or unintentionally by human actions(Figure 4.1). There are many ways to classify **mutagens**, which are the agents that cause mutation. We will classify mutagens here as being either biological, chemical, or physical.

入或缺失，或者是一段 DNA 序列与等长的另一段 DNA 序列间的**替换**。这些DNA序列的改变可由许多方式产生，有些基因突变是自发产生的，而有些则是来自于人类有意或无意的诱导（图 4.1）。基因突变的**诱变剂**有很多种分类方式，这里我们将诱变剂分为生物诱变剂、化学诱变剂和物理诱变剂 3 类。

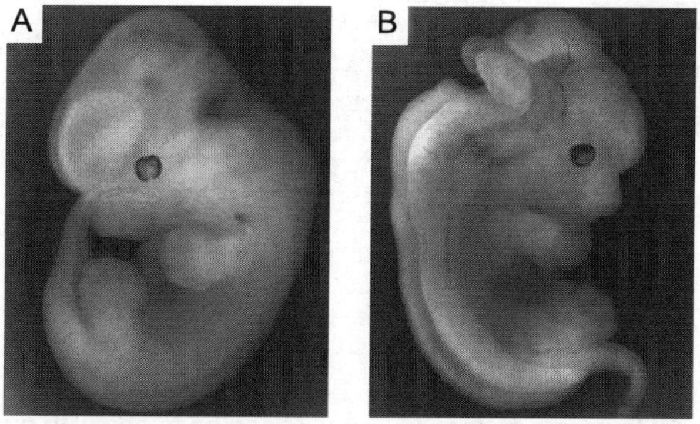

Figure 4.1 Examples of wild-type (A) and mutant (B) mouse embryos observed while screening for genes affecting cranium development

图 4.1 当筛选影响头盖骨发育基因时，所观察到的野生型小鼠(A)和突变体小鼠(B)胚胎

Biological 生 物 诱 变

A major source of spontaneous mutation is errors that arise during DNA replication. DNA polymerases are usually very accurate in adding a base to the growing strand that is the exact complement of the base on the template strand. However, occasionally, an incorrect base is inserted. In some cases, this is because rare and minor shifts in the chemical structure of nucleotides (called **tautomerism**) allow for unusual base pairs to form, such as G-T and C-A (Figure 4.2). Usually, the machinery of DNA replication will recognize and repair mispaired bases, but nevertheless, some errors become permanently incorporated in a daughter strand, and so become mutations that will be inherited by the cell's descendents (Figure 4.3).

自发突变主要来源于 DNA 复制过程中产生的错误。DNA 聚合酶通常会非常精确地将碱基加到与模板链互补的子链上。然而，偶尔也会有错误的碱基插入。在某些情况下，这是因为核苷酸化学结构的稀有、微小的改变（称作**互变异构现象**）允许了非正常碱基对的形成，如 G-T 和 C-A（图 4.2）。通常情况下，DNA 复制的机制能够识别和修复错配的碱基，尽管如此，有些错误却永久地存在于子链当中，因此产生了可以被下一代细胞遗传的基因突变（图 4.3）。

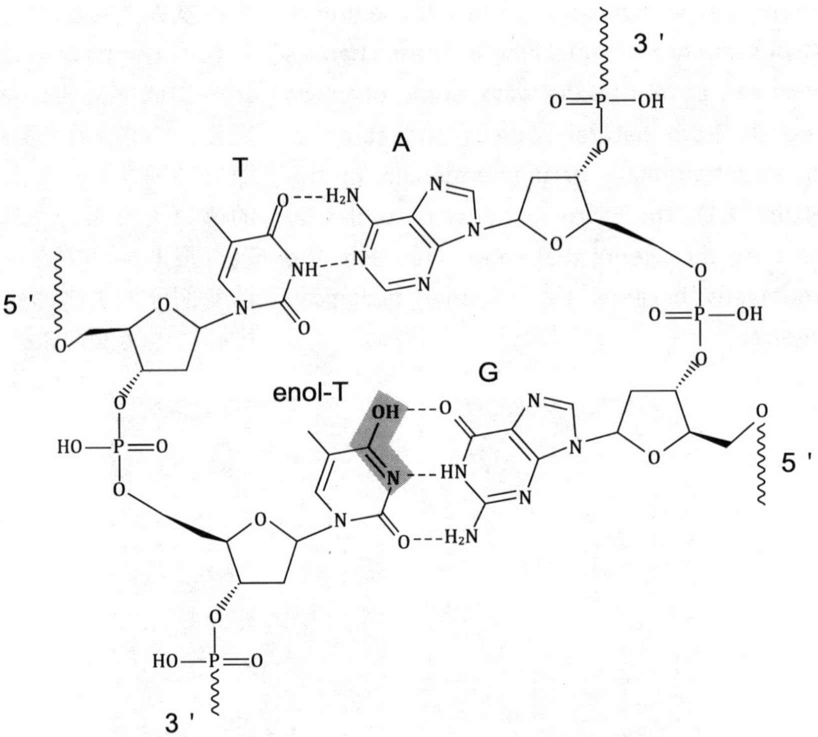

Figure 4.2 A rare, enol tautomer of thymine (enol-T) can base pair with guanine (G) rather than adenine (A). The enol tautomer can form spontaneously and is also stabilized by some types of mutagens

图 4.2 稀有的烯醇式互变体（5-溴尿嘧啶）可以与鸟嘌呤（G）而不是腺嘌呤（A）配对，烯醇式互变体可以自发形成也可以被某些类型的诱变剂所稳定

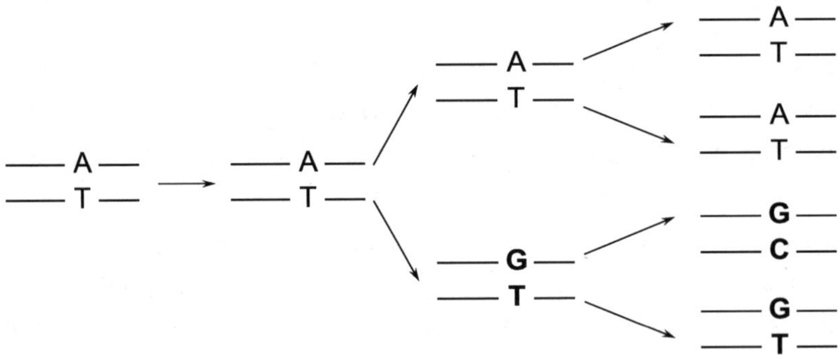

Figure 4.3 Mispairing of bases (e.g. G with T) can occur due to tautomerism, alkylating agents, or other effects. As a result, in this example the AT base pair in the original DNA strand will become permanently substituted by a GC based pair in some progeny. The mispaired GT basepair will likely be repaired or eliminated before further rounds of replication

图 4.3 由互变现象、烷化剂或其他因素引起的碱基错配（如 G 和 T）。其结果是，在原有 DNA 链上的 AT 碱基对在某些子代中会永久地被 GC 碱基对所取代。错配的 GT 碱基对可能在新一轮复制之前被修复或者淘汰

Another source of error introduced during replication is caused by a temporary misalignment of a few bases between the template strand and daughter strand (Figure 4.4). This causes one or more bases on either strand to be temporarily displaced in a **loop** that is not paired with the opposite strand. If this loop forms on the template strand, the bases in the loop may not be replicated, and a deletion will be introduced in the growing daughter strand. Conversely, if a region of the daughter strand that has just been replicated becomes displaced, this region may be replicated again, leading to an insertion of additional sequence in the daughter strand, as compared to the template strand. Regions of DNA that have several repeats of the same few nucleotides in a row are especially prone to this type of error during replication. These short-sequence repeats (**SSRs**) are also called microsatellites and tend to be highly polymorphic, and are therefore particularly useful in genetics.

复制过程中产生错误的另一个来源是模板链和子链之间几个碱基暂时的错位对齐（图 4.4）。这引起了一条链上的一个或多个碱基被暂时替换成还未与其互补链配对的一个**环形结构**。如果这个环形结构在模板链上形成，那么环形结构上的碱基可能不会被复制，从而导致复制的子链上的碱基缺失。相反地，与模板链相比较而言，如果已经复制的子链上的一个区域移位，这个区域可能会被再一次复制，这样就会导致子链上额外序列的插入。在 DNA 复制期间同一条链上有几段相同重复的核苷酸序列的 DNA 区域特别容易产生这种类型的错误。这些简单序列重复（**SSRs**）也被称作微卫星，而且趋于很高的多态性，因此在遗传学上特别具有使用价值。

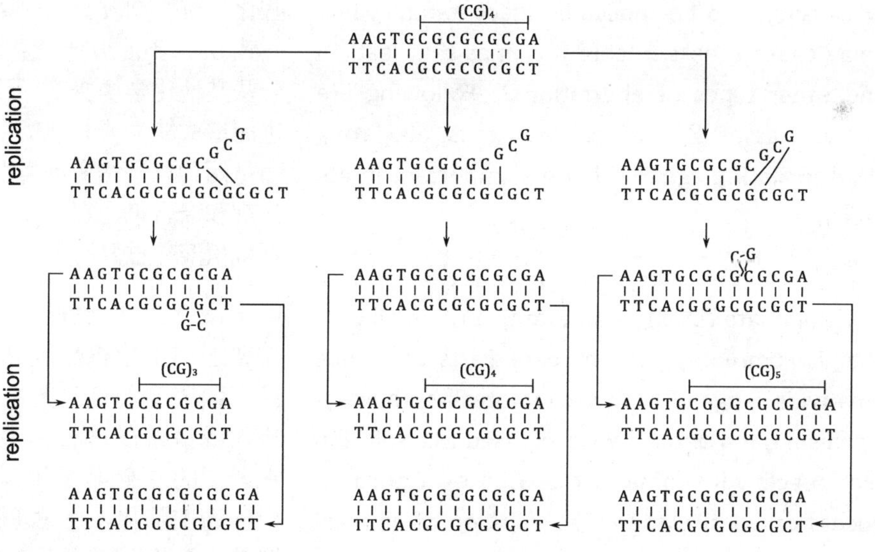

Figure 4.4 Improperly aligned basepairing during replication can occur occasionally, especially in regions with short, repeated sequences. This can lead to either deletion (left) or insertion (right) of sequences compared to the products of normal replication (center), depending on whether the template strand or daughter strand “loops-out” during replication

图 4.4 复制期间的错位对齐会偶然产生，尤其会发生在具有简单重复序列的区域，与正常复制的产物相比，这会导致序列的缺失或插入，缺失或插入取决于在复制时是模板链还是子链产生环形结构

Mutations can also be introduced by viruses, transposable elements, and other types of DNA that are naturally inserted at more or less random positions in chromosomes. The insertion may disrupt the coding sequence of a gene, or have other consequences including the fusion of part of one gene with another. These insertions occur spontaneously, and can also be intentionally stimulated in the laboratory as a method of mutagenesis. For example, a type of transposable element called a **P-element** is widely used as a biological mutagen in *Drosophila*, and **T-DNA**, which is an insertional element modified from a bacterial pathogen is used as a mutagen in some plant species.

基因突变也可以由随机插入在染色体任意位置上的病毒、转座元件和其他类型 DNA 而产生。插入可能会破坏基因的编码序列或有其他影响，如一个基因的一部分与另一个基因融合。这些插入自发地产生，也可能作为一种诱变方法在实验室有目的地诱导产生。例如，一种被称为 **P 因子**的转座元件被广泛地用作果蝇的生物诱变剂，而 **T-DNA**，一种由细菌病原体改造成的插入元件，也作为一种诱变剂应用在某些植物种当中。

Chemical 化学诱变

Many chemical compounds, whether natural or synthetic, can react with DNA. These reactions may change the chemical structure of particular bases, so that they are misread during replication. Other chemical mutagens distort the double helix causing it to be replicated inaccurately, while still others may cause breaks in chromosomes that lead to deletions and other types of aberrations. Following are examples of two classes of chemical mutagens, **alkylating agents**, and **intercalating agents**, that are important in genetics or medicine.

许多化合物无论是天然的还是合成的，都可以与 DNA 发生反应，这些化学反应可以改变某些特殊碱基的化学结构以至于使它们在复制时读错。一些化学诱变剂改变了 DNA 双螺旋结构导致 DNA 不能被精确复制，而且还有一些其他化学诱变剂导致染色体断裂进而造成缺失或其他类型的畸变。下面是两种化学诱变剂类型的例子，**烷化剂**和**嵌合剂**，它们在遗传学和医学领域扮演着重要的角色。

Ethane methyl sulfonate (**EMS**), is an example of an alkylating agent that is commonly used by geneticists to induce mutations in a wide range of both prokaryotes and eukaryotes. The organism is fed or otherwise exposed to a solution of EMS, which reacts with some of the G bases it encounters in a process called alkylation. The addition of an alkyl group to G changes the base pairing properties so that the next time the alkylated DNA strand is replicated, a T instead of a C will be inserted opposite to the alkylated-G in the daughter strand (Figure 4.5). The new strand therefore bears a mutation which will be inherited in all the strands that are subsequently replicated from it.

甲基磺酸乙酯（**EMS**）是被遗传学家普遍用于原核生物和真核生物诱导基因突变的烷化剂之一。生物体喂入或暴露在 EMS 溶液后会与一些它遇到的 G 碱基发生反应，这个过程称为烷基化。给 G 碱基增加一个烷基会改变碱基的配对特性从而导致下次烷基化的 DNA 链被复制时，子链上与烷基化的 G 对应的位置上插入的是 T 而不是 C（图 4.5），因此由新链作为模板而复制出来的所有 DNA 链上都会携带可遗传的突变。

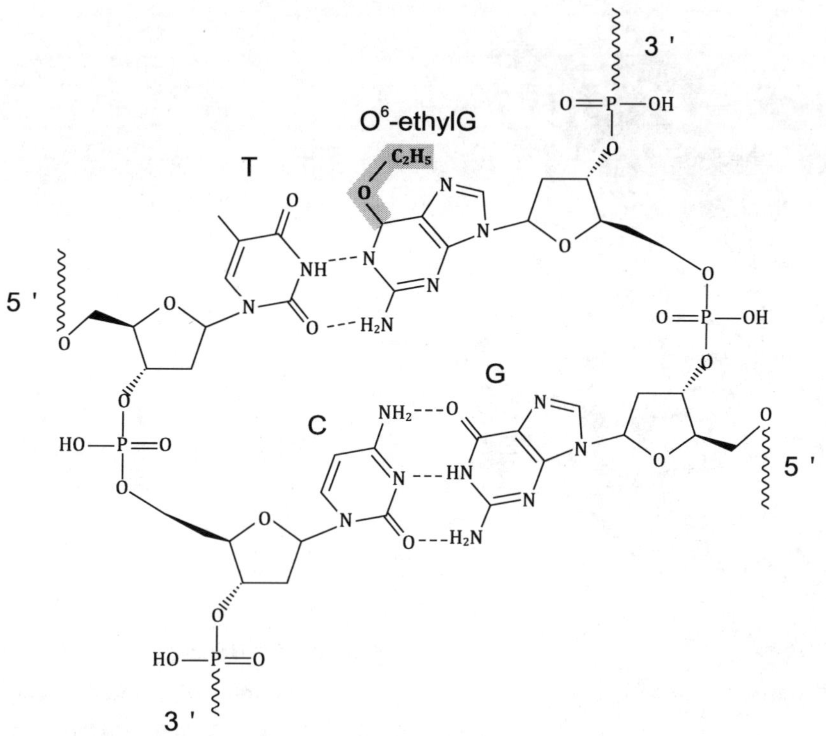

Figure 4.5 Alkylation of guanine (shown in shadow) allows G to bond with thymine rather than cytosine at replication

图 4.5 鸟嘌呤的烷基化（阴影部分）会使其在复制中与胸腺嘧啶而不是与胞嘧啶互补配对

Intercalating agents are another type of chemical mutagen. These induce mutations by inserting between the stacked bases at the center of the DNA helix (Figure 4.6). This intercalation distorts the shape of the DNA helix, which can cause the wrong bases to be added to a growing DNA strand during DNA synthesis. Intercalating agents tend to be flat, planar molecules such as **benzopyrene**, a component of wood and tobacco smoke. Another important intercalating agent is thalidomide, an anti-nausea drug whose harmful effects were unknown until its consumption by thousands of pregnant woman resulted in birth defects. Finally **ethidium bromide**, the dye that fluorescently stains DNA in laboratory assays, is also an intercalating agent. For this reason, molecular biologists are trained to handle this chemical carefully.

嵌合剂是另一种化学诱变剂。它是通过插入到 DNA 螺旋中心堆叠的碱基中而引起突变的（图 4.6）。插入的片段会使 DNA 双螺旋结构变形，从而导致在 DNA 合成时会有错误的碱基加到正在形成的 DNA 链上。嵌合剂一般是类似于一种扁平的二维结构分子，如**苯并芘**，它是树木和烟草烟雾中的一种成分。另一种重要的嵌合剂是萨立多胺，是一种高效止吐药（镇静剂），它的副作用直到数以千计的孕妇产下的新生儿是先天畸形才被人们所发现。最后，**溴化乙锭**（用于实验室鉴定分析 DNA 的荧光染色剂）也是一种嵌合剂。为此，必须训练分子生物学工作者小心使用这类化学药品。

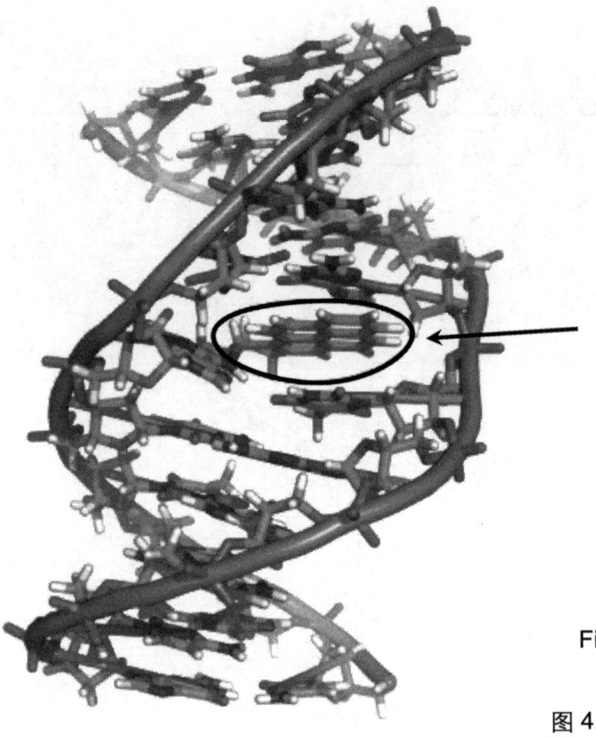

（彩图）

Figure 4.6 Benzopyrene (circled in black) is an example of an intercalating agent

图 4.6 苯并芘（黑色圈起部位，箭头所指）是嵌合剂的一个例子

Physical 物理诱变

Anything that damages DNA by transferring energy to it can be considered a physical mutagen. Usually this involves either radioactive particles, X-rays, or UV light. Smaller, fast moving particles may substitute or delete a single base, while larger, slightly slower particles induce larger deletions by breaking the double stranded helix. Physical mutagens can also create unusual structures in DNA, such as the thymine dimers formed by UV light (Figure 4.7). Thymine dimers disrupt normal base-pairing in the double helix, and may block replication altogether if not repaired by the cell.

任何通过转移能量而损伤 DNA 的物质都可以被称为物理诱变剂，通常包括放射性粒子、X 射线和紫外线。快速运动的较小粒子可能替换或删除一个单一碱基，而稍慢的较大的粒子通过破坏双螺旋结构而产生较大片段的缺失。物理诱变剂也能使 DNA 上产生异常结构，如由紫外线照射而形成的胸腺嘧啶二聚体（图 4.7）。胸腺嘧啶二聚体打破了双螺旋上正常的碱基配对原则，并且如果没有被细胞修复的话，它可能阻止 DNA 的复制。

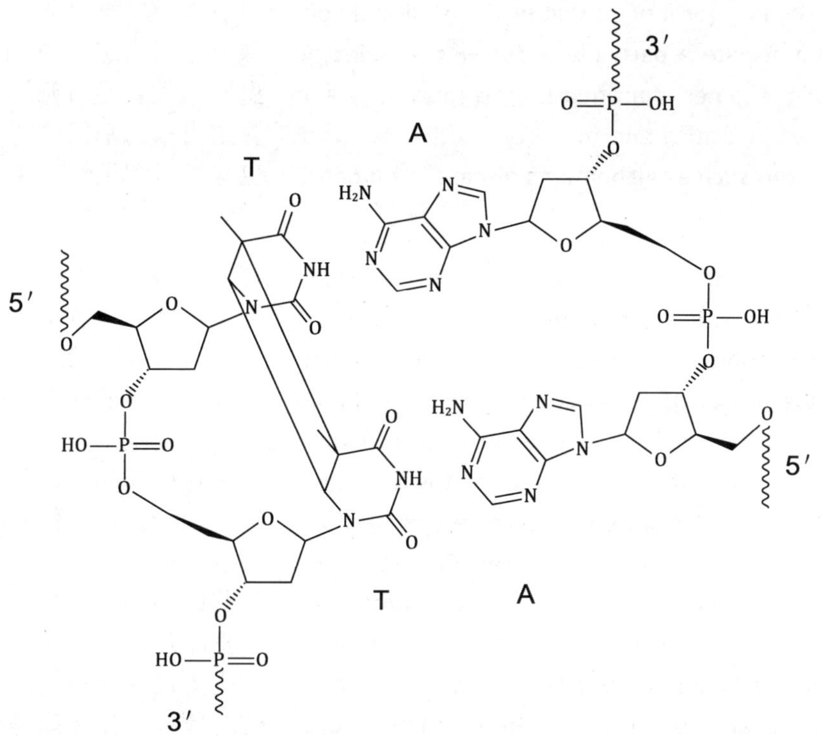

Figure 4.7 Thymine dimers are formed when adjacent thymine bases on the same DNA strand become covalently linked follow exposure to mutagens such as UV light. The dimers distort base pairing and can interrupt processes such as replication

图 4.7 当同一 DNA 链上的两个相邻的胸腺嘧啶核苷酸受到诱变剂，如紫外线的诱导后将以共价键结合，从而形成胸腺嘧啶二聚体，二聚体的形成扭曲了碱基的互补配对并且阻断了诸如复制的进程

MUTANT SCREENING: FORWARD GENETICS
突变体的筛选：正向遗传学

One way to identify genes that affect a particular biological process is to induce random mutations in a population, and then look for individuals with phenotypes that might be caused by a disruption of a particular biochemical pathway. This strategy of **mutant screening** has been used very effectively to better understand the molecular components of hundreds of different biological processes. For example, to better understand processes of memory and learning, researchers have screened mutagenized populations of *Dro-*

鉴定影响特定生物过程的基因的一种方法是在群体中诱发随机突变，然后找出可能由特定生化过程的中断而产生的突变表现型的个体。这种**突变体筛选**的策略已被非常有效地应用于理解不同的生物过程中的分子成分。例如，为了更好地了解记忆和学习的过程，研究人员已经筛选了果蝇的突变群体，从而鉴定

sophila to identify flies (or larvae) that lack the normal ability to learn to associate a particular odor with an electric shock. Some of the genes identified by this mutant screen may be relevant to learning and memory in other animals, including conditions such as Alzheimer's disease in humans.

出缺少通过学习能将电击和感受特殊气味联系在一起的果蝇（或幼虫）。一些由这种筛选突变体的方法鉴定出来的基因可能在其他动物上也与学习和记忆有关，其中包括人类的阿尔茨海默病（老年痴呆症）。

Exposure of an organism to a mutagen causes mutations in essentially random positions along the chromosomes. Most of the mutant phenotypes recovered from a genetic screen are caused by **loss-of-function** mutations. These are changes in the sequence of an allele that cause it to no longer produce the same level of active protein as the wild-type allele. Loss-of-function alleles tend to be recessive because the wild-type allele is haplosufficient (see Chapter 6). A loss-of-function allele that produces no active protein is called an **amorph**, or **null**. On the other hand, alleles with only a partial loss-of-function are called hypomorphic. More rarely, a mutant allele may have a **gain-of-function**, producing either more of the active protein (**hypermorph**) or producing an active protein with a new function (**neomorph**).

将生物体暴露于诱变剂后，几乎能在染色体的任意位置引发突变。大多数通过基因筛选获得的突变表现型都是由**功能缺失**的突变引起的。这些突变是由一个等位基因序列上的变化引起的，这些变化使其不能够再如野生型等位基因那样产生相同水平的活性蛋白。功能缺失的等位基因倾向于隐性，因为野生型等位基因是单倍充足的（见第 6 章）。产生无活性蛋白的功能性缺失的等位基因被称作**无效等位基因**或**无效基因**。此外，只有部分功能缺失的等位基因称作亚效等位基因。更稀有的是，突变的等位基因可能是**功能获得**的等位基因，从而产生更多的活性蛋白（为**超效等位基因**）或具有新功能的活性蛋白（为**新效等位基因**）。

In a typical mutant screen, researchers will treat a parental population with a mutagen. This may, for example, involve soaking seeds in EMS, or mixing this mutagen with the food fed to flies. The individuals that are directly exposed with the mutagen are called the M_0 generation. No phenotypes will be visible among the M_0 generation, in part because not all somatic (i.e. non-reproduce- tive) cells of the M_0 individuals will be affected in the same way. More important in the M_1 generation are the germline cells: gametes and any of their developmental precursors. Since a single gamete contributes half of the chromosomes to every cell of the next (M_2) generation, mutagenizing gametes or the cells that produce them is the easiest way to generate individu-

在一个典型的突变体筛选中，科研人员将用诱变剂处理一个亲本群体。其中包括，将种子浸泡在 EMS 中，或喂给果蝇混有这种诱变剂的食物。直接用诱变剂处理的个体称作 M_0 代。M_0 代的表现型特征是看不到的，可能因为并非所有的 M_0 代个体的体细胞（即非再生细胞）都会受到相同的影响。在 M_1 代中起到更重要作用的是生殖细胞，即配子和任何它们的发育前体细胞。由于配子只会将染色体一半的遗传信息传递给它的下一代（M_2 代），通

als in which every cell bears the same mutation. In most cases, however, the M_1 individual will be heterozygous for any induced mutation; this is because it would be very unlikely for the same gene to have been mutated in the other gamete that contributed to the M_1 individual. Because most induced mutations are recessive, the M_1 generation must therefore be selfed (i.e. crossed to siblings, or self-fertilization if the species is a hermaphrodite like worms and most plants), and the following generations (e.g. M_2, in which mutant alleles could potentially become homozygous) examined for the presence of novel phenotypes. Once a relevant mutant has been identified, geneticists can begin to make inferences about what the normal function of the mutated gene is, based on its mutant phenotype.

过诱变配子或细胞是获得突变个体最容易的方法，产生的突变个体中每个细胞携带相同的突变。然而大部分情况下，M_1代的个体将会是被诱导的突变的杂合体；这是因为在另一个形成个体的配子中很难能有同样的基因突变。因为大多数产生的突变是隐性的，所以 M_1代必须自交（即与姐妹株杂交，如果像蠕虫或大多数的植物雌雄同体时则需要自体受精或自交），并且在下一代（即 M_2，其突变体的等位基因可能变为纯合）检测出新的表现型。一旦相关的突变体被鉴定出来，遗传学家就可以根据其突变体的表现型推断出突变基因的正常功能。

SOME MUTATIONS MAY NOT HAVE DETECTABLE PHENOTYPES
一些突变可能没有可被检测的表现型

The vast majority of mutations (especially substitutions) have no effect on the phenotype. Often, this is because the mutation is **silent**; it changes the DNA sequence of a non-coding region of the DNA, or else the changes a base within a codon without changing the amino acid that it encodes (recall that the genetic code is degenerate; for example, GCT, GCC, GCA, and GCG all encode alanine). There are also cases where a mutation can cause a complete loss-of-function of a gene, yet not produce a phenotype even when the mutant allele is homozygous. This can often be attributed to genetic **redundancy**, i.e. the encoding of similar genes at more than one locus in the genome. It is important therefore to remember this important limitation of mutational analysis: genes with redundant functions cannot be easily identified by mutant screening.

绝大多数的突变（尤其是替换）对表现型无影响。这通常是因为突变是**沉默**的；它改变了非编码区的DNA序列，或者改变了密码子内部的碱基却没有改变它编码的氨基酸（回想一下，遗传密码是简并的，如 GCT、GCC、GCA 和 GCG 均编码丙氨酸）。也有这样的情况，突变能导致基因彻底的功能缺失而且当突变的等位基因是纯合时也不能产生突变的表现型。这经常归因于**基因冗余**，即在基因组中不止在一个基因位点上进行相似基因的编码。因此记住这个突变分析的限制因素是很重要的：具有冗余功能的基因不能轻易地通过突变体筛选鉴定出来。

Some phenotypes require individuals to reach a particular developmental stage before they can be scored. For exam-

一些表现型要求个体达到一个特殊的发育阶段才得以表现。例如，花

ple, flower color can only be scored in plants that are mature enough to make flowers, and eye color can only be scored in flies that have developed eyes. However, some alleles may not develop sufficiently to be included among the progeny that are scored according to their phenotype. Lethal alleles that arrest the development of an individual at an embryonic stage may therefore go unnoticed in a typical mutant screen. Furthermore, the progeny of a monohybrid cross involving an embryonic lethal recessive allele may therefore all be of a single phenotypic class, giving a phenotypic ratio of 1：0 (which is the same as 3：0).

色只能在足够成熟开花的植物中才能表现出来，而果蝇眼睛的颜色只能在发育出眼睛的果蝇身上体现。然而一些等位基因可能并不能在后代中充分发育，以至于不存在于后代的表现型中。在个体胚胎发育阶段阻止个体发育的致死基因很可能在典型的突变筛选中被忽视。此外，含胚胎致死隐性基因的单基因杂交子代因此可能导致后代为单一表现型，表现型比例为 1：0（基因型为 3：0）。

Many genes are first identified in mutant screens, and so they tend to be named after their mutant phenotypes. This can cause some confusion for students of genetics. For example, we have already encountered an X-linked gene named *white* in fruit flies. Null mutants of *white* have white eyes, but the normal function of the *white* gene is actually the production of a red pigment.

许多基因在突变筛选中首先被鉴定出来，因此人们倾向于以它们的突变表现型来命名，这可能会造成遗传学上的混淆。例如，我们已经在果蝇中遇到一个名为*white*基因的X染色体伴性遗传基因。果蝇 *white* 基因的无效突变体是白眼，但是实际上未突变的 *white* 基因正常功能是产生一种红色素。

Summary

- When a variation in DNA sequence originated recently, and is rare in a population, we call that change a mutation.

- DNA 序列上发生群体中稀有的变异，我们称这种改变为突变。

- When variations in DNA sequence co-exist in a population, and neither one can be meaningfully defined as wild-type, we call the variations polymorphisms.

- 当 DNA 序列中的变异共存于一个群体中，并且变异没有被明确定义野生型，我们称这些变异为多态性。

- Mutations may either occur spontaneously, or may be induced by exposure to mutagens.

- 突变可以自发产生，也可以利用诱变剂诱导产生。

- Mutations may result in either substitutions, deletions, or insertions.

- 突变可能导致替换、缺失或插入。

- Spontaneous mutations arise from many sources including natural errors in DNA replication, usually associated with base mispairing, or else insertion deletion especially within repetitive sequences.

- 自发性突变有许多来源，包括DNA复制时自发产生的错误，通常是碱基的错配，或者插入、缺失，特别是在重复序列上发生的插入和缺失。

- Induced mutations result from mispairing, DNA damage, or sequence interruptions caused by chemical, biological, or physical mutagens.

- 诱发突变起因于化学诱变剂、生物诱变剂或物理诱变剂引发的碱基错配、DNA损伤或DNA序列的中断。

- By randomly inducing mutations, then screening for a specific phenotype, it is possible to identify genes associated with specific biological pathways.

- 通过随机诱导突变，然后筛选特定表现型可能会鉴定出基因是否与特定的生物途径有关。

- The efficiency of mutant screening is limited by silent mutations, redundancy, and embyronic lethality.

- 突变体筛选的有效性受沉默突变、基因冗余和胚胎致死的限制。

Key Terms

mutation 突变
mutant 突变体
polymorphism 多态性
insertion 插入
deletion 缺失
substitution 替换
mutagen 诱变剂
biological mutagen 生物诱变剂
chemical mutagen 化学诱变剂
physical mutagen 物理诱变剂
tautomer 互变异构体
enol 烯醇式
mispairing 错配
loop 拱形结构
SSR 简单序列重复
insertional mutagen 插入突变
transposon 转座子
P-element P 元件
T-DNA
alkylation agent 烷化剂
EMS 甲基磺酸乙酯
intercalating agent 插入剂
benzopyrene 苯并芘
ethidium bromide 溴化乙锭
thymine dimer 胸腺嘧啶二聚体
mutant screen 突变体筛选
loss-of-function 功能缺失
gain-of-function 功能获得
amorph 无效等位基因
null 零基因
hypomorph 超效等位基因
hypermorph 亚效等位基因
neopmorph 新效等位基因
somatic 胚细胞的
germline 生殖细胞
M_0, M_1, M_2
silent mutation 沉默突变
redunancy 冗余
lethality 致死性

Study Questions

4.1 How are polymorphisms and mutations alike? How are they different?

4.1 多态性与突变有什么相似之处？它们又有什么区别？

4.2 What are all of the ways a substitution can occur in a DNA sequence?

4.2 DNA 序列中替换发生的方式有哪些？

4.3 What are all of the ways a deletion can occur in a DNA sequence?

4.3 DNA 序列中缺失发生的方式有哪些？

4.4 What are all of the ways an insertion can occur in a DNA sequence?

4.4 DNA 序列中插入发生的方式有哪些？

4.5 In the context of this chapter, explain the health hazards of smoking tobacco.

4.5 根据本章内容，试解释吸烟对健康的危害。

4.6 You have exposed a female fruit fly to a mutagen. Mating this fly with a non-mutagenized male produces offspring that appear to be completely normal. However there are twice as many females as males in the F_1 progeny of this cross.

a) Propose a hypothesis to explain these observations.

b) How could you test your hypothesis?

4.6 将雌性果蝇用诱变剂处理，让其与未突变的此类雄性果蝇交配，产生了表现型完全正常的子代。然而这种杂交方式产生的 F_1 代中雌性果蝇是雄性果蝇的 2 倍。

a）提出一个假说解释这种现象。

b）你怎样证明你的假说？

4.7 You decide to use genetics to investigate how your favourite plant makes its flowers smell good.

a) What steps will you take to identify some genes that are required for production of the sweet floral scent? Assume that this plant is a self-pollinating diploid.

b) One of the recessive mutants you identified has fishy-smelling flowers, so you name the mutant (and the mutated gene) fishy. What do you hypothesize about the normal function of the wild-type fishy gene?

c) Another recessive mutant lacks floral scent altogether, so you call it nosmell. What could you hypothesize about the normal function of this gene?

4.7 你决定用遗传学知识研究你最喜欢的植物是怎样使它的花更具有香气。

a）假设这种植物是自花授粉的二倍体植物，你会采取哪些步骤来鉴定出产生花香的基因？

b）你鉴定出的一个隐性突变体的花具有鱼腥味，所以你给这个突变体（和突变基因）命名为鱼腥味型。那么你假设的野生型鱼腥味基因的正常功能是什么？

c）另一个隐性突变体完全没有花香，因此你称它为无香型，那么你假设的这个基因的正常功能是什么？

4.8. Suppose you are only interested in finding dominant mutations that affect floral scent.

a) What do you expect to be the relative frequency of dominant mutations, as compared to recessive mutations, and why?

b) How will you design your screen differently than in the previous question, in order to detect dominant mutations specifically?

c) Which kind of mutagen is most likely to produce dominant mutations, a mutagen that produces point mutations, or amutagen that produces large deletions?

4.8.假设你只对寻找影响花香的显性突变有兴趣。

a）与隐性突变相比，你希望相对显性突变频率是多少？为什么？

b）为了特定地检测出显性突变，你将怎样设计不同于前面问题的筛选？

c）哪种诱变剂最可能诱导显性突变？是产生点突变的诱变剂还是产生大片段缺失的诱变剂？

Chapter 5

PEDIGREES AND POPULATIONS
系谱与群体

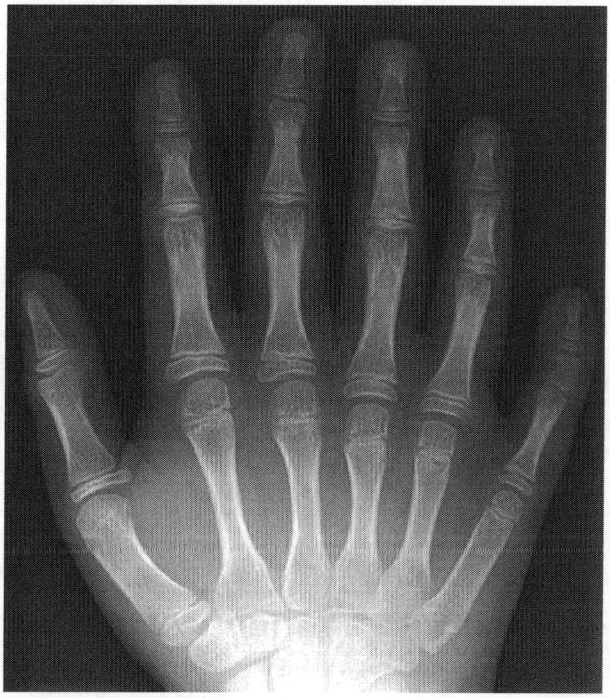

Polydactyly is an example of a human trait that can be studied by pedigree analysis
多指（趾）是一个用系谱分析方法研究人类性状的实例

The basic concepts of genetics described in the preceding chapters can be applied to almost any eukaryotic organism. However, some techniques, such as test crosses, can only be performed with model organisms or other species that can be experimentally manipulated. To study the inheritance patterns of genes in humans and other species for which controlled matings are not possible, geneticists use techniques including the analysis of pedigrees and populations.

在前述的章节里所叙述的遗传学基本概念几乎适用于所有真核生物。然而，一些方法，如测交试验等仅能够在模式生物或者其他能够实验操作的物种中进行。为了研究人类及其他不太可能控制其交配的物种的基因遗传模式，遗传学家采用了包括系谱和群体分析的技术来进行研究。

PEDIGREE ANALYSIS 系谱分析

Pedigrees use a standardized set of symbols to represent an individual's sex, family relationships and phenotype. These diagrams are used to determine the **mode of inheritance** of a particular disease or trait, and to predict the probability of its appearance among offspring. Pedigree analysis is therefore an important tool in both basic research and **genetic counseling**.

系谱用一套标准符号来表示个体性别、家族关系及表现型。这些示意图用来确定某一特定疾病或者性状的**遗传模式**，而且也可以用来预测后代中这一疾病或性状可能发生的概率。因此，系谱分析是基础研究及**遗传咨询**中的一个重要工具。

Each pedigree represents all of the available information about the inheritance of a single trait (most often a disease) within a family. The pedigree is therefore drawn from factual information rather than theoretical predictions, but there is always some possibility of errors in this information, especially when relying on family members' recollections or even clinical diagnoses. In real pedigrees, further complications can arise due to incomplete penetrance (including age of onset) and variable expressivity of disease alleles, but for the examples presented in this book, we will presume complete accuracy of the pedigrees. A pedigree may be drawn when trying to determine the nature of a newly discovered disease, or when an individual with a family history of a disease wants to know the probability of passing the disease on to their children. In either case, a tree is drawn, as shown in Figure 5.1, with circles to represent females, and squares to represent males. If an individual is known to have symptoms of the disease, the symbol is filled in. Sometimes a half-filled in symbol is used to indicate a **carrier** of a disease; this is someone who does not have any symptoms of the disease, but who passed the disease on to subsequent generations. Note that when a pedigree is constructed, it is often unknown whether a particular individual is a carrier or not, so not all carriers are always explicitly indicated in a pedigree. For simplicity, we will assume that the pedigrees presented in this chapter are accurate, and represent fully penetrant traits.

每一个家族的系谱代表了关于某一性状（通常是疾病）遗传特性的所有有用的信息。因此，系谱是根据实际信息而非理论预测得出的，但在这一信息中常可能会有一些错误产生，尤其是当这些信息依赖于家族成员的回忆或是临床诊断时。在真实的系谱中，由于致病等位基因的**不完全外显**（包括疾病的发病年龄）及可变表现度可能会导致更复杂的情况产生，但在本书所呈现的例子中，我们假定系谱完全正确。如果想确定一种新发现疾病的性质或者具有一种遗传病家族病史的人想知道这种疾病遗传给后代的可能性时，我们就可以绘制系谱。在任何情况下，绘制如图5.1的系谱树时，用圆圈代表雌性，方框代表雄性。如果已知某个个体具有某种疾病的症状，则用实体图形表示。一般用半填充图形表示疾病**携带者**，这种人不表现疾病症状，但会将疾病遗传给后代。值得一提的是，系谱构建之初，常常不知道某一特定个体是否是疾病的携带者，所以并非所有的携带者都能在系谱中明确地表示出来。为简

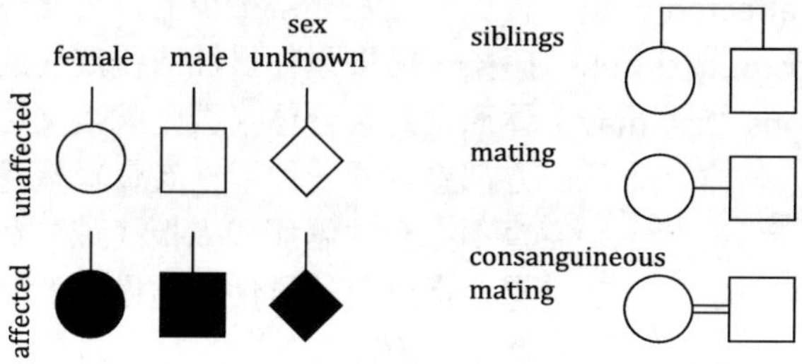

便起见，我们假设在这一章中所有的系谱都是正确的，代表完全外显的性状。

Figure 5.1 Symbols used in drawing a pedigree

图 5.1 绘制系谱中用到的符号

INFERRING THE MODE OF INHERITANCE 遗传模式的推断

Given a pedigree of an uncharacterized disease or trait, one of the first tasks is to determine the mode of inheritance, as this information is essential in calculating the probability that the trait will be inherited in offspring. We will consider four major types of inheritance: autosomal dominant (AD), autosomal recessive (AR), X-linked dominant (XD), X-linked recessive (XR).

给定一个无特征的疾病或性状的系谱，首要任务之一就是确定该疾病的遗传模式，因为在计算该特征遗传给后代的可能性时，此信息是非常重要的。我们将主要考虑 4 种主要遗传类型：常染色体显性遗传（AD）、常染色体隐性遗传（AR）、X 连锁显性遗传（XD）、X 连锁隐性遗传（XR）。

Autosomal dominant (AD) 常染色体显性（AD）

When a disease is caused by a dominant allele of a gene, every person with that allele will show symptoms of the disease (assuming complete penetrance), and only one disease allele needs to be inherited for an individual to be affected. Thus, every affected individual must have an affected parent. A pedigree with affected individuals in every generation is typical of AD diseases(Figure 5.2). However, beware that other modes of inheritance can also show the disease in every generation, as described below. It is also possible for an affected individual with an AD disease to have a family without any affected children, if the affected parent is a heterozygote. This is particularly true in small families, where the probability of every child inheriting the normal, rather than disease allele is not extremely small. Note that AD diseases are usually rare within populations, therefore affected individuals with AD diseases tend to be heterozygotes (oth-

如果一种疾病是由显性等位基因引起的，那么携带此等位基因的每个个体都会患病（假设是完全外显）；此时只要一个致病基因被遗传，个体就会患病。所以，患病个体必有一个亲本患病。在家族系谱里，每一代中都有患病个体是典型的常染色体显性遗传疾病（图 5.2）。然而，注意下面所描述的其他遗传模式中也可能每一代都有患病个体。如果患病的双亲是杂合体，那么感染常染色体遗传病的个体也可能具有健康的后代。这在小家族中常常出现，也就是说每一个孩子遗传正常基因而不是致病基因的概率也不是非常小。注意在人类中常染色体显性遗

erwise, both parents would have had to been affected with the same rare disease). Achondroplastic dwarfism, and polydactyly are both examples of human conditions that may follow an AD mode of inheritance.

传疾病还是非常稀少的，因此每个感染了常染色体显性遗传疾病的个体通常是杂合体（否则就是父母双方都患有同一种罕见疾病）。软骨发育不完全侏儒症和多指（趾）症是符合常染色体显性遗传模式的两种遗传疾病。

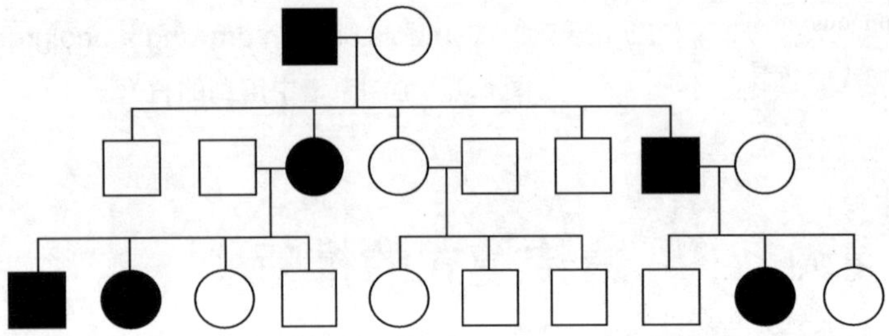

Figure 5.2 A pedigree consistent with AD inheritance

图 5.2 常染色体显性遗传的一个系谱

X-linked dominant (XD) X 连锁显性 (XD)

In X-linked dominant inheritance, the gene responsible for the disease is located on the X-chromosome, and the allele that causes the disease is dominant to the normal allele. Because females have twice as many X-chromosomes as males, females tend to be affected more frequently than males in XD pedigrees. However, not all pedigrees provide sufficient information to distinguish XD and AD. One definitive indication that a trait is inherited as AD rather than XD is that an affected father passes the disease to a son; this type of transmission is <u>not</u> possible with XD, since males inherit their X chromosome from their mothers (Figure 5.3, Figure 5.4).

在 X 连锁显性遗传中，致病基因位于 X 染色体上，致病基因对于正常基因是显性的。由于女性 X 染色体的数目是男性的 2 倍，所以在 X 连锁显性遗传中，女性比男性更容易患病。然而并非所有的系谱都能提供足以区分 X 连锁显性遗传和常染色体显性遗传的所有信息。区别 AD 而非 XD 的一个明确特征是患有常染色体显性遗传疾病的父亲会把疾病传染给儿子，这种遗传方式对于 X 连锁显性遗传疾病来说是<u>不可能</u>的：因为男性只能从母亲那里遗传获得 X 染色体（图 5.3、图 5.4）。

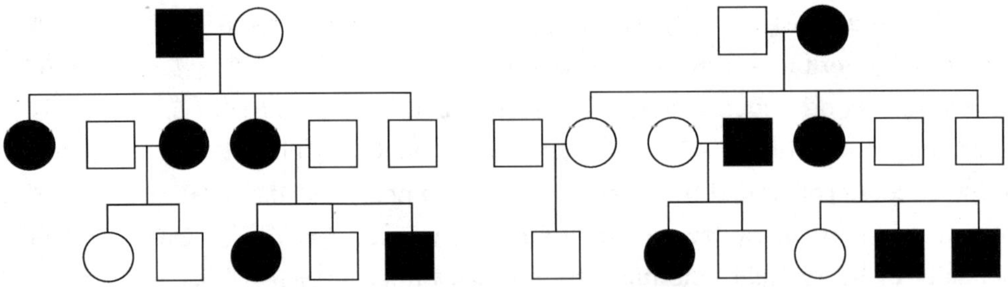

Figure 5.3 Two pedigrees consistent with XD inheritance

图 5.3 X 连锁显性遗传的两个系谱

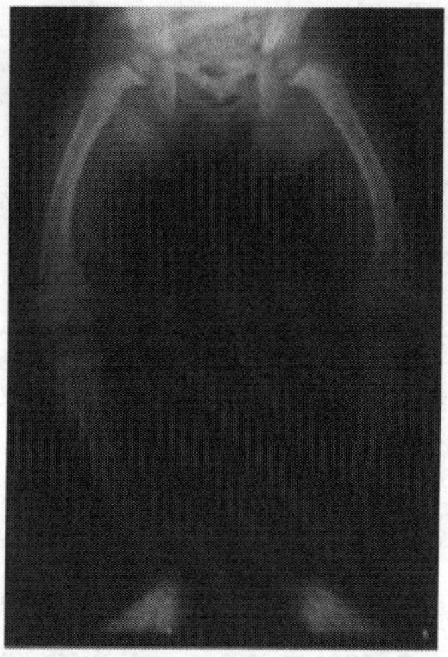

Figure 5.4 Some types of rickets may follow an XD mode of inheritance

图 5.4 一些类型的佝偻病遵循 X 连锁显性遗传模式

Autosomal recessive (AR) 常染色体隐性（AR）

Diseases that are inherited in an autosomal recessive pattern require that both parents of an affected individual carry at least one copy of the disease allele. With AR traits, many individuals in a pedigree can be carriers, probably without knowing it. Compared to pedigrees of dominant traits, AR pedigrees tend to show fewer affected individuals and are more likely than AD or XD to "skip a generation". Thus, the major feature that distinguishes AR from AD or XD is that unaffected individuals can have affected offspring (Figure 5.5, Figure 5.6).

按常染色体隐性模式遗传的疾病需要患病个体的双亲分别携带至少一个致病的等位基因。由于常染色体隐性遗传的特点，系谱中的许多个体都有可能是致病基因的携带者，但是我们可能并不知道这些个体是携带者。与显性性状的系谱相比，常染色体隐性系谱更倾向于患病个体较少，并且比常染色体显性遗传和 X 连锁显性遗传更易隔代遗传。因此，区分常染色体隐性遗传和常染色体显性遗传或者 X 连锁显性遗传的一个主要特征就是未患病的个体却有患病的后代（图 5.5、图 5.6）。

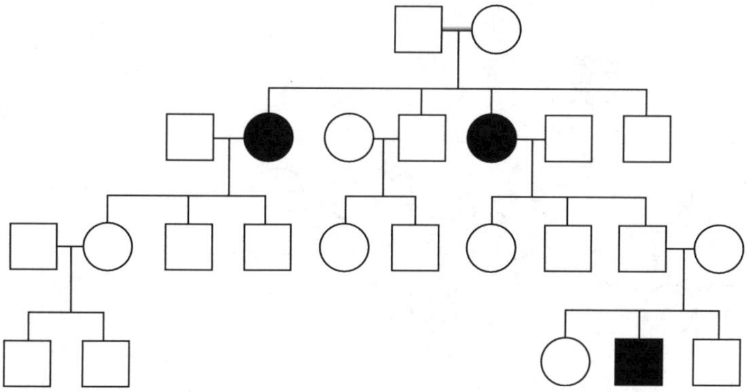

Figure 5.5 A pedigree consistent with AR inheritance

图 5.5 常染色体隐性遗传的一个系谱

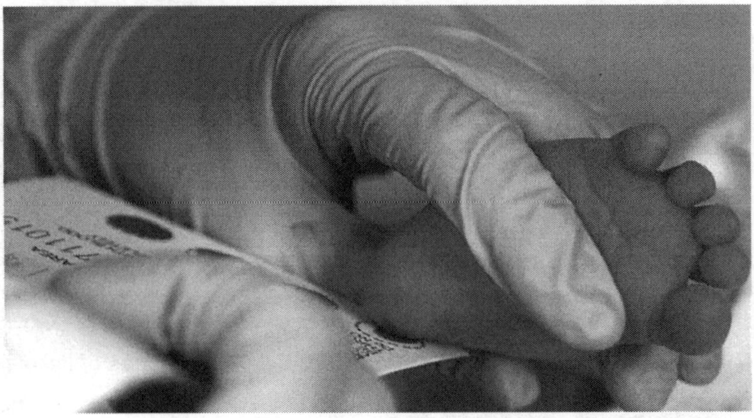

Figure 5.6 Many inborn errors of metabolism, such as phenylketonuria (PKU) are inherited as AR. Newborns are often tested for a few of the most common metabolic diseases

图 5.6 许多先天代谢疾病，如苯丙酮尿症（PKU）就是常染色体隐性遗传。新生儿常被检测是否患有几种最常见的代谢疾病

X-linked recessive (XR) X 连锁隐性（XR）

Because males have only one X-chromosome, any male that inherits an X-linked recessive disease allele will be affected by it (assuming complete penetrance). Therefore, in XR modes of inheritance, males tend to be affected more frequently than females (Figure 5.7). This is in contrast to AR and AD, where both sexes tend to be affected equally, and XD, in which females are affected more frequently. Note, however, that in the small sample sizes typical of human

由于男性只有一条 X 染色体，遗传带有 X 连锁隐性致病等位基因的任何男性都会患病（假设完全外显）。因此，在 X 连锁隐性遗传模式中，男性比女性患病频率更高（图 5.7）。对比 AR、AD 和 XD：在 AR 和 AD 中，两个性别患病比例均等；在 XD 中，女性患病频率

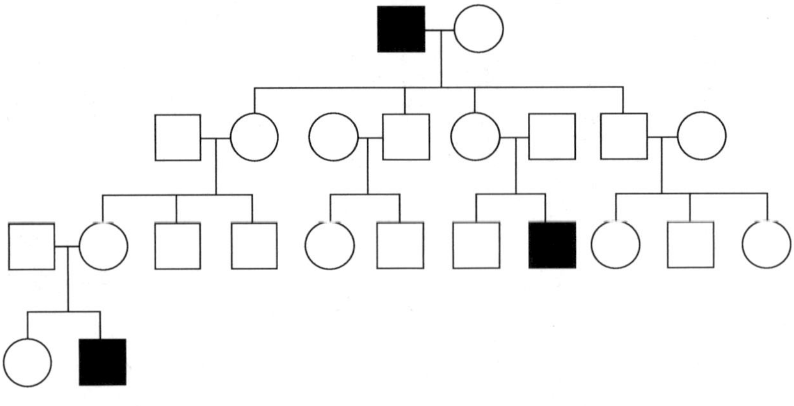

Figure 5.7 A pedigree consistent with XR inheritance

图 5.7 X 连锁隐性遗传系谱

families, it may not be possible to accurately determine whether one sex is affected more frequently than others. On the other hand, one feature of a pedigree that can be used to definitively establish that an inheritance pattern is not XR is the presence of an affected daughter from unaffected parents; because she would have had to inherit one X-chromosome from her father, he would also have been affected in XR.

更高。然而，在一些数目小的典型家族中，精确地确定是否一个性别比另外一个性别患病频率更高是不太可能的。另外，明确确定一种遗传模式不是 X 连锁隐性遗传的系谱特征就是双亲未患病，而其女儿却是患者，因为她继承父亲的 X 染色体，如果是 X 连锁隐性遗传模式，那么父亲也必将患病，女儿才可能患有该病。

(彩图)

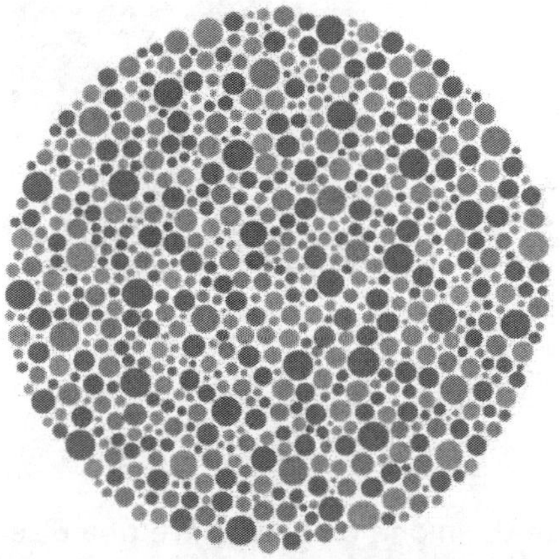

Some forms of colour blindness are inherited as XR-traits. Colour blindness is diagnosed using tests such as this Ishihara Test

几种色盲形式均属于 X 连锁隐性遗传模式。通过石原检测等方法诊断其是否为色盲

SPORADIC AND NON-HERITABLE DISEASES 散发性和非遗传疾病

Only a fraction of all of the known human traits and diseases have been proven to be caused by alleles of a single gene. Many other diseases have a heritable component, but have more complex inheritance patterns due to the involvement of multiple genes and environmental factors. On the other hand, some diseases may appear to be heritable, because they affect multiple members of the same family, but this could also be because the family members are exposed to the same toxins or other environmental factors in their homes. Finally, diseases with similar symptoms may have different causes, so of which may be genetic while others are not. One example of this is ALS (amyotrophic lateral sclerosis); approximately 5%～10% of cases are inherited in an AD

在所有的人类性状和疾病中只有一小部分被证实是由一个基因的等位基因引起的。其他的许多疾病包含有可遗传的组分，同时由于多基因及环境因子的参与而具有更复杂的遗传模式。此外，许多疾病显示出具有遗传性是因为同一家族的许多成员均患此病，但是这有可能是因为这些家族成员在家里受到同一种毒素或者环境因子的影响。结果，具有相似病征的疾病也许是由不同原因造成的，所以有的可遗传而有的不能遗传。举一个

pattern, while the majority of the remaining cases appear to be **sporadic**, in other words, not caused by a mutation inherited from a parent. We now know that different genes or proteins are affected in the inherited and sporadic forms of ALS. The physicist Stephen Hawking (Figure 5.8) and baseball player Lou Gehrig both suffered from sporadic ALS.

例子就是肌萎缩侧索硬化症（ALS）；5%～10%符合常染色体显性（AD）遗传模式，而剩余的大多数病例是**散发性的**，换句话说并非由于遗传自父母的突变造成的。我们现在已获知在遗传性和散发性的肌萎缩侧索硬化症中分别是不同基因和蛋白质受到了影响。物理学家史蒂芬·霍金（图 5.8）和棒球运动员卢·格里克都患有散发性的肌萎缩侧索硬化症。

Figure 5.8 Stephen Hawking

图 5.8 史蒂芬·霍金

CALCULATING PROBABILITIES 概率计算

Once the mode of inheritance of a disease or trait is known, some inferences about the genotype of individuals in a pedigree can be made, based on their phenotypes. Given these genotypes, it is possible to calculate the probability of a particular genotype being inherited in subsequent generations. This can be useful in genetic counseling, for example when prospective parents wish to know the likelihood of their offspring inheriting a disease for which they have a family history.

一旦了解了疾病或性状的遗传模式，就可以在系谱中基于表现型对个体的基因型进行推测。给定基因型，就可以计算某一特定基因型在后代中遗传的比例。这在遗传咨询中是非常有用的。例如，当父母想知道他们的后代是否有可能患有某种家族遗传史疾病时。

Probabilities in pedigrees are calculated using the same basic methods as are used in other fields. The first formula is the **product rule**: the joint probability of two independent events is the product of their individual probabilities; this is the probability of one event AND another event occurring. For example, the probability of a rolling a “five” with a single throw of a single six-sided die is 1/6, and the probability of rolling “five” in each of three successive rolls is 1/6×1/6×1/6= 1/216. The second useful formula is the **sum rule**,

在系谱概率计算时所用的基本方法与在其他领域中所用的基本方法是一样的。第一个公式就是**乘积法则**，两个独立事件共同发生的概率为每个个体概率的乘积，这是一个事件和另一个事件共同发生的概率。例如，在投掷六面骰子的过程中出现“5”的概率是 1/6，那么在连续 3 次投掷中均出现“5”

which states that the combined probability of two independent events is the sum of their individual probabilities. This is the probability of one event OR another event occurring. For example, the probability of rolling a five or six in a single throw of a dice is 1/6 + 1/6 = 1/3.

的概率是 1/6×1/6×1/6，即 1/216。第二个有用的公式是**加和法则**，也就是说两个独立事件组合发生的概率是单个事件概率之和。这是一个事件或者其他事件发生的概率。例如，在投掷骰子的过程中出现“5”或者“6”的概率是 1/6+1/6=1/3。

With these rules in mind, we can calculate the probability that two carriers (i.e. heterozygotes) of an AR disease will have a child affected with the disease as 1/2×1/2 = 1/4, since for each parent, the probability of any gametes carrying the disease allele is 1/2. This is consistent with what we already know from calculating probabilities using a Punnett Square (e.g. in a monohybrid cross *Aa*×*Aa*, 1/4 of the offspring are *aa*). We can likewise calculate probabilities in the more complex pedigree shown in Figure 5.9.

记住这些规则我们就可以计算两个携带常染色体隐性遗传疾病（即杂合体）的父母，他们的后代患病的概率是 1/2×1/2，即 1/4。因为对于双亲之一而言，配子携带致病等位基因的概率是 1/2。这与我们在计算概率时常用的旁氏棋盘法是一致的（如在 *Aa*×*Aa* 杂交中，*aa* 出现的概率是 1/4）。同理我们可以计算更复杂的系谱中患病的概率（图 5.9）。

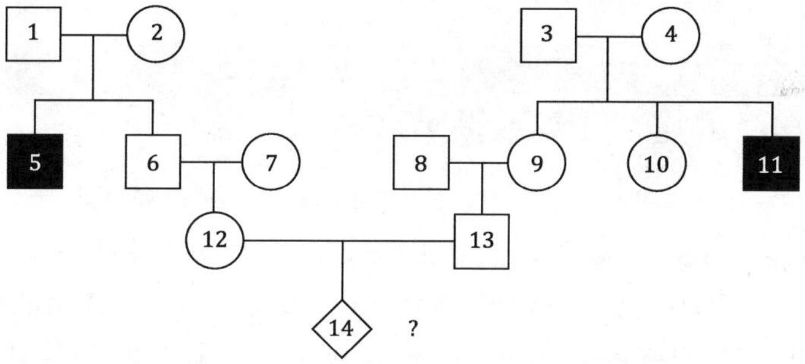

Figure 5.9 Individuals in this pedigree are labeled with numbers to make discussion easier

图 5.9 为了论述得更清楚，系谱中的个体用数字进行了标记

Assuming the disease has an AR pattern of inheritance, what is the probability that individual 14 will be affected? We can assume that individuals #1, #2, #3 and #4 are heterozygotes (*Aa*), because they each had at least one affected (*aa*) child, but they are not affected themselves. This means that there is a 2/3 chance that individual #6 is also *Aa*. This is because according to Mendelian inheritance, when two heterozygotes mate, there is a 1∶2∶1 distribution of genotypes

假设这是一种常染色体隐性遗传疾病，个体 14 患病的概率是多大？我们可以假设个体 1、2、3、4 是杂合体（*Aa*），因为他们每个人至少有一个遗传了此病的孩子，但他们自己不表现病征。这就意味着个体 6 的基因型是 *Aa* 的概率是 2/3。这是因为根据孟德尔的遗传

AA：*Aa*：*aa*. However, because #6 is unaffected, he can't be *aa*, so he is either *Aa* or *AA*, but the probability of him being *Aa* is twice as likely as *AA*. By the same reasoning, there is likewise a 2/3 chance that #9 is a heterozygous carrier of the disease allele.

定律：当两个杂合体（*Aa*）交配时，后代基因型（*AA*、*Aa*、*aa*）的比例是 1：2：1，由于个体 6 未患病，就不可能是 *aa*，所以其基因型是 *AA* 或 *Aa*，但是 *Aa* 的概率是 *AA* 的 2 倍。同理，个体 9 携带杂合等位基因的可能性也是 2/3。

If individual 6 is a heterozygous for the disease allele, then there is a 1/2 chance that #12 will also be a heterozygote (i.e. if the mating of #6 and #7 is *Aa* × *AA*, half of the progeny will be *Aa*; we are also assuming that #7, who is unrelated, does not carry any disease alleles). Therefore, the combined probability that #12 is also a heterozygote is 2/3 × 1/2 = 1/3. This reasoning also applies to individual #13, i.e. there is a 1/3 probability that he is a heterozygote for the disease. Thus, the overall probability that both individual #12 and #13 are heterozygous, and that a particular offspring of theirs will be homozygous for the disease alleles is 1/3×1/3×1/4 = 1/36.

如果个体 6 在致病等位基因上是杂合的，那么个体 12 为杂合体的可能性为 1/2（即我们假设个体 7 不携带任何致病等位基因，如果个体 6 和个体 7 的配子是 *Aa*×*AA*，那么后代中有一半的基因型是 *Aa*）。因此，个体 12 也为杂合体的概率是 2/3×1/2=1/3。此推理过程也适用于个体 13，其为杂合体的可能性为 1/3。因此，个体 12 和个体 13 是杂合体，以至于其后代是纯合体的可能性为 1/3×1/3×1/4 = 1/36。

POPULATION GENETICS 群体遗传学

A **population** is a large group of individuals of the same species, who are capable of mating with each other. It is useful to know the frequency of particular alleles within a population, since this information can be used to calculate disease risks. Population genetics is also important in ecology and evolution, since changes in allele frequencies may be associated with migration or natural selection.

群体是指一群相同物种的个体，在这个群体里能够相互交配。了解某特定基因在群体里出现的频率是非常有用的，因为此信息可以用来计算患病风险。群体遗传学在生态学和进化论中也是非常重要的，因为等位基因频率的变化与种群迁徙及自然选择是相关的。

When calculating the frequency of two alleles of the same locus (e.g. *A*,*a*), we use the symbol ***p*** to represent the frequency of the dominant allele within the population, and ***q*** for the frequency of the recessive allele. Because there are only two possible alleles, we can say that the frequency of *p* and *q* together represent 100% of the alleles in the popula-

当计算同一位点两个等位基因（如 *A* 和 *a*）出现的频率时，我们用 ***p*** 代表群体中显性等位基因出现的频率，而隐性等位基因频率用 ***q*** 表示。由于只有两个可能的等位基因，我们可以认为在群体中 *p* 和 *q*

tion ($p+q=1$).

代表100%的等位基因，即 $p+q=1$。

Allele frequencies may also be studied on the population level

等位基因的频率可以在群体水平上研究

If we know the genotypes of a representative sample of individuals in a population, we can calculate the values of p and q by simply counting the alleles and dividing by the total number of alleles examined; for a give allele, homozygotes will count for twice as much as heterozygotes. For example, given:

genotype	number of individuals
AA	320
Aa	160
aa	20

p =[2 (*AA*) + *Aa*]/total alleles counted=[2(320)+160]/[2(320) + 2(160) + 2(20)] = 0.8

q=[2 (*aa*)+ *Aa*]/total alleles counted=[2(20) + 160]/[2(320) + 2(160) + 2(20)] = 0.2

Given the allele frequencies within a population we can use an extension of the Punnett Square, and the product rule, to calculate the expected frequency of each genotype following matings of the entire population. This is the basis of the

如果我们知道某一群体中代表性个体的基因型，我们就可以简单计算等位基因数量除以检测的等位基因总数而得出 p 值和 q 值。例如，对于一个给定的等位基因，纯合体是杂合体的2倍：

基因型	个体数
AA	320
Aa	160
aa	20

p=[2(*AA*)+*Aa*]/等位基因总数=[2(320)+160]/[2(320)+2(160)+ 2(20)] =0.8

q=[2(*aa*)+*Aa*]/等位基因总数=[2(20)+160]/[2(320)+2(160)+ 2(20)]= 0.2

在群体中，给出等位基因的频率，我们就可以用旁氏棋盘法和乘积法则来计算每个基因型的预期频率。这是**哈迪-温伯格公式**的基础：

Hardy-Weinberg formula: $\boldsymbol{p^2 + 2pq + q^2=1}$, where p^2 is the frequency of homozygotes *AA*, where $2pq$ is the frequency of the heterozygotes, and q^2 is the frequency of homozygotes *aa*.

$\boldsymbol{p^2 + 2pq + q^2=1}$，其中 p^2 是纯合体 *AA* 的频率，$2pq$ 是杂合体的频率，q^2 是纯合体 *aa* 的频率。

	***A* (*p*)**	***a* (*q*)**
***A* (*p*)**	p^2	***pq***
***a* (*q*)**	***pq***	q^2

Notice that if we substitute the allele frequencies we calculated above (p=0.8, q=0.2) into the formula $\boldsymbol{p^2 + 2pq + q^2=1}$, we obtain expected probabilities for each of the genotypes that exactly match our original observations:

注意如果我们把以上计算的等位基因的频率（p=0.8, q=0.2）带入公式 $\boldsymbol{p^2 + 2pq + q^2=1}$ 中，就会得到符合原始观察值的每个基因型的预期概率：

$p^2=0.8^2=0.64$ $\quad$ $0.64\times500 = 320$

$2pq= 2(0.8)(0.2)=0.32$ $\quad$ $0.32\times500 = 160$

$q^2=0.2^2=0.04$ $\quad$ $0.04\times500 = 20$

This is a demonstration of the **Hardy-Weinberg equilibrium** , which states that both the genotype frequencies and allele frequencies in a population remain unchanged following successive matings within a population, if certain conditions are met. These conditions are listed in Table 5.1. Few natural populations actually satisfy all of these conditions. Nevertheless, large populations of many species, including humans, appear to approach Hardy-Weinberg equilibrium for many loci. In these situations, deviations of a particular gene from Hardy-Weinberg equilibirum can be an indication that one of the alleles affects the reproductive success of organism, for example through natural selection or **assortative mating**.

这就是**哈迪-温伯格平衡**的论证过程，它表明了某一群体在满足一定条件的情况下，进行连续交配后其基因型频率和等位基因频率保持不变。少数几个自然群体能满足表5.1 中的这些条件。然而，许多物种的大群体，包括人类，在许多基因位点上接近哈迪-温伯格平衡。在这些情况下，一个特定基因与哈迪-温伯格平衡相背离的现象就意味着一个等位基因影响着生物体的繁殖成功率，如通过自然选择或者同型交配来繁殖。

Table 5.1 Conditions for the Hardy-Weinberg equilibrium

1. Random mating: Individuals of all genotypes mate together with equal frequency. Assortative mating, in which certain genotypes preferentially mate together, is a type of non-random mating
2. No natural selection: All genotypes have equal fitness
3. No migration: Individuals do not leave or enter the population
4. No mutation: The allele frequencies do not change due to mutation
5. Large population: Random sampling effects in mating (i.e. genetic drift) are insignificant in large populations

表 5.1 哈迪-温伯格平衡的条件

1. 随机交配：所有基因型的个体以相等频率交配。选型交配是非随机交配的一种类型，即某一特定基因型可以优先交配
2. 非自然选择：所有基因型具有同等的适应性
3. 非迁移：个体不会离开或进入一个群体
4. 非突变：等位基因的频率不会由于突变而发生变化
5. 大群体：在大群体中交配时的随机取样效应是可以忽略的（即遗传漂移）

The Hardy-Weinberg formula can also be used to estimate allele frequencies, when only the frequency of one of the genotypic classes is known. For example, if 0.04% of the population is affected by a particular genetic condition, and all of the affected individuals have the genotype *aa*, then we assume that $q^2 = 0.0004$ and we can calculate *p*, *q*, and 2*pq* as follows:

当知道一个基因型的频率时，也可以用哈迪-温伯格公式来估计等位基因的频率。例如，如果群体的0.04%被特定遗传因素影响，并且所有受到影响的个体都具有基因型 *aa*，我们假设 $q^2 = 0.0004$，我们可以计算 *p*、*q* 和 2*pq*：

$$q^2 = 0.04\% = 0.0004$$
$$q=0.02$$
$$p= 1-q = 0.98$$
$$2pq = 2(0.98)(0.02) = 0.04$$

Thus, approximately 4% of the population is expected to be heterozygous (i.e. a carrier) of this genetic condition. Note that while we recognize that the population is probably not exactly in Hardy-Weinberg equilibrium for this locus, application of the Hardy-Weinberg formula nevertheless can give a reasonable estimate of allele frequencies, in the absence of any other information.

因此，在这个遗传条件下大约群体中的 4%预期是杂合的（即携带者）。注意，当我们认识到在这个基因位点上群体不精确符合哈迪-温伯格平衡时，尽管如此，在缺少任何其他信息的情况下，用哈迪-温伯格公式仍可以对等位基因频率做出合理的估计。

Summary

- Pedigree analysis can be used to determine the mode of inheritance of specific traits such as diseases.

- 系谱分析可以用来决定特定性状（如疾病）的遗传模式。

- If the mode of inheritance is known, a pedigree can be used to calculate the probability of inheritance of a particular genotype by an individual.

- 如果遗传模式已知，可用系谱来计算一个个体中特定基因型的遗传概率。

- The frequencies of all alleles and genotypes remain unchanged through successive generations of a population in Hardy-Weinberg equilibrium.

- 在哈迪-温伯格平衡中，群体经过连续几代后所有等位基因和基因型频率保持不变。

- Populations in true Hardy-Weinberg equilibrium have random mating, and no genetic drift, no migration, no mutation, and no selection with respect to the gene of interest.

- 就目的基因而言，真正的哈迪-温伯格平衡群体应具有随机交配、非遗传漂移、非迁徙、非突变、非自然选择等条件。

- The Hardy-Weinberg formula can be used to estimate allele and genotype frequencies given only limited information about a population.

- 假设只给了关于一个群体的有限信息，哈迪-温伯格公式可以用来估计等位基因和基因型频率。

Key Terms

mode of inheritance　遗传模式
genetic counseling　遗传咨询
carrier　携带者
autosomal dominant　常染色体显性
autosomal recessive　常染色体隐性
X-linked dominant　X 连锁显性
X-linked recessive　X 连锁隐性
product rule　乘积法则
sum rule　加和法则
population　群体
$p+q=1$
Hardy-Weinberg formula　哈迪-温伯格公式
$p^2 + 2pq + q^2=1$
Hardy-Weinberg equilibrium　哈迪-温伯格平衡
assortative mating　选型交配
random mating　随机交配
migration　迁移
genetic drift　遗传漂移

Study Questions

5.1 What are some of the modes of inheritance that are consistent with this pedigree?

5.1 根据该系谱，此疾病的遗传模式是什么？

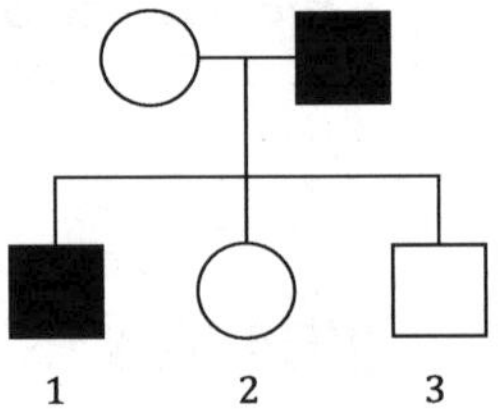

5.2 In this pedigree in question 5.1, the mode of inheritance cannot be determined unambiguously. What are some examples of data (e.g. from other generations) that, if added to the pedigree would help determine the mode of inheritance?

5.2 在问题 5.1 中，遗传模式不能被清楚确定。你认为在系谱中加入什么数据（如从其他世代中）有助于确定遗传模式？

5.3 For each of the following pedigrees, name the most likely mode of inheritance (AR=autosomal recessive, AD=autosomal dominant, XR=X-linked recessive, XD=X-linked dominant). (These pedigrees were obtained from various external sources.)

5.3 对于下面的每个系谱，指明最可能的遗传模式（AR=常染色体隐性，AD=常染色体显性，XR=X连锁隐性，XD=X连锁显性）。（这些系谱来自各种外部资源。）

a)

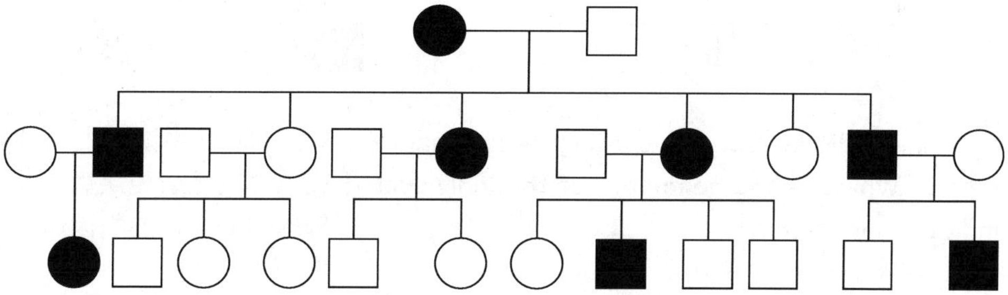

b)

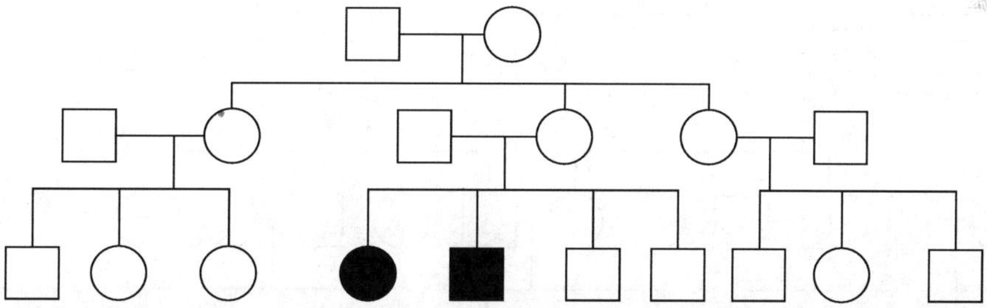

c)

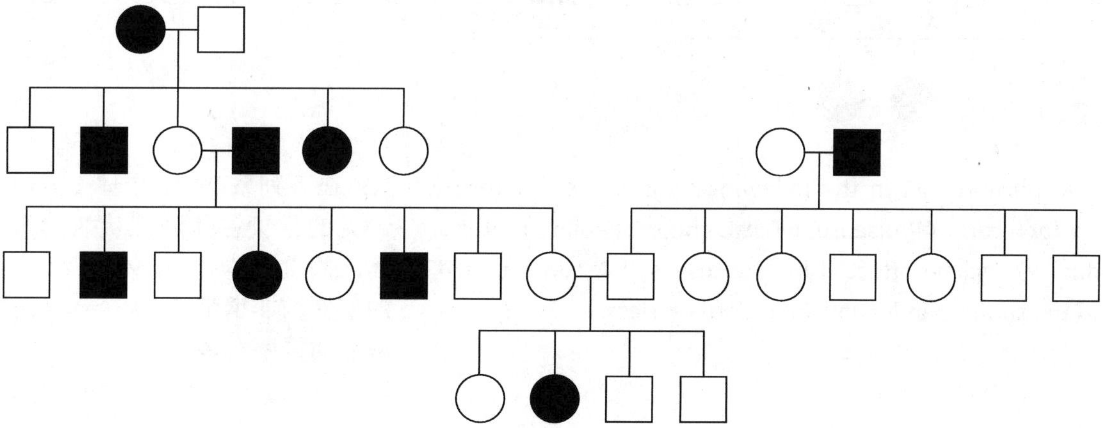

d)

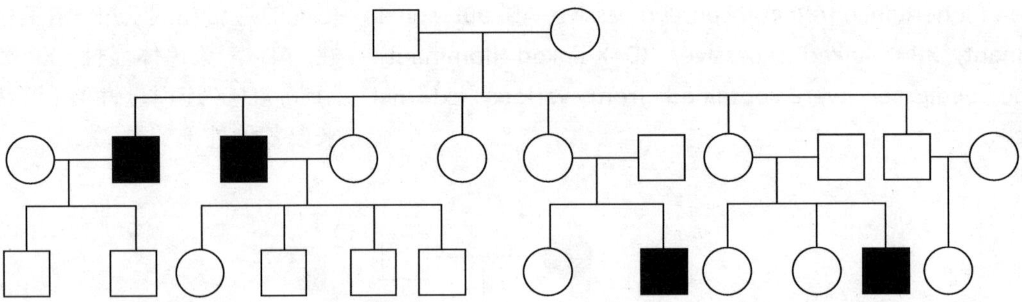

5.4 The following pedigree represents a rare, autosomal recessive disease. What are the genotypes of the individuals who are indicated by letters?

5.4 下面的系谱代表一种罕见的常染色体隐性遗传疾病。系谱中用字母标明的个体的基因型是什么？

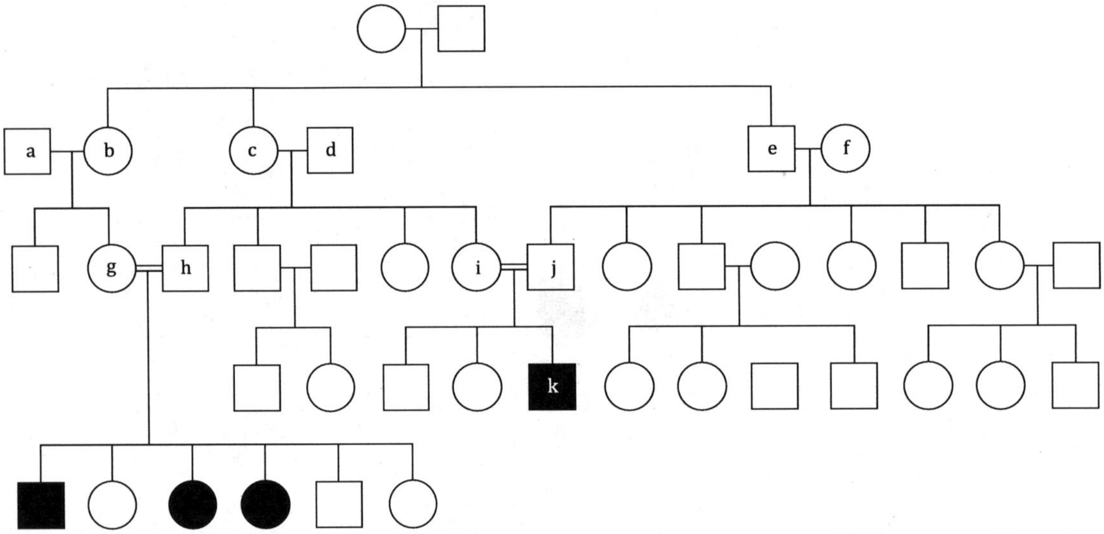

5.5 If individual #1 in the following pedigree is a heterozygote for a rare, AR disease, what is the probability that individual #7 will be affected by the disease? Assume that #2 and the spouses of #3 and #4 are not carriers.

5.5 在下列系谱中，个体 1 为一种罕见的常染色体隐性疾病的杂合体，假设个体 2、个体 3 及个体 4 的配偶均非携带者，则个体 7 可能患病的概率有多大？

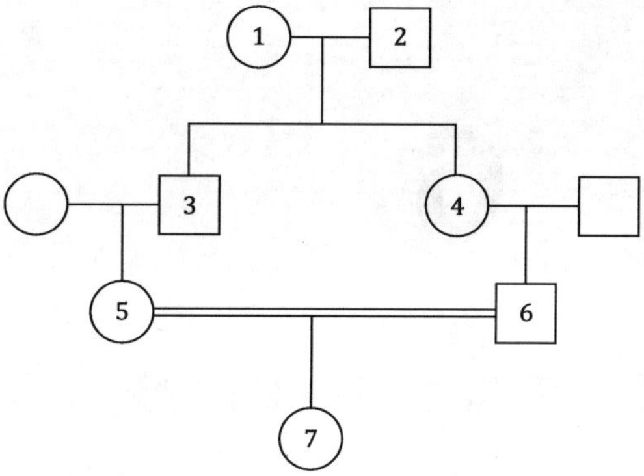

5.6 You are studying a population in which the frequency of individuals with a recessive homozygous genotype is 1%. Assuming the population is in Hardy-Weinberg equilibrium, calculate:

a) The frequency of the recessive allele.

b) The frequency of dominant allele.

c) The frequency of the heterozygous phenotype.

d) The frequency of the homozygous dominant phenotype.

5.7 Determine whether the following population is in Hardy-Weinberg equilibrium.

genotype	number of individuals
AA	432
Aa	676
aa	92

5.8 Out of 1200 individuals examined, 432 are homozygous dominant (*AA*)for a particular gene. What numbers of individuals of the other two genotypic classes (*Aa, aa*) would be expected if the population is in Hardy-Weinberg equilibrium?

5.9 Propose an explanation for the deviation between the genotypic frequencies calculated in question 5.8 and those observed in the table in question 5.7.

5.6 假设有一处于哈迪-温伯格平衡的群体，此群体中的个体携带隐性纯合基因型的概率是 1%，试计算：

a）隐性等位基因的概率。

b）显性等位基因的概率。

c）杂合表现型的概率。

d）纯合显性表现型的概率。

5.7 计算一下群体是否属于哈迪-温伯格平衡？

基因型	个体数
AA	432
Aa	676
aa	92

5.8 在 1200 个个体中，432 个个体具有纯合显性基因（*AA*），如果此群体是哈迪-温伯格平衡，那么其他两个基因型（*Aa*、*aa*）个体的数目各为多少？

5.9 请对问题 5.8 中计算的基因型频率和问题 5.7 观察到的表格中数据偏离的状况给出解释。

Chapter 6

GENETIC ANALYSIS OF TWO LOCI

两个位点的遗传学分析

Coat color in animals is an example of a trait that affected by more than one locus (see the cover)

动物皮毛颜色是受多个位点控制的性状（见封面）

The principles of genetic analysis that we have described for a single locus can be extended to the study of two genes simultaneously. Analysis of two genes in parallel is required for genetic mapping and can also reveal gene interactions. These techniques can be very useful for both basic and applied research. Before discussing these techniques in detail,

我们曾讲过的一个基因位点的遗传分析原理可以扩展来同时研究两个基因。遗传作图需要对两个基因进行平行分析，这样也能揭示基因的互作关系。这些技术对于基础和应用研究都十分有用。在详细讨论这

we will first revisit Mendel and his groundbreaking experiments.

些方法之前，我们再回顾一下孟德尔进行的具有开创性意义的试验。

MENDEL'S SECOND LAW 孟德尔第二定律

Before Mendel, it had not yet been established that heritable traits were controlled by discrete factors. An important question was therefore whether distinct traits could be shown to be controlled by factors that were inherited independently. To answer this, Mendel took two apparently unrelated traits, such as seed shape and seed color, and studied their inheritance in the same individuals. He studied two variants of each trait: seed color was either yellow or green, and seed shape was either round or wrinkled. When either of these traits was studied alone, the phenotypes segregated in a 3 : 1 ratio among the progeny of a monohybrid cross (Figure 6.1), with 3/4 of the seeds yellow and 1/4 green in one cross, and 3/4 round and 1/4 wrinkled in the other cross. To analyze the segregation of the two traits at the same time, he crossed a pure breeding line of green, round peas with a pure breeding line of yellow, wrinkled peas to produce F_1 progeny that were all yellow and round, and which were also **dihybrids**; they carried two alleles at each of two loci (Figure 6.3).

在孟德尔之前，人们还不知道遗传特性是由独立因子所控制。因此，一个重要的问题就是不同性状是否由独立的遗传因子所控制。为了回答这个问题，孟德尔选择两种明显不相关的性状，如种子形状和种子颜色，来研究在同一个体中它们的遗传情况。每一性状研究两种变异型，种子颜色为黄色或绿色，种子形状为圆粒或皱粒。对这些性状单独进行研究时，在单基因杂种杂交的后代中表现型呈 3：1 的分离比率（图 6.1）。一次杂交中 3/4 是黄粒，1/4 是绿粒；在另一杂交中，3/4 是圆粒，1/4 是皱粒。为了同时分析两个性状的分离情况，孟德尔采用纯合的绿色圆粒与纯合的黄色皱粒杂交，得到的 F_1 代都是黄色圆粒，也就是**双基因杂种**，在每个遗传位点上各携带两个不同的等位基因（图 6.3）。

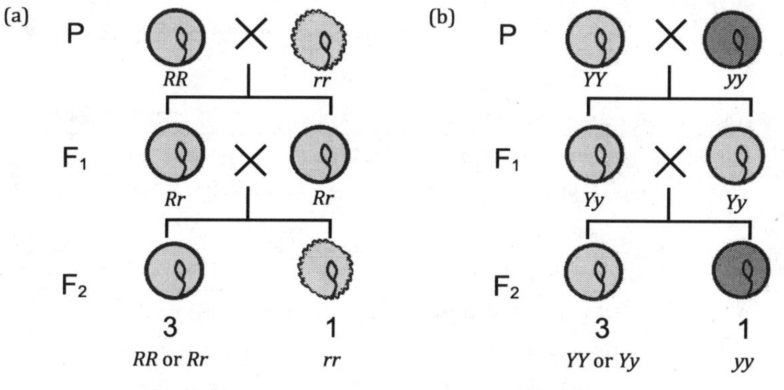

Figure 6.1 Monohybrid crosses involving two distinct traits in peas (see the color figure)

图 6.1 在豌豆单基因杂种杂交中涉及的两个明显的性状（见彩版）

If the inheritance of seed color was truly independent of seed shape, then when the F_1 dihybrids were crossed to each other, a 3:1 ratio of one trait should be observed within each phenotypic class of the other trait (Figure 6.2). Using the product law, we would therefore predict that if 3/4 of the progeny were yellow, and 3/4 of the progeny were round, then 3/4 × 3/4 = 9/16 of the progeny would be both round and yellow (Table 6.1). Likewise, 3/4 × 1/4 = 3/16 of the progeny would be both round and green, and so on. By applying the product rule to all of these combinations of phenotypes, we can predict a **9 : 3 : 3 : 1** phenotypic ratio among the progeny of a dihybrid cross, if certain conditions are met, including the independent segregation of the alleles at each locus. Indeed, 9 : 3 : 3 : 1 is very close to the ratio Mendel observed in his studies of dihybrid crosses, leading him to state his Second Law, the **Law of Independent Assortment**, which we now express as follows: two loci assort independently of each other during gamete formation.

如果种子颜色的遗传确实独立于种子形状的遗传，那么当 F_1 代中双基因杂种相互杂交时，观察到的每一个性状都会呈现 3 : 1 的比例（图 6.2）。用乘积法则我们就能预测出，如果子代的 3/4 是黄色的，3/4 是圆粒的，那么子代黄色圆粒的比例应该是 3/4 × 3/4 = 9/16（表 6.1）。同理，子代是绿色圆粒的比例应该是 3/4 × 1/4 = 3/16，以此类推。如果符合特定的条件，包括每个位点的等位基因独立分离，通过对所有重组性状应用乘积法则计算，就能预测出在双基因杂种杂交后代中表现型的比为 9 : 3 : 3 : 1。实际上 9 : 3 : 3 : 1 已非常接近孟德尔的双基因杂种杂交研究中所观察到的比例，于是他表述了他的第二定律，即**独立分配（又称自由组合）定律**，现在我们表述如下：在配子形成过程中，两个位点彼此独立地分配到配子中去。

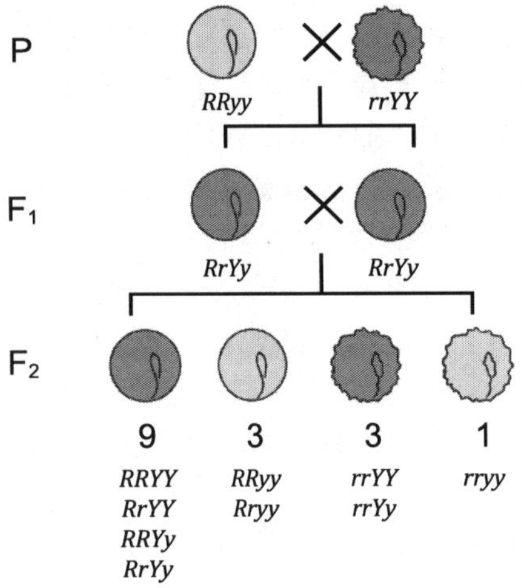

Figure 6.2 Pure-breeding lines are crossed to produce dihybrids in the F_1 generation. The cross of these particular dihybrids produces four phenotypic classes (see the color figure)

图 6.2 纯育系杂交为使 F_1 代得到双基因杂交种。这些特定的双基因杂交种杂交会形成 4 种表现型（见彩版）

Table 6.1 Phenotypic classes expected in monohybrid and dihybrid crosses for two seed traits in pea

Frequency of phenotypic crosses within separate monohybrid crosses		
seed shape:	3/4round	1/4wrinkled
seed color:	3/4 yellow	1/4 green
Frequency of phenotypic crosses within a dihybrid cross		
3/4 round ×3/4 yellow = 9/16		round &yellow
3/4 round×1/4 green = 3/16		round & green
1/4 wrinkled×3/4 yellow = 3/16		wrinkled & yellow
1/4 wrinkled×1/4 green = 1/16		wrinkled & green

表 6.1 单基因杂种和双基因杂种中的预期表现型

不同单基因杂种杂交中的表型频率		
种子形状：	3/4 圆粒	1/4 皱粒
种子颜色：	3/4 黄色	1/4 绿色
在双基因杂种杂交中的表现型频率		
3/4 圆粒 × 3/4 黄粒	= 9/16	黄色圆粒
3/4 圆粒 × 1/4 绿粒	= 3/16	绿色圆粒
1/4 皱粒 × 3/4 黄粒	= 3/16	黄色皱粒
1/4 皱粒 × 1/4 绿粒	= 1/16	绿色皱粒

The 9 : 3 : 3 : 1 phenotypic ratio that we calculated using the product rule can also be obtained using Punnett Square (Figure 6.3). First, we list the genotypes of the possible gametes along each axis of the Punnett Square. In a diploid with two heterozygous genes of interest, there are up to four combinations of alleles in the gametes of each parent. The gametes from the respective rows and column are then combined in the each cell of the array. When working with two loci, genotypes are written with the symbols for both alleles of one locus, followed by both alleles of the next locus (e.g. *AaBb*, not *ABab*). Note that the order in which the loci are written does not imply anything about the actual position of

9 : 3 : 3 : 1 的表现型比率不仅能用乘积法则计算得到，也可以用旁氏棋盘法来计算（图 6.3）。首先在旁氏棋盘上沿着旁氏棋盘一个轴线列出所有可能的配子基因型。在一个有两个杂合基因的二倍体中，来自亲本的配子中有多达 4 种的等位基因组合。然后来自相应行列的配子在表格中的各个单元格中组合在一起。当同时有两个位点时，书写基因型时，一个位点的两个等位基因符号后跟着另一位点的两个等

	RY	*Ry*	*rY*	*ry*
RY	*RRYY*	*RRYy*	*RrYY*	*RrYy*
Ry	*RRYy*	*RRyy*	*RrYy*	*Rryy*
rY	*RrYY*	*RrYy*	*rrYY*	*rrYy*
ry	*RrYy*	*Rryy*	*rrYy*	*rryy*

Figure 6.3 A Punnett Square showing the results of the dihybrid cross from Figure 6.2. Each of the four phenotypic classes is represented by a different color of shading: round & yellow (yellow); round & green (blue); wrinkled & yellow (red); wrinkled & green (green) (see the color figure)

图 6.3 旁氏棋盘法表示出图 6.2 的双基因杂种杂交结果。4 类表现型分别由不同底色表示：黄色圆粒(黄)；绿色圆粒(蓝)；黄色皱粒(红)；绿色皱粒(绿)（见彩版）

the loci on the chromosomes.

位基因符号(如 *AaBb*,而非 *ABab*)。要注意位点的书写位置和这个位点在染色体上的实际位置并没有关系。

To calculate the expected phenotypic ratios, we assign a phenotype to each of the 16 genotypes in the Punnet Square, based on our knowledge of the alleles and their dominance relationships. In the case of Mendel's seeds, any genotype with at least one *R* allele and one *Y* allele will be round and yellow; these genotypes are shown in the nine, yellow-shaded cells in Figure 6.3. We can represent all of four of the different genotypes shown in these cells with the notation (*R_Y_*), where the blank line (__), means "any allele". The three offspring that have at least one *R* allele and are homozygous recessive for *y* (i.e. *R_yy*) will have a round, green phenotype. Conversely the three progeny that are homozygous recessive *r*, but have at least one *Y* allele (*rrY_*) will have wrinkled, yellow seeds. Finally, the rarest phenotypic class of wrinkled, green seeds is produced by the doubly homozygous recessive genotype, *rryy*, which is expected to occur in only one of the sixteen possible offspring represented in the square.

为了计算预期的表现型比率,基于我们对等位基因的知识和它们的显隐性关系,在旁氏棋盘上将一个表现型分成 16 个基因型。在孟德尔种子的例子中,任何一个基因型带有至少一个 *R* 基因和一个 *Y* 基因的都是黄色圆粒的,这些基因型在图 6.3 中显示为 9 个黄色的单元格。在单元格中我们用符号(*R_Y_*)来表示 4 种不同的基因型,空白画线处意为任何等位基因。至少有一个 *R* 等位基因且有纯合隐性基因 *y*(如 *R_yy*)的 3 个子代将会呈现绿色圆粒表现型。相反地,携带纯合隐性 *r* 基因而且携带至少一个 *Y* 等位基因(*rrY_*)的 3 个子代会出现黄色皱粒种子。最后,最少的表现型就是绿色皱粒种子,是双重纯合隐性基因型(*rryy*),就是在棋盘中显示的 16 个子代中才能得到 1 个这样的基因型。

ASSUMPTIONS OF THE 9 : 3 : 3 : 1 RATIO
9 : 3 : 3 : 1 比率的假定条件

Both the product rule and the Punnett Square approaches showed that a 9 : 3 : 3 : 1 phenotypic ratio is expected among the progeny of a dihybrid cross such as Mendel's *RrYy* × *RrYy*. In making these calculations, we assumed that: both loci assort independently; one allele at each locus is completely dominant; and each of four possible phenotypes can be distinguished unambiguously, with no interactions between the two genes that would alter the phenotypes. Devi-

基于乘积法则和旁氏棋盘法,双基因杂种杂交,如孟德尔式的 *RrYy*×*RrYy* 的后代预期表现型比例为 9 : 3 : 3 : 1。在作出上述计算时,我们假定各个位点独立分配,每个位点的 1 个等位基因是完全显性的;并且 4 种可能表现型的任何一种都能被显著区分,且 2 个基因间没

ations from the 9 : 3 : 3 : 1 phenotypic ratio may indicate that one of more of these conditions has not been met. Modified ratios in the progeny of a dihybrid cross can therefore reveal useful information about the genes involved. **Linkage** is one of the most important reasons for distortion of the ratios expected from independent assortment. Linked genes are located close together on the same chromosome, which affects which combinations of alleles assort together most frequently. We will return to the concept of linkage in Chapter 7. Deviations from 9 : 3 : 3 : 1 ratios can also be due to interactions between genes; these interactions will be discussed throughout the remainder of this chapter. For simplicity, we will focus on examples that involve easily scored phenotypes, such as pigmentation. Nevertheless, keep in mind that the analysis of segregation ratios can provide insight into a wide range of biological processes.

有能改变表现型的基因互作。偏离 9 : 3 : 3 : 1 表现型比例可能预示着该杂交尚未达到上述条件。双基因杂种杂交后代偏离的比率能够揭示相关基因的有用信息。**连锁**是与独立分配定律预期结果产生差异的一个重要原因。连锁的基因在同一条染色体上相距很近，从而常常使等位基因共同分离。第 7 章我们会回顾连锁的概念。9 : 3 : 3 : 1 比率的偏差也可归结于基因间的互作。这些互作将会在本章余下内容中进行讨论。为了简单起见，我们将专注于容易区分的表现型的例子，如着色。不过，牢记分离比率的分析能够深刻理解广泛的生物学过程。

EPISTASIS AND OTHER GENE INTERACTIONS 上位效应和其他基因互作

Some dihybrid crosses produce a phenotypic ratio that differs from 9 : 3 : 3 : 1 because of epistasis. Epistasis (which means "standing upon") occurs when the phenotype of one locus masks the phenotype of another locus. Thus, following a dihybrid cross with epistasis, fewer than four phenotypic classes will be observed, with ratios such as 9 : 3 : 4, 12 : 3 : 1, 9 : 7, or 15 : 1. Note that each of these modified ratios can be obtained by summing one or more of the 9 : 3 : 3 : 1 classes expected from our original dihybrid cross. In the following paragraphs, we will look at some modified phenotypic ratios obtained from dihybrid crosses and what they might tell us about interactions between genes.

由于上位效应，一些双基因杂种杂交形成表现型比率不同于 9 : 3 : 3 : 1 的比率。当一个位点的表现型掩盖了另一位点的表现型时就产生了上位效应(意为"占上位")。因此，带有上位效应的双基因杂种杂交会观察到少于 4 种表现型的情况。比率会出现 9 : 3 : 4、12 : 3 : 1、9 : 7 或 15 : 1 的情况。值得注意的是，这些不同的比率都能通过最原始的双基因杂种杂交预期的 9 : 3 : 3 : 1 比例求和得出。在接下来的段落中，我们将会看到一些双基因杂种杂交后一些表现型比率变化的现象，以此来告诉大家基因间的互作。

Recessive epistasis 隐性上位

As we have already discussed, in the absence of epistasis, there are four phenotypic classes among the progeny of a dihybrid cross. The four phenotypic classes correspond to the genotypes: *A_B_*, *A_bb*, *aaB_*, and *aabb*. If either of the singly homozygous recessive genotypes (i.e. *A_bb* or *aaB_*) has the same phenotype as the double homozygous recessive (*aabb*), then a **9：3：4** phenotypic ratio will be obtained. For example, in the Labrador Retriever breed of dogs (Figure 6.4), the *B* locus encodes a gene for an important step in the production of melanin. The dominant allele, *B* is more efficient at pigment production than the recessive *b* allele, thus *B_* hair appears black, and *bb* hair appears brown. A second locus, which we will call *A*, regulates the production of melanin. At least one functional *A* allele is required to produce any pigment, whether it is black or brown. Thus, all retrievers that are *aa* fail to produce any melanin (and so appear pale yellow), regardless of the genotype at the *B* locus (Figure 6.5). The *aa* genotype is therefore said to be epistatic to both the *B* and *b* alleles, since the homozygous *aa* phenotype masks the phenotype of the *B* locus. Because the masking allele is in this case is recessive, this is called **recessive epistasis** (Figure 6.5).

我们已经讨论过，在没有上位效应的情况下，双基因杂种杂交后代中有 4 种表现型。4 种表现型对应的基因型分别是：*A_B_*、*A_bb*、*aaB_* 和 *aabb*。如果任何一个单一纯合隐性的基因型（如 *A_bb* 或 *aaB_*）和双重纯合隐性基因型（*aabb*）有着相同的表现型，那么就会得到 **9：3：4** 的表现型比率。例如，在拉布拉多猎犬中，*B* 位点编码黑色素形成过程中重要步骤的一个基因（图 6.4）。这个显性的等位基因 *B* 远比隐性等位基因 *b* 在色素形成上功能强，因此 *B_* 型毛发表现出黑色，*bb* 型毛发表现出棕色。第二个位点我们称为 *A*，调节黑色素的形成。不论是黑色还是棕色，至少需要一个功能性的等位基因 *A* 来形成色素。所以，不管 *B* 位点是什么基因型，所有的 *aa* 型的猎犬都不能产生黑色素（所以呈现出浅黄色）。因此，*aa* 基因型就称为对于 *B* 和 *b* 等位基因上位，因为纯合 *aa*

Figure 6.4 Labrador Retrievers with different coat colors: (from left to right) black, chocolate, yellow (see the color figure)

图 6.4 不同毛色的拉布拉多猎犬（从左至右）黑色、巧克力色、黄色（见彩版）

表现型掩盖了 *B* 位点的表现型。因为在这个例子中有掩盖作用的等位基因是隐性的，故称为**隐性上位**（图 6.5）。

	AB	*Ab*	*aB*	*ab*
AB	*AABB*	*AABb*	*AaBB*	*AaBb*
Ab	*AABb*	*AAbb*	*AaBb*	*Aabb*
aB	*AaBB*	*AaBb*	*aaBB*	*aaBb*
ab	*AaBb*	*Aabb*	*aaBb*	*aabb*

Figure 6.5 Genotypes and phenotypes among the progeny of a dihybrid cross of Labrador Retrievers heterozygous for two loci affecting coat color. The phenotypes of the progeny are indicated by the shading of the cells in the table: black coat (black, *A_B_*); chocolate coat (brown, *A_bb*); yellow coat (yellow, *aaB_* or *aabb*) (see the color figure)

图 6.5 当两个位点影响拉布拉多猎犬不同毛色时，双基因杂种杂交后代的遗传型和表现型。表格中底色指示后代的表现型：黑色表皮（黑色, *A_B_*）；巧克力色表皮(棕色, *A_bb*)；黄色表皮（黄色, *aaB_* 或 *aabb*）（见彩版）

Dominant epistasis 显 性 上 位

In some cases, a dominant allele at one locus may mask the phenotype of a second locus. This is called **dominant epistasis**, which produces a segregation ratio such as **12 : 3 : 1**, which can be viewed as a modification of the 9 : 3 : 3 : 1 ratio in which the *A_B_* class is combined with one of the other genotypic classes that contains a dominant allele. One of the best known examples of a 12 : 3 : 1 segregation ratio is fruit color in some types of squash (Figure 6.6). Alleles of a locus that we will call *B* produce either yellow (*B_*) or green (*bb*) fruit. However, in the presence of a dominant allele at a second locus that we call *A*, no pigment is produced at all, and fruit are white. The *A* allele is therefore epistatic to both *B* and *bb* combinations (Figure 6.7). One possible biological interpretation of this segregation pattern is that the function of the *A* allele somehow blocks an early stage of pigment synthesis, before either yellow or green pigments are produced.

在某些情况下，一个位点的显性等位基因可能掩盖了第二个位点的表现型，这种现象叫做**显性上位**，其分离比例会出现 **12 : 3 : 1** 的情况，可以被视为变化的 9 : 3 : 3 : 1 比例，即由于基因型为 *A_B_* 的表现型和基因型中含有一个显性等位基因（*A_*）的表现型一样，被视为同一种表现型来计算比例。最好的 12 : 3 : 1 的分离比率的例子是一些类型南瓜的果实颜色（图 6.6）。一个位点的等位基因 *B* 能产生黄色（*B_*）或是绿色（*bb*）果实。但是，当第二个位点的显性等位基因 *A* 出现时则不能产生任何色素，果实呈现白色。等位基因 *A* 就对 *B* 和 *bb* 组合上位（图 6.7）。对于这个分离模式的一个合理的生物学解释就是在黄色或绿色色素形成之前，等位基因 *A* 以某种方式在色素合成前期阻碍了色素合成。

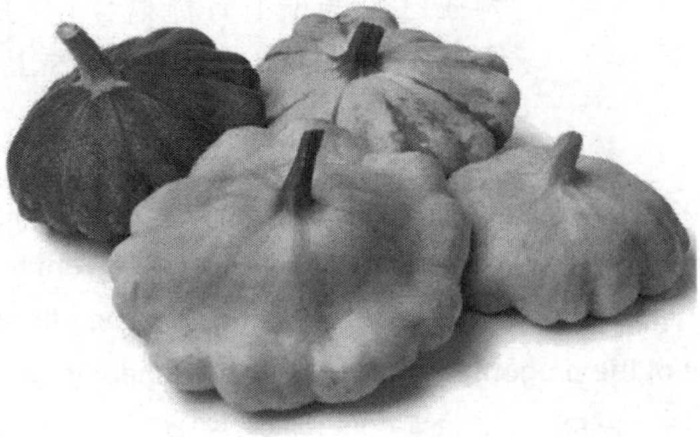

Figure 6.6 Green, yellow, and white fruits of squash (see the color figure)

图 6.6 绿色、黄色、白色南瓜果实（见彩版）

	AB	*Ab*	*aB*	*ab*
AB	*AABB*	*AABb*	*AaBB*	*AaBb*
Ab	*AABb*	*AAbb*	*AaBb*	*Aabb*
aB	*AaBB*	*AaBb*	*aaBB*	*aaBb*
ab	*AaBb*	*Aabb*	*aaBb*	*aabb*

Figure 6.7 Genotypes and phenotypes among the progeny of a dihybrid cross of squash plants heterozygous for two loci affecting fruit color

图 6.7 当两个位点影响南瓜果实颜色时，双基因杂种杂交后代中的基因型和表现型

Complementary gene action 基因互补作用

The progeny of a dihybrid cross may produce just two phenotypic classes, in an approximately **9：7** ratio. An interpretation of this ratio is that the loss of function of either *A* or *B* gene function has the same phenotype as the loss of function of both genes, due to **complementary gene action** (meaning that the functions of both genes work together to produce a final product). For example, consider a simple biochemical pathway in which a colorless substrate is converted by the action of gene *A* to another colorless product, which is then converted by the action of gene *B* to a visible pigment (Figure 6.8). Loss of function of either *A* or *B*, or both, will have the same result: no pigment production. Thus *A_bb*, *aaB_*, and *aabb* will all be colorless, while only *A_B_* genotypes will produce pigmented product (Figure 6.9). The modified 9：7 ratio may therefore be obtained when two genes act together in the same biochemical pathway, and when their loss of function phenotypes are indistinguishable from each other or from the loss of both genes.

在双基因杂种杂交中只产生两种表现型，近似 **9：7** 的比例。对这种比例的解释是由于基因互补作用，*A* 或 *B* 基因中的任何一个基因功能缺失与两种基因功能都缺失产生同样的表现型，**基因互补**意味着两个基因共同作用产生最终的产物。例如，考虑一个简单的生化途径，一个无色底物被基因 *A* 转换成另一个无色产物，然后由于基因 *B* 的作用变成可见的色素（图 6.8）。缺少基因 *A* 或 *B* 或都缺失会产生相同的结果：没有色素产生。所以 *A_bb*、*aaB_*和 *aabb* 都呈现无色，而只有 *A_B_*型产生色素（图 6.9）。在同一个生化途径中，当两种基因同时起作用时会出现 9：7 的比例，同时当缺失它们中的任何一个基因和两个基因全都缺失的表现型一样。

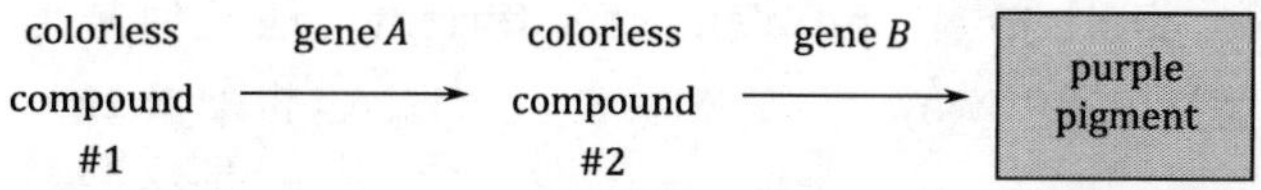

Figure 6.8 A simplified biochemical pathway showing complementary gene action of *A* and *B*. Note that in this case, the same phenotypic ratios would be obtained if gene *B* acted before gene *A* in the pathway

图 6.8 一个表示 *A* 和 *B* 基因互补作用的简化生化途径。这个例子中值得注意的是，如果基因 *B* 在这个途径中先于基因 *A* 作用，会得到同样的表现型比率

	AB	***Ab***	***aB***	***ab***
AB	*AABB*	*AABb*	*AaBB*	*AaBb*
Ab	*AABb*	*AAbb*	*AaBb*	*Aabb*
aB	*AaBB*	*AaBb*	*aaBB*	*aaBb*
ab	*AaBb*	*Aabb*	*aaBb*	*aabb*

Figure 6.9 Genotypes and phenotypes among the progeny of a dihybrid cross of a hypothetical plant heterozygous for two loci affecting flower color

图 6.9 假定两个位点影响花的颜色时，植物双基因杂种杂交后代的基因型和表现型

Duplicate gene action 基因重复作用

When a dihybrid cross produces progeny in two phenotypic classes in a 15 : 1 ratio, this can be because the two loci have redundant functions within the same biological pathway. Yet another pigmentation pathway, in this case in wheat, provides an example of this **duplicate gene action**. The biosynthesis of red pigment near the surface of wheat seeds (Figure 6.10) involves many genes, two of which we will label *A* and *B*. Normal, red coloration of the wheat seeds is maintained if function of either of these genes is lost in a homozygous mutant (e.g. in either *aaB_* or *A_bb*). Only the doubly recessive mutant (*aabb*), which lacks function of both genes, shows a phenotype that differs from that produced by any of the other genotypes (Fig. 6.10 and Figure 6.11). A reasonable interpretation of this result is that both genes encode the

当双基因杂种杂交产生的后代出现两种表现型，且呈 15 : 1 的比率时，是因为两个位点在同一个生物途径中出现冗余功能。小麦色素形成途径是**基因重复作用**的典型例子。小麦种皮上红色色素的生物合成（图 6.10）涉及多个基因，我们标注其中两个分别为 *A* 和 *B* 基因。正常来讲，即使产生了缺失任何一个基因的纯合突变体，小麦种子红色着色仍能够维持（如 *aaB_* 或 *A_bb*）。只有发生双重隐性突变（*aabb*）时，即同时缺少两种基因的功能时，该种子表现出不同于其

same biological function, and either one alone is sufficient for the normal activity of that pathway.

他任何基因型的表现型（图 6.10 和图 6.11）。这一结果的合理解释就是这两种基因有着相同的生物功能，任何一种单独存在都足以维持这一途径的正常活动。

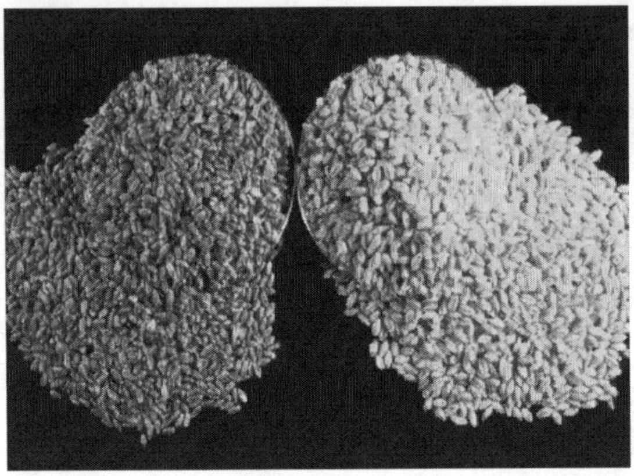

Figure 6.10 Red (left) and white (right) wheat seeds (see the color figure)

图 6.10 红色（左侧）和白色（右侧）小麦种子（见彩版）

	AB	*Ab*	*aB*	*ab*
AB	*AABB*	*AABb*	*AaBB*	*AaBb*
Ab	*AABb*	*AAbb*	*AaBb*	*Aabb*
aB	*AaBB*	*AaBb*	*aaBB*	*aaBb*
ab	*AaBb*	*Aabb*	*aaBb*	*aabb*

Figure 6.11 Genotypes and phenotypes among the progeny of a dihybrid cross of a wheat plants heterozygous for two loci affecting seed color

图 6.11 当两个位点影响小麦种子颜色时，双基因杂种杂交后代的基因型和表现型

ENHANCER/SUPPRESSOR SCREENS 增强子/抑制子筛选

From the examples of genetic interactions already discussed in this chapter, it should be apparent that the analysis of phenotypes at two loci simultaneously can provide insight into the functions of genes and biochemical pathways. Accordingly, geneticists sometimes attempt to identify interacting genes through mutant screening, using a technique called enhancer/suppressor screening. Typically, a researcher will mutagenize a population that is already has an interesting mutant phenotype in one gene (*aa*), then screen through the progeny of the remutagenized individuals to find additional mutations that either make the original *aa* mutants look more like wild-type (i.e. **suppressors** or **revertants**), or else increase (i.e. **enhance**) the severity of the original *aa*

基因间互作的例子已经在本章讨论过了，很明显的是两个位点表现型分析同时能够让人们深刻理解基因的功能和生化途径。于是，遗传学家也尝试着通过突变筛选来鉴定互作的基因，该技术叫做增强子/抑制子筛选。典型的方法是：研究人员会对一个感兴趣的基因（*aa*）突变体进行诱导突变，然后筛选第二次突变个体的后代，找到突变后使之前的 *aa* 突变体看起来更像是野生型（即**抑制子**或**回复子**）的突变体，或者找到增加（**增

phenotype. Note that this use of the term enhancer is unrelated to its use in the context of transcriptional gene regulation (see Chapter 10).

强）原始的 *aa* 突变表现型的突变体。值得注意的是这里使用的增强子概念与转录基因调控内容所使用的增强子概念是完全不相干的（见第 10 章）。

Reversions, as implied by their name, are mutation that reverses the sequence changes caused by a preceding mutation. Reversions therefore restore the wild-type function of a gene. For example, if the first mutation introduced a stop codon within the coding sequence of a gene, a reversion would result from mutation of that stop codon to again code for an amino acid that restores normal function of the protein. Reversions are genetically less interesting than some other potential outcomes of an enhancer/suppressor screen.

回复突变，顾名思义，就是突变体中突变的序列通过第二次突变得到了复原。因此回复突变恢复了野生型基因的功能。例如，如果第一个突变在一个基因的编码序列引入了一个终止密码子，那么回复突变就能使终止密码子再次突变回原来的序列，从而使氨基酸恢复编码蛋白质的功能。在遗传学上，回复突变体不如增强子/抑制子筛选出的潜在结果更有意义。

Suppressors also restore some or all of the wild-type function that is lost in an existing mutant (*aa*), either through mutation of a different site within the same gene (i.e. an **intragenic** suppressor), or by mutation of a different gene (i.e. an **intergenic** suppressor). There are many mechanisms by which intergenic suppressor mutations may restore wild-type function. One way is through the modification of an interacting protein. For example, imagine that proteins produced by genes *A* and *B* must physically connect with each other to perform their normal function (Figure 6.12). If a mutant allele (*a*) was structurally altered in some way that made it unable to interact with the protein produced by *B*, then there would be a blockage of the biochemical pathway normally catalyzed by the two wild-type genes. However, if through additional random mutagenesis, *B* was mutated in a way that changed its structure to allow it to again connect with a, then the wild-type function of the protein complex might be restored. In this case, *b* would be said to suppress *aa*. In this way, a novel gene (*B*) that normally interacts with the original gene of interest (*A*), could be identified through the mutagenesis of a mutant.

无论是通过同一基因不同位点的突变（**基因内**的抑制子）还是通过不同基因的突变（**基因间**的抑制子），抑制子能够恢复现有突变体（*aa*）所丢失的某些或全部野生型功能。通过基因间抑制子的突变恢复野生型功能具有许多机制。其中一种方式就是通过改变相互作用的蛋白质。例如，想象通过基因 *A* 和 *B* 产生的蛋白质必须物理上彼此互作才能执行它们的正常功能（图 6.12）。如果突变的等位基因 *a* 结构上以某种方式突变了，以至于它不能够和基因 *B* 产生的蛋白质共同作用，那就必然阻碍两个野生型基因所催化的生化途径。然而，如果通过另外的随机突变，B 蛋白结构以某种方式发生了突变，并恰好可以和 a 蛋白互作，从而使这一蛋白复合体的功能又得到了恢复。在这个例子中，可以说 *b* 抑制了 *aa*。在这种情况下，与之前感兴趣的基因（*A*）相互作用的新基因（*B*）能在突变体发生突变中鉴定出来。

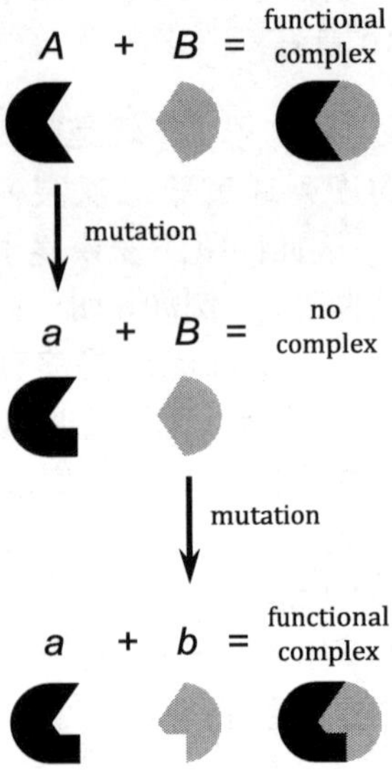

Figure 6.12 Mutation in allele *A* leads to a loss of function because of a failure to form an active complex with *B*. However, a second (suppressor) mutation allows the two mutant alleles to again connect in a functional complex

图 6.12 等位基因 *A* 突变导致功能缺失，使其与基因 *B* 不能形成活性复合体。但是第二个突变能够使两个突变基因再次互作形成功能性复合体

Enhancer mutations increase or expand an existing mutant phenotype, often by reducing the function of other genes that normally interact cooperatively or redundantly within a biochemical pathway. Like revertants and suppressors, enhancers can be identified by screening after mutagenesis of a (usually homozygous) mutant (e.g. *aa*).

通常通过降低其他基因功能，增强子突变增加或者说放大了已存在的突变体表现型，这些基因在一个生化途径中与增强子协同作用或冗余地互作。就像回复突变体和抑制子一样，增强子能够在突变体发生突变时就被鉴定出来（通常为纯合体）。

A particularly interesting example of a gene identified by enhancer screening is provided by *Arabidopsis*. Researchers had already identified mutants of *Arabidopsis* called *apetala1* (*ap1*) that lacked the outer organs (sepals, petals) of the flower. To find additional genes that interact with *ap1*, the researchers attempted an enhancer/suppressor screen by mutagenizing *ap1*/*ap1* plants, and then looking for novel mutant phenotypes among their selfed (F_2) progeny. One of the novel, enhanced phenotypes caused structures that looked like tiny cauliflowers to be produced in place of the *ap1* flowers. They named the enhancer gene *CAULIFLOWER* (*CAL*), and further analysis showed that the cauliflower phenotype was produced only when both *ap1* and *cal* were homozygous mutant; in fact *cal*/*cal* alone looked just like

在拟南芥中有一个特别有趣的通过增强子筛选鉴定基因的例子。研究者已经在拟南芥中筛选出了花中缺少外部器官（萼片和花瓣）的突变体——*apetala1*（*ap1*）。为找到与 *ap1* 相互作用的其他基因，研究人员尝试诱变 *ap1*/*ap1* 突变体来进行增强子/抑制子筛选，然后通过自交后代来找到新的突变体表现型。其中一个新的增强突变的表现型是产生了类似微小花椰菜结构的花，这种花替代了 *ap1* 的花，于是将该增强子命名为 *CAULIFLOWER* 基因（*CAL*），并且进

wild-type. Since *Arabidopsis* is in the same taxonomic family as cauliflower, cabbage, they hypothesized that something like the *Arabidopsis cal and ap1* mutations might be what makes the vegetable, cauliflower, look the way that it does. Indeed, analysis of cauliflower from a grocery store ultimately showed that its distinct appearance is the result of mutation in genes like *cal/cal* and *ap1/ap1*. This is just one example of the unexpected information that can come from enhancer/suppressor screening.

一步分析表明，花椰菜表现型是仅当 *ap1* 和 *cal* 共同突变并纯合时才能形成的；实际上 *cal/cal* 单独突变时看起来就像是野生型。由于拟南芥、花椰菜和甘蓝在分类上属于同一科，研究人员设想可能类似于拟南芥 *cal* 和 *ap1* 突变的一些改变使花椰菜形成了现在的外观。实际上，从超市中买到的花椰菜分析表明，它的不寻常表现型就是类似于 *cal/cal* 和 *ap1/ap1* 基因突变的结果。这就是通过增强子/抑制子筛选而获得意想不到信息的例子。

Summary

- The alleles of different genes are inherited independently of each other, unless they are genetically linked.
- 如果不同基因的等位基因之间遗传上不连锁，它们彼此独立遗传。
- The expected phenotypic ratio of a dihybrid cross is 9∶3∶3∶1, except in cases of linkage or gene interactions that modify this ratio.
- 双基因杂种杂交的表现型预期比例为 9∶3∶3∶1，但基因连锁或者基因互作的比例除外，它们具有不同的比例。
- Epistasis occurs when the phenotype of one gene masks the phenotype of another gene. This usually indicates that the two genes interact within the same biological pathway.
- 当一个基因的表现型覆盖了另一个基因的表现型就发生了上位效应，这通常是在同一生化途径中两个基因相互作用的结果。
- Enhancer/suppressor screening is a way to identify genetically interacting genes through further mutagenesis of an existing mutant.
- 增强子/抑制子筛选是通过对已存在的突变体进一步突变来鉴定遗传上互作基因的方法。

Key Terms

Mendel's Second Law 孟德尔第二定律
dihybrid 双基因杂种
9∶3∶3∶1
9∶3∶4
9∶7
12∶3∶1
15∶1
recessive epistasis 隐性上位
dominant epistasis 显性上位
complementary action 互补作用
redundancy 冗余
duplicate gene action 重复基因作用
enhancer/suppressor 增强子/抑制子
revertant 回复突变体

independent assortment 独立分配
linkage 连锁
epistasis 上位效应
intergenic 基因间的
intragenic 基因内的
CAULIFLOWER

Study Questions

Answer questions 6.1~6.3 using the following biochemical pathway for fruit color. Assume all mutations (lower case allele symbols) are recessive, and that *either* precursor 1 or precursor 2 can be used to produce precursor 3. If the alleles for a particular gene are not listed in a genotype, you can assume that they are wild-type.

用下图产生果实颜色的生化途径回答 6.1～6.3 的问题。假设所有的突变（小写符号的等位基因）是隐性的，前体 1 或前体 2 能被用作产生前体 3。如果在一个基因型中没有列出一个特定基因的等位基因，你可以假定它是野生型。

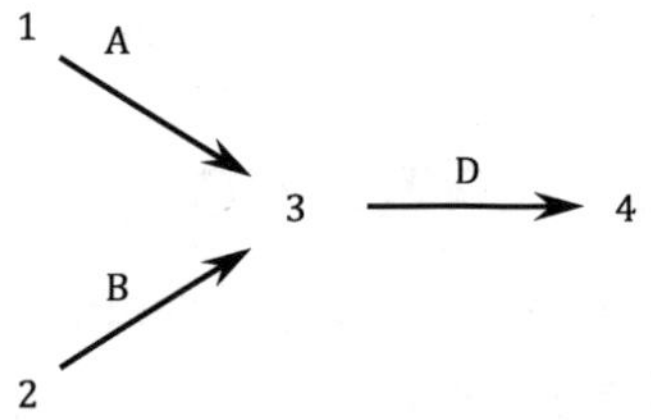

6.1 If 1 and 2 and 3 are all colorless, and 4 is red, what will be the phenotypes associated with the following genotypes?

a) *aa*
b) *bb*
c) *dd*
d) *aabb*
e) *aadd*
f) *bbdd*
g) *aabbdd*
h)What will be the phenotypic ratios among the offspring of a cross *AaBb*×*AaBb*?
i) What will be the phenotypic ratios among the offspring of a cross *BbDd*×*BbDd*?
j) What will be the phenotypic ratios among the offspring of a cross *AaDd*×*AaDd*?

6.1 如果 1、2 和 3 都是无色的，4 是红色的，下面基因型的表现型是什么样的？

a）*aa*
b）*bb*
c）*dd*
d）*aabb*
e）*aadd*
f）*bbdd*
g）*aabbdd*
h）*AaBb*×*AaBb* 杂交后代的表现型比率是多少？
i）*BbDd*×*BbDd* 杂交后代的表现型比率是多少？
j）*AaDd*×*AaDd* 杂交后代的表现型比率是多少？

6.2 If 1 and 2 are both colorless, and 3 is blue and 4 is red, what will be the phenotypes associated with the following genotypes?
a) *aa*
b) *bb*

6.2 如果 1 和 2 都是无色的，而 3 是蓝色的，4 是红色的，下面基因型的表现型是什么样的？
a）*aa*
b）*bb*

c) *dd*
d) *aabb*
e) *aadd*
f) *bbdd*
g) *aabbdd*
h) What will be the phenotypic ratios among the offspring of a cross *AaBb*×*AaBb*?
i) What will be the phenotypic ratios among the offspring of a cross *BbDd*×*BbDd*?
j) What will be the phenotypic ratios among the offspring of a cross *AaDd*×*AaDd*?

c) *dd*
d) *aabb*
e) *aadd*
f) *bbdd*
g) *aabbdd*
h) *AaBb*×*AaBb* 杂交后代的表现型比率是多少?
i) *BbDd*×*BbDd* 杂交后代的表现型比率是多少?
j) *AaDd*×*AaDd* 杂交后代的表现型比率是多少?

6.3 If 1 is colorless, 2 is yellow and 3 is blue and 4 is red, what will be the phenotypes associated with the following genotypes?
a) *aa*
b) *bb*
c) *dd*
d) *aabb*
e) *aadd*
f) *bbdd*
g) *aabbdd*
h) What will be the phenotypic ratios among the offspring of a cross *AaBb*×*AaBb*?
i) What will be the phenotypic ratios among the offspring of a cross *BbDd*×*BbDd*?
j) What will be the phenotypic ratios among the offspring of a cross *AaDd*×*AaDd*?

6.3 如果 1 是无色的, 2 是黄色的，3 是蓝色的，4 是红色的，下面基因型的表现型是什么样的?
a) *aa*
b) *bb*
c) *dd*
d) *aabb*
e) *aadd*
f) *bbdd*
g) *aabbdd*
h) *AaBb*×*AaBb* 杂交后代的表现型比率是多少?
i) *BbDd*×*BbDd* 杂交后代的表现型比率是多少?
j) *AaDd*×*AaDd* 杂交后代的表现型比率是多少?

6.4 Which of the situations in questions 6.1～6.3 demonstrate epistasis?

6.4 在什么情况下问题 6.1～6.3 属于上位效应。

6.5 You recover mutants from an enhancer/suppressor screen that look like wild-type. How can you tell whether the restoration of the phenotype is due to a mutation in the same gene as was originally mutated. or it a second gene has been mutated?

6.5 你通过增强子/抑制子筛选恢复了一个突变体,使其看起来像野生型。你怎样判断该表现型的恢复是由于原始突变基因的二次突变产生的还是不同基因被突变产生的?

6.6 If the genotypes written within the Punnett Square are from the F_2 generation, what would be the phenotypes and

6.6 如果在旁氏棋盘法中基因型来自 F_2 代，F_1 代和亲代的表现型

genotypes of the F_1 and P generations for:
a) Figure 6.5
b) Figure 6.7
c) Figure 6.9
d) Figure 6.11

和基因型是哪一个图:
a）图 6.5
b）图 6.7
c）图 6.9
d）图 6.11

6.7 To better understand how genes control the development of three-dimensional structures, you conducted a mutant screen in *Arabidopsis* and identified a recessive point mutation allele of a single gene (*g*) that causes leaves to develop as narrow tubes rather than the broad flat surfaces that develop in wild-type (*G*). Allele *g* causes a complete loss of function. Now you want to identify more genes involved in the same process. Diagram a process you could use to identify other genes that interact with gene *g*. Show all of the possible genotypes that could arise in the F_1 generation.

6.7 为了更好理解基因怎样控制三维结构的发育，你在拟南芥中做了一个突变体筛选试验，鉴定了一个单基因（*g*）的等位基因隐性点突变，这将会促使叶片发育为狭长的管状物而不是野生型（*G*）发育的宽的扁平表面。等位基因 *g* 使该功能完全丧失。现在你要鉴定该过程中更多的基因。图示你用来鉴定与基因 *g* 相互作用的其他基因的过程。请列出所有在 F_1 代可能产生的基因型。

6.8 With reference to question 6.7, if the recessive allele, *g* is mutated again to make allele *g**, what are the possible phenotypes of a homozygous *g* g** individual?

6.8 参考问题 6.7，如果隐性等位基因 *g* 再次突变为等位基因 *g**，纯合 *g* g**个体的表现型是什么？

6.9 Again, in reference to question 6.7, what are the possible phenotypes of a homozygous *aagg* individual, where a is a recessive allele of a second gene? In each case, also specify the phenotypic ratios that would be observed among the F_1 progeny of a cross of *AaGg*×*AaGg*.

6.9 再参考问题 6.7，纯合的 *aagg* 个体可能的表现型是什么，在这个个体中 *a* 是第二个基因的隐性等位基因吗？在每一个案例中，请详细说明 *AaGg*×*AaGg* 杂交的 F_1 后代所观察到的表现型比率。

6.10 Calculate the phenotypic ratios from a dihybrid cross involving the two loci shown in Figure 6.12. There may be more than one possible set of ratios, depending on the assumptions you make about the phenotype of allele *b*.

6.10 计算图 6.12 所示的两个位点的双基因杂种杂交的表现型比率。这里可能不止一套比率，这主要决定你对等位基因 *b* 表现型的假定。

6.11 Use the product rule to calculate the phenotypic ratios expected from a trihybrid cross. Assume independent assortment and no epistasis/gene interactions.

6.11 使用乘积原则计算三基因杂种杂交的预期的表现型比率。假定独立分配并且没有上位效应和基因互作。

Chapter 7

Linkage and Mapping
连锁与作图

(彩图)

Linkage affects the frequency at which some combinations of traits are observed

连锁会影响观察到的一些性状组合的比例

As we learned in Chapter 6, Mendel reported that the pairs of genes he observed behaved independently of each other; for example, the segregation of seed color alleles was inde-

我们在第 6 章已经学过，孟德尔报道了他所观察到的基因对在遗传上是各自独立的，如决定种子颜色的等位

pendent from the segregation of alleles for seed shape. This observation was the basis for his Second Law, and contributed greatly to our understanding of heredity. However, further research showed that Mendel's Second Law did not apply to every pair of genes that could be studied. In fact, we now know that alleles of genes that are located close together on the same chromosome tend to be inherited together. This phenomenon is called **linkage**, and is a major exception to Mendel's Second Law. Understanding linkage is important to natural processes of heredity and evolution, and we will learn how researchers use linkage to determine the location of genes along chromosomes in a process called genetic mapping.

基因分离和决定种子形状的等位基因分离彼此是独立的。这项观察报道是孟德尔第二定律的基础，同时它也有助于加深我们对遗传的理解。然而，进一步的研究表明，孟德尔第二定律并不适用于我们所研究的每一对基因。事实上，我们现在知道，往往位于同一条染色体上并且彼此靠近的等位基因会趋向于被共同遗传，这种现象称为**连锁**，而且对于孟德尔第二定律来说连锁也是一个主要的例外现象。正确理解连锁规律对于理解遗传和进化的自然过程是重要的，同时通过一个叫做遗传作图的过程，我们可以领会到研究者是如何运用连锁规律沿着染色体进行基因定位的。

RECOMBINATION 重　组

Recombination is term that is used in several different contexts in genetics. In reference to heredity, **recombination** is defined as any process that results in gametes with combinations of alleles that were not present in the gametes of a previous generation (see Figure 7.1). Recombination may occur either through random assortment of alleles that are on different chromosomes, or through **crossovers** between loci on the same chromosomes (as described below). It is important to remember that in both of these cases, recombination is a process that occurs during meiosis (mitotic recombination may also occur in some species, but it is relatively rare). If meiosis results in recombination, the products are said to have a **recombinant** genotype. On the other hand, if no recombination occurs during meiosis, the products are said to have a non-recombinant, or **parental** genotype. Recombination is important because it contributes to the variation that may be observed between individuals within a population.

重组这一术语可以被用于遗传学的不同语境中。在遗传上，**重组**是指产生与前一代配子的等位基因组合不同的配子的过程（图 7.1）。重组的发生要么是位于不同染色体上等位基因的随机组合，要么是位于同一条染色体上各位点之间的**交换**（如下述）。重要的是要记住，在这两种情况下重组是发生在减数分裂过程中（在一些物种的有丝分裂过程中或许也会发生重组，但是比较少见）。如果在减数分裂过程中发生了重组，那么就会产生**重组**基因型。另一方面，如果在减数分裂过程中没发生重组，那么就称为非重组基因型或**亲本**基因型。重组是非常重要的，因为它会使群体内个体间产生可观察到的变异。

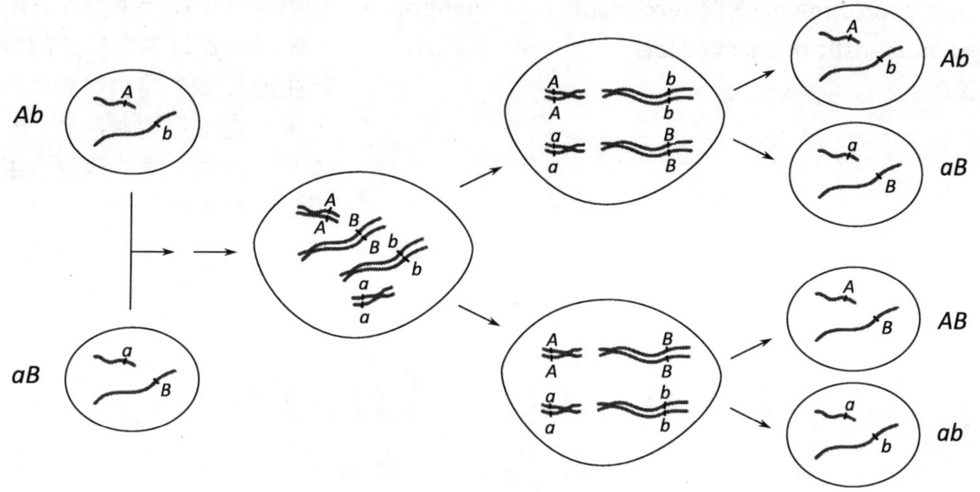

Figure 7.1 When two loci are on non-homologous chromosomes, their alleles will segregate in combinations identical to those present in the parental gametes (*Ab*, *aB*), and in recombinant genotypes (*AB*, *ab*) that are different from the parental gametes

图 7.1 当两个基因位点于非同源染色体上时，它们的等位基因通过分离重组将会产生与亲本型配子相同的配子（*Ab*, *aB*）和与亲本型配子不同的重组型配子（*AB*, *ab*）

As an example of recombination, consider loci on two different chromosomes as shown in Figure 7.1. We know that if these loci are on different chromosomes, there are no physical connections between them, so they are **unlinked** and will segregate independently as did Mendel's traits. When loci are unlinked, can we predict which combinations of alleles will segregate together in any given meiosis? No, not with certainty: the segregation depends on the relative orientation of each pair of chromosomes at metaphase. Since the orientation is random and independent of other chromosomes, each of the arrangements (and their meiotic products) is equally possible for two unlinked loci as shown in Figure 7.1. More precisely, there is a 50% probability of recombinant genotypes, and a 50% probability of parental genotypes within the gametes produced by unlinked loci. Indeed, if we examined all of the gametes produced by this individual (which are the products of multiple independent meioses), we would note that approximately 50% of the gametes would be recombinant, and 50% would be parental. **Recombination frequency** is simply the number of recombinant gametes, divided by the total number of gametes. A

图 7.1 是重组的一个例子，两个不同染色体之间的位点重组。我们知道，如果这些基因位于不同的染色体上，那么它们之间就不存在实体上的连接，因此它们是彼此**不连锁的**，且它们会像孟德尔性状一样独立地进行分离。那么当位点不连锁时，我们能够在任何给定的减数分裂过程中预测出哪组等位基因组合会在一起进行分离吗？答案是不确定的：基因分离受细胞分裂中期每对染色体的相对方向的影响。由于染色体方向是随机的，不依赖于其他染色体，所以同图 7.1 所示，对于两个不连锁的基因位点（和它们的减数分裂产物），任何一种排列的概率都是相等的。更确切地说，即由两个不连锁的位点产生的配子中出现重组基因型的概率是 50%，出现亲本基因型的概率也是 50%。而事实上也的确如此，如果

frequency of approximately 50% recombination is therefore a defining characteristic of unlinked loci.

检测某一个体产生的所有配子（这些配子是通过多个独立的减数分裂产生的），我们将会注意到约有 50%的配子是重组型基因型，50%是亲本型基因型。简单地说**重组率**是指重组型配子数目占配子总数目的百分率。因此约 50%的重组率是非连锁位点的一个最典型的特征。

LINKAGE SUPPRESSES RECOMBINATION 连锁抑制了重组

Having considered unlinked loci, let us turn to the opposite situation, in which two loci are so close together on a chromosome that the parental combinations of alleles always segregate together (Figure 7.2). This is because alleles at the two loci are physically attached and so they always follow each other into the same gamete. In this case, no recombinants will be detected following meiosis, and the recombination frequency will be 0%. **Complete linkage** is rare, as the loci must be so close together that crossovers are never detected between them.

研究过非连锁的位点后，我们再来研究一下相反的情况，也就是当两个位点在同一条染色体上非常接近的情况下，其等位基因的亲本型组合总是一起进行分离（图 7.2）。这是因为位于两个位点上的两对等位基因存在实体上的连接，所以它们总是能够一起进入相同的配子。所以在这种情况下，在减数分裂后是检测不到重组的，即重组率为 0%。**完全连锁**是很少见的，因为这种情况的发生要求位点之间相距特别近以至于它们之间不能发生交换。

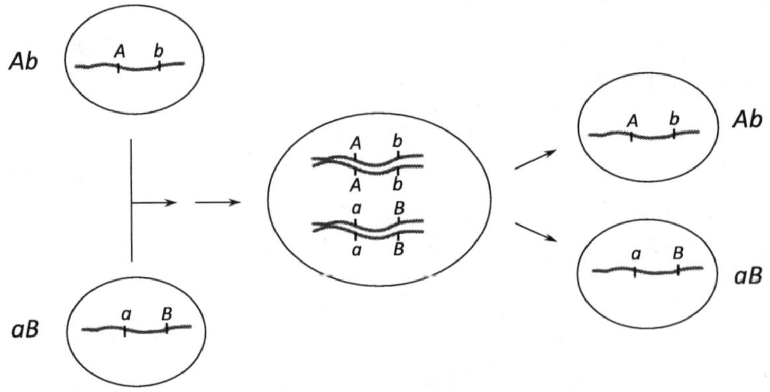

Figure 7.2 If two loci are completely linked, their alleles will segregate in combinations identical to those present in the parental gametes (*Ab*, *aB*). No recombinants will be observed

图 7.2 如果两个基因是完全连锁的，则两对等位基因将连锁在一起分离，会产生与亲本基因型完全相同的配子（*Ab*, *aB*），所以观察不到重组体

CROSSOVERS ALLOW RECOMBINATION BETWEEN LINKED LOCI
交换使两个连锁位点发生重组

Thus far, we have only considered situations with either no linkage (50% recombination) or else complete linkage (0% recombination). It is also possible to obtain recombination frequencies between 0% and 50%, which is a situation we call partial linkage or **incomplete linkage**. Incomplete linkage occurs when two loci are located on the same chromosome (i.e. they are physically linked), but the loci are far enough apart so that crossovers occur between them during some, but not all, meioses.

到目前为止，我们仅考虑了不发生连锁（50%重组）和完全连锁（0%重组）这两种情况。但是也存在重组率为 0%～50%的情况，我们称之为部分连锁或**不完全连锁**。当两个基因位于同一条染色体上（即它们是实体上连接的），并且这两个基因之间相距足够远以至于在一些（但不是所有的）减数分裂的过程中能够发生交换时才会发生不完全连锁。

Crossovers occur during prophase I of meiosis, when pairs of homologous chromosomes have aligned with each other in a process called **synapsis**. Crossing over begins with the double-strand breakage of a pair of non-sister chromatids. The breaks usually occur at corresponding positions on two chromatids, and then the broken ends of non-sister chromatids are connected to each other resulting in a reciprocal exchange of double- stranded DNA (Figure 7.3). Generally every pair of chromosomes has at least one (and often more) crossovers during meioses (Figure 7.4).

在减数分裂前期 I，当同源染色体在**联会**过程中彼此配对时就会发生交换。交换开始于双链断裂的一对非姐妹染色单体。而断裂通常发生在两个染色单体的相应位置，然后非姐妹染色单体的裂口末端会彼此相连，从而使双链 DNA 相互交换（图 7.3）。一般来讲，在减数分裂过程中每对同源染色体至少会有一处（或更多的）交换（图 7.4）。

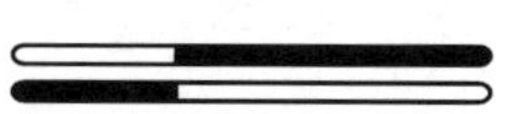

Figure 7.3 A depiction of a crossover from Morgan's 1916 manuscript. Only one pair of non-sister chromatids is shown

图 7.3 摩尔根在其 1916 年的文稿中表示的交换示意图。图中仅用一对非姐妹染色单体来表示

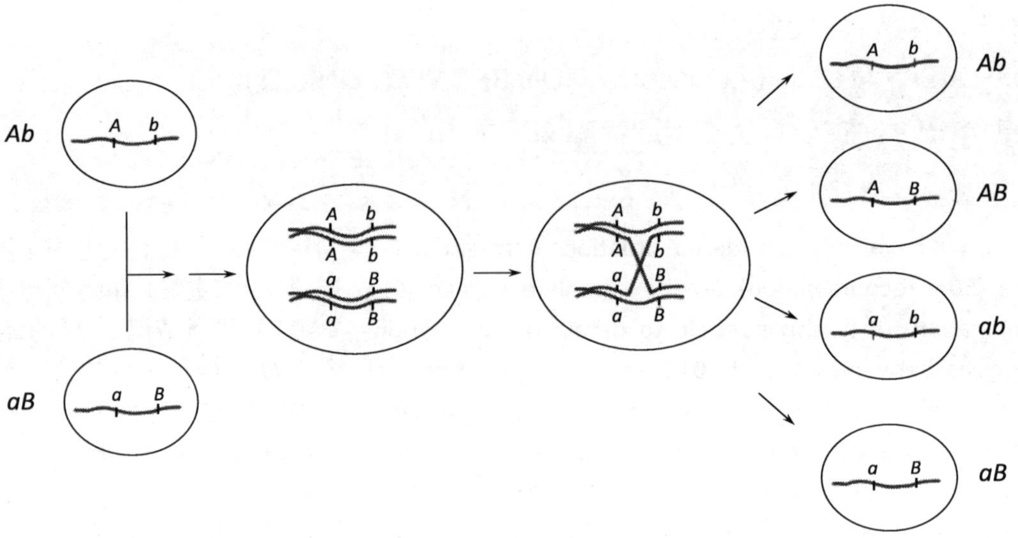

Figure 7.4 A crossover between two linked loci can generate recombinant genotypes (*AB*, *ab*), from the chromatids involved in the crossover. Remember that multiple, independent meioses occur in each organism, so this particular pattern of recombination may not be observed among all the gametes from this individual

图 7.4 两个连锁的基因位点之间发生交换，由发生交换的染色单体产生重组基因型（*AB*,*ab*）。还记得前面提到在每个生物体内发生的多个独立的减数分裂，所以重组不可能在该个体中的所有配子中被观察到

Because the location of crossovers is essentially random, the greater the distance between two loci, the more likely it is that a crossover will occur between them. Furthermore, loci that are on the same chromosome, but are sufficiently far apart from each other, will have crossovers so often that they will behave as though they are completely unlinked. A recombination frequency of 50% is therefore the maximum recombination frequency that can be observed, and is indicative of loci that are either on separate chromosomes, or are located very far apart on the same chromosome.

因为交换的位点本质上是随机的，因此一般认为两个位点距离越远，它们之间发生交换的可能性越大。而且，位于同一条染色体上距离足够远的基因位点常会发生交换，以至于这种交换的产生就像两位点间完全不连锁一样。因此 50%的重组率是所能观测到的最大的重组率，并且这也意味着基因位点不在同一条染色体上，或在同一条染色体上但相距甚远。

INFERRING RECOMBINATION FROM GENETIC DATA
依据遗传数据推测重组

In the preceding examples, we had the advantage of knowing

从前面的例子可知，我们在计算重

the approximate chromosomal positions of each allele involved, before we calculated the recombination frequencies. Knowing this information beforehand made it relatively easy to define the parental and recombinant genotypes, and to calculate recombination frequencies. However, in most experiments, we cannot directly examine the chromosomes, or even the gametes, so we must infer the arrangement of alleles from the phenotypes over two or more generations. Importantly, it is generally not sufficient to know the genotype of individuals in just one generation; for example, given an individual with the genotype *AaBb*, we do not know from the genotype alone whether the loci are located on the same chromosome, and if so, whether the arrangement of alleles on each chromosome is or *AB* and *ab* (also called the ***cis*** , or **coupling** arrangement; Figure 7.5) or *Ab* and *aB* (***trans***, or **repulsion**).

组率之前，可以比较容易地推知各等位基因在染色体上的大概位置。事先掌握这些信息，就能够相对容易地确定亲本基因型和重组基因型，进一步计算重组率。然而，在大多数实验中，我们不能直接去检测染色体或者是配子中各等位基因的排列方式，因此我们不得不通过连续两代（或两代以上）的表现型去推断各等位基因之间的排列方式。关键是仅仅在一个世代中也不足以确定个体的基因型。例如，给定一个基因型为 *AaBb* 的个体，那么我们不能仅通过其基因型去确定这两个基因是否在同一条染色体上，即便是在同一条染色体上，也不能确定基因在染色体上的排列是 *AB* 和 *ab*（也称为**顺式排列**或**耦合排列**，图 7.5）还是 *Ab* 和 *aB*（也称为**反式排列**或**相斥排列**）。

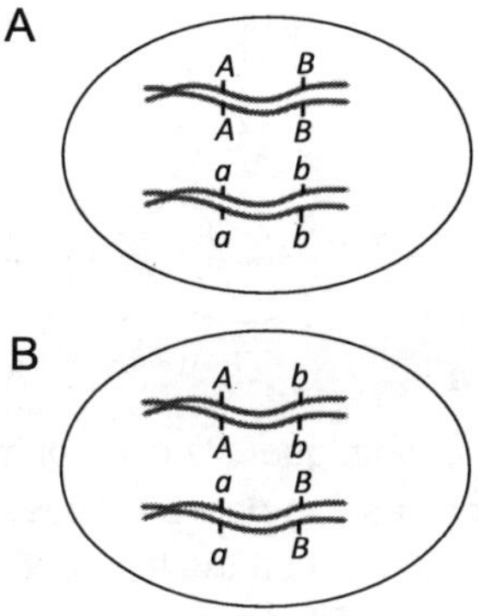

Figure 7.5 Alleles in *cis* configuration (A) or *trans* configuration (B)

图 7.5 等位基因之间的顺式结构（A）和反式结构（B）

Fortunately for geneticists, the arrangement of alleles can sometimes be inferred if the genotypes of a previous generation are known. For example, if the parents of *AaBb* had genotypes *AAB*B and *aabb* respectively, then the parental gametes that fused to produce *AaBb* would have been genotype *AB* and genotype *ab*. Therefore, prior to meiosis in the dihybrid, the arrangement of alleles would likewise be *AB* and *ab* (Figure 7.6). Conversely, if the parents of *AaBb* had genotypes *aaBB* and *AAbb*, then the arrangement of alleles on the chromosomes of the dihybrid would be *aB* and *Ab*. Thus, the genotype of the previous generation can determine which of an individual's gametes are considered recombinant, and which are considered parental.

对于遗传学家来说幸运的是，如果知道上一代的基因型，有时就可以推断出各等位基因之间的排列方式。例如，假设基因型为 *AaBb* 的亲本基因型分别为 *AABB* 和 *aabb*，那么产生 *AaBb* 的亲本的配子基因型就为 *AB* 和 *ab*。因此，在双基因杂合体减数分裂前，等位基因的排列方式应该也是 *AB* 和 *ab*（图 7.6）。相反，假设子代基因型为 *AaBb*，其亲本的基因型为 *aaBB* 和 *AAbb*，那么双基因杂合体的等位基因在染色体上的排列方式会是 *aB* 和

Ab。所以，由上一代的基因型能够确定个体的配子是重组基因型还是亲本基因型的。

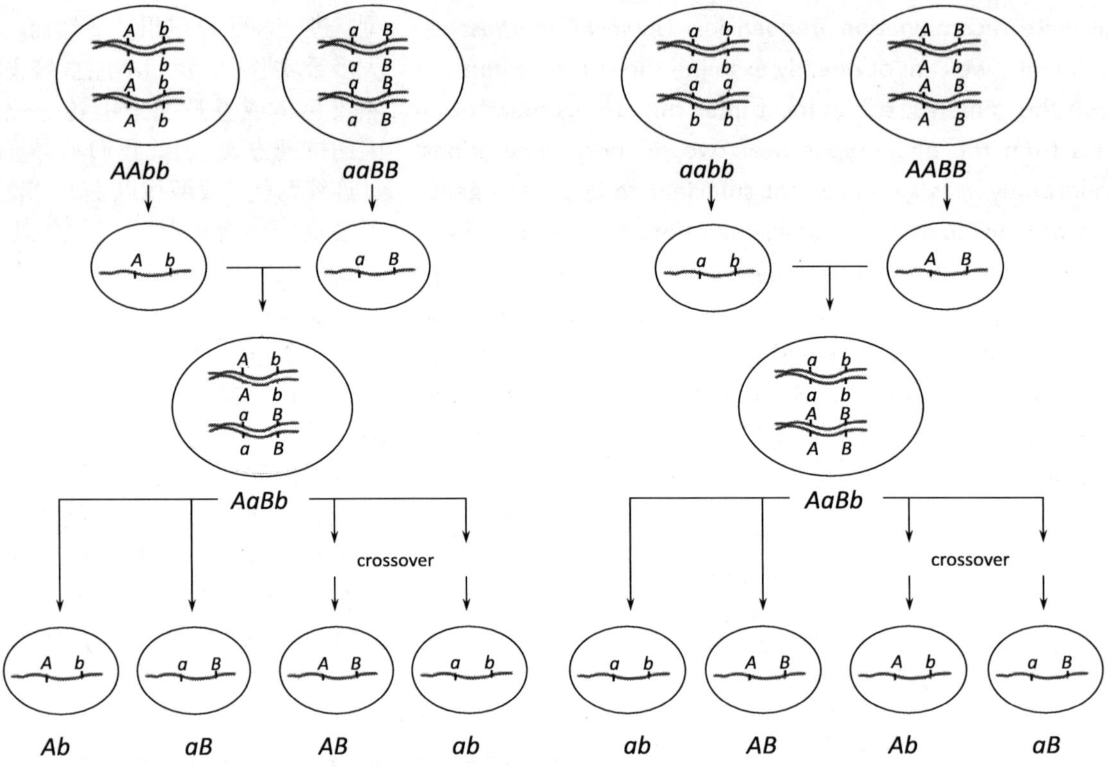

Figure 7.6 The genotype of gametes can be inferred unambiguously if the gametes are produced by homozygotes. However, recombination frequencies can only be measured among the progeny of heterozygotes (i.e. dihybrids). Note that the dihybrid on the left contains a different configuration of alleles than the dihybrid on the right due to differences in the genotypes of their respective parents. Therefore, different gametes are defined as recombinant and parental among the progeny of the two dihybrids. In the cross at left, the recombinant gametes will be genotype *AB* and *ab*, and in the cross on the right, the recombinant gametes will be *Ab* and *aB*

图 7.6 如果配子由纯合体产生，配子的基因型能够清楚地推断出来。然而，重组率仅仅能在杂合子（双基因杂种）的子代中计算出来。注意，由于亲本基因型不同，所以图中左边双基因杂种与右边双基因杂种的等位基因结构不同。因此，不同的双基因杂合体所产生的配子中，各自所谓的重组基因型和亲本基因型是不同的。在左边的树形图中，重组型配子是 *AB* 和 *ab*；在右边的树形图中，重组型配子是 *Ab* 和 *aB*

Let us now consider a complete experiment in which our objective is to measure recombination frequency (Figure 7.7). We need at least two alleles for each of two genes, and we must know which combinations of alleles were present in the parental gametes. The simplest way to do this is to start with pure-breeding lines that have contrasting alleles at two loci. For example, we could cross short-tailed mice, brown mice

为了计算重组率，让我们现在来看一个完整的实验（图 7.7)。我们首先需要选择至少两组基因，且每个基因有两个等位基因，并且必须要知道其在亲本配子中的等位基因的组合形式。那么最简单的方法就是在实验开始就选择等位基因之间具

(*aaBB*) with long-tailed, white mice (*AAbb*). Based on the genotypes of the parents, we know that the parental gametes will be *aB* or *Ab* (but not *ab* or *AB*), and all of the progeny will be dihybrids, *AaBb*. We do not know at this point whether the two loci are on different pairs of homologous chromosomes, or whether they are on the same chromosome, and if so, how close together they are.

有鲜明对比的纯育系进行交配。例如，我们可以用短尾棕鼠（*aaBB*）和长尾白鼠（*AAbb*）进行杂交。基于亲本的基因型我们可以知道，亲本的配子应该是 *aB* 和 *Ab*（不存在 *ab* 和 *AB*），且所有的子代将都是双基因杂种（*AaBb*）。但是我们还不能知道这两组等位基因是否在不同的同源染色体上，或者是否它们在同一染色体上，如果在同一条染色体上，它们又相距多远呢？

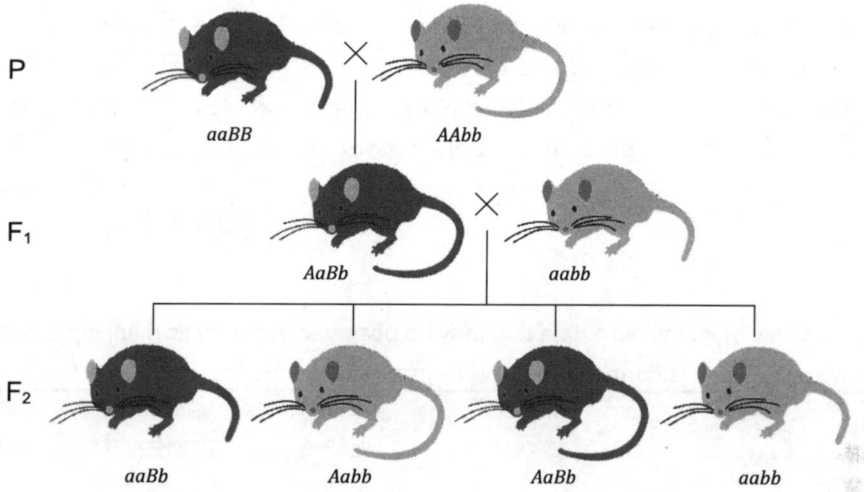

Figure 7.7 An experiment to measure recombination frequency between two loci. The loci affect coat color and tail length

图 7.7 两个位点之间重组率的检测实验。这两个位点分别影响毛色和尾巴的长度

The recombination events that may be detected will occur during meiosis in the dihybrid individual. If the loci are completely or partially linked, then prior to meiosis, alleles *aB* will be located on one chromosome, and alleles *Ab* will be on the other chromosome (based on our knowledge of the genotypes of the gametes that produced the dihybrid). Thus, recombinant gametes produced by the dihybrid will have the genotypes *ab* or *AB*, and non-recombinant (i.e. parental) gametes will have the genotypes *aB* or *Ab*.

可以检测到的重组事件将在双基因杂种减数分裂的过程中发生。如果这两个位点之间是完全连锁或部分连锁的，那么在减数分裂前期，等位基因 *aB* 会在一条染色体上，而 *Ab* 则在另一条染色体上（基于我们对产生双基因杂种的配子基因型的知识）。因此，双基因杂种产生的重组配子基因型是 *ab* 或 *AB*，非重组配子（即亲本型）基因型是 *aB* 或 *Ab*。

How do we determine the genotype of the gametes produced by the dihybrid individual? The most practical method is to use a testcross (Figure 7.7), in other words to mate *AaBb* to an individual that has only recessive alleles at both loci (*aabb*). This will give a different phenotype in the F_2 generation for each of the four possible combinations of alleles in the gametes of the dihybrid. We can then infer unambiguously the genotype of the gametes produced by the dihybrid individual, and therefore calculate the recombination frequency between these two loci. For example, if only two phenotypic classes were observed in the F_2 (i.e. short tails and brown fur (*aaBb*), and white fur with long tails (*Aabb*) we would know that the only gametes produced following meiosis of the dihybrid individual were of the parental type: *aB* and *Ab*, and the recombination frequency would therefore be 0%. Alternatively, we may observe multiple classes of phenotypes in the F_2 in ratios such as shown in Table 7.1.

我们怎么确定某一双基因杂种所产生的配子的基因型呢？最可行的方法就是测交（图 7.7），也就是说将 *AaBb* 与双隐性（*aabb*）个体交配。这使得双基因杂种配子的 4 种可能组合在 F_2 代中具有不同的表现型。我们完全可以推断出双基因杂种产生的配子基因型，且据此可以计算出这两个位点的重组率。例如，如果在 F_2 代中仅观察到两种表现型[即短尾棕毛（*aaBb*）和长尾白毛（*Aabb*）]，我们就能知道双基因杂种在减数分裂过程中产生的配子应该全是亲本型的：*aB* 和 *Ab*，且重组率也因此为 0%。如果不是上述情况，我们或许就可以在 F_2 代中观察到如表 7.1 所示的表现型比率分布。

Table 7.1 An example of quantitative data that may be observed in a genetic mapping experiment involving two loci. The data correspond to the F_2 generation in the cross shown in Figure 7.7

tail phenotype	fur phenotype	number of progeny	gamete from dihybrid	genotype of F_2 from test cross	Parental or Recombinant
short	brown	48	*aB*	*aaBb*	P
long	white	42	*Ab*	*Aabb*	P
short	white	13	*ab*	*aabb*	R
long	brown	17	*AB*	*AaBb*	R

表 7.1 在确定两个位点遗传作图的实验中我们可以观察到表中的数据。这个数据与图 7.7 中所显示的 F_2 代表现型是一致的

尾部表型	毛色表型	子代数	双基因杂合体的配子	测交得到的 F_2 代基因型	亲本型(P)/重组型(R)
短尾	棕色	48	*aB*	*aaBb*	P
长尾	白色	42	*Ab*	*Aabb*	P
短尾	白色	13	*ab*	*aabb*	R
长尾	棕色	17	*AB*	*AaBb*	R

Given the data in Table 7.1, the calculation of recombination frequency is straightforward

根据表 7.1 中的数据，可以直接计算重组率

$$\text{recombination frequency} = \frac{\text{number of recombinant gametes}}{\text{total number of gametes scored}}$$

$$\text{R.F.} = \frac{13+17}{48+42+13+17} = 25\%$$

$$\text{重组率} = \frac{\text{重组型配子数}}{\text{配子总数}}$$

$$\text{R.F.} = \frac{13+17}{48+42+13+17} = 25\%$$

GENETIC MAPPING 遗传作图

Because the frequency of recombination between two loci (up to 50%) is proportional to the chromosomal distance between them, we can use recombination frequencies to produce genetic maps. The units of genetic distance are called centiMorgans (cM, also called map units), in honor of Thomas Hunt Morgan. We can easily convert recombination frequencies to cM: the recombination frequency in percent is the same as the map distance in cM. For example, if two loci have a recombination frequency of 25% they are said to be 25cM apart on a chromosome (Figure 7.8). Note that the map distance of two loci alone does not tell us anything about the orientation of these loci relative to other features on the chromosome.

因为两基因位点在染色体上的距离与它们的重组率（不超过 50%）是相对应的，所以可以利用重组率来绘制遗传图谱。后人为了纪念托马斯·亨特·摩尔根，将遗传距离的单位用厘摩尔根（cM，也称作图距单位）表示。我们可以很容易地将重组率转换为 cM：以重组率表示的百分率数值与以 cM 为单位的图距数值是一致的。例如，如果两个基因的重组率为 25%，那么它们在染色体上的图距为 25cM（图 7.8）。但要注意的是，单凭两基因位点的图距我们无法知道相对于其他特征来说它们在染色体上的方向。

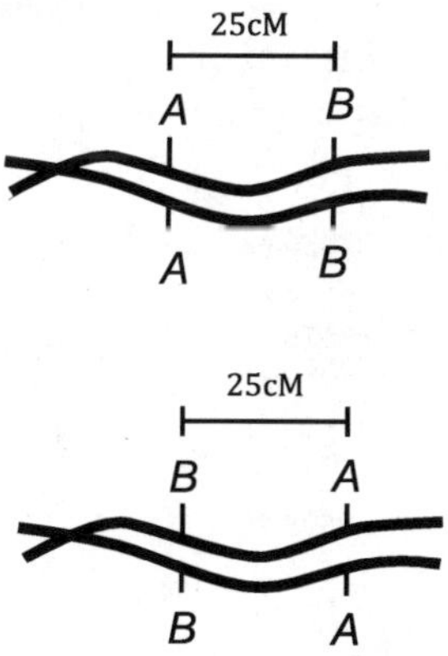

Figure 7.8 Two genetic maps consistent with a recombination frequency of 25% between *A* and *B*

图 7.8 基因 *A* 与 *B* 之间的重组率为 25%可表示两种可能的遗传图谱

Map distances are always calculated for one pair of loci at a time. However, by combining the results of multiple calculations, a genetic map of many loci on a chromosome can be produced (Figure 7.9). A genetic map shows the map distance, in cM, that separates any two loci, and the position of these loci relative to all other mapped loci. The map distance

图距经常计算的是一对基因位点之间的遗传距离。但是，对大量的计算结果进行综合，我们就可以获得一条染色体上许多基因位点的遗传图谱（图 7.9）。遗传图谱以 cM 为单位表示了任意两基因位点之间的图距，也

corresponds roughly to the physical distance, i.e. the amount of DNA between two loci. For example, in *Arabidopsis*, 1.0cM corresponds roughly to 150 000bp and contains approximately 5000 genes. The exact number of DNA bases in a cM depends on the organism, and on the particular position in the chromosome; some parts of chromosomes ("hot spots") have slightly higher rates of recombination than others.

表示了这些基因位点相对于其他基因位点的相对位置。图距基本与基因的物理距离（即两基因之间的 DNA 碱基数）相一致。例如，在拟南芥中 1.0cM 约等于 150 000bp，约包含 5000 个基因。基于 cM 的准确的 DNA 碱基数取决于不同的生物体和在染色体上的特殊位置；染色体上的某些区域（“热点区域”）重组率略高于其他区域。

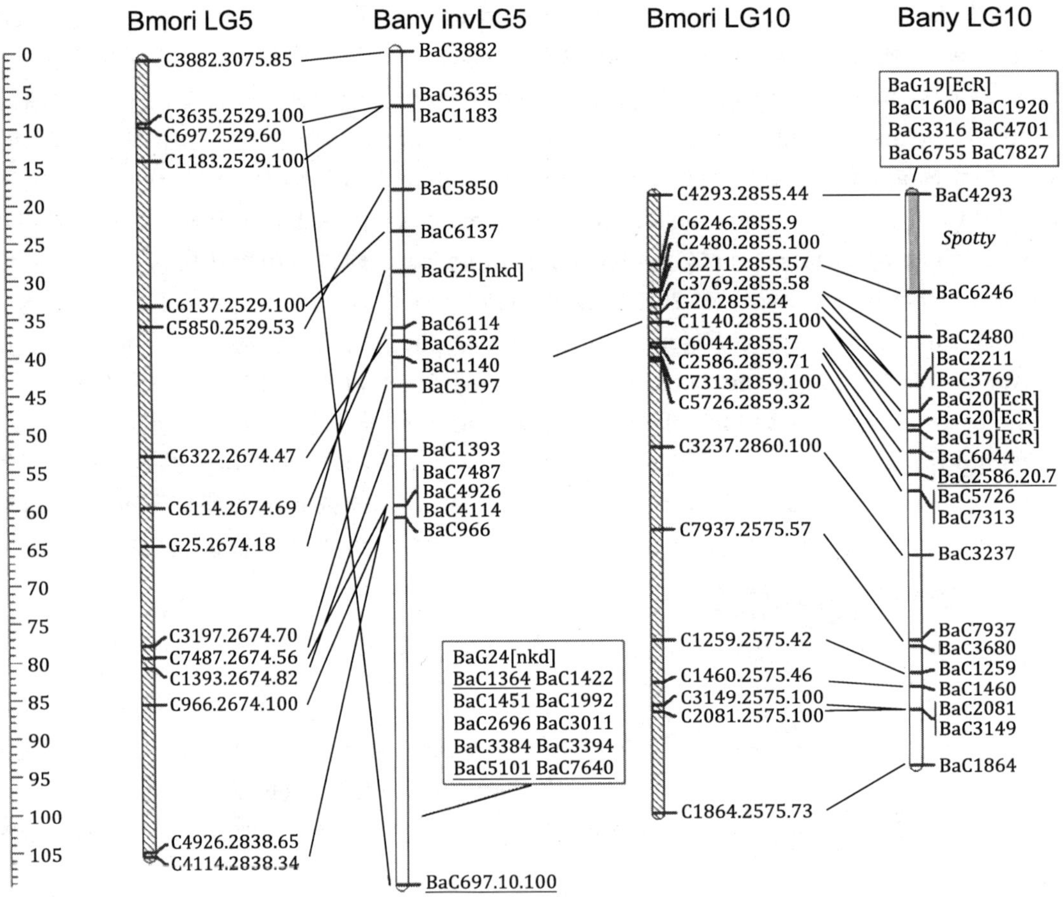

Figure 7.9 Genetic maps for regions of two chromosomes from two species of the moth, *Bombyx*. The scale at left shows distance in cM, and the position of various loci is indicated on each chromosome. Diagonal lines connecting loci on different chromosomes show the position of corresponding loci in different species

图 7.9 此遗传图谱为家蚕属两个飞蛾种的两条染色体区域遗传图谱。左边的刻度表示图距（单位 cM），且每条染色体上的各位点也已在图中标明。连接两条染色体上的位点之间的连线标明了这两个物种间相应位点的位置

When a novel gene is identified by mutation or polymorphism, its approximate position on a chromosome can be determined by crossing it with previously mapped genes, and then calculating the recombination frequency. If the novel gene and the previously mapped genes show complete or partial linkage, the recombination frequency will indicate the approximate position of the novel gene within the genetic map. This information is useful in isolating (i.e. cloning) the specific fragment of DNA that encodes the novel gene, through a process called map- based cloning. Genetic maps are also useful in breeding crops and animals, in studying evolutionary relationships between species, and in determining the causes and individual susceptibility of some human diseases.

当一个新的基因通过突变体或多态性分析被鉴定出来时，我们可以选取前面遗传图谱上的基因，通过与该新基因之间的杂交和重组率的计算分析来确定新基因在染色体上的大概位置。如果该新基因与遗传图谱上的某现有基因表现出完全连锁或部分连锁，那么通过重组率就可以确定新基因在遗传图谱上的大致位置。这有助于通过图位克隆的方法分离（即克隆）编码该基因的 DNA 特定片段。遗传图谱也在作物育种、动物繁育、物种间进化关系的研究和人类一些疾病的病因及个体敏感性等方面都有所应用。

Genetic maps are useful tools, but genetic map distances are only an approximation of the actual physical distance between loci. The correlation between recombination frequency and chromosomal distance is more accurate for short distances than long distances. Observed recombination frequencies between two relatively distant markers tend to underestimate the actual number of crossovers that occurred. This is because as the distance between loci increases, so also increases the possibility of having two crossovers occur between the loci. This is a problem for geneticists, because with respect to the loci being studied, these double-crossovers produce gametes with the same genotypes as if no recombination events had occurred (Figure 7.10). Researchers will sometimes use specific mathematical functions to adjust large recombination frequencies to account for the possibility of multiple crossovers.

遗传图谱是很有用的工具，但是图谱上的基因位点距离仅仅是两个位点间实际物理距离的一个近似值。基因位点之间相距越短，重组率和基因位点在染色体上的距离之间的一致性就越强。对于两个相对较远的标记，观察到的重组率常常会低估实际发生的交换频率。这是因为随着两基因位点距离的增加，在基因位点间发生两次交换的可能性也会增加。这对遗传学家来说是个难题，因为就研究的基因位点而言，双交换产生的配子与没发生重组产生的配子基因型是一样的（图 7.10）。研究者有时也用专门的数学函数调整较大的重组率，以解释发生多次交换的可能性。

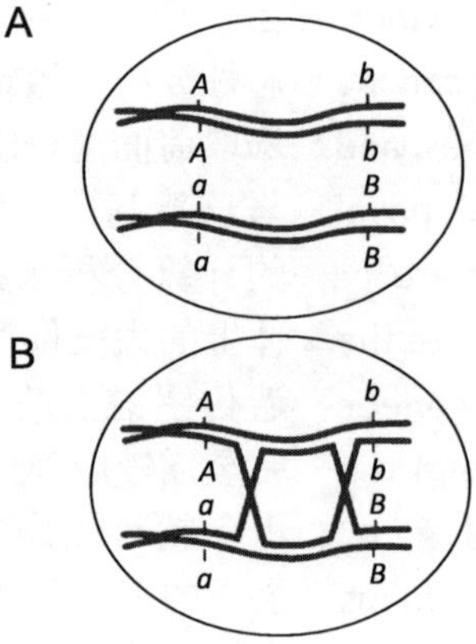

Figure 7.10 A double crossover between two loci (B) will produce gametes with parental genotypes (with respect to these loci)

图 7.10 两基因之间发生双交换（B）产生亲本基因型配子（就这两位点而言）

MAPPING WITH THREE-POINT CROSSES 用三点测交法作图

A particularly efficient method of mapping genes is the **three-point cross**, which allows the order and distance between three potentially linked genes to be determined in a single experiment (Figure 7.11). The basic strategy is the same as for the dihybrid mapping experiment described above; pure breeding lines with contrasting genotypes are crossed to produce an individual heterozygous at three loci (a trihybrid), which is then testcrossed to determine the recombination frequency between each pair of genes.

三点测交法是一种特别有效的基因定位的方法，它通过一次性实验就可以确定 3 个潜在连锁的基因之间的顺序和距离（图 7.11）。三点测交的基本策略和上面描述的双基因杂种绘图实验类似；选用基因型具有明显差异的纯育系进行杂交，产生在 3 个基因位点杂合的杂合体（三基因杂种），然后再进行测交，最后确定每对基因间的重组率。

One useful feature of the three-point cross is that the order of the loci relative to each other can usually be determined by a simple visual inspection of the F_2 segregation data. If the genes are linked, there will often be two phenotypic classes that are much more infrequent than any of the others. In these cases, the rare phenotypic classes are usually those that arose from two crossover events, in which the locus in the middle is flanked by a crossover on either side of it. Thus, among the two rarest recombinant phenotypic classes, the one allele that differs from the other two alleles relative to the parental genotypes likely represents the locus that is in the middle of the other two loci. For example, based on the phenotypes of the pure-breeding parents in Figure 7.11, the parental genotypes are *aBC* and *AbC* (remember the order of

三点测交法的一个有用功能就是通过对 F_2 代分离数据进行简单的目测，就可以确定基因间彼此的相对顺序。如果基因之间是连锁的，那么有两类表现型的个体总是比其他表现型的个体明显少很多。在这种情况下，表现型中个体较少的类型常常发生了两次交换，这样使得中间的那个基因位点交换到了另一条染色体上。因此，在个体最少的这两种重组类型中，相对于亲本基因型来说，有一个等位基因不同于其他两个等位基因，则代表这个位点在其他两个基因位点的中

the loci is unknown, and it is not necessarily the alphabetical order in which we wrote the genotypes). Because we can deduce from the outcome of the testcross (Table 7.2) that the rarest genotypes were *abC* and *ABc*, we can conclude that locus *A* that is most likely located between the other two loci, since it would require a recombination event between both *A* and *B* and between *A* and *C* in order to generate these gametes. Thus, the order of loci is *BAC* (which is equivalent to *CAB*).

间。例如，依据图 7.11 中纯育系亲本的表现型，将亲本基因型定义为 *aBC* 和 *AbC*（注意，这些基因的顺序是未知的，并且未必按我们写的字母顺序那样排列）。从测交结果（表 7.2）中可以推断出数目最少的表现型的基因型为 *abC* 和 *ABc*，所以我们可以知道最可能是基因 *A* 位于其他两个基因的中间，因为要产生上述配子必须在 *A* 与 *B*、*A* 与 *C* 之间都发生重组。因而基因的顺序应该是 *BAC*（或 *CAB*）。

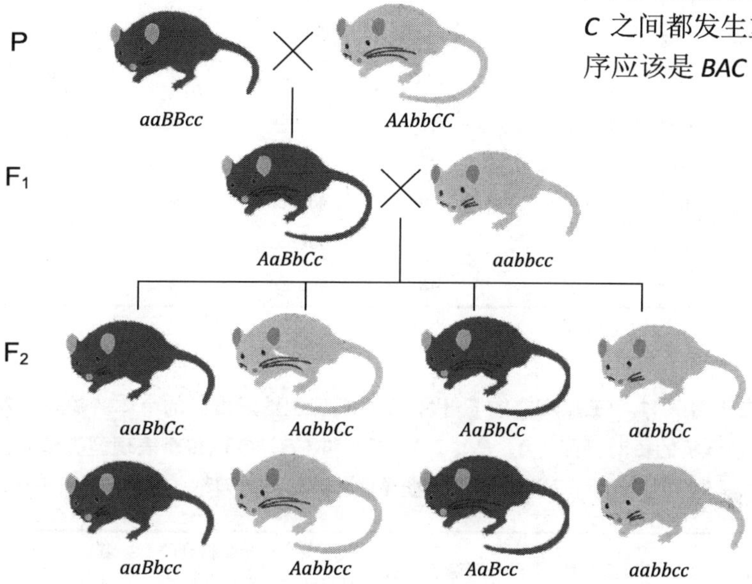

Figure 7.11 A three point cross for loci affecting tail length, fur color, and whisker length

图 7.11 控制尾长、毛色和须长的基因的三点测交

Recombination frequencies may be calculated for each pair of loci in the three-point cross as we did before for one pair of loci in our dihybrid (Figure 7. 7).

因为在前面我们在双基因杂种（图 7.7）中已经计算过一对位点的重组率，所以用同样的方法可以计算出三点测交实验中每对位点的重组率。

$$\text{loci } A,B \text{ R.F.} = \frac{1+16+12+1}{120} = 25\%$$

$$\text{loci } A,C \text{ R.F.} = \frac{1+5+1+5}{120} = 10\%$$

$$\text{loci } B,C \text{ R.F.} = \frac{5+16+12+5}{120} = 32\%$$

(not corrected for double crossovers)

$$\text{基因 } A,B \text{ R.F.} = \frac{1+16+12+1}{120} = 25\%$$

$$\text{基因 } A,C \text{ R.F.} = \frac{1+5+1+5}{120} = 10\%$$

$$\text{基因 } B,C \text{ R.F.} = \frac{5+16+12+5}{120} = 32\%$$

(不考虑双交换)

Table 7.2 An example of data that might be obtained from the F_2 generation of the three-point cross shown in Figure 7.11. The rarest phenotypic classes correspond to double recombinant gametes *ABc* and *abC*. Each phenotypic class and the gamete from the trihybrid that produced it can also be classified as parental (P) or recombinant (R) with respect to each pair of loci (*A*,*B*), (*A*,*C*), (*B*,*C*) analyzed in the experiment

tail phenotype	Fur phenotype	whisker phenotype	number of progeny	gamete from trihybrid	genotype of F_2 from test cross	loci *A, B*	loci *A, C*	loci *B, C*
short	brown	long	5	*aBC*	*aaBbCc*	P	R	R
long	white	long	38	*AbC*	*AabbCc*	P	P	P
short	white	long	1	*abC*	*aabbCc*	R	R	P
long	brown	long	16	*ABC*	*AaBbCc*	R	P	R
short	brown	short	42	*aBc*	*aaBbcc*	P	P	P
long	white	short	5	*Abc*	*Aabbcc*	P	R	R
short	white	short	12	*abc*	*aabbcc*	R	P	R
long	brown	short	1	*ABc*	*AaBbcc*	R	R	P

表 7.2 图中的数据来自于图 7.11 中三点测交的 F_2 代，其中表现型数量最少的个体就是来自双重组配子 *ABc* 和 *abC*。对于在实验中被分析的每对基因（*A*，*B*）、（*A*，*C*）和（*B*，*C*），每个表现型类型和三基因杂合体产生的配子也可分为亲本基因型（P）和重组基因型（R）

尾部表型	毛色表型	须长表型	子代数	三基因杂合体的配子	测交得到的 F_2 代基因型	基因 *A, B*	基因 *A, C*	基因 *B, C*
短尾	棕色	长须	5	*aBC*	*aaBbCc*	P	R	R
长尾	白色	长须	38	*AbC*	*AabbCc*	P	P	P
短尾	白色	长须	1	*abC*	*aabbCc*	R	R	P
长尾	棕色	长须	16	*ABC*	*AaBbCc*	R	P	R
短尾	棕色	短须	42	*aBc*	*aaBbcc*	P	P	P
长尾	白色	短须	5	*Abc*	*Aabbcc*	P	R	R
短尾	白色	短须	12	*abc*	*aabbcc*	R	P	R
长尾	棕色	短须	1	*ABc*	*AaBbcc*	R	R	P

However, note that in the three point cross, the sum of the distances between *A-B* and *A-C* (35%) is less than the distance calculated for *B-C* (32%)(Figure 7.12). this is because of double crossovers between *B* and *C*, which were undetected when we considered only pairwise data for *B* and *C*. We can easily account for some of these double crossovers, and in-

然而值得注意的是，在三点测交实验的结果中，*A-B* 和 *A-C* 之间的图距之和（35%）小于 *B-C* 之间的图距（32%）（图 7.12）。这是因为当仅仅成对地考虑 *B* 和 *C* 之间的重组率时，我们检测不到 *B* 和 *C* 之间发

clude them in calculating the map distance between *B* and *C*, as follows. We already deduced that the map order must be *BAC* (or *CAB*), based on the genotypes of the two rarest phenotypic classes in Table 7.2. However, these double recombinants, *ABc* and *abC,* were not included in our calculations of recombination frequency between loci *B* and *C*.

生双交换的情况。如下所示，我们可以容易地对双交换做出解释，并且确定 *B* 和 *C* 之间的准确遗传图距。根据表 7.2 中两种表现型数目最少个体的基因型已经知道基因图谱顺序是 *BAC*（或 *CAB*）。但是在位点 *B* 和 *C* 重组率的计算过程中，如 *ABc* 和 *abC* 这样的双重组型没有包括在内。

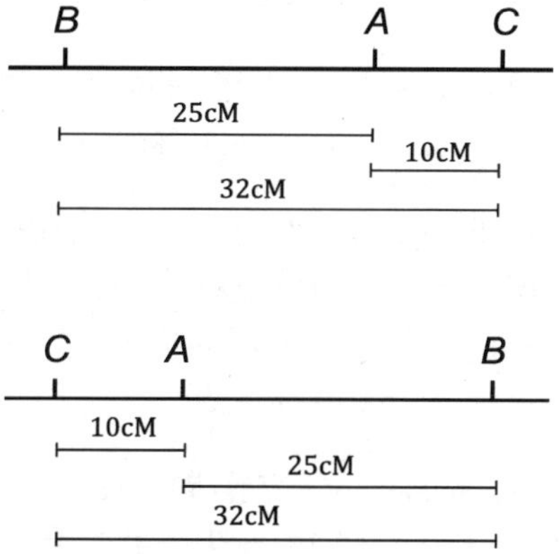

Figure 7.12 Equivalent maps based on the data in Table 7.2 (without correction for double crossovers)

图 7.12 基于表 7.2 的两种可能的连锁图谱（不考虑双交换）

If we included these double recombinant classes (multiplied by 2, since they each represent two recombination events), the calculation of recombination frequency between *B* and *C* is as follows, and the result is now more consistent with the sum of map distances between *A-B* and *A-C*.

如果我们包含了这些双重组类型（即乘以 2，因为它们都代表发生了两次重组事件），那么基因 *B* 和 *C* 之间的重组率就应如下计算，并且计算结果与 *A-B* 和 *A-C* 之间的图距之和是一致的。

$$\text{loci } B,C \text{ R.F.} = \frac{5+16+12+5+2(1)+2(1)}{120} = 35\%$$

(corrected for double recombinants)

基因 *B,C*
（对于双重组进行了校正）

$$\text{R.F.} = \frac{5+16+12+5+2(1)+2(1)}{120} = 35\%$$

Thus, the three point cross was useful for determining the order of three loci relative to each other, calculating map distances between the loci, and detecting some of the double crossover events that would otherwise lead to an underestimation of map distance. However, it is possible that other, double crossovers events remain undetected, for example double crossovers between loci *A,B* or between loci *A,C*. Geneticists have developed a variety of mathematical procedures to try to correct for things like double crossovers during large-scale mapping experiments.

因此，三点测交法被用于确定三个位点彼此的相对顺序，计算位点间的图距并且检测双交换，否则容易导致图距被低估。然而，该方法还是检测不到另外一些双交换，如基因 *A* 和 *B*、基因 *A* 和 *C* 之间的双交换。遗传学者已经发展了一系列的数学程序，试图来校正在大型的绘图实验中出现的像双交换这样的事件。

Summary

- Recombination is defined as any process that results in gametes with combinations of alleles that were not present in the gametes of a previous generation.
- 重组是指产生具有不同等位基因组合的配子的过程,且这些配子的基因型在上一代配子中未出现过。
- The recombination frequency between any two loci depends on their relative chromosomal locations.
- 两位点间的重组率取决于基因在染色体上的相对位置。
- Unlinked loci show a maximum 50% recombination frequency.
- 非连锁位点之间的重组率最大，为 50%。
- Loci that are close together on a chromosome are linked and tend to segregate with the same combinations of alleles that were present in either parent.
- 位于同一条染色体上紧密靠近的位点是连锁的,并且常以与任一亲本基因型相同的等位基因组合进行分离。
- Crossovers are a normal part of most meioses, and allow for recombination between linked loci.
- 交换常常在大多数减数分裂过程中发生，并且会伴随连锁位点的重组。
- Measuring recombination frequency is easiest when starting with pure-breeding lines with two alleles for each locus, and with suitable lines for test crossing.
- 用每个位点的两个等位基因纯育系和合适的测交系作为材料开始确定基因间的重组率是最容易的。
- Because recombination frequency is proportional to the distance between loci, recombination frequencies can be used to create genetic maps.
- 因为重组率与位点间距离是相对应的,所以重组率被用于遗传作图。
- Recombination frequencies tend to underestimate map distances, especially over long distances, since double crossovers may be genetically indistinguishable from non-recombinants.
- 由于从遗传角度难以区别双交换和非重组,所以重组率常常会低估图距，特别是距离较大的位点。
- Three-point crosses can be used to determine the order and map distance between of three loci, and can correct for some of the double crossovers between the two outer loci.
- 三点测交法被用于确定 3 个位点之间的顺序和图距，并且能够校正两个外部位点之间发生的双交换。

Key Terms

linkage 连锁
recombination 重组
crossover 交换
recombinant 重组的
synapsis 联会
cis 顺式
coupling 耦合
trans 反式

parental 亲代的
linked 连锁的
unlinked 非连锁的
complete linkage 完全连锁
recombination frequency 重组率
repulsion 相斥
cM 厘摩
linkage map 连锁图谱
genetic map 遗传图谱

Study Questions

7.1 Compare recombination and crossover. How are these similar? How are they different?

7.1 比较重组和交换的相似点和不同点。

7.2 Explain why it usually necessary to start with pure-breeding lines when measuring genetic linkage by the methods presented in this chapter.

7.2 请解释在本章检测基因连锁采用的方法中，为什么一开始必须要采用纯育系？

7.3 If you knew that a locus that affected earlobe shape was tightly linked to a locus that affected susceptibility to cardiovascular disease human, under what circumstances would this information be clinically useful?

7.3 如果你知道一个影响耳垂形状的基因与一个影响人类对心血管疾病敏感性的基因是紧密连锁的，那么在什么情况下这个信息能够用于临床？

7.4 In a previous chapter, we said a 9 : 3 : 3 : 1 phenotypic ratio was expected among the progeny of a dihybrid cross, in absence of gene interaction.

7.4 在前面一章双基因杂种杂交产生的子代中，我们预期的表现型比率应该是 9 : 3 : 3 : 1，因为这些基因间没有相互作用。

a) What does this ratio assume about the linkage between the two loci in the dihybrid cross?

a）假设在双基因杂种杂交时两个位点是连锁的，那么表现型比率应该是怎么样的？

b) What ratio would be expected if the loci were completely linked? Be sure to consider every possible configuration of alleles in the dihybrids.

b）如果基因位点是完全连锁的，那么表现型预期比率会是怎么样的？在双基因杂种中一定要考虑等位基因间各种可能的结构。

7.5 Given a dihybrid with the genotype *CcEe*:

7.5 有一个基因型为 *CcEe* 的双基因杂种：

a) If the alleles are in cis-configuration, what will be the genotypes of the parental and recombinant progeny from a test-cross?

a）如果两等位基因是顺式结构，那么请写出通过测交产生的亲本型和重组型子代的基因型。

b) If the alleles are in trans-configuration, what will be the genotypes of the parental and recombinant progeny from a test-cross?

b）如果两等位基因是反式结构，那么请写出通过测交产生的亲本型和重组型子代的基因型。

7.6 Imagine the white flowers are recessive to purple flowers,

7.6 假设花的白色对紫色是隐性性

and yellow seeds are recessive to green seeds. If a green-seeded, purple-flowered dihybrid is testcrossed, and half of the progeny have yellow seeds, what can you conclude about linkage between these loci? What do you need to know about the parents of the dihybrid in this case?

状，种子的黄色对绿色是隐性性状。如果绿色种子、紫色花的个体通过测交产生一半的黄色种子个体，那么你可以得到这两位点连锁方面的什么信息？此时你还需要知道双基因杂种亲本的什么信息？

7.7 In corn (i.e. maize, a diploid species), imagine that alleles for resistance to a particular pathogen are recessive and are linked to a locus that affects tassel length (short tassels are recessive to long tassels). Design a series of crosses to determine the map distance between these two loci. You can start with any genotypes you want, but be sure to specify the phenotypes of individuals at each stage of the process. Outline the crosses similar to what is shown in Figure 7.7, and specify which progeny will be considered recombinant. You do not need to calculate recombination frequency.

7.7 在玉米中（即苞米，二倍体种），假设一等位基因对某特殊病原菌抗性是隐性性状并且与影响穗长的位点（穗短对穗长是隐性性状）是连锁的。那么，请设计系列杂交试验确定这两基因位点间的图距。你可以选择以你想要的基因型为开始，但是请确定在试验的每个阶段中个体的表现型。将杂交过程画成与图 7.7 类似的流程图，请说明哪一个子代的表现型被考虑是重组体。不必计算重组率。

7.8 In a mutant screen in *Drosophila*, you identified a gene related to memory, as evidenced by the inability of recessive homozygotes to learn to associate a particular scent with the availability of food. Given another line of flies with an autosomal mutation that produces orange eyes, design a series of crosses to determine the map distance between these two loci. Outline the crosses similar to what is shown in Figure 7.7, and specify which progeny will be considered recombinant. You do not need to calculate recombination frequency.

7.8 在果蝇突变体筛选中，经鉴定一个基因与记忆有关，因为证据是：隐性纯合体缺乏学习将食物和食物的味道相联系的能力。还有一个常染色体发生突变的品系能产生橙眼果蝇。那么，请设计系列杂交试验确定这两位点间的图距。将杂交过程画成与图 7.7 类似的流程图，请说明哪一个子代的表现型被考虑是重组体。不必计算重组率。

7.9 Image that methionine heterotrophy, chlorosis (loss of chlorophyⅡ), and absence of leaf hairs (trichomes) are each caused by recessive mutations at three different loci in *Arabidopsis*. Given a triple mutant, and assuming the loci are on the same chromosome, explain how you would determine the order of the loci relative to each other.

7.9 在拟南芥中，假设甲硫氨酸异养、失绿病（缺乏叶绿素Ⅱ）和无叶毛（表皮毛）是 3 个不同的基因位点由隐性突变所引起的。现有一个三基因位点都发生突变的个体，并且假设这 3 个位点位于同一条染色体上，请说明怎样确定位点间彼此的相对顺序。

7.10 If the progeny of the cross *aaBB*×*AAbb* is testcrossed,

7.10 如果对 *aaBB*×*AAbb* 的杂交

and the following genotypes are observed among the progeny of the testcross, what is the frequency of recombination between these loci?

子代再进行测交，并且观察确定了测交子代的基因型。请计算这两个位点间的重组率。

AaBb	135
Aabb	430
aaBb	390
aabb	120

7.11 Three loci are linked in the order *B-C-A*. If the *A-B* map distance is 1cM, and the *B-C* map distance is 0.6cM, given the lines *AaBbCc* and *aabbcc*, what will be the frequency of *Aabb* genotypes among their progeny if one of the parents of the dihybrid had the genotypes *AABBCC*?

7.11 假设3个位点以*B-C-A*的顺序连锁，且*A-B*之间的图距是1cM，*B-C*之间的图距是0.6cM，现有品种*AaBbCc*和*aabbcc*，如果双基因杂种的亲本之一是*AABBCC*，那么在它们的子代中基因型为*Aabb*的比率是多少？

7.12 Genes for body color (*B* black dominant to *b* yellow) and wing shape (*C* straight dominant to *c* curved) are located on the same chromosome in flies. If single mutants for each of these traits are crossed (i.e. a yellow fly crossed to a curved-wing fly), and their progeny is testcrossed, the following phenotypic ratios are observed among their progeny.

7.12 决定果蝇身体颜色的基因（黑色*B*对黄色*b*是显性）和决定翼形的基因（直翅*C*对弯翅*c*是显性）位于同一条染色体上。如果用上述特征的单一突变体进行杂交（即黄色果蝇与弯翅果蝇杂交），并且对它们的子代再测交，新产生的子代表现型及比率如下：

black, straight	黑体、直翅	17
yellow, curved	黄体、弯翅	12
black, curved	黑体、弯翅	337
yellow, straight	黄体、直翅	364

a) Calculate the map distance between *B* and *C*.

b) Why are the frequencies of the two smallest classes not exactly the same?

a）请计算*B*和*C*之间的图距。

b）为什么两个最小的表现型数目不是完全相同的？

7.13 Given the map distance you calculated between *B-C* in question 7.12, if you crossed a double mutant (i.e. yellow body and curved wing) with a wild-type fly, and testcrossed the progeny, what phenotypes in what proportions would you expect to observe among the F_2 generation?

7.13 现已知问题7.12中*B-C*之间的图距，如果用双突变体（即黄体和弯翅）与野生型果蝇杂交，并且对它们的子代再测交，那么预测在F_2代中个体有什么样的表现型及各类表现型的比率？

7.14 In a three-point cross, individuals *AAbbcc* and *aaBBCC* are crossed, and their F_1 progeny is testcrossed. Answer the

7.14 利用三点测交法，首先让个体*AAbbcc*和*aaBBCC*杂交，F_1代再

following questions based on these F_2 frequency data.

aaBbCc	480
AaBbcc	15
AaBbCc	10
aaBbcc	1
aabbCc	13
Aabbcc	472
AabbCc	1
aabbcc	8

a) Without calculating recombination frequencies, determine the relative order of these genes.

b) Calculate pair-wise recombination frequencies (without considering double cross overs) and produce a genetic map.

c) Recalculate recombination frequencies accounting for double recombinants.

进行测交。根据 F_2 代频率回答下列问题：

aaBbCc	480
AaBbcc	15
AaBbCc	10
aaBbcc	1
aabbCc	13
Aabbcc	472
AabbCc	1
aabbcc	8

a）先不计算基因间的重组率，请确定基因间的相对顺序。

b）请计算各对基因间的重组率（不考虑双交换）并作出遗传图谱。

c）若考虑双交换，请重新计算基因间的重组率。

7.15 Wild-type mice have brown fur and short tails. Loss of function of a particular gene produces white fur, while loss of function of another gene produces long tails, and loss of function at a third locus produces agitated behaviour. Each of these loss of function alleles is recessive. If a wild-type mouse is crossed with a triple mutant, and their F_1 progeny is test-crossed, the following recombination frequencies are observed among their progeny. Produce a genetic map for these loci.

fur	tail	behaviour	
white	short	normal	16
brown	short	agitated	0
brown	short	normal	955
white	short	agitated	36
white	long	normal	0
brown	long	agitated	14
brown	long	normal	46
white	long	agitated	933

7.15 老鼠的野生型为棕毛短尾。某一基因功能缺失会产生白毛个体，另一基因功能的缺失会产生长尾个体，第三个位点功能的缺失会产生亢奋个体。这些基因功能缺失的基因是隐性性状。假设一个野生型老鼠和一个三基因突变体进行杂交，F_1 代再进行测交，根据测交产生的子代计算位点间的重组率并做出遗传图谱。

毛色	尾长	行为表现	
白色	短尾	正常	16
棕色	短尾	亢奋	0
棕色	短尾	正常	955
白色	短尾	亢奋	36
白色	长尾	正常	0
棕色	长尾	亢奋	14
棕色	长尾	正常	46
白色	长尾	亢奋	933

Chapter 8

TECHNIQUES OF MOLECULAR BIOLOGY

分子生物学技术

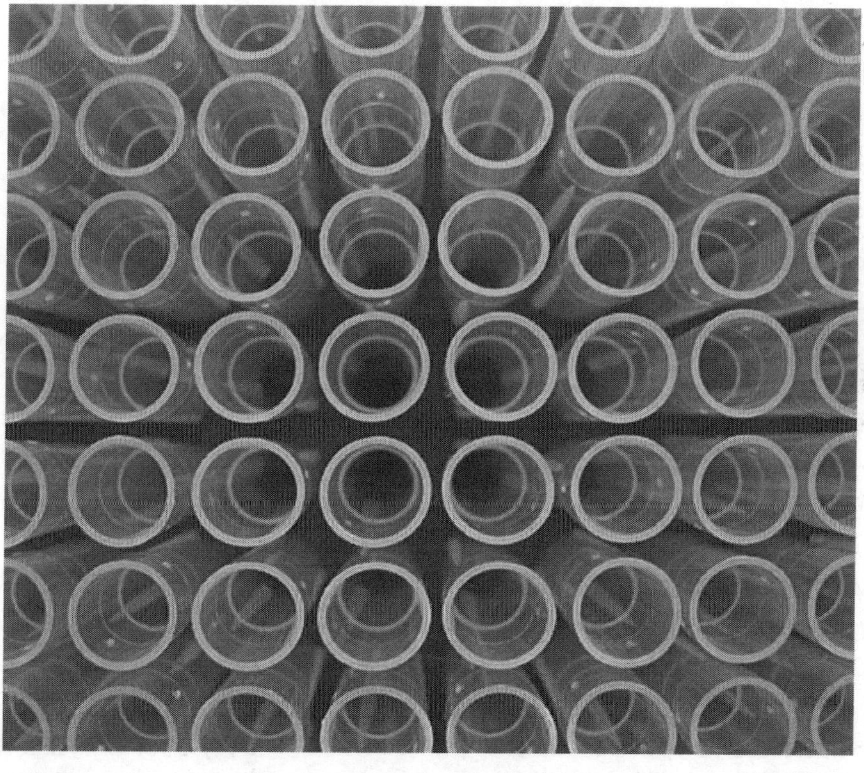

Disposable tips for a pipette are used to distribute microliter volumes of liquid in molecular biology (see the cover)

分子生物学中安装在用于分装微升体积液体的取样器上的一次性吸头（见封面）

Genetics is the study of the inheritance and variation of biological traits. We have previously noted that it is possible to conduct genetic research without directly studying DNA. In-

遗传学是研究生物性状的遗传和变异的学科。之前我们可以注意到，在不直接研究 DNA 的情况下

deed some of the greatest geneticists had no special knowledge of DNA at all, but relied instead on analysis of phenotypes and their ratios in carefully designed crosses. Today, classical genetics is often complemented by **molecular biology**, which is the study of DNA and other **macromolecules** that have been isolated from an organism. Usually, molecular biology experiments involve some combination of techniques to isolate, then analyze the DNA or RNA of a particular gene. In some cases, the DNA may be subsequently manipulated by mutation or by recombination with other DNA fragments. Techniques of molecular biology have wide application in many fields of biology, as well as forensics, biotechnology, and medicine.

也可以研究遗传学，事实上一些伟大的遗传学家也没有关于 DNA 的专业知识，而是依靠表现型和精细设计的杂交中表现型比率分析来得出结论。**分子生物学**是研究 DNA 和其他从生物中分离出来的**大分子**的科学，现在经常用来补充经典遗传学内容。通常分子生物学实验需要结合一系列技术去分离、分析某一特定基因的 DNA 或 RNA。接下来，在某些情况下会通过突变或与其他 DNA 片段重组技术来操作 DNA。分子生物学技术在许多生物学及法医学、生物技术和医学等领域都有广泛的应用。

ISOLATING GENOMIC DNA 基因组 DNA 分离

DNA purification strategies rely on the chemical properties of DNA that distinguish it from other molecules in the cell, namely that it is a very long, negatively charged molecule. To extract purified DNA from a tissue sample, cells are broken open by grinding or **lysing** in a solution that contains chemicals that protect the DNA while disrupting other components of the cell (Figure 8.1). These chemicals may include **detergents**, which dissolve membranes and denature proteins. A cation such as Na^+ helps to stabilize the negatively charged DNA and separate it from proteins including histones. A **chelating agent**, such as **EDTA**, is added to protect DNA by sequestering Mg^{2+}, which can otherwise serve as a necessary co-factor for **nucleases** (enzymes that digest DNA). As a result, free, double-stranded DNA molecules are released from the chromatin into the extraction buffer, which also contains proteins and all other cellular components.

DNA 纯化策略是根据 DNA 的化学性质在细胞中将其与其他分子区分开来，换句话说，DNA 是一条长的、带负电荷的分子。为了从组织样品中提取纯化的 DNA，要在含有保护 DNA 完整而破坏细胞中其他成分的化学溶液中进行研磨或者**裂解**，从而破裂细胞（图 8.1）。这些化学成分可能包括**清洁剂**，它能溶解细胞膜并使蛋白质变性。阳离子如 Na^+能稳定带有负电荷的 DNA 并且能使它与蛋白质(包括组蛋白)分离。添加**螯合剂**，如 **EDTA**，可以保护 DNA，隔离 Mg^{2+}，Mg^{2+} 是核酸酶（降解 DNA 的酶类）形成必需的辅助因子。这样，从染色质释放出来的游离双链 DNA 分子进入到提取缓冲液中，其中仍然包含蛋白质和细胞的所有其他成分。

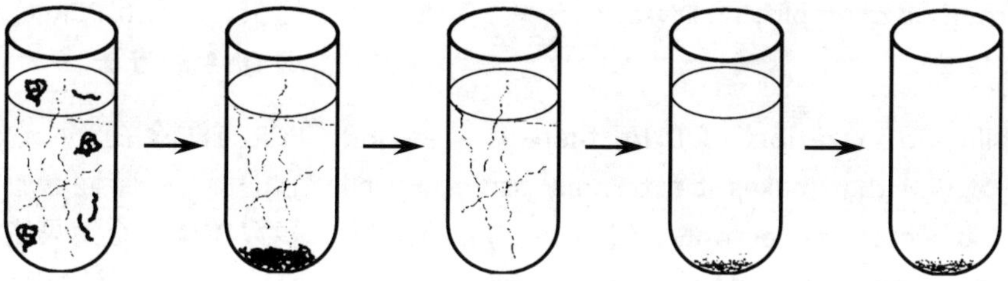

Figure 8.1 Extraction of DNA from a mixture of solubilized cellular components by successive precipitations. Proteins are precipitated, then DNA (in the supernatant) is precipitated in ethanol, leaving a pellet of DNA

图 8.1 通过一系列的沉淀从溶解细胞成分的混合液中提取 DNA。蛋白质沉淀，然后上清液中的 DNA 沉淀在乙醇中，留下 DNA 沉淀

The free DNA molecules are subsequently isolated by one of several methods, such as adjusting the salt concentration so that proteins precipitate. The supernatant, which contains DNA and other, smaller metabolites, is then mixed with ethanol, which causes the DNA to precipitate. A small **pellet** of DNA can be collected by centrifugation, and after removal of the ethanol, the DNA pellet can be dissolved in water (usually with a small amount of EDTA and a pH buffer) for the use in other reactions. Note that this process has purified all of the DNA from a tissue sample; if we want to further isolate a specific gene or DNA fragment, we must use additional techniques, such as PCR.

游离的 DNA 分子可以通过几种不同的方法分离出来，如可以调节盐浓度来沉淀蛋白质。上清液，包括 DNA 和其他小的代谢产物，与乙醇混合，从而沉淀 DNA。小的 DNA **沉淀物**通过离心收集，然后倒掉乙醇，DNA 沉淀可以融入水中（通常使用少量 EDTA 和 pH 缓冲液），以备用于其他反应。注意这个过程从组织样品中纯化了全部的 DNA，如果我们想要进一步分离某一特定基因或 DNA 片段，则需进一步使用其他的技术，如 PCR 等。

ISOLATING OR DETECTING A SPECIFIC SEQUENCE BY PCR
通过 PCR 方法分离或检测特异序列

The **Polymerase Chain Reaction (PCR)** is a method of DNA replication that is performed in a test tube (i.e. *in vitro*). Here "polymerase" refers to a DNA polymerase enzyme extracted from bacteria, and "chain reaction" refers to the ability of this technique produce millions of copies of a DNA molecule, by using each newly replicated double helix as a template to synthesize two new DNA double helices. PCR is therefore a

聚合酶链反应（PCR）是一种在试管中进行 DNA 复制的方法（即在体外）。“聚合酶”是指从细菌中提取的一种 DNA 聚合酶，“链反应”是指这种技术用每一个新复制的双螺旋作模板合成新的 DNA 双螺旋结构，从而产生数百万的 DNA 分子

very efficient method of amplifying DNA.

拷贝。因此，PCR 是一种高效的扩增 DNA 的方法。

Besides its ability to make lots of DNA, there is a second characteristic of PCR that makes it extremely useful. Recall that most DNA polymerases can only add nucleotides to the end of an existing strand of DNA, and therefore require a **primer** to begin the process of replication. For PCR, chemically synthesized primers of about 16 nucleotides are used. In an ideal PCR, primers only hybridize to their exact complementary sequence on the template strand (Figure 8.2).

PCR 方法除了产生大量的 DNA 外，它的第二个特性更加有用。因为大多数 DNA 聚合酶只能将核苷酸加到已经存在的双链 DNA 末端上，所以要求有一个**引物**开始复制过程。而在 PCR 中，使用化学合成的约 16 个核苷酸组成的引物。在理想的 PCR 中，引物只能和模板链上精确互补的序列发生杂交（图 8.2）。

```
          5′ CATGGTCATACCAT 3′ ———→
             ||||||||||  |||
3′----GTCAGTACCAGTATCGTAAATGCTGTGAA------5′

          5′ CAGGACTATACCAT 3′
             ||  ||   |||  |||
3′----GTCAGTACCAGTATCGTAAATGCTGTGAA------5′
```

Figure 8.2 The primer-template duplex at the top part of the figure is perfectly matched, and will be stable at a higher temperature than the duplex in the bottom part of the figure, which contains many mismatches and therefore fewer hydrogen bonds. If the annealing temperature is sufficiently high, only the perfectly matched primer will be able to initiate extension (grey arrow) from this site on the template

图 8.2 图的上部引物模板二聚体是完全配对的，在高温下比图下部二聚体更稳定存在，图下部复合体包含许多错配和更少量的氢键。如果退火温度足够高，只有完全配对的引物才能从模板上该位点开始延伸（箭头处）

The experimenter can therefore control exactly what region of a DNA template is amplified by controlling the sequence of the primers used in the reaction.

实验者可以通过控制反应中引物的序列严格控制 DNA 模板需要扩增的区域。

To conduct a PCR, an experimenter combines in a small, thin-walled tube (Figure 8.3), all of the necessary components for DNA replication, including DNA polymerase and solutions containing nucleotides (dATP, dCTP, dGTP, dTTP), a DNA template, DNA primers, a pH buffer, and ions (e.g. Mg^{2+}) required by the polymerase. Successful PCR reactions have been conducted using a single DNA molecule as a template, but in practice, most PCR reactions contain many thousands of template molecules. The template DNA (e.g. total genomic DNA) has usually already been purified from cells or tissues

进行 PCR 反应时，实验者将 DNA 复制需要的所有必要的成分，包括 DNA 聚合酶、核苷酸溶液（dATP、dCTP、dGTP、dTTP）、DNA 模板、DNA 引物、pH 缓冲液及聚合酶需要的离子（Mg^{2+}等）放在一个小薄壁管中进行（图 8.3）。成功的 PCR 反应用单一的 DNA 分子作为模板，但实际上大多数 PCR 反应中包含成百上千个模板分子。通常 DNA

using the techniques described above. However, in some situations it is possible to put whole cells directly in a PCR reaction for use as a template.

模板（总基因组 DNA）是已经用前面描述的方法从细胞或组织中纯化出来的。然而，有些情况下也会用整个细胞直接作为模板进行 PCR 反应。

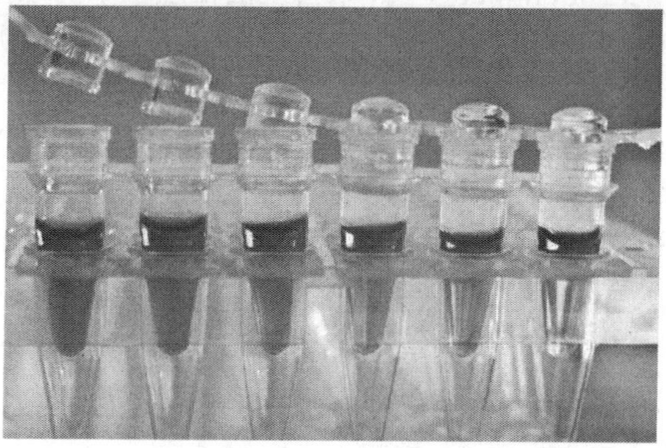

Figure 8.3 A strip of PCR tubes

图 8.3 一条 PCR 管

An essential aspect of PCR is **thermalcycling**, meaning the exposure of the reaction to a series of precisely defined temperatures (Figure 8.4). The reaction mixture is first heated to 95°C. This causes the hydrogen bonds between the strands of the template DNA molecules to melt, or **denature**. This produces two single-stranded DNA molecules from each double helix (Figure 8.5). In the next step (**annealing**), the mixture is cooled to 45~65°C (the exact temperature depends on the primer sequence used and the objectives of the experiment). This allows the formation of double stranded helices between complementary DNA molecules, including the annealing of primers to the template. In the final step (**extension**) the mixture is heated to 72°C. This is the temperature at which the particular DNA polymerase used in PCR is most active. During extension, the new DNA strand is synthesized, starting from the 3' end of the primer, along the length of the template strand. The entire PCR process is very quick, with each temperature phase usually lasting 30 seconds or less. Each cycle of three temperatures (denaturation, annealing, extension) is usually repeated about 30 times, amplifying the target region approximately 2^{30}-fold. Notice from the figure 8.5 that most of the newly synthesized strands in PCR begin and end with sequences either identical to or complementary to the primer sequences; although a few strands are longer than this, they are in such a small minority that they can almost always be ig-

热循环是 PCR 反应的一个重要部分，即反应在精细设定好的一系列温度下进行（图 8.4）。反应混合物首先在 95℃加热，模板间的氢键熔解或**变性**，这就会从每个 DNA 双螺旋中产生两条单链（图 8.5）。第二步**退火**，将温度降为 45～65℃（精确的温度由引物序列和实验目的决定）。包括引物在内互补的 DNA 分子就会形成双链螺旋。最后一步是**延伸**，混合物加热到 72℃，这是大多数 PCR 反应聚合酶活性最大的温度。在延伸的过程中，从引物的 3′端开始沿着模板长度合成新 DNA。整个 PCR 过程非常快速，每个温度段持续 30s 或是更短。变性、退火、延伸为一次循环，通常进行 30 次循环，大约扩增目标区域 2^{30} 倍。从图 8.5 中我们看到绝大多数新合成链的末尾和开头序列是与引物序列相同或互补的，尽管有少数链的序列比这些长，但是由于数量相对非常少可被忽略。最早的 PCR 反应中的聚合酶来自大肠杆菌，因为变性阶段的高温可以破坏聚合酶，所以不得不

nored. The earliest PCR reactions used a polymerase from *E. coli*. Because the high temperature of the denaturation step destroyed the enzyme, new polymerase had to be added after each cycle. To overcome this, researchers identified thermostable DNA polymerases such as ***Taq* DNA pol**, from *Thermus aquaticus*, a thermophilic bacterium that lives in hot springs. *Taq* cannot usually amplify fragments longer than about 3kb, but under some specialized conditions, PCR can amplify fragments up to approximately 10kb.

在每个循环后添加新的聚合酶，为了克服这个问题，研究者鉴定出了耐热的聚合酶，如 ***Taq* DNA 聚合酶**，来自生活在温泉中的水生栖热菌（*T. aquaticus*）。*Taq* 酶通常不能扩增大于 3kb 的片段，但是在一些特殊条件下，可以扩增大约 10kb 的片段。

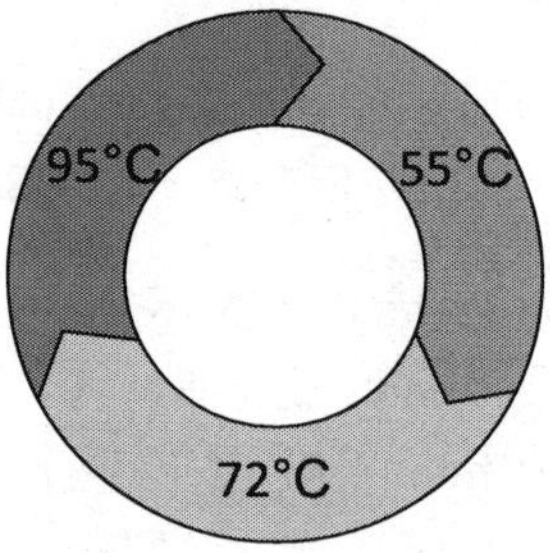

Figure 8.4 Example of a thermal cycle, in which the annealing temperature is 55°C

图 8.4 PCR 热循环举例，退火温度为 55°C

After completion of the thermal cycling, part of the PCR reaction is usually loaded onto an **electrophoretic gel** (described below) to determine whether a DNA fragment of the expected length was amplified or not. Usually, the template DNA will be so dilute that it will not show up on the gel, so the presence of a sharp band of the expected length indicates that PCR was able to amplify its target. If the purpose of the PCR was to test for the presence of a particular template sequence, this is the end of the experiment. Otherwise, the remaining PCR product can be used as starting material for a variety of other techniques such as sequencing or cloning.

热循环完成后，取一部分 PCR 产物进行**凝胶电泳**（后面将描述），检测是否扩增到了预期大小的 DNA 片段。通常，PCR 中模板 DNA 将被稀释，在凝胶中无法观察到，所以在凝胶中看到预期大小的清晰条带就是 PCR 反应能够扩增的目的片段。如果 PCR 的目的是为了检测特定的模板序列的存在，那么实验就可以结束了。此外，PCR 产物可以用作其他技术的起始材料，如测序、克隆。

An application of PCR: the StarLink affair

PCR 反应应用实例：StarLink 事件

PCR is sensitive (meaning it can amplify very small starting amounts of DNA), and specific (meaning it can amplify only the target sequence from a mixture of many DNA sequences). This made PCR the perfect tool to test whether genetically modified corn was present in consumer products on supermarket shelves. Although the majority of corn in the

PCR 反应非常灵敏（可以由数目非常少的 DNA 开始扩增），并且特异性强（可以从多种 DNA 混合样品中扩增出目的基因序列）。因此，PCR 反应成了一种检测超市货架上是否出售遗传修饰玉米的完美

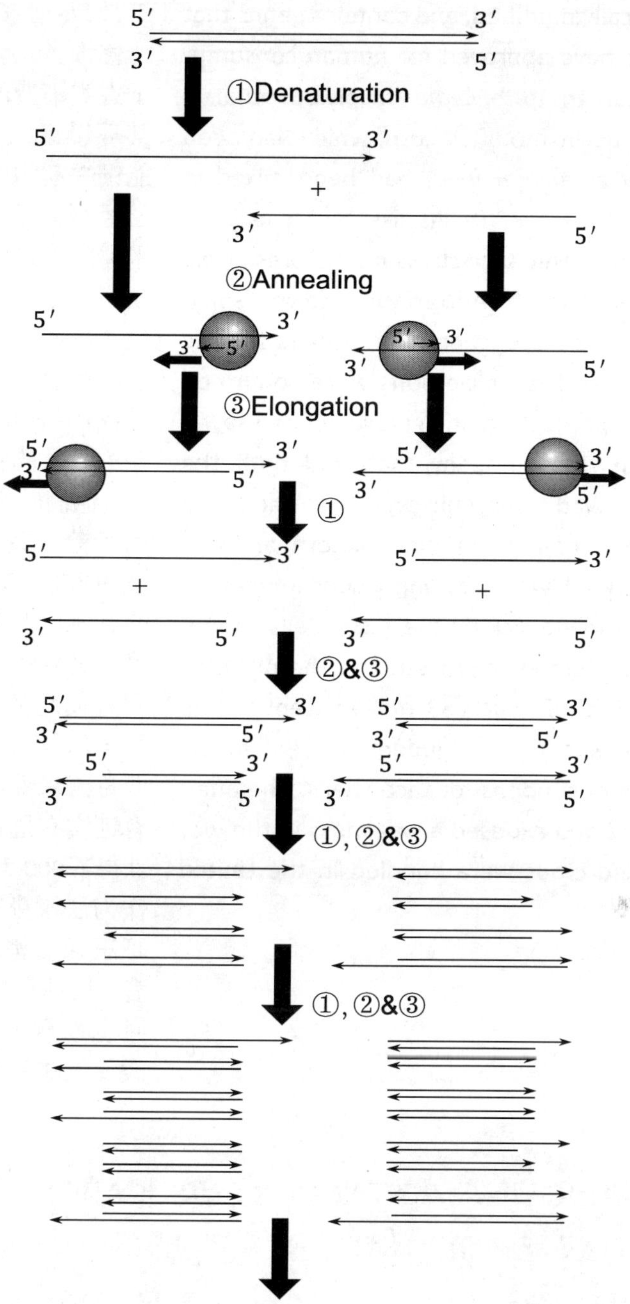

Figure 8.5 PCR with the three phases of the thermal cycle numbered. The template strand (blue) is replicated from primers (red), with newly synthesized strands in green. The green strands flanked by two primer binding sites will increase in abundance exponentially through successive PCR cycles (see the color figure)

图 8.5 用数字标出热循环的 3 个阶段的 PCR 反应。蓝色的模板链从红色的引物开始复制，新合成的为绿色。随着连续的 PCR 循环，两侧与引物结合位点的绿色链呈指数增长（见彩版）

United States is genetically modified, and contains genes that government regulators have approved for human consumption, an environmental group became suspicious that a different strain of genetically modified corn, which had been approved for use only as animal feed, had been mixed in with corn used in production of things like taco shells. To prove this, the group purchased taco shells from stores in the Washington DC area, extracted DNA from the taco shells and used it as a template in a PCR reaction with primers specific to the unauthorized gene. Their suspicions were confirmed when they ran this PCR product on an agarose gel and saw a band of expected size. The company that sold both the approved and non-approved transgenic seed to farmers had to pay for the destruction of large amounts of corn, and was the target of a class action law-suit by angry consumers who claimed they had been made sick by the taco shells. No legitimate cases of harm were ever proven, and the plaintiffs were awarded $9 million, of which $3 million went to the legal fees, and the remainder of the judgment went to the consumers in the form of coupons for taco shells. The affair destroyed the company, and exposed a weakness in the way the genetically modified crops were handled in the United States at the time.

工具。尽管在美国大多数玉米被遗传修饰了，包括政府已经批准可用于人类消费的遗传修饰玉米，但是某环境组织开始怀疑某个批准只能饲喂动物的遗传修饰玉米品种，已经混入了用于生产像墨西哥玉米卷的玉米中去。为了验证这个问题，该组织购买了华盛顿特区商店里的墨西哥玉米卷，从墨西哥玉米卷中提取了 DNA 作为 PCR 反应的模板，并使用与这种未获准的基因序列互补的特异引物进行 PCR 反应。他们的怀疑被证实是对的，在琼脂糖凝胶中看到了一个预期大小的条带。公司同时出售这种获准的和未经批准的转基因种子给农民，必须赔偿大量被摧毁的玉米，同时愤怒的消费者也起诉该公司要求赔偿，他们宣称因食用这种墨西哥玉米卷而患疾病。在法律上没有证实有危害消费者的实例，原告获得了 900 万美元赔偿，其中 300 万作为法律费用，剩余的费用以墨西哥玉米卷消费券的形式分给消费者。这件事情毁掉了这个公司，同时也暴露出那时候美国处理基因改良农作物的一个弱点。

CUTTING AND PASTING DNA: RESTRICTION AND LIGATION
剪切和粘贴 DNA：酶切和链接

Many bacteria have enzymes that recognize specific DNA sequences (usually 4 or 6 nucleotides) and then cut the double stranded DNA helix at this sequence (Figure 8.6). These enzymes are called site-specific **restriction endonucleases**, or more simply "restriction enzymes", and they naturally function as part of bacterial defenses against viruses and

许多来自细菌的酶可以识别特异的 DNA 序列（通常是 4 或 6 个核苷酸）并在这个序列切断双链 DNA 螺旋（图 8.6）。这些酶被称作位点特异**限制性内切核酸酶**，或简称限制酶。它们作为细菌的天然防御工

other sources of foreign DNA. To cut DNA at known locations, researchers use restriction enzymes that have been purified from various bacterial species, and which can be purchased from commercial sources. These enzymes are usually named after the bacterium from which they were first isolated. For example, ***Eco*R** Ⅰ and *Eco*R Ⅴ are both enzymes from *E. coli*. *Eco*R Ⅰ cuts double stranded DNA at the sequence GAATTC, but note that this enzyme, like many others, does not cut in exactly the middle of the restriction sequence (Figure 8.7). The ends of a molecule cut by *Eco*R Ⅰ have an overhanging region of single stranded DNA, and so are sometimes called **sticky-ends**. On the other hand, *Eco*R Ⅴ is an example of an enzyme that cuts both strands in exactly the middle of its recognition sequence, producing what are called **blunt-ends**, which lack overhangs.

具的一部分可以防御病毒和其他来源的外源 DNA。研究者使用从多种细菌中纯化出来的限制酶切断已知位置的 DNA 序列，这些酶可以由商业途径购买。这些酶按照它们最初分离的细菌命名。例如，***Eco*R** Ⅰ和 *Eco*R Ⅴ都是从大肠杆菌（*E.coli*）中分离得到的。*Eco*R Ⅰ在 GAATTC 序列处切断双链 DNA，但是我们注意到像其他许多酶一样，它并不是恰好切断这个限制性序列中间部分（图 8.7）。在 *Eco*R Ⅰ切断的分子末端会形成一个突出的单链 DNA 区域，这就是通常所说的**黏性末端**。另外，*Eco*R Ⅴ恰好在识别序列的中间切断双链，没有突出末端，而产生**平末端**。

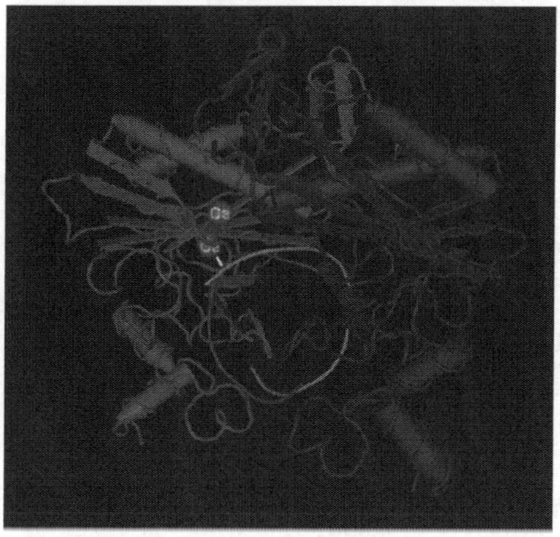

Figure 8.6 An *Eco*R Ⅰ dimer (blue, purple) sits like a saddle on a double helix of DNA (one strand is green, one is brown). This image is looking down the center of the helix (see the color figure)

图 8.6 *Eco*R Ⅰ的二聚体像 DNA 双螺旋上坐了一个马鞍(一条链是绿色，另一条是棕色)。这是一张螺旋结构中间俯瞰图（见彩版）

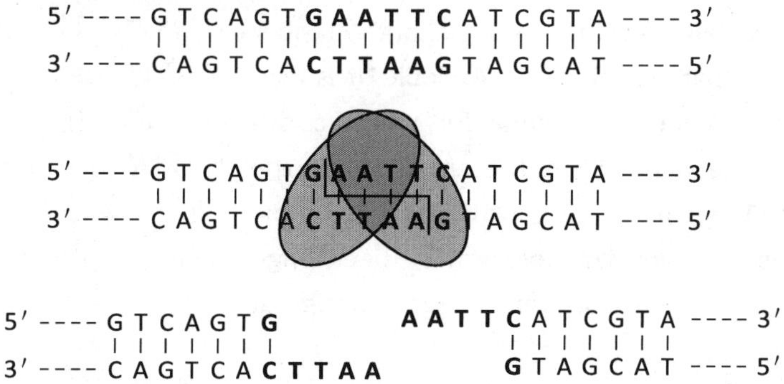

Figure 8.7 The recognition sequence for *Eco*R Ⅰ (bold) is cleaved by the enzyme (grey). This particular enzyme cuts DNA at a position offset from the center of the restriction site. This creates an overhanging, sticky-end

图 8.7 *Eco*R Ⅰ的识别位点（粗体）被酶（灰色）切开。这种特殊的酶在偏移识别位点中心切断 DNA，产生突出的黏性末端

The process of **ligation** occurs when double-stranded DNA molecules are covalently joined, end-to-end, through the action of an enzyme called **ligase**. Ligation is therefore central to the production of recombinant DNA, including the insertion of a cloned DNA fragment into a plasmid. Sticky-ended molecules with complementary overhanging sequences are said to have **compatible ends.** Likewise, two blunt-ended sequences are also considered compatible, although they may not ligate together as efficiently as sticky-ends. On the other hand, sticky-ended molecules with non-complementary sequences cannot be ligated together.

通过一种叫做**连接酶**的作用，双链DNA分子可以头尾相接，共价结合，产生连接反应。因此，连接是产生重组DNA的核心，包括将DNA片段插入质粒中。带有互补突出序列的黏性末端分子就叫做具有**互补末端**。同样，平末端序列也需要具有互补的分子，尽管它们不能像黏性末端那样有效连接。另外，不具有互补序列的黏性末端分子不能连接到一起。

CLONING DNA: PLASMID VECTORS 克隆DNA：质粒载体

Many bacteria contain extra-chromosomal DNA elements called **plasmids**. These are usually small, circular, double stranded molecules that replicate independently of the chromosome and can be present in high copy numbers within a cell. Plasmids can be transferred between individuals during bacterial mating and are sometimes even transferred between different species. Plasmids are particularly important in medicine because they often carry some genes for pathogenicity and drug-resistance.

许多细菌具有染色体外的DNA分子叫做**质粒**。它们通常是小的、环状双链分子，能独立于染色体外复制，在一个细胞内具有高拷贝数。质粒可以通过细菌交配而在个体间转移，有时也能在不同的物种间转移。由于质粒携带许多致病性和抗药性基因，所以在医学上特别重要。

To insert a DNA fragment into a plasmid, both the fragment and the plasmid are cut using a restriction enzyme that produces compatible ends (Figure 8.8). Given the large number of restriction enzymes that are currently available, it is usually not too difficult to find an enzyme for which corresponding recognition sequences are present in both the plasmid and the DNA fragment, particularly because most plasmid vectors used in molecular biology have been engineered to contain recognition sites for a large number of endonucleases.

为了将DNA片段插入质粒中，片段和质粒都要用限制酶酶切产生互补末端（图8.8）。现在有大量限制酶可以利用，要找到一种在质粒和片段中互补的识别序列并不难，特别是用在分子生物学的大多数质粒载体是人工改造的，具有大量的限制酶识别位点。

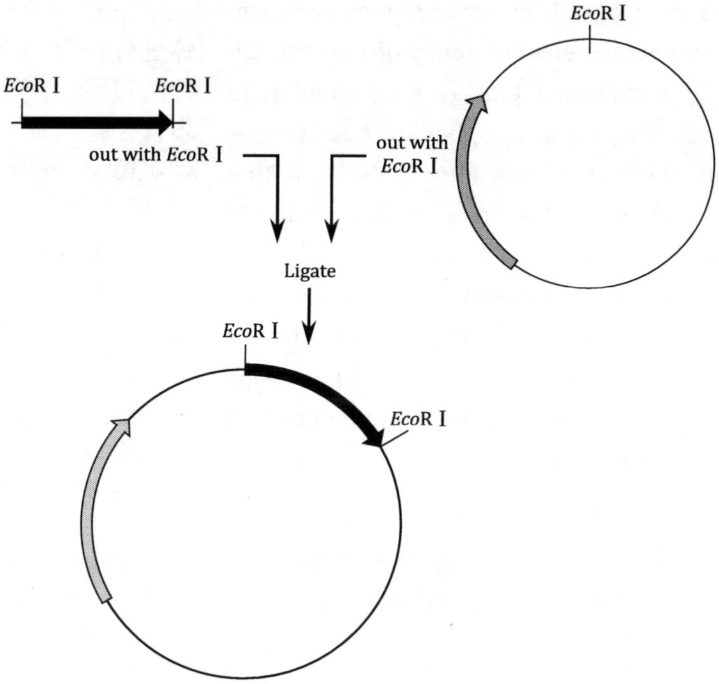

Figure 8.8 Cloning of a DNA fragment (black) into a plasmid vector. The vector already contains a selectable marker gene (light grey)

图 8.8 将一个 DNA 片段（黑色部分）克隆进质粒载体。载体已经包含一个可选择标记基因（浅灰色部分）

After restriction digestion, the desired fragments may be further purified before they are mixed together with ligase. Following a short incubation, the newly ligated plasmids, containing the gene of interest are **transformed** into *E. coli*. Transformation is accomplished by mixing the ligated DNA with *E. coli* that has been specially prepared (i.e. made **competent**) to uptake DNA when exposed to compounds such as $CaCl_2$ or to electrical fields (**electroporation**). Because only a small fraction of cells that are mixed with DNA will actually be transformed, a **selectable marker**, such as a gene for antibiotic resistance, is usually also present on the plasmid. After combining DNA with competent cells, bacteria are therefore spread on a plate containing an appropriate antibiotic so that only cells that have actually incorporated the plasmid will grow and form colonies for further study.

限制酶酶切后，将要得到的片段进一步纯化然后再与连接酶混合。进行短暂的温育后，将包含目的基因的新连接的质粒载体**转化**进大肠杆菌中。将连接的 DNA 和特殊处理的大肠杆菌（如**感受态**细胞）混合，转化就完成了，这种特殊状态是大肠杆菌预先经过 $CaCl_2$ 或电场（电转化）处理的，能够吸收进 DNA。因为实际上只有一少部分与 DNA 混合的细胞能够转化进 DNA，所以质粒载体就需要一个**选择标记**，如一个具有抗抗生素的基因。将 DNA 与感受态细胞混合后，将细菌涂布在含有相应抗生素的平板上，只有含有重组质粒的细胞才能生长，形成菌落后再做进一步研究。

Molecular biologists use plasmids as **vectors** to contain, amplify, transfer, and sometimes express genes of interest. Often, the first step in a molecular biology experiment is to **clone** (i.e. copy) a gene into a plasmid, then introduce transform this recombinant plasmid back into bacteria so that essentially unlimited copies of the gene (and the plasmid that carries it) can be made as the bacteria reproduce. This is a practical necessity for further manipulations of the DNA, since most techniques of molecular biology are not sensitive enough to work with just a single molecule at a time. Many molecular cloning and recombination experiments are therefore iterative processes in which:

分子生物学家有时用质粒作为**载体**进行整合、扩增、转化表达感兴趣的基因。分子生物学实验的第一步首先是**克隆**（即复制）一个基因到质粒中，然后将重组质粒转化进细菌中，这样当细菌繁殖时基因（包含携带该基因的质粒）就能产生无限的拷贝数。因为分子生物学技术还没有灵敏到一次用单个分子实验的程度，所以这是进一步进行 DNA 实际操作的必需工作。因此，许多分子克隆和重组是反复进行下面这些过程：

- a DNA fragment (usually isolated by PCR and/or restriction digestion) is cloned into a plasmid cut with a compatible restriction enzyme
- the recombinant plasmid is transformed into bacteria
- the bacteria are allowed to divide, usually in liquid culture
- a large quantity of the recombinant plasmid DNA is isolated from the bacterial culture
- further manipulations (such as site directed mutagenesis or the introduction of another piece of DNA) are conducted on the recombinant plasmid
- the modified plasmid is again transformed into bacteria, prior to further manipulations, or for expression

- 将 DNA 片段（通常由 PCR 或酶切分离得到）克隆进被相应限制酶酶切的质粒载体中
- 重组质粒转化到细菌中
- 通常在液体培养基中培养细菌
- 从培养的细菌中分离大量重组质粒 DNA
- 在重组质粒上进一步操作（如定点突变、引入其他 DNA 片段）
- 改造的质粒再转化进细菌中，再进一步操作或表达

An application of molecular cloning: production of recombinant insulin

分子克隆的应用：生产重组胰岛素

Purified insulin is critical to the treatment of diabetes. Historically, insulin for clinical use was isolated from human cadavers or from slaughtered animals such as pigs. Human-derived insulin generally had better pharmacological properties, but was in limited supply and carried risks of disease transmission. By cloning the human insulin gene and expressing it in *E. coli*, large quantities of insulin identical to

提纯胰岛素是治疗糖尿病的关键。在历史上，临床上使用的胰岛素是从人尸体或屠宰的动物（如猪）中分离得到的。通常人源的胰岛素有更好的药理性质，但是供应有限，而且具有传播疾病的风险。通过克隆人胰岛素基因并转化进细菌中

the human hormone could be produced in fermentors, safely and efficiently. Production of recombinant insulin also allows specialized variants of the protein to be produced: for example, by changing a few amino acids, longer-acting forms of the hormone can be made. The active insulin hormone contains two peptide fragments of 21 and 30 amino acids, respectively. Today, essentially all insulin is produced from recombinant sources (Figure 8.9), i.e. human genes and their derivatives expressed in bacteria or yeast.

表达，和人类激素一样的大量胰岛素就可以安全有效地在发酵罐中生产了。生产胰岛素也会产生特别的蛋白质变体，如改变少数氨基酸，可以制成长效的激素。有效的胰岛素包含两个肽链，分别含 21 和 30 个氨基酸。现在，基本上所有的胰岛素都是来源于重组体（图 8.9），即在细菌或酵母菌中表达的人类基因和它们的衍生物。

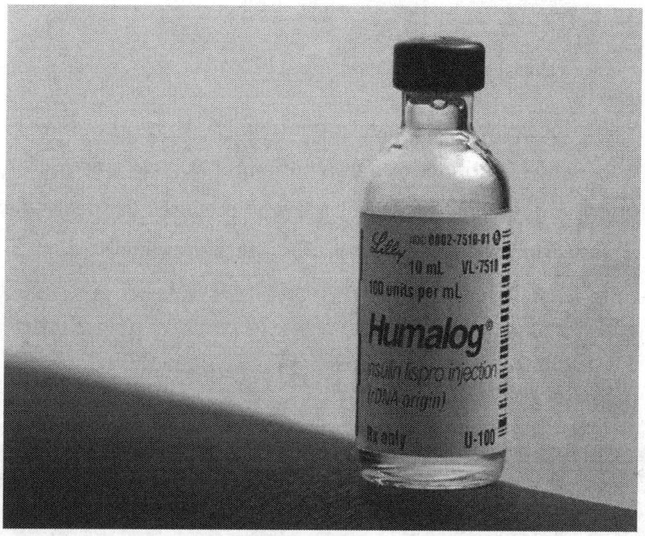

Figure 8.9 A vial of insulin. Note that the label lists the origin as "rDNA", which stands for recombinant DNA

图 8.9 胰岛素药瓶。标签区域列着起源"rDNA"，代表重组 DNA

DNA ANALYSIS: GEL ELECTROPHORESIS DNA 分析：凝胶电泳

A solution of DNA is colorless, and except for being viscous at high concentrations, is visually indistinguishable from water. Therefore, techniques such as **gel electrophoresis** have been developed to detect and analyze DNA (Figure 8.10). To start, a solution of DNA is deposited at one end of a gel slab. This gel is made from polymers such as **agarose**, which is a polysaccharide isolated from certain seaweed. The DNA is then pulled through the gel by an electrical current, with DNA

DNA 溶液无色，除了在高浓度时具有黏稠性，在视觉上不能和水区分。因此人们发明了**凝胶电泳**技术用来检测和分析 DNA（图 8.10）。一开始，DNA 溶液加在凝胶的一端，凝胶是用聚合物制成的，如从海藻中分离的多聚糖——**琼脂糖**。通过电流作用DNA在凝胶上运动，

molecules moving toward the positive electrode (Figure 8.11).

DNA 分子向阳极移动（图 8.11）。

Figure 8.10 Apparatus for agarose gel electrophoresis. A waterproof tank is used to pass current through a slab gel, which is submerged in a buffer in the tank. The current is supplied by an adjustable power supply. A gel (stained blue by a dye sometimes used when loading DNA on the gel) sits in a tray, awaiting further analysis

图 8.10 琼脂糖凝胶电泳仪器。在一个防水槽中电流通过平板凝胶，凝胶沉在水槽内的缓冲液中。电流由可调节的电源供电。凝胶（当上样 DNA 到凝胶时，有时使用蓝色染料作为指示剂）放在一个托盘里，等待进一步分析

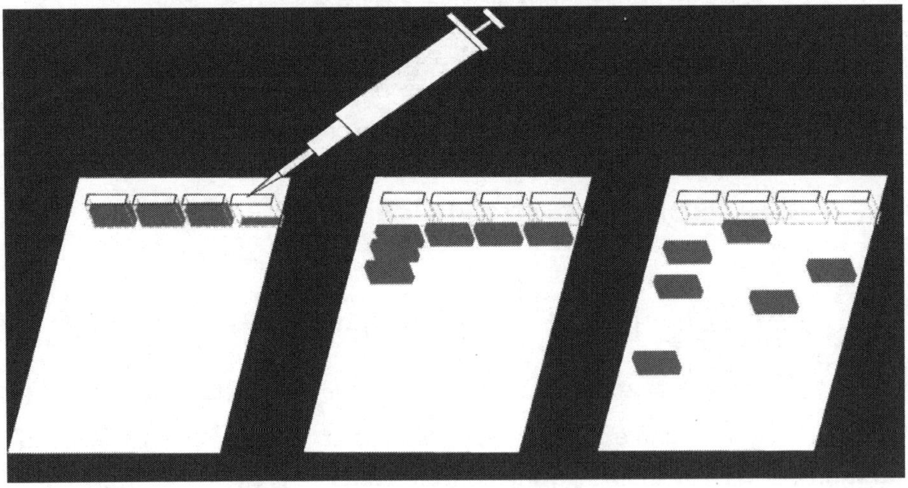

Figure 8.11 Agarose gel electrophoresis. DNA is loaded into wells at the top of a gel. A current is passed through the gel, pulling DNA towards the positively charged electrode. The DNA fragments are separated by size, with smaller fragments moving fastest towards the electrode

图 8.11 琼脂糖凝胶电泳。DNA 加到凝胶顶端的孔内。电流通过凝胶，将 DNA 拉向阳极。DNA 片段按照大小分开，小的片段向阳极运动得最快

As it migrates, each strand of DNA threads its way through the pores that form between the polymers of the gel. Because shorter fragments move through these pores faster than longer fragments, gel electrophoresis separates molecules based on their size, with smaller DNA fragments moving faster than long ones. This process also concentrates DNA fragments of a similar size in one location in each gel, called a **band**. Concentrating DNA fragments of similar size in this way make it easy to visualize DNA after staining the DNA with a fluorescent dye such as **ethidium bromide** (Figure 8.12). By electrophoresing a mixture of DNA fragments of known size in adjacent lanes on the same gel, the length of an uncharacterized DNA fragment can be estimated. Bands can also be cut out of the gel, and the DNA in the band can be extracted and used in other types of reactions.

随着移动，每一条 DNA 在凝胶多聚物形成的空隙中穿过。因为短的片段通过空隙的速度比大的片段快，所以凝胶电泳可以基于片段的大小分离分子。电泳的过程也是凝聚相同大小的 DNA 片段在凝胶的一个位置，成为一条**带**。用这种方法将相同大小的 DNA 富集，再经如**溴化乙锭**的荧光染料染色后，DNA 就清晰可见（图 8.12）。通过邻近凝胶泳道电泳分离已知大小的 DNA 片段的混合物，可以估计未知 DNA 片段的大小。可以将凝胶中的条带切掉，提纯其中的 DNA 用于其他反应。

Figure 8.12 An agarose gel stained with ethidium bromide and illuminated by UV light. The stain associated with DNA is fluorescent (see the color figure)

图 8.12 用紫外灯照射溴化乙锭染色的琼脂糖凝胶。有 DNA 的凝胶发出荧光（见彩版）

DNA ANALYSIS: BLOTTING AND HYBRIDIZATION
DNA 分析：印迹和杂交

DNA only forms distinct bands in gel electrophoresis if most of the DNA molecules are of the same size, such as following

如果大多数 DNA 分子大小相同，如 PCR 产物，或者质粒酶切产物，凝

a PCR reaction, or restriction digestion of a plasmid. In other situations, such as after restriction digestion of chromosomal DNA, there will be so many molecules of so many different sizes, that the mixture will appear as a smear, rather than distinct bands. In this case, it is necessary to use additional techniques to detect the presence of a specific DNA sequence within the electrophoretic gel.

胶中能形成明显的 DNA 条带。另外，如果限制酶酶切染色体 DNA，就会形成许多大小不同的分子，混合物就会呈现弥散状，而不能区分出条带。在这种情况下，我们需要用另外的技术检测凝胶电泳中存在的特殊 DNA 序列。

In a **Southern blotting** (the technique is named after Ed Southern, its inventor), DNA that has been digested with restriction enzymes is separated by gel electrophoresis, and then a sheet of nylon or similar material is laid under the gel and the DNA is transferred to the nylon by drawing the liquid out of the gel, in a process called **blotting** (Figure 8.13). The blotted DNA is usually covalently attached to the nylon **membrane** by briefly exposing the blot to UV light. Transferring the DNA to the nylon is necessary be because the fragile gel would fall apart during the next steps in the process: **hybridization** and **washing**. For hybridization, a piece of DNA that is complementary in sequence to the target molecule is

在 **Southern 印迹**（这个技术是按照它的发明人 Ed Southern 命名的）中，DNA 经限制酶酶切后在凝胶上分离，然后将一张尼龙或类似材料的膜放在凝胶下，通过把液体拉出凝胶将 DNA 转移到尼龙膜上，这个过程叫做**印迹**（图 8.13）。DNA 印迹经紫外光下短暂曝光后可以共价地附着在尼龙膜上。将 DNA 转移到尼龙膜上是必需的，因为在随后的**杂交**和**洗涤**步骤中易断凝胶可能随时断裂破损。杂交时，将

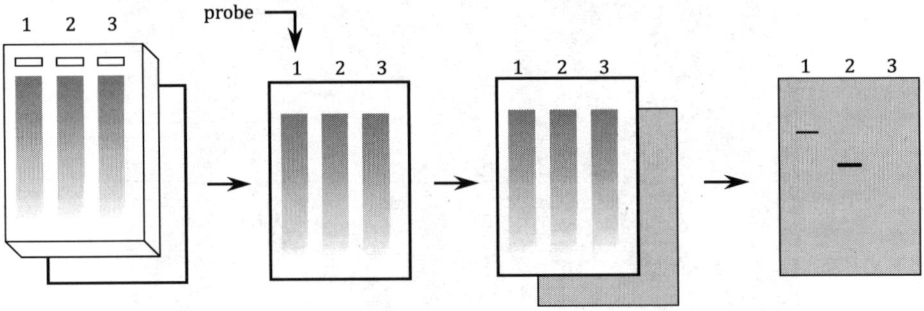

Figure 8.13 An example of Southern blotting. Genomic DNA that has been digested with a restriction enzyme is separated on an agarose gel, then the DNA is transferred from the gel to a nylon membrane (thick outline) by blotting. The DNA is immobilized on the membrane, then probed with a radioactively labeled DNA fragment that is complementary to a target sequence. After stringent washing, the blot is exposed to X-ray film to detect where the probe is bound. In this case, the probe bound to different-sized fragments in lanes 1 and 2, and no fragments in lane 3

图 8.13 Southern 印迹举例。基因组 DNA 酶切后在琼脂糖凝胶上分离，然后将 DNA 通过印迹转移到尼龙膜（粗边框）上。DNA 被固定在膜上，然后用放射性物质标记的 DNA 片段探测出与靶序列互补的 DNA 片段。经过严格的洗涤，将印迹在 X 线片上放射自显影，找出探针结合的部位。图中探针在 1、2 泳道与不同大小的片段结合，3 泳道中没有

labeled using fluorescent or radioactive molecules, and then this labeled **probe** is flooded over the surface of the nylon membrane prior to denaturing the DNA on the membrane.

目标分子序列互补的 DNA 片段用荧光或放射性分子标记，标记的**探针**（标记的 DNA 片段）在膜上 DNA 变性之前就会覆盖在尼龙膜的表面。

If the hybridization is performed properly, the probe DNA will form a stable helix only with those DNA molecules on the membrane that exactly match it, and the radioactive or fluorescent signal will appear in a distinct band after washing off the unbound probe. In this way, the presence of a particular DNA sequence within a mixture of DNA can be detected. The temperature of the hybridization and washing solutions is important to the **stringency** of the hybridization. At maximum stringency (higher temperature), probes will only hybridize with target sequences that are perfectly complementary and therefore form the maximum number of hydrogen bonds. At lower temperatures, probes will be able to hybridize to targets to which they do not match exactly.

如果杂交做得正确的话，探针 DNA 会和尼龙膜上准确匹配的 DNA 分子形成稳定的螺旋结构，在洗掉未结合的探针后放射性或荧光信号会呈现可区分的条带。通过这种途径，可以检测出混合 DNA 中是否存在的特定 DNA 序列。杂交和洗涤的温度对于杂交的**严谨性**是非常重要的。在最大的严谨性上（高温），探针只能和完全互补的靶序列杂交，因此形成最大数量的氢键。在较低的温度时，探针可能和不完全匹配的靶序列结合。

Southern blotting is useful when trying to detect the presence of a DNA sequence within a mixture of DNA molecules. Southern blotting was invented before PCR, and although PCR has replaced blotting in some applications, Southern blots are still useful when detecting fragments larger than those normally amplified by PCR, and when trying to detect fragments that may be only distantly related to a known sequence. Applications of Southern blotting will be discussed further in the context of molecular markers in a subsequent chapter.

当要检测混合 DNA 分子中存在的 DNA 序列时，Southern 印迹非常有用。它的发明早于 PCR 技术，尽管在许多应用中 PCR 技术取代了印迹法，但是当要检测的片段大于常规 PCR 技术扩增的片段时，或要检测序列与已知序列不相关时，Southern 印迹仍然有用。在以后的分子标记章节中 Southern 印迹的应用还要进一步讨论。

Following the development of the Southern blotting, other types of blotting techniques were invented, including the Northern blot (in which RNA is separated on a gel before probing), and the Western blot (protein is separated on a gel before probing with an antibody).

随着 Southern 印迹技术的发展，其他种类的印迹技术也相继出现，包括 Northern 印迹（在凝胶上分离 RNA，然后与探针结合），Western 印迹（在凝胶上分离蛋白质，然后与抗体探针结合）。

Summary

- Molecular biology involves the isolation and analysis of DNA and other macromolecules.
- 分子生物学包含 DNA 和其他大分子的分离与分析。

- Isolation of total genomic DNA involves separating DNA from protein and other cellular components, for example by ethanol precipitation of DNA.
- 分离基因组总 DNA 包括将 DNA 与蛋白质和细胞其他成分分开，如 DNA 的乙醇沉淀。

- PCR can be used as part of a sensitive method to detect the presence of a particular DNA sequence.
- PCR 技术可以用作检测特殊 DNA 序列是否存在的灵敏方法。

- PCR can also be used as part of a method to isolate and prepare large quantities of a particular DNA sequence.
- PCR 技术也可以作为分离和制备大量特殊 DNA 序列的方法。

- Restriction enzymes are natural endonucleases used in molecular biology to cut DNA sequences at specific sites.
- 限制酶是在分子生物学上用于在特异位点上切割 DNA 的天然的核酸内切酶。

- DNA fragments with compatible ends can be joined together through ligation. If the ligation produces a sequence not found in nature, the molecule is said to be recombinant.
- 通过连接可以将末端相匹配的 DNA 结合。如果连接产生了自然界中没有的分子，这个分子就叫做重组体。

- Transformation is the introduction of DNA (usually recombinant plasmids) into bacteria.
- 转化是 DNA 分子（通常是重组质粒）转入细菌的过程。

- Cloning of genes in *E. coli* is a common technique in molecular biology, since it allows large quantities of a DNA for gene to made, which allows further analysis or manipulation.
- 在大肠杆菌中克隆基因是分子生物学中的常规技术，因为它可以产生大量带有基因的 DNA 供以后分析和操作。

- Cloning can also be used to produce useful proteins, such as insulin, in microbes.
- 克隆可用来生产有用的蛋白质，如在微生物中生产胰岛素。

- Southern blotting can be used to detect the presence of any sequence that matches a probe, within a mixture of DNA (such as total genomic DNA).
- Southern 印迹可以用来检测任何与探针结合的，并且在混合 DNA（如总基因组 DNA）中存在的序列。

- The stringency of hybridization in blotting and in PCR is dependent on physical parameters such as temperature.
- 在印迹法和 PCR 中杂交的严谨性取决于物理参数，如温度。

Key Terms

macromolecules 大分子
lysis 裂解
detergent 清洁剂
chelating agent 螯合剂
EDTA 乙二胺四乙酸
nuclease 核酸酶
pellet 沉淀物
PCR 聚合酶链反应
primer 引物
thermal cycle 热循环
denature 变性
anneal 退火
extend 延伸
Taq DNApol *Taq* DNA 聚合酶
electrophoretic gel 电泳凝胶
restriction endonuclease 限制性内切核酸酶
*Eco*R Ⅰ
sticky end 黏性末端
blunt end 平末端
compatible end 互补末端
ligation 连接
ligase 连接酶
plasmid 质粒
transformation 转化
competent 感受态
electroporation 电转化
selectable marker 选择标记
agarose 琼脂糖
vector 载体
band 条带
ethidium bromide 溴化乙锭
Southern blotting Southern 印迹
membrane 膜
hybridization 杂交
washing 洗涤
probe 探针
stringency 严谨性
Northern blotting Northern 印迹
Western blotting Western 印迹

Study Questions

8.1 What information, and what reagents would you need to use PCR to detect HIV in a blood sample?

8.1 用 PCR 检测血样中的 HIV，需要什么信息和试剂？

8.2 A 6000bp PCR fragment flanked by recognition sites for the *Hind*Ⅲ restriction enzyme is cut with *Hind*Ⅲ then ligated with a 3kb plasmid vector that has also been cut with *Hind*Ⅲ. This recombinant plasmid is transformed into *E. coli* and a large preparation of plasmid is digested with *Hind*Ⅲ.

a) When the product of the *Hind*Ⅲ digestion is analyzed by gel electrophoresis, what will be the size of the bands observed?

b) What bands would be observed if the recombinant plasmid was cut with *Eco*R Ⅰ, which has only one site, directly in the middle of the PCR fragment?

8.2 一个两端具有 *Hind*Ⅲ 酶切位点的 6000bp 的 PCR 产物片段，用 *Hind*Ⅲ酶切后与一个也用 *Hind*Ⅲ酶切后的 3kb 质粒载体相连接。将重组质粒转化进大肠杆菌中并制备大量的质粒后，质粒用 *Hind*Ⅲ酶切。

a）在凝胶电泳上分析 *Hind*Ⅲ酶切产物时，会观察到哪些大小的条带？

b）重组体只有一个 *Eco*R Ⅰ 酶切位点，恰好在 PCR 产物中间，那么用 *Eco*R Ⅰ 酶切重组质粒会看到什么样的条带？

c) What bands would be observed if the recombinant plasmid was cut with both *Eco*R Ⅰ and *Hind*Ⅲ at the same time?

c）如果重组质粒同时用 *Eco*R Ⅰ 和 *Hind*Ⅲ双酶切，会看到什么样的带？

8.3 If you started with 10 molecules of double stranded DNA template, what is the maximum number of molecules you would you have after 10 PCR cycles?

8.3 如果开始用 10 个 DNA 分子作模板，完成 10 次 PCR 循环后能得到最大 DNA 的分子数是多少？

8.4 What is present in a PCR tube at the end of a reaction? With this in mind, why do you usually only see a single, sharp band on a gel when a successful PCR reaction is analyzed by electrophoresis?

8.4 在反应最后 PCR 管中有什么？如果是这样，那么为什么在凝胶电泳中分析一个成功的 PCR 反应时只看到一条清晰的条带？

8.5 A coat protein from a particular virus can be used to immunize children against further infection. However, inoculation of children with proteins extracted from natural viruses sometimes causes fatal disease, due to contamination with live viruses. How could you use molecular biology to produce an optimal vaccine?

8.5 特殊病毒的外壳蛋白可以使孩子获得免疫防止进一步感染。但是，接种从天然病毒提取的蛋白质却能引发疾病，因为污染了活体病毒。你如何应用分子生物学技术生产最佳疫苗呢？

8.6 How would cloning be different if there were no selectable markers?

8.6 如果没有选择标记，克隆会有什么不同呢？

8.7 You believe that a particular form of cancer is caused by a 200bp deletion in a particular human gene that is normally 2kb long.

a) Explain how you would use Southern blotting to diagnose the disease.

b) How would the blotting appear in a heterozygote?

c) How would the blotting appear in a homozygote with the deletion?

d) How would the blotting appear in a homozygote without the deletion?

e) How would any of the blots appear if you hybridized and washed at very low temperature?

8.7 一个特殊的人类基因正常是 2kb，你认为某种特殊癌症的形成是因为其中的 200bp 缺失。

a）解释你如何利用 Southern 印迹诊断这种疾病？

b）在杂合体中印迹是什么样的？

c）在缺失的纯合体中印迹是什么样的？

d）在没有缺失的纯合体中印迹是什么样的？

e）如果你在非常低的温度下杂交和洗涤，以上的任何一个杂交会是什么样的？

8.8 Refer to question 8.7.

a) Explain how you would detect the presence of the same deletion using PCR, rather than Southern blotting.

b) How would the results appear in a heterozygote?

c) How would the results appear in a homozygote with the

8.8 有关问题 8.7。

a）解释你如何利用 PCR 技术而不是Southern 印迹法检测这种缺失？

b）在杂合体中呈现什么结果？

c）在缺失的纯合体中呈现什么结

deletion?

d) How would the results appear in a homozygote without the deletion?

e) How would any of the blots appear if you annealed at very low temperature?

果？

d）在没有缺失的纯合体中呈现什么结果？

e）如果你的退火温度很低，以上印迹结果是什么样的？

8.9 You have a PCR fragment for a human olfactory receptor gene (perception of smells). You want to know what genes a dog might have that are related to this human gene. How can you use your PCR fragment and genomic DNA from a dog to find this out?

8.9 你有一个人类嗅觉受体基因的 PCR 片段（感受嗅觉的）。你想知道狗中与人类这个基因相关的基因。你如何利用这个 PCR 片段和来自狗的基因组 DNA 找到这个基因？

8.10 You mix ligase with a sticky-ended plasmid and stick-ended insert fragment, which both have compatible ends. Unbeknownst to you, someone in the lab left the stock of ligase enzyme out of the freezer and it no longer works. Explain in detail what will happen in your ligation experiment in this situation.

8.10 将连接酶和具有黏性末端的质粒及插入片段混合，两个黏性末端相匹配。你不知道实验室中有人将酶拿出冰箱而使酶失效了，解释在这种情况下你的连接实验会发生什么情况？

Chapter 9

MOLECULAR MARKERS AND QUANTITATIVE TRAITS

分子标记与数量性状

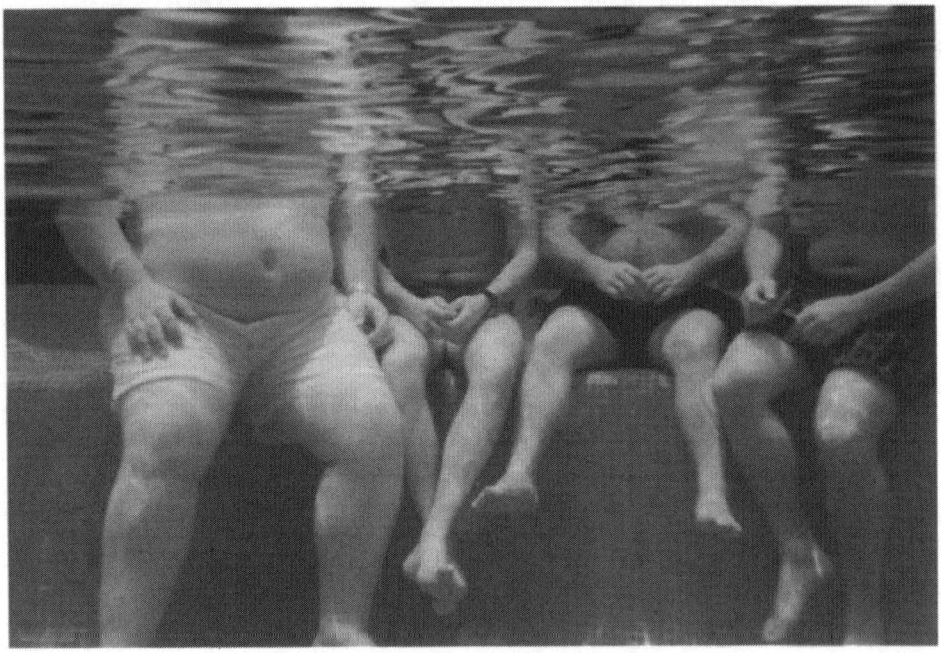

Many interesting traits, such as body mass, show continuous variation. Although environment obviously also affects this trait, some of the variation observed between individuals is heritable, and is dependent on interactions involving multiple genes. The study of quantitative traits is one of many applications of molecular markers

许多有趣的性状如体重显示了连续变异。尽管环境也明显地影响了这个性状，但是在个体之间观察到的一些变异是可遗传的，而且依靠多基因的相互作用。数量性状的研究也是分子标记的应用领域之一

Imagine that you could compare the complete DNA of any two people you meet today. Although their genomic DNA sequences would be very similar, they would not be identical at each of the 3 billion base pair positions you examined (unless, perhaps, your subjects were identical twins). In fact, the genomic sequences of almost any two unrelated people differ at millions of nucleotide positions. Some of these polymorphisms are found in the regions of genes that code for proteins. Other polymorphisms might affect the amount of transcript that is made for a particular gene. A person's health, appearance, behavior, and other characteristics depend in part on these polymorphisms. However, the vast majority of DNA polymorphisms have no effect on protein sequences, because they occur within regions of DNA that neither encode proteins, nor regulate the expression of genes. These polymorphisms are nevertheless very useful because they can be used as **molecular markers** in medicine, forensics, ecology, agriculture, and many other fields. In most situations, molecular markers obey the same rules of inheritance that we have already described for other types of loci, and so can be used to create genetic maps and to identify linked genes.

想象你能够比较今天你遇到的任何两个人的全部 DNA。尽管他们的基因组 DNA 序列会非常相似，但是你检测的 30 亿个碱基位置上的每个碱基也不会完全相同（除非或者也许你的实验对象是双胞胎）。事实上，几乎任何两个不相关的人的基因组序列在数以百万计的核苷酸位置上都会有所不同。在编码蛋白质的基因区域上可以发现一些这样的多态性。而其他的多态性也许会影响某一个特定基因的转录水平。一个人的健康、相貌、行为和其他特征在一定程度上取决于这些多态性。然而，绝大多数的 DNA 多态性对蛋白质序列没有影响，因为它们存在于既不编码蛋白质也不调控基因表达的 DNA 区域。然而这些多态性却是非常有用的，因为它们能够在医药、法医学、生态学、农业和许多其他领域作为**分子标记**使用。大多数情况下，分子标记遵循我们已经描述的与其他类型位点相同的遗传法则，所以也能够用分子标记建立遗传图谱和鉴定连锁基因。

ORIGINS OF MOLECULAR POLYMORPHISMS 分子多态性的起源

Mutations of DNA sequences can arise in many ways (Chapter 4). Some of these changes occur during DNA replication processes, resulting in an insertion, deletion, or substitution of one or a few nucleotides. Larger mutations can be caused by mobile genetic elements such as transposons, which are inserted more or less randomly into chromosomal DNA, sometimes occurring in clusters. In these and other types of **repetitive DNA** sequences, the number of repeated units is prone to change through unequal crossovers and other

DNA 序列能以多种方式发生突变（第 4 章）。一些变化发生在 DNA 的复制过程中，从而导致 DNA 插入、缺失或者一个或多个核苷酸的替换。移动的基因元件如转座子会导致更大的突变，它或多或少地被随机地插入到染色体 DNA 中，有时成簇出现。在这些和其他类型的**重复 DNA** 序列中，通过不均等交

rare events.

换和其他罕见情况很容易改变重复单元的数量。

CLASSIFICATION AND DETECTION OF MOLECULAR MARKERS
分子标记的分类和检测

Regardless of their origins, molecular markers can be classified as polymorphisms that either vary in the length of a DNA sequence, or vary only in the identity of nucleotides at a particular position on a chromosome (Figure 9.1). In both cases, because two or more alternative versions of the DNA sequence exist, we can treat each variant as a different allele of a single locus. Each allele gives a different molecular phenotype. For example, polymorphisms of **SSR** (short sequence repeat) can be distinguished based on the length of PCR products: one allele of a particular SSR locus might produce a 100bp band, while the same primers used with a different allele as a template might produce a 120bp band (Figure 9.2). A different type of marker, called a **SNP** (single nucleotide polymorphism), is an example of polymorphism that varies in nucleotide identity, but not length. SNPs occur at the highest density of any molecular markers, and the genotypes of thousands of SNP loci can be determined in parallel, using new, hybridization based instruments are one the of the most common types of Note that the alleles of most molecular markers are co-dominant, since it is possible to distinguish the phenotype of a heterozygote from either homozygote.

不考虑分子标记的来源，分子标记多态性能够根据 DNA 序列长度不同或者仅仅是染色体上某一特定位置核苷酸的不同进行分类（图 9.1）。在上述两种情况下，因为两个或者多个不同DNA序列的存在，我们能够把每个变异作为在某个单独位点上的一个不同的等位基因。每个等位基因都有不同的分子表现型。例如，**SSR**（简单重复序列）的多态性能够根据 PCR 产物的长度被区别开来；某个特定的 SSR 位点的一个等位基因也许会产生一个 100bp 的条带，而相同的引物用于一个不同的等位基因模板也许会产生一个 120bp 的条带（图 9.2）。另外一个不同类型的标记被称为 **SNP**（单核苷酸多态性），是核苷酸碱基类型而非长度的多态性的一个例子。SNP 是发生密度最高的分子标记，并且使用最常见类型的、新的、基于杂交的设备能够平行地鉴定出数千个 SNP 位点的基因型。值得注意的是，大多数分子标记的等位基因是共显性的，因为可以将一个杂合体的表现型和任意一个纯合体区分开。

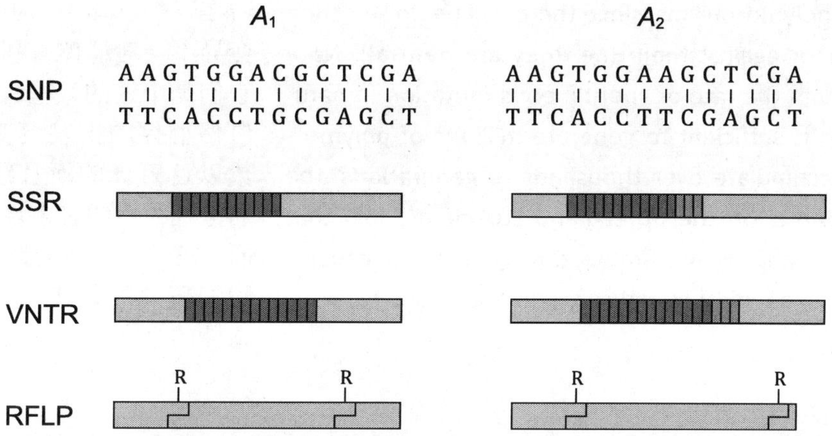

Figure 9.1 Some examples of DNA polymorphisms. The variant region is marked in blue, and each variant sequence is arbitrarily assigned one of two allele labels. Abbreviations: SNP (single nucleotide polymorphism); SSR (simple sequence repeat) = SSLP (simple sequence length polymorphism); VNTR (variable number of tandem repeats); RFLP (restriction fragment length polymorphisms. VNTRs and SSR differ in the size of the repeat unit; VNTR are larger than SSR (see the color figure)

图 9.1 DNA 多态性的一些例子。变异区域被标记成蓝色，并且每个变异序列随机地定为两个等位基因中的一个。缩写：SNP（单核苷酸多态性）；SSR（简单重复序列）=SSLP(简单序列长度多态性)；VNTR（可变数目串联重复序列）；RFLP（限制性片段长度多态性）。VNTR 与 SSR 在重复单元大小上不同；VNTR 重复单元比 SSR 大（见彩版）

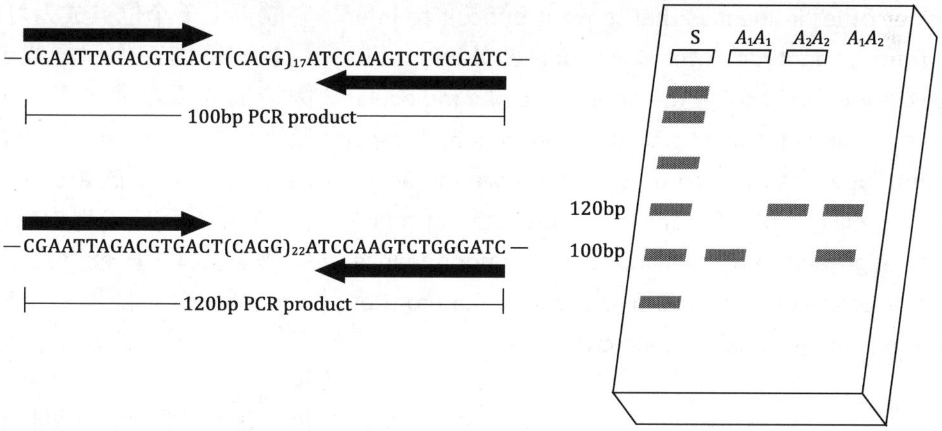

Figure 9.2 Determining the genotype of an individual at a single SSR locus using a specific pair of PCR primers and agarose gel electrophoresis. S= size standard

图 9.2 用一对特异的 PCR 引物和琼脂糖凝胶电泳决定在某一 SSR 位点的个体基因型。S=分子质量标准

Mutations that do not affect the function of protein sequences or gene expression are likely to be retained in a

不会影响蛋白质功能或者基因表达的变异有可能作为多态性被保

population as polymorphisms, since there will be no selection either in favor or against them (i.e. they are **neutral**). Note that the although the rate of spontaneous mutation in natural populations is sufficient to generate millions of polymorphisms that accumulate over thousands of generations, the rate of mutation is on the other hand sufficiently low that existing polymorphisms are stable throughout the generations we study in a typical genetic experiment.

留在一个群体中，因为选择这样的变异不会对群体有利或者有害（即它们是**中性的**）。要注意到，尽管自然群体的自发突变率足以产生数以百万计的而且经过数以千计的世代积累的多态性，但是另一方面，在一个典型的遗传实验中，在我们研究的数代中产生稳定的多态性的突变率还是很低的。

APPLICATIONS OF MOLECULAR MARKERS 分子标记的应用

Several characteristics of molecular markers make them useful to geneticists. Because of the way DNA polymorphisms arise and are retained, they are present at high density throughout the genome. Because they are phenotypically neutral, they can also be highly polymorphic, meaning that it is relatively easy to find markers that differ between two individuals. The neutrality of molecular markers makes it possible to study hundreds of loci without worrying about gene interactions or other influences that make it difficult to infer genotype from phenotype. Moreover, unlike visible traits such as eye color or petal color, the phenotype of a molecular marker can be detected in any tissue or developmental stage, and the same type of assay can be used to score molecular phenotypes at millions of different loci. Thus, the neutrality, high density, high degree of polymorphism, co-dominance, and ease of detection of molecular markers have lead to their wide adoption in many areas of research.

分子标记的几个特征对遗传学家是相当有用的。因为 DNA 多态性的出现和保留方式，使得它们在整个基因组中的密度相当大。因为它们在表现型上是中性的且具有很高的多态性，这意味着能够相对容易地找到在两个个体之间不同的标记。分子标记的中性使得我们研究成百上千个位点成为可能，而不用担心基因互作问题或者其他原因造成的很难通过表现型来推断基因型的问题。并且，不像看得见的性状，如眼睛的颜色或花瓣的颜色，分子标记的表现型能在任何组织或者发育阶段被检测到，并且同一类型的分析能够用于检测在数以百万计不同位点上的分子表现型。因此，分子标记的中性、高密度、高度多态性、共显性和易于检测性等众多特点使得分子标记在许多研究领域都有广泛的应用。

It is worth emphasizing again that DNA polymorphisms are a natural part of most genomes. Geneticists discover these polymorphisms in various ways, including comparison of random DNA sequence fragments from several individuals

值得再一次强调的是，DNA 多态性是大多数基因组的自然组成部分。遗传学家通过各种方式发现这些多态性，包括在一个群体中几个个

in a population. Once molecular markers have been identified, they can be used in many ways.

体的随机 DNA 片段序列的比较。一旦分子标记被确定，它们就能被应用在许多方面。

DNA fingerprinting DNA 指纹图谱

By comparing the genotypes of several molecular markers, it is possible to determine the relationship between two DNA samples. For example, a forensic scientist can demonstrate that some of the blood on a weapon came from a particular suspect, or even that leaves in the back of a suspect's pick-up truck came from a particular tree at a crime scene (Figure 9.3). DNA fingerprinting is also useful in paternity testing and in commercial applications such as verification of species of origin of certain foods and herbal medicines.

通过比较几个分子标记的基因型，很容易确定两个 DNA 样本之间的关系。例如，一个法医科学家能够证实武器上的一些血是否来自于某个特定嫌疑犯，或者甚至可以证明在嫌疑犯的轻运货车后面的树叶是否来自于犯罪现场的某一棵树（图 9.3）。DNA 指纹图谱技术能够用于亲子鉴定；在商业应用上，如确认某种食品和草药的起源物种，也可以应用这项技术。

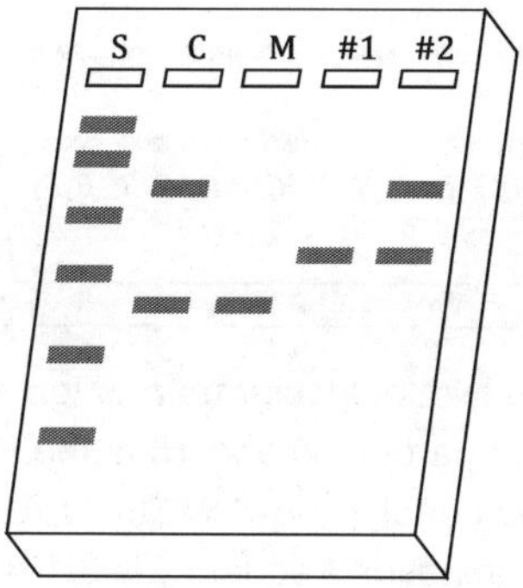

Figure 9.3 Paternity testing. Given the molecular phenotype of the child (C) and mother (M), only one of the possible fathers (#2) has alleles that are consistent with the child's phenotype

图 9.3 亲子鉴定。基于孩子 (C) 和母亲 (M)的分子表现型，两个可能的父亲中仅有一个父亲(#2)具有与孩子的表现型一致的等位基因

Construction of genetic linkage maps 基因连锁图谱的构建

By calculating the recombination frequency between pairs of molecular markers, a map of each chromosome can be generated for almost any organism (Figure 9.4). These maps are calculated using the same mapping techniques described for genes in Chapter 7, however, the high density and ease with which molecular markers can be genotyped makes them more useful than other phenotypes for constructing genetic maps. These maps are useful in further studies, including map-based cloning of protein coding genes that were identified by mutation.

通过计算数对分子标记之间的重组率，几乎能建立任何一个生物体上每个染色体的图谱（图 9.4）。通过与第 7 章中描述用于基因的相同作图技术能够作出这些图谱，然而，由于具有高密度和简易性等特点，在构建基因图谱上，分子标记被作为基因型比使用其他表现型更加实用。这些图谱在未来的研究中非常有用，包括通过突变鉴定出来的编码蛋白基因的图位克隆。

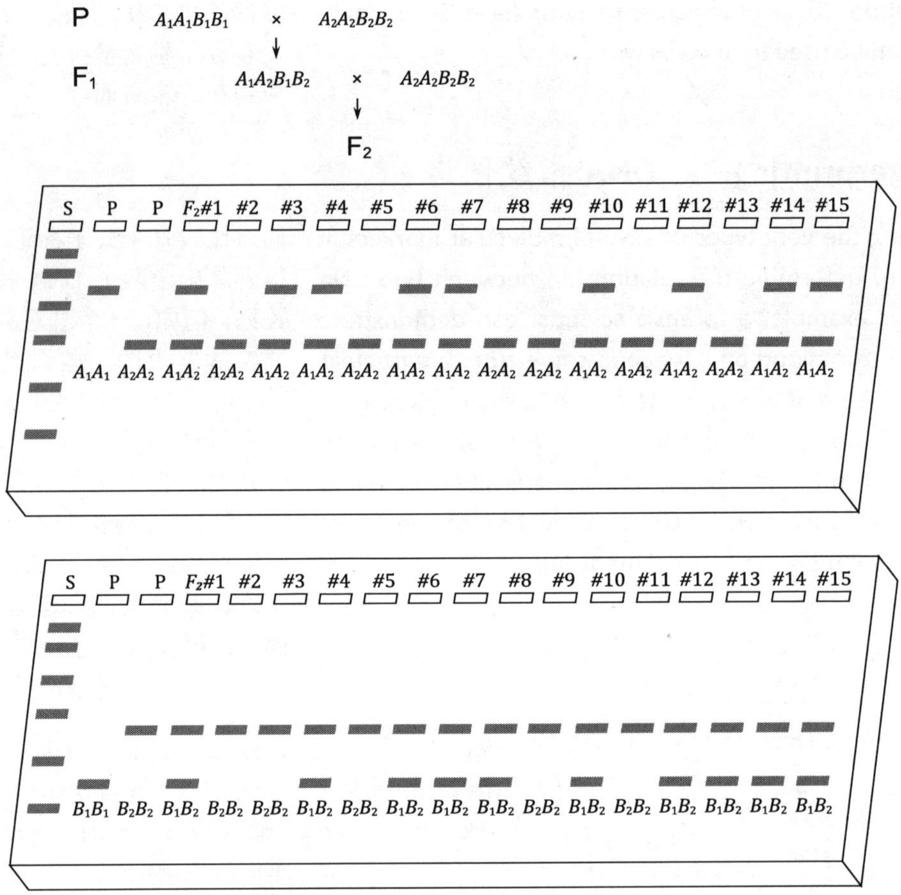

Figure 9.4 Measuring recombination frequency between two molecular marker loci, *A* and *B*. A different pair of primers is used to amplify DNA from either parent (P) and 15 of the F_2 offspring from the cross shown. Recombinant progeny will have the genotype $A_1A_2B_2B_2$ or $A_2A_2B_1B_2$. Individuals #3, #8, #13 are recombinant, so the recombination frequency is 3/15=20%

图 9.4 测定 *A* 和 *B* 两个分子标记位点之间的重组率。如图所示，用一对不同的引物来扩增亲本(P)和 15 个 F_2 杂交后代的 DNA 样本。重组后代有基因型 $A_1A_2B_2B_2$ 或 $A_2A_2B_1B_2$。个体#3、#8、#13 是重组体，所以重组率是 3/15=20%

Population studies 群体研究

As described in Chapter 5, the observed frequency of alleles, including alleles of molecular markers, can be compared to frequencies expected for populations in Hardy-Weinberg equilibrium to determine whether the population is in equilibrium. By monitoring molecular markers, ecologists and wildlife biologists can make inferences about migration, selection, diversity, and other population-level parameters. Molecular markers can also be used by anthropologists to

如第 5 章所述，已经观察到的等位基因的频率，包括分子标记的等位基因，与 Hardy-Weinberg 平衡定律中群体的期望频率相比较来决定群体是否处于平衡之中。通过追踪分子标记，生态学家和野生生物学家能够推理出关于迁移、选择、物种多样性和其他群体水平参数。人

study migration events in human ancestry.

类学家可以利用分子标记来研究人类祖先的迁移情况。

Identification of linked traits 连锁性状的鉴定

It is often possible to identify an allele of a molecular marker whose presence is correlated with a particular disease or other trait of interest. One way to make this correlation is to obtain genomic DNA samples from hundreds of individuals with a particular disease, as well as samples from a control population of healthy individuals. The genotype of each individual is scored at hundreds or thousands of molecular marker loci (e.g. SNP), to find alleles that are usually present in persons with the disease, but not in healthy subjects. The molecular marker is presumed to be tightly linked to the gene that causes the disease, although this protein-coding gene may itself be unknown. The presence of a particular molecular polymorphism may therefore be used to diagnose a disease, or to advise an individual of susceptibility to a disease.

我们常常能够鉴定出一个与特定疾病或者其他感兴趣的性状相关的分子标记等位基因，获得这种相关性的途径之一是从患有某种特定疾病的数百个个体中和作为对照组的健康个体的群体中获取基因组 DNA 样品。每个个体的基因型用成百个或者上千个分子标记位点进行标记（如 SNP），来找到通常存在于患病个体而不存在健康个体的等位基因。分子标记被认为与导致这种疾病的基因紧密连锁，尽管这个编码蛋白的基因本身是未知的。因此某种分子多态性的存在能够被用来诊断疾病，或者报道某一个体对这种病的易感性。

Molecular markers may also be used in a similar way in agriculture. For example, markers associated with desirable traits can be identified by screening both the traits and molecular marker genotypes of hundreds of individuals. Markers that are linked to desirable traits can then be used during breeding to select varieties with economically useful combinations of traits, even when the genes underlying the traits are not known.

分子标记也可以类似地应用在农业中。例如，通过筛选数百个个体的性状和分子标记基因型能够鉴定出与目标性状连锁的标记，在育种中，即使构成性状的基因是未知的，也可以通过与目标性状连锁的标记来选择具有优异经济性状组合的品种。

Quantitative trait locus (QTL) mapping 数量性状位点（QTL）图谱

Molecular markers can be used to identify regions of chromosomes that contain genes that act together to produce complex traits. This process involves finding combinations of alleles of molecular markers that are correlated with a quantitative phenotype such as body mass, or intelligence. QTL mapping is described in more detail in the following section.

使用分子标记能够鉴定出共同作用进而产生复杂性状的含有多个基因的染色体区域。这个过程包括发现与数量性状，如体重或智力等表现型有关的分子标记的等位基因组合。在下面的部分将更加详细地描述 QTL 作图。

QUANTITATIVE TRAIT LOCUS ANALYSIS 数量性状位点分析

Most of the phenotypic traits commonly used in introductory genetics are qualitative, meaning that the phenotype exists in only two (or possibly a few more) alternative forms, such as either purple or white flowers, or red or white eyes. These qualitative traits are therefore said to exhibit **discrete variation**. On the other hand, many interesting and important traits exhibit **continuous variation**; these exhibit a continuous range of phenotypes that are usually measured quantitatively, such as intelligence, body mass, blood pressure in animals including humans, and yield, water use, or vitamin content in crops. Traits with continuous variation are often complex, and do not show the simple Mendelian segregation ratios (e.g. 3 ∶ 1) observed with some qualitative traits. Many complex traits are also influenced heavily by the environment. Nevertheless, complex traits can often be shown to have a component that is heritable, and which must therefore involve one or more genes.

在入门遗传学中普遍应用的大多数表现型性状是质量性状的，意味着表现型仅仅存在两种（或者也可能几种）可选择的形式，如不是紫花就是白花，不是红眼就是白眼。这些质量性状因此表现为**不连续变异**。但是，许多有趣和重要的性状则表现出**连续变异**；这些表现通常是在数量上测量出的连续的表现型范围，如动物（包括人类在内）的智力、体重、血压和作物的产量、用水量或者维生素含量等。连续变异的性状通常是复杂的，不能显示出在一些质量性状上观察到的简单的孟德尔分离比率（如 3∶1）。许多复杂的性状受环境影响很大。然而，复杂性状有时显现出某一部分是可遗传的，因此必然与一个或者多个基因有关。

How can genes, which are inherited (in the case of a diploid) as at most two variants each, explain the wide range of continuous variation observed for many traits? The lack of an immediately obvious explanation to this question was one of the early objections to Mendel's explanation of the mechanisms of heredity. However, upon further consideration, it becomes clear that the more loci that contribute to trait, the more phenotypic classes may be observed for that trait (Figure 9.5). If the number of phenotypic classes is sufficiently large, individual classes may become indistinguishable from each other (particularly when environmental effects are included), and the result is continuous variation (Figure 9.6). Thus, quantitative traits are sometimes called **polygenic traits**, because it is assumed that their phenotypes are controlled by the combined activity of many genes. Note that

在遗传上至多有两个变量的基因（以二倍体为例），那么怎么解释许多已观察到的性状在大范围内的连续变异呢？缺乏对这个问题的明确迅速的解释是早期很多人反对孟德尔遗传机制的原因之一。然而，通过进一步思考，很显然与性状有关的位点越多，这个性状观察到的表现型类型也就越多（图 9.5）。如果表现型类型的数量足够大，个体之间也会很难分类（特别是当环境影响也被包括进去时），结果就是连续变异（图 9.6）。因此，数量性状有时也被称为**多基因性状**，因为数量性状被认为它们的表

	A	a
A	AA	Aa
a	Aa	aa

	AB	Ab	aB	ab
AB	AABB	AABb	AaBB	AaBb
Ab	AABb	AAbb	AaBb	Aabb
aB	AaBB	AaBb	aaBB	aaBb
ab	AaBb	Aabb	aaBb	aabb

	ABC	ABc	AbC	Abc	aBC	aBc	abC	abc
ABC	AABBCC	AABBCc	AABbCC	AABbCc	AaBBCC	AaBBCc	AaBbCC	AaBbCc
ABc	AABBCc	AABBcc	AABbCc	AABbcc	AaBBCc	AaBBcc	AaBbCc	AaBbcc
AbC	AABbCC	AABbCc	AAbbCC	AAbbCc	AaBbCC	AaBbCc	AabbCC	AabbCc
Abc	AABbCc	AABbcc	AAbbCc	AAbbcc	AaBbCc	AaBbcc	AabbCc	Aabbcc
aBC	AaBBCC	AaBBCc	AaBbCC	AaBbCc	aaBBCC	aaBBCc	aaBbCC	aaBbCc
aBc	AaBBCc	AaBBcc	AaBbCc	AaBbcc	aaBBCc	aaBBcc	aaBbCc	aabbCc
abC	AaBbCC	AaBbCc	AabbCC	AabbCc	aaBbCC	aaBbCc	aabbCC	aabbCc
abc	AaBbCc	AaBbcc	AabbCc	Aabbcc	aaBbCc	aaBbcc	aabbCc	aabbcc

Figure 9.5 Punnett Squares for one, two, or three loci. We are using a simplified example of up to three semi-dominant genes, and in each case the effect on the phenotype is additive, meaning the more “upper case” alleles present, the stronger the phenotype. Comparison of the Punnett Squares and the associated phenotypes shows that under these conditions, the larger the number of genes that affect a trait, the more intermediate phenotypic classes that will be expected (see the color figure)

图 9.5 在旁氏棋盘法中表示 1 个、2 个或者 3 个位点。我们使用 1 个到 3 个主效基因的简化例子，并且在每种情况下这 3 个基因对表现型的影响是加性的，意味着越多“大写”等位基因存在，表现型越强。比较旁氏棋盘方格和相关的表现型，在这些条件下影响一个性状的基因数目越多，就会有越多期望的中间表现型类型（见彩版）

this does not imply that each of the individual genes has an equal influence on a polygenic trait. Furthermore, any give gene may influence more than one trait, whether these traits are quantitative or qualitative traits.

现型是受多基因的综合作用所决定的。注意这并不是指每一个基因对一个多基因性状有均等的影响。此外，任何一个特定的基因也许会影响一个以上的性状，无论这些性状是数量性状还是质量性状。

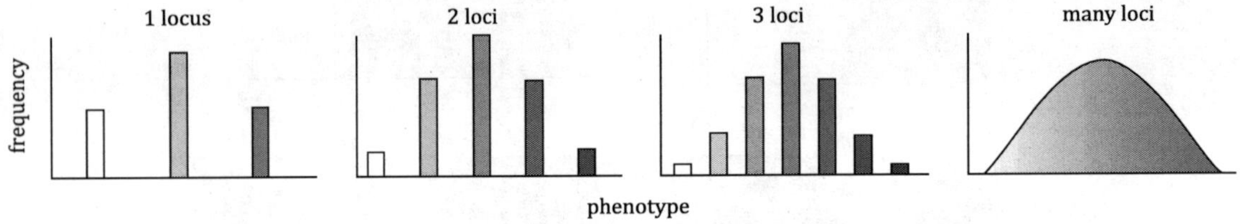

Figure 9.6 The more loci that affect a trait, the larger the number of phenotypic classes that can be expected. For some traits, the number of contributing loci is so large that the phenotypic classes blend together in apparently continuous variation (see the color figure)

图 9.6 影响一个性状的位点越多，预期表现型类型的数目就越多。对于一些性状，相关位点的数目很多以至于表现型类型融合在一起呈现出明显的连续变异（见彩版）

We can use molecular markers to identify at least some of the genes that affect a given quantitative trait. This is essentially an extension of the mapping techniques we have already considered for discrete traits. A QTL mapping experiment will ideally start with two pure-breeding lines that differ greatly from each other in respect to one or more quantitative traits (Figure 9.7). The parents and all of their progeny should be raised in under similar environmental conditions, to ensure that observed variation is due to genetic rather than external factors. These parental lines must also be polymorphic for a large number of molecular loci, meaning that they must have different alleles from each other at hundreds of loci. The parental lines are crossed, and then this F_1 individual, in which recombination between parental chromosomes has occurred is self-fertilized (or back-crossed). Because of recombination, each of the F_2 individuals will contain a different combination of molecular markers, and also a different combination of alleles for the genes that control the quantitative trait of interest (Table 9.1). By comparing the molecular marker genotypes of several hundred F_2 individuals with their quantitative phenotypes, a researcher can iden-

我们至少能用分子标记鉴定影响某一数量性状的一部分基因。这主要是进一步使用我们在不连续性状上应用的作图技术。一个 QTL 作图试验最好从两个在一个或多个数量性状上有很大差别的纯育系开始（图 9.7）。亲本和它们的所有后代应该在相似的环境条件下成长，从而确保观察到的变异是由于遗传而非外部因素造成的。这些亲本也必须在许多分子位点上是具有多态性的，也就是说必须在数百个位点上有不同的等位基因。亲本杂交，然后获得 F_1 代个体，亲本染色体的重组是通过 F_1 代自交（或者回交）发生的。由于重组，F_2 代的每个个体都会有一个不同的分子标记组合，也是一个控制目标数量性状的不同等位基因组合（表 9.1）。通过比较几百个 F_2 代个体的分子标记基因型和数量性

tify molecular markers for which the presence of particular alleles is always associated with extreme values of the trait (Figure 9.8). In this way, regions of chromosomes that contain genes that contribute to quantitative traits can be identified. It then takes much more work (further mapping and other experimentation) to identify the individual genes in each of the regions that control the quantitative trait.

状的表现型，一个研究者能够鉴定出总是与性状极值连锁的特定等位基因的分子标记（图 9.8）。通过这种方式，含有与数量性状相关基因的染色体区域能够被鉴定出来。要鉴定出控制数量性状的每个区域的单个基因，还要进行更多的工作（进一步作图和其他实验）。

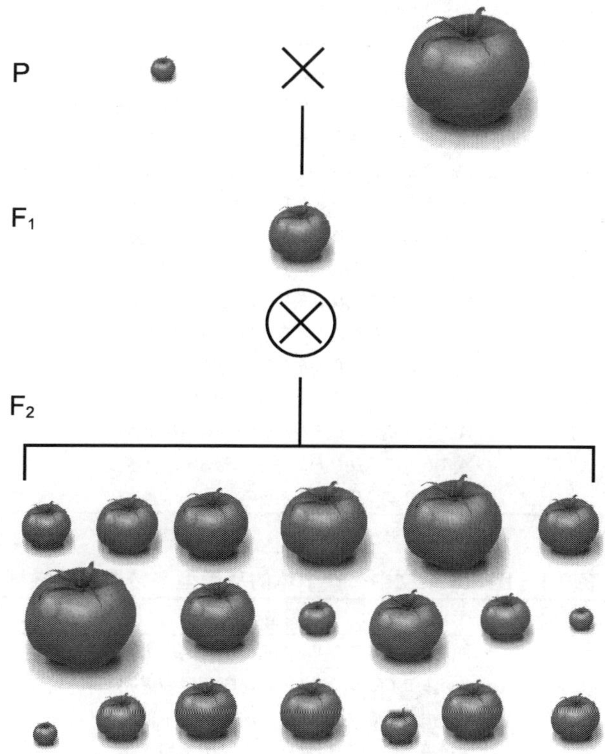

Figure 9.7 Strategy for a typical QTL mapping experiment. Two parents that differ in a quantitative trait (e.g. fruit mass) are crossed, and the F_1 is self-fertilized (as shown by the cross-in-circle symbol). The F_2 progeny will show a range of quantitative values for the trait. The task is then to identify alleles of markers from one parent that are strongly correlated with the quantitative trait. For example, markers from the large-fruit parent that are always present in large-fruit F_2 individuals (but never in small-fruit individuals) are likely linked to loci that control fruit mass

图 9.7 一个典型的 QTL 作图试验策略。数量性状（如果实质量）不同的两个亲本进行杂交，F_1 代进行自交（用中间带有叉号的圆表示）。F_2 代会显示出这个性状的一个数值范围。接下来的任务就是确定出来源于一个亲本、与数量性状紧密连锁的标记等位基因。例如，总是存在于大果 F_2 个体（绝不存在于小果个体中）中来源于大果亲本的标记很可能与控制果实质量的位点连锁

Table 9.1 Genotypes and quantitative data for some individuals from the crosses shown in Figure 9.8

	genotype	fruit mass
P	$A_1A_1B_1B_1C_1C_1D_1D_1E_1E_1F_1F_1G_1G_1H_1H_1J_1J_1K_1K_1$	10g
P	$A_2A_2B_2B_2C_2C_2D_2D_2E_2E_2F_2F_2G_2G_2H_2H_2J_2J_2K_2K_2$	90g
F_1	$A_1A_2B_1B_2C_1C_2D_1D_2E_1E_2F_1F_2G_1G_2H_1H_2J_1J_2K_1K_2$	50g
F_2 #001	$A_1A_1B_1B_2C_1C_1D_2D_2E_1E_2F_1F_2G_1G_2H_1H_1J_1J_2K_1K_2$	80g
F_2 #002	$A_1A_2B_1B_2C_1C_2D_1D_1E_1E_2F_1F_2G_2G_2H_1H_2J_2J_2K_1K_1$	10g
F_2 #003	$A_2A_2B_1B_2C_2C_2D_1D_2E_1E_2F_1F_2G_1G_1H_1H_2J_1J_2K_1K_2$	50g
F_2 #004	$A_1A_2B_1B_2C_1C_2D_1D_2E_1E_2F_1F_2G_1G_2H_1H_2J_1J_2K_2K_2$	60g
F_2 #005	$A_1A_2B_1B_1C_1C_2D_2D_2E_1E_2F_1F_2G_1G_2H_1H_2J_1J_1K_2K_2$	90g
F_2 #006	$A_1A_2B_2B_2C_1C_2D_1D_2E_1E_2F_1F_2G_2G_2H_1H_2J_1J_2K_1K_2$	60g
F_2 #007	$A_2A_2B_1B_1C_1C_2D_2D_2E_1E_2F_1F_2G_1G_1H_1H_2J_1J_1K_1K_2$	80g
F_2 #008	$A_1A_1B_1B_2C_1C_2D_1D_2E_1E_2F_1F_2G_1G_2H_1H_2J_1J_2K_1K_2$	50g
F_2 #009	$A_1A_2B_1B_2C_2C_2D_1D_2E_1E_2F_1F_2G_1G_2H_1H_2J_1J_2K_1K_2$	50g
F_2 #010	$A_1A_2B_1B_2C_1C_2D_1D_2E_1E_2F_1F_2G_1G_2H_1H_2J_1J_2K_2K_2$	30g
F_2 #011	$A_1A_2B_1B_2C_1C_2D_2D_2E_1E_1F_1F_2G_1G_2H_1H_2J_1J_2K_1K_2$	80g
F_2 #012	$A_1A_1B_1B_2C_1C_2D_1D_1E_1E_2F_2F_2G_1G_2H_1H_2J_1J_2K_2K_2$	30g
F_2 #013	$A_2A_2B_1B_1C_1C_2D_1D_1E_1E_2F_1F_1G_1G_2H_2H_2J_1J_1K_1K_1$	10g
F_2 #014	$A_2A_2B_1B_1C_1C_1D_2D_2E_1E_2F_1F_2G_1G_2H_1H_2J_1J_1K_1K_1$	70g
F_2 #015	$A_2A_2B_2B_2C_1C_2D_1D_2E_1E_2F_2F_2G_1G_2H_1H_1J_2J_2K_1K_2$	40g
F_2 #016	$A_1A_2B_2B_2C_1C_2D_1D_1E_1E_2F_1F_1G_2G_2H_1H_1J_1J_2K_1K_1$	10g
F_2 #017	$A_1A_2B_2B_2C_1C_2D_2D_2E_2E_2F_1F_1G_2G_2H_1H_2J_1J_2K_2K_2$	90g
F_2 #018	$A_1A_2B_2B_2C_1C_2D_1D_2E_1E_2F_1F_1G_2G_2H_1H_2J_1J_2K_1K_1$	40g
F_2 #019	$A_1A_1B_1B_2C_1C_2D_1D_1E_1E_2F_2F_2G_1G_2H_1H_1J_1J_2K_1K_2$	20g
F_2 #100	$A_1A_1B_1B_2C_1C_2D_2D_2E_1E_2F_1F_2G_2G_2H_1H_2J_2J_2K_1K_2$	80g

表 9.1 图 9.8 杂交中一些个体的基因型和数量性状数据

	基因型	果实质量
P	$A_1A_1B_1B_1C_1C_1D_1D_1E_1E_1F_1F_1G_1G_1H_1H_1J_1J_1K_1K_1$	10g
P	$A_2A_2B_2B_2C_2C_2D_2D_2E_2E_2F_2F_2G_2G_2H_2H_2J_2J_2K_2K_2$	90g
F_1	$A_1A_2B_1B_2C_1C_2D_1D_2E_1E_2F_1F_2G_1G_2H_1H_2J_1J_2K_1K_2$	50g
F_2 #001	$A_1A_1B_1B_2C_1C_1D_2D_2E_1E_2F_1F_2G_1G_2H_1H_1J_1J_2K_1K_2$	80g
F_2 #002	$A_1A_2B_1B_2C_1C_2D_1D_1E_1E_2F_1F_2G_2G_2H_1H_2J_2J_2K_1K_1$	10g
F_2 #003	$A_2A_2B_1B_2C_2C_2D_1D_2E_1E_2F_1F_2G_1G_1H_1H_2J_1J_2K_1K_2$	50g
F_2 #004	$A_1A_2B_1B_2C_1C_2D_1D_2E_1E_2F_1F_2G_1G_2H_1H_2J_1J_2K_2K_2$	60g
F_2 #005	$A_1A_2B_1B_1C_1C_2D_2D_2E_1E_2F_1F_2G_1G_2H_1H_2J_1J_1K_2K_2$	90g
F_2 #006	$A_1A_2B_2B_2C_1C_2D_1D_2E_1E_2F_1F_2G_2G_2H_1H_2J_1J_2K_1K_2$	60g
F_2 #007	$A_2A_2B_1B_1C_1C_2D_2D_2E_1E_2F_1F_2G_1G_1H_1H_2J_1J_1K_1K_2$	80g
F_2 #008	$A_1A_1B_1B_2C_1C_2D_1D_2E_1E_2F_1F_2G_1G_2H_1H_2J_1J_2K_1K_2$	50g
F_2 #009	$A_1A_2B_1B_2C_2C_2D_1D_2E_1E_2F_1F_2G_1G_2H_1H_2J_1J_2K_1K_2$	50g
F_2 #010	$A_1A_2B_1B_2C_1C_2D_1D_2E_1E_2F_1F_2G_1G_2H_1H_2J_1J_2K_2K_2$	30g
F_2 #011	$A_1A_2B_1B_2C_1C_2D_2D_2E_1E_1F_1F_2G_1G_2H_1H_2J_1J_2K_1K_2$	80g
F_2 #012	$A_1A_1B_1B_2C_1C_2D_1D_1E_1E_2F_2F_2G_1G_2H_1H_2J_1J_2K_2K_2$	30g
F_2 #013	$A_2A_2B_1B_1C_1C_2D_1D_1E_1E_2F_1F_1G_1G_2H_2H_2J_1J_1K_1K_1$	10g
F_2 #014	$A_2A_2B_1B_1C_1C_1D_2D_2E_1E_2F_1F_2G_1G_2H_1H_2J_1J_1K_1K_1$	70g
F_2 #015	$A_2A_2B_2B_2C_1C_2D_1D_2E_1E_2F_2F_2G_1G_2H_1H_1J_2J_2K_1K_2$	40g
F_2 #016	$A_1A_2B_2B_2C_1C_2D_1D_1E_1E_2F_1F_1G_2G_2H_1H_1J_1J_2K_1K_1$	10g

续表

	基因型	果实质量
F_2 #017	$A_1A_2B_2B_2C_1C_2D_2D_2E_2E_2F_1F_1G_2G_2H_1H_2J_1J_2K_2K_2$	90g
F_2 #018	$A_1A_2B_2B_2C_1C_2D_1D_2E_1E_2F_1F_1G_2G_2H_1H_2J_1J_2K_1K_1$	40g
F_2 #019	$A_1A_1B_1B_2C_1C_2D_1D_1E_1E_2F_2F_2G_1G_1H_1H_1J_1J_2K_1K_2$	20g
F_2 #100	$A_1A_1B_1B_2C_1C_2D_2D_2E_1E_2F_1F_2G_2G_2H_1H_2J_2J_2K_1K_2$	80g

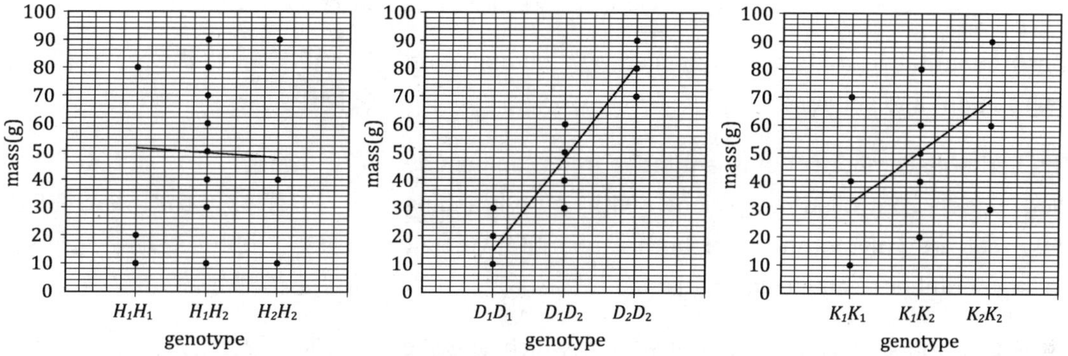

Figure 9.8 Plots of fruit mass and genotype for selected loci from Table 9.1. For most loci (e.g. *H*), the genotype shows no significant correlation with fruit weight. However, for some molecular markers, the genotype will be highly correlated with fruit weight. Both *D* and *K* influence fruit weight, but the effect of genotype at locus *D* is larger than at locus *K*.

图 9.8 表 9.1 中被选位点的果实质量和基因型的坐标图。对大多数位点（如 *H*），基因型显示出与果实质量没有显著相关性。然而，对于一些分子标记，基因型与果实质量紧密相关。*D* 和 *K* 都影响果实质量，但是位点 *D* 的基因型的影响比位点 *K* 大

Summary

- Natural variations in the length or identity of DNA sequences occur at millions of locations throughout most genomes.

- 在大多数基因组中数以百万计的位点存在着 DNA 长度和序列的自然变异。

- DNA polymorphisms are often neutral, but because of linkage may be used as molecular markers to identify regions of genomes that contain genes of interest.

- DNA 多态性经常是中性的，但是由于连锁的原因，DNA 多态性可以用作分子标记来鉴定包含感兴趣基因的基因组区域。

- Molecular markers are useful because of their neutrality, co-dominance, density, allele frequencies, ease of detection, and expression in all tissues.

- 分子标记是有用的，因为它具有中性、共显性、密度、等位基因频率、易于检测和能在所有组织中检测等特点。

- Molecular markers can be used for any application in which the identity of two DNA samples is to be compared, or

- 分子标记能够被用来比较两个 DNA 样本是否一致的任何一项应

when a particular region of a chromosome is to be correlated with inheritance of a trait.

用中，或者应用于检测一个染色体的某一特定区域是否与某一性状的遗传相关。

- Many important traits show continuous, rather than discrete variation. These are also called quantitative traits.

- 许多重要性状显示连续而非不连续变异。这些性状也被称为数量性状。

- Many quantitative traits are influenced by a combination of environment and genetics.

- 许多数量性状受环境和遗传的共同影响。

- The heritable component of quantitative traits can best be studied under controlled conditions, with pure-breeding parents that are polymorphic for both a quantitative trait and a large number of molecular markers.

- 在可控条件下，通过数量性状和许多分子标记都具多态性的纯育系亲本，能够很好地研究数量性状的可遗传部分。

- Molecular markers can be identified for which specific alleles are tightly correlated with the quantitative value of a particular phenotype. The genes that are linked to these markers can be identified through subsequent research.

- 与特定表现型的数量性状数值紧密连锁的某一等位基因能够用分子标记来鉴定。通过后续研究能够鉴定出与这些标记连锁的基因。

Key Terms

molecular marker 分子标记
repetitive DNA 重复 DNA
neutral mutation 中性突变
discrete variation 不连续变异
continuous variation 连续变异
polygenic 多基因的

Study Questions

9.1 Three different polymorphisms have been identified at a particular molecular marker locus. A single pair of PCR primers will amplify either a 50bp fragment (B_2), a 60bp fragment (B_3), or a 100bp fragment (B_4).

9.1 在特定的分子标记位点上鉴定出有 3 个不同的多态性。PCR 引物会扩增出一个 50bp 片段（B_2），一个 60bp 片段（B_3），或者一个 100bp 片段（B_4）。

Draw the PCR bands that would be expected if these primers were used to amplify DNA from individuals with each of the following genotypes:

a) B_2B_2
b) B_4B_4
c) B_2B_3
d) B_2B_4

如果用这些引物扩增以下每个基因型的 DNA，画出预期的 PCR 条带：

a）B_2B_2
b）B_4B_4
c）B_2B_3
d）B_2B_4

9.2 In addition to the primers used to genotype locus B (de-

9.2 除了被用于基因型位点 B 的引

scribed above), a separate pair of primers can amplify another polymorphic SSR locus *E*, with either a 60bp product (E_1) or a 90bp (E_2) product. DNA was extracted from six individuals (#1~#6), and DNA from each individual was used as a template in separate PCR reactions with primers for either locus *B* or primers for locus *E*, and the PCR products were visualized on electrophoretic gels as shown below.

物（如上所述），一对独立的引物能够扩增另外一个多态性 SSR 位点*E*，带有或者一个 60bp 产物(E_1)或者一个 90bp（E_2）产物。从 6 个个体中提取出 DNA（#1～#6），并且每个个体的 DNA 作为一个模板用位点*B*或者位点*E*的引物进行单独的 PCR 反应，PCR 产物经过凝胶电泳后显示如下 。

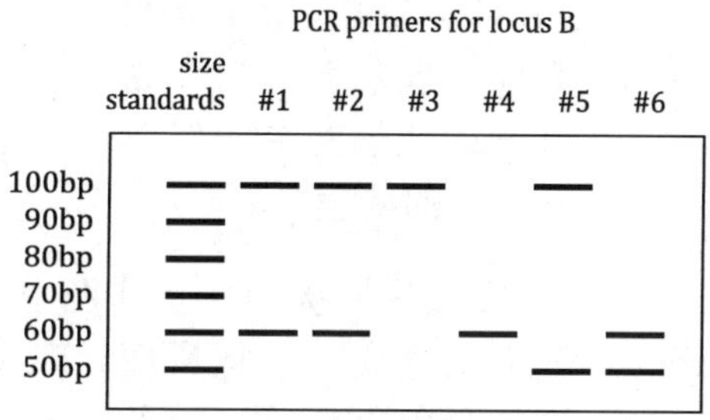

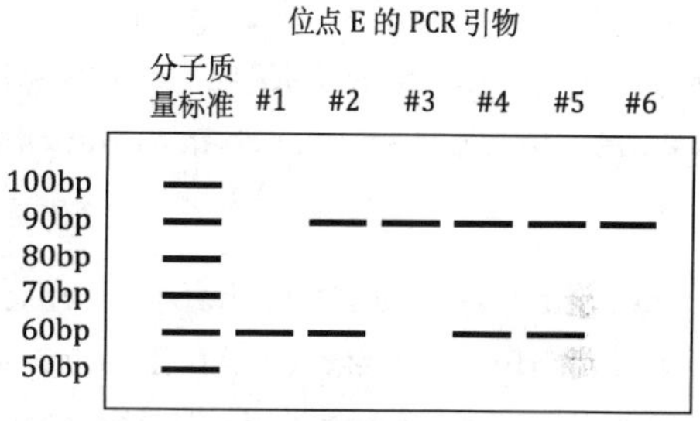

Based on the following PCR banding patterns, what is the full genotype of each of the six individuals?

根据以下的 PCR 条带类型，6 个个体的基因型是什么？

9.3 Based on the genotypes you recorded in Question 9.2, can you determine which of the individuals could be a parent of individual #1?

9.3 根据在问题 9.2 中记录的基因型，你能确定哪个个体是个体#1的亲本吗？

9.4 Here is part of the DNA sequence of a chromosome:

9.4 以下是一个染色体的部分 DNA 序列：

```
TAAAGGAATCAATTACTTCTGTGTGTGTGTGTGTGTGTGTGTGTGTTCTTAGTTGTTTAAGTTTTAAGTTGTGA
||||||||||||||||||||||||||||||||||||||||||||||||||||||||||||||||||||||||||
ATTTCCTTAGTTAATGAAGACACACACACACACACACACACACACAAGAATCAACAAATTCAAAATTCAACACT
```

Identify the following features on the sequence:

a) the region of the fragment that is most likely to be polymorphic

b) any simple sequence repeats

c) the best target sites for PCR primers that could be used to detect polymorphisms in the length of the simple sequence repeat region in different individuals

标出序列的以下特征：

a）最可能呈现多态性的片段区域

b）任一简单重复序列

c）在不同个体中检测简单重复序列长度多态性的 PCR 引物的最好的目标位置

9.5 In a particular diploid plant, seed color is a polygenic trait. If true-breeding plants that produce red seeds are crossed with true breeding plants that produce white seeds, the F_1 produces seeds that are intermediate in color (i.e. pink).

9.5 在某一二倍体植物中，种子颜色是一个多基因性状。如果产生红色种子的纯育系植物与产生白色种子的纯育系植物杂交，F_1代产生

When an F_1 plant self-fertilizes, white seeds are observed in the next generation. How many genes are involved in seed color for each of the following frequencies of white seeds in the F_2 generation?

a) 1/4 white seeds
b) 1/16 white seeds
c) 1/64 white seeds
d) 1/256 white seeds

的种子是介于两者之间的颜色（如粉色）。F_1代自交，在下一代会出现白色的种子。下面分别是在F_2代中白色种子出现的频率，在这些频率下涉及种子颜色有多少基因？

a）1/4 白色种子
b）1/16 白色种子
c）1/64 白色种子
d）1/256 白色种子

9.6 If height in humans is a polygenic trait, explain why it occasionally happens that two tall parents have a child who grows up to be much shorter than either of them.

9.6 假设身高是多基因性状，解释为什么偶尔会有两个高个父母的孩子比他们两个的任何一个都要矮得多的情况。

9.7 In quantitative trait (QTL) mapping, researchers cross two parents that differ in expression of some quantitative trait, then allow chromosomes from these parents to recombine randomly, and after several generations of inbreeding, produce a large number of offspring ("recombinant inbred lines"). Because the position of crossovers is random, each of the offspring contain a different combination of chromosomal regions from each of the two parents. The researchers then use molecular markers to determine which chromosomal regions have the greatest influence on the quantitative trait, e.g. in tall offspring, which chromosomal regions always come from the tall parent?

9.7 在数量性状（QTL）作图中，研究人员杂交一些数量性状表现不同的两个亲本，然后允许这些亲代的染色体随机重组，在几代的自交后，产生大量后代（“重组自交系”）。由于交换的位置是随机的，每个后代包含着与亲代不同的染色体区域组合。研究人员用分子标记确定哪个染色体区域对数量性状影响最大，如高的后代，哪个染色体区域总是来自于高的亲本？

Imagine that two mice strains have been identified that differ in the time required to complete a maze, which may be an indication of intelligence. The time for maze completion is heritable and these parental strains "breed true" for the same completion time in each generation. Imagine also that their chromosomes are different colors and we can track the inheritance of chromosomal regions from each parent based on this color.

假设用走出迷宫所需要的时间以区分两个老鼠品系的智力水平。走出迷宫的时间是可遗传的，并且这些纯合的亲代品系每个世代用相同的时间完成。想象它们的染色体是不同颜色的并且我们也能追踪基于这种颜色的每个亲代的染色体区域的遗传。

Based on the following diagrams of one chromosome from each individual in a pedigree, identify a chromosomal region that may contain a gene that affects time to complete a maze. The time for each individual is shown below each

根据下面系谱中每个个体的一个染色体的图解，确定一个包含影响走完迷宫时间基因的一个染色体区域。每个个体花费的时间显示在

chromosome. Assume that all individuals are homozygous for all loci.

每个染色体下。假设所有位点的所有个体都是纯合的。

Parents:

Selected individuals from among F_8 progeny of the above parents:

在以上亲本的 F_8 后代中选择的个体:

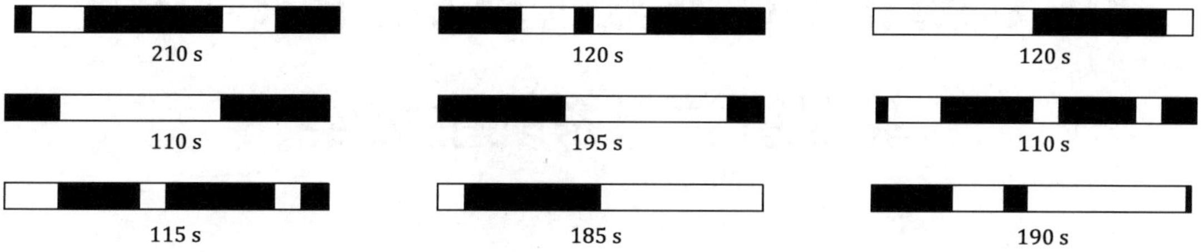

9.8 In a more realistic situation (as compared to question 9.7), where you could not distinguish the parental origin of different chromosomal regions just by appearance of chromosomes, explain how you could identify which parent was the source of a particular region of a chromosome in recombinant offspring.

9.8 在更为现实的情况下（与问题 9.7 相比较），你不可能根据染色体的外观区分不同染色体区域的亲本来源，解释你如何鉴别出在重组后代中某个染色体的特定区域来源于哪个亲本。

Chapter 10

GENOMICS AND SYSTEMS BIOLOGY

基因组学与系统生物学

（彩图）

An artist's depiction of part of an *E.coli* ce1 showing many different types of molecules in their typical abundance. mRNA appears as white lines associated with purple ribosomes, while DNA and proteins such as histones are yellow

艺术家绘制的大肠杆菌部分细胞，细胞中以典型丰度显示了很多种不同类型的分子，mRNA 用白线条表示，与紫色的核糖体相连，而 DNA 和蛋白质，如组氨酸等用黄色表示

Imagine that you could identify and quantify every molecule within a cell in a single assay. You could use this ability to better understand almost any aspect of biology. For example, by comparing the molecular profiles of plants that differed in their resistance to drought, you might discover which combination of genes or proteins makes a crop drought tolerant. The complete set of DNA within an organism is called its **genome.** Although it is not currently possible to

想象在一次分析过程中就能够鉴定并量化细胞内的每一个分子。运用这项技能，可以更好地全方位理解生物学。例如，通过比较植物在抵御干旱的过程中分子轮廓的差异，就可以发现许多基因或蛋白质共同作用使植物具有抗旱性。一个生物体内的全套 DNA 叫做**基因**

study literally every molecule in a cell in a single experiment, recent advances in molecular biology have made it possible to study many genes (or their products) in parallel. **Genomics** is therefore the large-scale application of techniques of molecular biology; the study of many genes or even many thousands of genes at once. This type of research is facilitated by technologies that increase throughput (i.e. rate of analysis), and decrease cost The **-omics** suffix has been used to indicate high-throughput analysis of many types of molecules, including transcripts **(transcriptomics)**, proteins **(proteomics)**, and the products of enzymatic reactions, or metabolites **(metabolomics;** Figure 10.1). Interpretation of the large data sets generated by -omics research depends on a combination of computational, biological, and statistical knowledge provided by experts in **bioinformatics.** Attempts to combine information from different types of -omics studies is sometimes called **systems biology.**

组。尽管目前不可能在一次独立试验中对细胞内的每一个分子进行逐一地研究，但是分子生物学的新进展已经使得一次平行研究许多基因（或其产物）成为可能。因此，**基因组学**是分子生物学技术的大规模应用，是一次对于许多基因，甚至是同时对成千上万的基因进行研究。高通量（即分析率）、低成本的技术促进了该方面的研究。**-omics** 后缀已经被用作在多种类型分子的高通量分析上，包括转录产物（**转录组学**）、蛋白质（**蛋白组学**）及酶反应产物或代谢产物（**代谢组学**；图 10.1）。组学研究得到大量数据需要**生物信息学**专家结合计算机学、生物学和统计学方面的知识进行解释。人们试图将这些信息与不同类型的组学信息结合在一起称之为**系统生物学**。

Figure 10.1 A word cloud listing some of the different -omics technologies. Terms that are more widely used are written in the largest characters

图 10.1 该词汇云列举了一些不同的组学技术。广泛使用的术语用大号字体表示

DNA SEQUENCING DNA 测 序

The purpose of DNA sequencing is to determine the order of

DNA 测序的目的是对于给定的一

nucleotide bases within a given fragment of DNA. This information can be used to infer the protein sequence encoded by the gene, from which further inferences may be made about the gene's function and its relationship to other genes. DNA sequence information is also useful in studying the regulation of gene expression. If DNA sequencing is applied to the study of many genes, or even a whole genome, it is considered an example of genomics.

段 DNA 序列来确定其核苷酸序列的顺序。这些测序信息可用于推断基因编码的蛋白质序列，甚至进一步推测这些基因的功能及与其他基因的关系。DNA 测序也可以用在研究基因表达调控上。如果 DNA 测序被应用于对多个基因甚至是整个基因组的研究上，那么就会被视为基因组学研究的范畴。

Recall that DNA polymerases incorporate nucleotides (dNTP) into a growing strand of DNA. DNA polymerases can generally add a new base only to the 3′-OH group of an existing strand of DNA; this is why primers are required in natural DNA synthesis and in techniques such as PCR. Most of the currently used DNA sequencing techniques rely on modified nucleotides called terminators. Examples of terminators are the dideoxy nucleotides **(ddNTP),** which lack a 3′-OH group and therefore cannot serve as an attachment site for the addition of new bases to a growing strand of DNA (Figure 10.2). Thus, after a ddNTP is incorporated into a strand of DNA, no further elongation can occur. Terminators labeled with fluorescent dyes specific to each of the four nucleotide bases are particularly useful in DNA sequencing.

回想一下，DNA 聚合酶将核苷酸（dNTP）依据模板链序列结合在正在延伸的 DNA 链上。一般 DNA 聚合酶只能将新的单一碱基加到已有 DNA 链的 3′-OH 基团上，所以在天然 DNA 合成和一些实验技术，如 PCR 中需要引物。当前使用的大部分 DNA 测序技术依赖于随机掺入叫做终止子的修饰核苷酸。终止子的一个例子是缺少 3′-OH 基团的双脱氧核苷酸（**ddNTP**），在 DNA 延伸链中它不能够为新碱基的加入提供附着位点（图 10.2）。在一个双脱氧核苷酸分子与 DNA 链结合之后，延伸终止。被特殊荧光染料标记的四种核苷酸的终止子在 DNA 测序中特别有用。

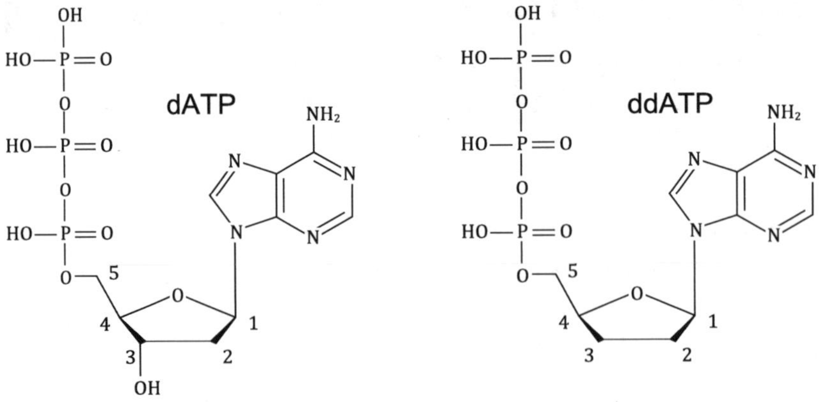

Figure 10.2 Structure of a terminator (ddATP) compared to a regular nucleoside. Note the absence of the hydroxyl group in the 3' position of ddATP

图 10.2 常用的核苷酸和终止子的结构对比。注意 ddATP 在 3'端缺乏羟基集团

To sequence a DNA fragment, you need many copies of that fragment (Figure 10.3). Unlike PCR, DNA sequencing does not amplify the target sequence. In another difference from PCR, only one primer is used in DNA sequencing. This primer is hybridized to the denatured template DNA, and determines where on the template strand the sequencing reaction will begin. A mixture of dNTPs, fluorescently labeled terminators, and DNA polymerase is added to a tube containing the primer-template hybrid. The DNA polymerase will then synthesize a new strand of DNA until a fluorescently labeled nucleotide is incorporated. Because the reaction contains millions of template molecules, a corresponding number of shorter molecules is synthesized, each ending in a fluorescent label that corresponds to the last base incorporated. The newly synthesized strands can be denatured from the template, and then separated electrophoretically based on their length (Figure 10.4). Since each band differs in length by one nucleotide, and the identity of that nucleotide is known from its fluorescence, the DNA sequence can be read simply

在对一个 DNA 片段测序时，需要这个片段的许多拷贝（图 10.3）。与 PCR 不同，DNA 测序并不会扩增目标序列。此外，DNA 测序仅需一种引物，这也是区别 PCR 的另一方面。这种引物与变性的 DNA 模板链杂交，并确定模板链上的反应起始位置。将 dNTP 混合物、荧光标记的终止子、DNA 聚合酶加入到含有引物-模板混合物的管中。DNA 聚合酶会合成一条新的 DNA 链直到加入荧光标记的核苷酸为止。由于反应包含数百万个模板分子，其中有相当数量的短的分子被合成，每个结尾掺入都是荧光标记的碱基。每个新合成的链能够从模板变性下来，然后根据它们的长度通过电泳进行分离（图 10.4）。由于每一条带都会有一个碱基的长

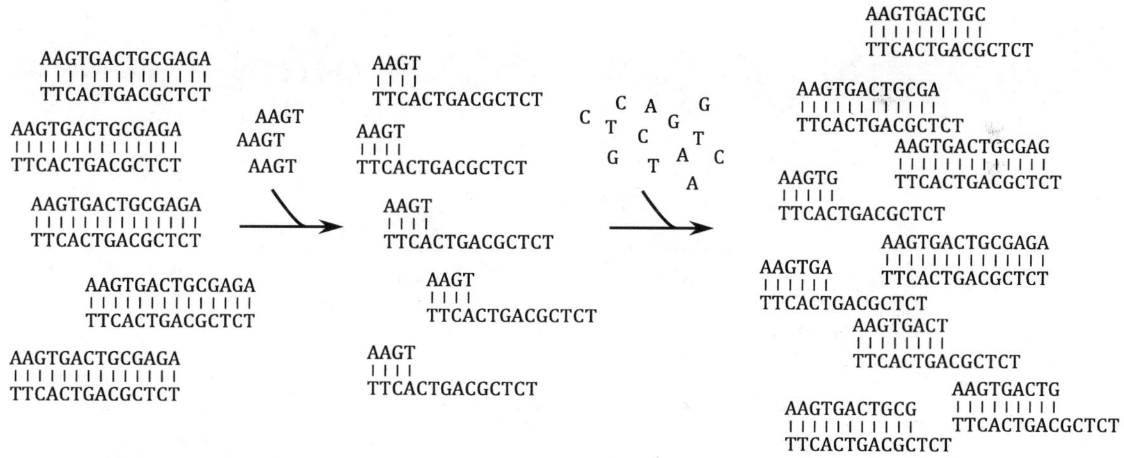

Figure 10.3 A sequencing reaction begins with many identical copies of a template DNA fragment. The template is denatured, then primers are annealed to the template. Following the addition of polymerase, regular dNTPs, and fluorescently labeled terminators, extension begins at the primer site. Elongation proceeds until a fluorescently labeled terminator (shown here in color) is incorporated

图 10.3 测序反应从模板 DNA 片段的多个相同拷贝开始进行，模板变性，然后引物与模板退火。再加入聚合酶、普通的 dNTP、荧光标记的终止子等，从引物处开始延伸，当荧光标记的终止子掺入时延伸终止

from the order of the colors in successive bands. In practice, the maximum length of sequence that can be read from a single sequencing reaction is about 700bp.

度差异，并且根据荧光标记能够知道核苷酸的种类，这样就可以按照连续的条带颜色顺序简单地读出DNA序列。在实践中，每次独立测序反应所能读出的序列长度的最大值约为700bp。

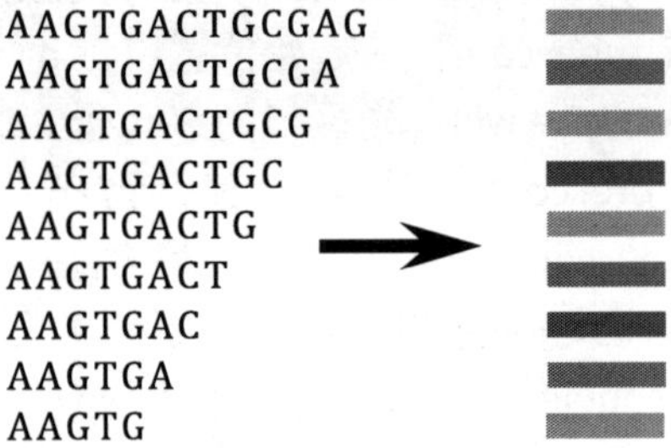

Figure 10.4 Fluorescently labeled products can be separated electrophoretically based on their length (see the color figure)

图 10.4 可以根据荧光标记的DNA片段长度用电泳进行分离（见彩版）

A particularly sensitive electrophoresis method used in the analysis of DNA sequencing reactions is called **capillary electrophoresis** (Figure 10.5). In this method, a current pulls the sequencing products through a gel-like matrix that is encased in a fine tube of clear plastic. As in conventional electrophoresis, the smallest fragments move through the capillary the

DNA 测序反应分析中用到一种特别灵敏的电泳方法叫做**毛细管电泳法**（图 10.5）。在这种方法中，电流拉动测序产物通过由透明塑料制成的细管内部的凝胶基质，像常规电泳一样，最小的片段最先通

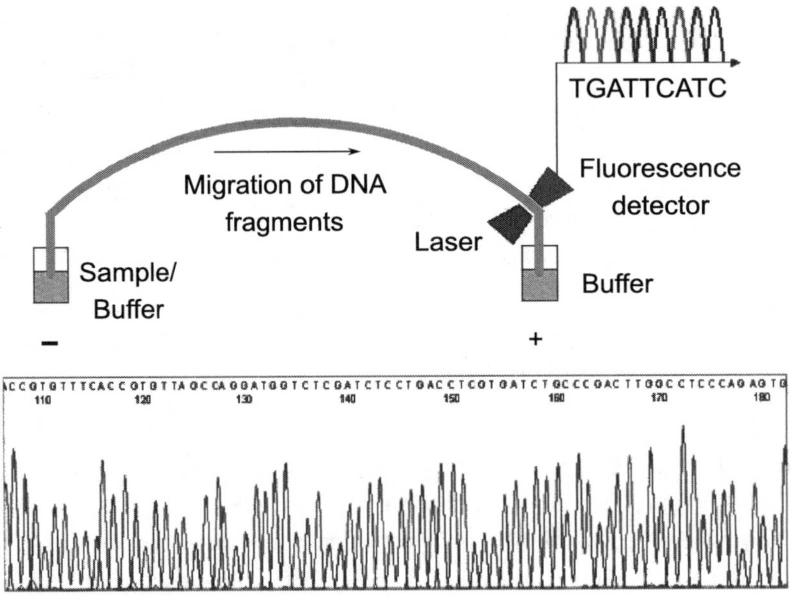

Figure 10.5 Fluorescently labeled products can be separated by capillary electrophoresis, generating a chromatogram from which the sequence can be read (see the color figure)

图 10.5 荧光标记的产物可以通过毛细管电泳进行分离，产生能够读取序列的色谱（见彩版）

fastest As they pass through a point near the end of the capillary, the fluorescent intensity of each dye is read. This produces a graph called a chromatogram (Figure 10.6). The sequence is determine by identifying the highest peak (i.e. the dye with the most intense fluorescent signal) at each position.

过毛细管，速度最快。当它们通过毛细管接近尾端的一点时，每个片段带有的荧光染料的荧光密度将被读取。由此而产生的图称为色谱（图 10.6）。通过鉴定每个位置的最高峰值（即染料带有最强荧光信号时）来确定序列。

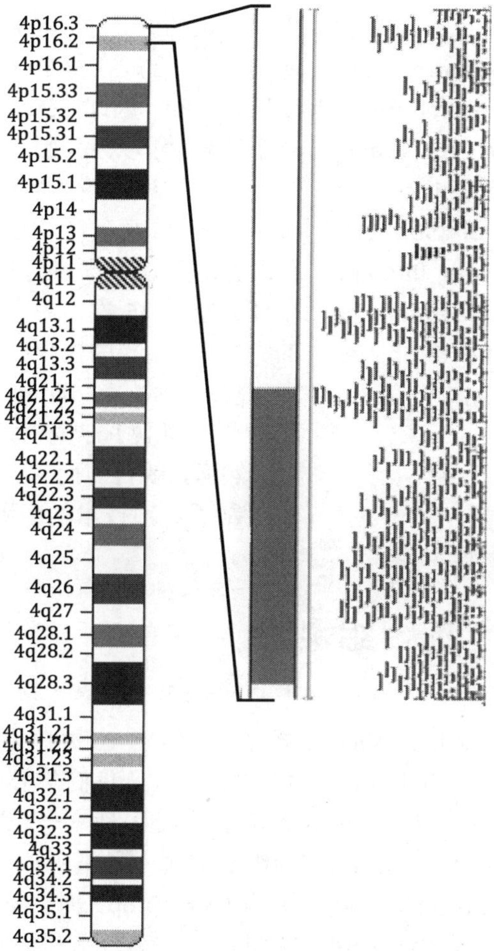

Figure 10.6 A portion of a physical map for human chromosome 4. The entire chromosome is shown at left. The physical map is made up of the small lines, each of which represents a cloned piece of DNA approximately 100kb in length

图 10.6 人类 4 号染色体的一部分物理图谱，左边的是完整染色体，物理图谱由小短线构成，每个短线代表长约 100kb 的 DNA 克隆

Advances in technology over the past two decades have increased the speed and quality of sequencing, while decreasing the cost This has become especially true with the most recently developed methods called **next-generation** sequencing. Not all of these new methods rely on terminators, but one that does is a method used in instruments sold by a company called **Illumina.** Illumina sequencers use a special variant of PCR called bridge PCR to make many thousands of

在过去的 20 年中，技术的发展不仅提高了测序的速度和质量，同时也降低了成本。随着近来被称为下一代测序技术的发展，这些已经成为现实。所有的这些新技术并非都依赖于终止子，但是一家名为 **Illumina** 的仪器销售商使用了终止子技术。Illumina 测序仪应用一项

copies of a short (45bp) template fragment. Each of these short template fragments is attached in a cluster in a small spot on a reaction surface. Millions of other clusters, each made by different template fragment, are located at other positions on the reaction surface. DNA synthesis at each template strand then proceeds using dye-labeled terminators that are used are reversible. Synthesis is therefore terminated (temporarily) after the incorporation of each nucleotide. Thus, after the first nucleotide is incorporated in each strand, a camera records the color of fluorescence emitted from each cluster. The terminators are then modified, and a second nucleotide is incorporated in each strand, and again the reaction surface is photographed. This cycle is repeated a total of 45 times. Because millions of 45bp templates are sequenced in parallel in a single process, Illumina sequencing is very efficient compared to other sequencing techniques. However, the short length of the templates currently limits the application of the technology.

与众不同的、被称为桥接 PCR 的 PCR 技术来获得成千上万个短的（45bp）模板片段拷贝。每个小模板片段都在反应表面的一个小点上形成簇。由不同的模板链获得的百万个不同模板簇分别位于反应表面的不同位置。DNA 在每条模板链上合成，然后继续用之前用过染料标记的终止子，这种反应是可逆的。因此合成在每个核苷酸掺入后暂时停止。因此，在每条链的第一个核苷酸掺入后，照相机开始记录每个簇发出的荧光颜色。然后终止子被修饰，每条链结合第二个核苷酸并对反应表面进行拍照。整个循环共重复 45 次。由于数百万计的大小为 45bp 的模板在一个循环中进行平行测序，Illumina 测序仪相对于其他测序技术而言十分高效。然而，就目前而言，模板长度短限制了这项技术的应用。

WHOLE GENOME SEQUENCING 全基因组测序

Given that the length of a single sequencing read is somewhere between 45bp and 700bp, we are faced with a problem when we want to determine the sequence of longer fragments, including each of the chromosomes in an entire genome such as that of humans (3×10^9 bp). Obviously, we need to break the genome into smaller fragments. There are two different strategies for doing this: clone-by-clone sequencing, which relies on the creation of a physical map, and whole genome shotgun sequencing, which does not require a physical map.

给定一次独立测序的长度为 45~700bp，当我们想要确定一个更长的片段序列——包括整个基因组上的每一条染色体，如人类染色体（3×10^9bp）时，我们就会面临问题。显然，我们需要将基因组打碎成小的片段。有两种不同的方法可以解决这个问题：依赖于建立物理图谱的逐步克隆测序法和不需要物理图谱的全基因组鸟枪测序法。

Physical mapping 物 理 图 谱

A **physical map** is a representation of a genome that is comprised of cloned fragments of DNA (Figure 10.6). The map is therefore made of physical entities (pieces of DNA) rather than abstract concepts such as the linkage frequencies and genes that make up a genetic map. It is usually possible to correlate genetic and physical maps, for example by identifying the clone that contains a particular molecular marker. The connection between physical and genetic maps allows the genes underlying particular mutations to be identified through a process called **map-based cloning.**

一个**物理图谱**是对一个基因组的描述，包括 DNA 克隆片段（图 10.6）。该图谱是由物理实体（DNA 片段）构成而不是像连锁频率和基因构成遗传图谱那样的抽象概念。通常将遗传图谱和物理图谱相关联，举例来说，对含有特定分子标记的克隆进行鉴定。通过物理图谱和遗传图谱之间的联系，可以通过一个叫做**图位克隆**的过程鉴定引起特定突变的基因。

To create a physical map, large fragments of the genome are cloned into plasmid vectors, or into larger vectors called bacterial artificial chromosomes **(BAC).** BACs can contain approximately 100kb fragments. The set of BAC produced in a cloning reaction will be redundant, meaning that different clones will contain DNA from the same part of the genome. Because of this redundancy, it is useful to select the minimum set of clones that represent the entire genome, and to order these clones respective to the sequence of the original chromosome. Note that this is all to be done without knowing the sequence of each BAC. Making a physical map may therefore rely on techniques related to Southern blotting: DNA from the ends of one BAC is used as a probe to find another clone that contains at least part of the same sequence. By repeating this process, a series of clones can be identified that together contain the sequence of a larger part of a chromosome.

为了创建一个物理图谱，需将基因组大片段克隆到质粒载体上，或克隆到更大的称为**细菌人工染色体**（BAC）的载体上。一套 BAC 能够包含约 100kb 的片段。在克隆反应过程中产生的系列 BAC 是冗余的，意味着不同的克隆会包含基因组同一部分的 DNA。由于这种冗余的情况，筛选能够代表全部基因组的最小一套克隆，并且该套克隆可以在原来的染色体上按各自顺序排列，将是非常有用的。请注意，这里所操作的一切都是在不知道每个 BAC 的完整序列的前提下。因此，制作一个物理图谱可能会依赖于与 Southern 印迹相关的技术：以一个 BAC 末端的 DNA 作为探针，找到至少包含部分相同序列的另一个克隆。通过重复这样的过程，包含染色体大部分序列的一系列克隆就会被鉴定出来。

Clone-by-clone genome sequencing 逐步克隆测序

Physical mapping was once considered a pre-requisite for whole genome sequencing. The **clone-by-clone** sequencing

物理图谱，曾一度被认为是全基因组测序的首要条件。**逐步克隆**测序

process would begin by breaking the genome into BAC-sized pieces, arranging these BAC into a map, then breaking each BAC up into successively smaller clones, which were usually then also mapped. Eventually, a minimum set of clones would be identified, each of which was small enough to be sequenced. Because the order of clones relative to the complete chromosome was known prior to sequencing, the resulting sequence information could be easily assembled into a complete chromosome at the end of the project clone-by-clone sequencing therefore minimizes the number of sequencing reactions that must be performed, and makes sequence assembly straightforward. However, a drawback of this sequencing strategy is the tedious process of building a physical map.

过程首先将基因组打断成 BAC 大小的片段，将这些 BAC 整理进图谱，然后将每个 BAC 分散成连续的更小的克隆，然后通常也整理在图谱上。最后，鉴定出最小的一套克隆，每一个都小到可以被测序。测序前已知完整染色体相关的克隆顺序，这样测序结果信息能很容易地被组装成一个完整的染色体。因此，逐步克隆测序将必要的测序反应数量降至最小，并且使测序组装直截了当。然而，这种测序方法的缺点是创建物理图谱的繁杂过程。

Whole genome shotgun sequencing 全基因组鸟枪法测序

Rather than making a physical map, why not simply break the genome into fragments that are small enough to be sequenced, then reassemble complete chromosome sequences simply by finding overlaps in the small fragments? This **whole genome shotgun** avoids the process of making a physical map. However, this requires many more sequencing reactions than the clone-by-clone method, because in the shotgun approach, there is no way to avoid sequencing redundant fragments. There is also a question of the feasibility of assembling complete chromosomes based simply on the sequence of many small fragments. This is particularly a problem when the size of the fragments is smaller than the length of a repetitive region of DNA. Nevertheless, it has now been demonstrated in the sequencing of rice, human, and many other large genomes, that whole genome shotgun sequencing is an efficient way to obtain nearly complete genome sequence. However, shotgun assemblies often contain some gaps particularly in repeat-rich regions. The human genome project, for example, relied on a combination of shotgun sequence and physical mapping to produce contiguous sequence for the length of each arm of each chromosome. Note that because of the highly repetitive nature of centromeric and telomeric DNA, sequencing projects rarely include these

为什么不将基因组打断成足够被测序的小片段，然后根据每个片段序列相重叠的部分简单地进行基因组组装呢？**全基因组鸟枪法**就可以避免建立物理图谱的过程。然而，在应用鸟枪法的时候，比逐步克隆测序的方法需要更多的测序反应，不可避免地要对一些冗余的片段进行测序。基于简单通过小片段测序的方法组装整个染色体组的想法，还存在可行与否的问题。尤其是当片段的大小比 DNA 重复区域的长度还要小的时候。不过，全基因组鸟枪法测序是获得几乎所有基因组序列的行之有效的一种方法，这在水稻、人类及其他大型基因组中都得到了证实。然而鸟枪组装经常包含一些缺口，尤其在重复富集区域。以人类基因组计划为例，将鸟枪测序法和物理图谱相结合，才产生与每条染色体的每个臂长度都十分接近的序列。需要注意的是，由于着丝粒和端粒 DNA

heterochromatic regions.

的高重复本质，测序方案很少包含这些异染色质区域。

Genome annotation 基因组注释

No matter which strategy is used to obtain genomic sequence, the result is a string of millions of A's,T's,G's, and C's. Which of these nucleotides encode proteins, and which of them represent other features of genes and their regulatory elements, or non-coding DNA with no evident function? The process of **genome annotation** relies on computers to define features such a start and stop codons, introns, exons, and splice sites. However, none of the predictions made by these programs are entirely accurate, and must be verified experimentally for any gene of particular importance.

无论用哪种技术来获得基因组序列，结果都是成千上万的 A、T、G、C 的字符串。哪些核苷酸编码蛋白质？哪些代表基因的其他特性、它的调控元件及没有明显功能的非编码 DNA？**基因组注释**的过程需要计算机来定义诸如起始密码子、终止密码子、内含子、外显子、剪切位点这些元件。然而，这些程序所做的预测没有一个是完全精确的，在特殊情况下对于一个特定基因往往需要试验验证。

FUNCTIONAL GENOMICS 功能基因组学

Having identified putative genes within a genome sequence, how do we determine their function? Techniques of functional genomics are an experimental approach to address this question. One widely used technique in functional genomics is called microarray analysis. Microarrays measure the abundance of mRNA for hundreds or thousands of genes at once. The abundance of mRNA of a particular gene is sometimes correlated with its activity. For example, genes that are involved in neuronal development generally produce more mRNA in brain tissue than in heart tissue. We can therefore use microarrays and related technologies to identify genes whose transcripts are abundant in one tissue sample, but not in another.

前面我们已经在基因组序列中鉴定了假定的基因，那么我们要如何来确定它们的功能呢？功能基因组学技术是一项解决这一问题的试验途径。功能基因组学中被广泛应用的一项技术为微阵列分析。微阵列能够一次对成百上千个基因的 mRNA 丰度进行检测。这些特定基因的 mRNA 丰度通常与这些基因的活性相关。举例来说，与神经元发育紧密相关的基因在脑组织中产生的 mRNA 远比在心脏组织中产生的多。因此，我们可以用微阵列和相关技术鉴定那些在一个组织样品中转录而在另一个样品中不转录的基因。

One type of microarray analysis begins with the immobilization of DNA in tens of thousands of small (100μm) spots on the surface of a specially treated microscope slide. Within each spot, there are hundreds of thousands of copies of DNA for the same gene, but each of the spots represents a different gene. The DNA on the surface of this microarray is denatured, making it single-stranded. Then RNA is extracted from two tissue samples that a researcher wants to compare, for example biopsies of cancerous and healthy tissues. The RNA from each sample is labeled with a contrasting fluorescent dye and is usually also reverse transcribed into cDNA, for stability. In our example, all of the transcripts from the tumor sample might be labeled red, and all of the transcripts from the normal sample might be labeled green. These labeled molecules are then hybridized to the surface of the microarray at high stringency, so that they will bind only at spots that contain complementary sequence. Importantly, the labeled cDNA molecules will bind at each spot in proportion to their relative abundance in the original mixture of transcripts from the two samples. Thus, if a gene produced more transcripts in a tumor sample than in a normal sample, the corresponding spot on the microarray would be more red than green. Conversely, a gene that was silenced in a tumor, but was expressed at high levels in a normal tissue would have a spot on the microarray that was more green than red (Figure 10.7). By analyzing images of fluorescent signals from microarrays, researchers can then identify genes whose expression is highly correlated with one physiological state but not another. Accordingly, microarrays have been used to study everything from psychiatric disorders to wood formation in trees.

一种微阵列分析开始于在特殊处理的显微镜载玻片上把 DNA 固定在成千上万的小点（100μm）上。在每个点上有同一基因的成百上千个拷贝，每一个点代表不同的基因。在微阵列上的 DNA 被变性为单链。然后研究者从要对比的两个样品中提取 RNA，如从癌症和健康活组织中。从每个样品中提取的 RNA 用明显不同的荧光标记，为了稳定性，RNA 通常也被反转录为 cDNA。在我们的例子中，所有来自肿瘤样品的转录本被标记成红色，所有来自正常样品的转录本被标记成绿色。然后这些标记的分子与微阵列表面进行高严谨性杂交，这些转录本仅仅能够结合在包含互补序列的点上。重要的是，结合在点上的标记的 cDNA 分子数量将与来自两个样品的原来转录本混合物丰度成比例。因此，如果一个基因在肿瘤样品中相比正常样品产生更多的转录本，在微阵列的相应点将会有比绿色更多的红色。相反，一个基因在肿瘤中沉默，而在正常细胞中高水平表达，在微阵列的相应点上会有比红色更多的绿色（图 10.7）。通过分析微阵列上的荧光信号图像，研究者就能鉴定出与一种生理状态高度相关的基因的表达。因此，微阵列能被用于从精神方面的疾病到树木中木材形成的所有研究中。

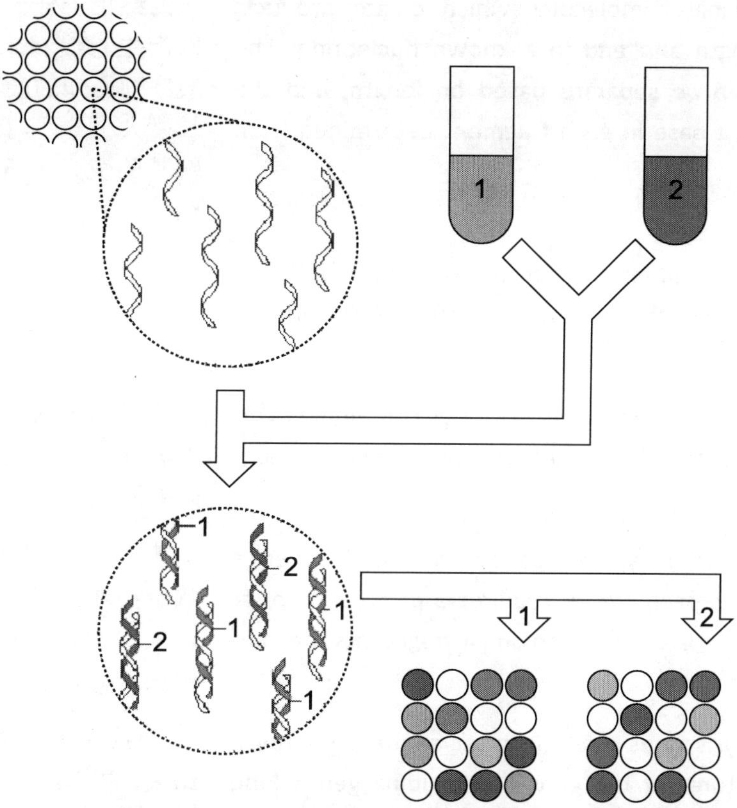

Figure 10.7 An example of a type of DNA microarray. Fluorescently labeled molecules derived from the transcripts of two tissue samples are hybridized immobilized DNA molecules on the surface of an array. The labeled molecules will bind in proportion to their abundance in the original tissue samples. Thus spots on the microarray that are more green than red represent genes that are more abundant in the tissue sample from which green-labeled molecules were derived (see the color figure)

图 10.7 一个典型的 DNA 微阵列的例子。来自两个组织样品转录的荧光标记的分子与微阵列表面固定的 DNA 分子杂交。标记的分子将与原来组织样品的转录丰度在数量上成比例地结合。因此，在微阵列上的点的绿色多于红色，代表绿色标记的组织样品分子丰度更高（见彩版）

Summary

- Genomics and related technologies differ from other techniques of molecular biology largely because of their scale; they allow many molecules to by studied in parallel.

- 在规模上基因组学及其相关技术与其他分子生物学技术不同，这些技术允许对众多分子进行平行研究。

- DNA sequencing can be applied to either a single gene, or in the case of genomics, to a large number of genes.

- DNA 测序既可以应用到单个基因测序上，也可以应用到以基因组为例的大量基因的测序上。

- Most DNA sequencing relies on the incorporation of

- 大多数 DNA 测序依赖于染色标

dye-labeled terminator molecules which create products that differ in length and end in a known nucleotide. The products can then be separate based on length, and the identity of the last base in each fragment determined from its fluorescence.

记的终止子分子的掺入，终止子可以产生长度和末端均不同但核苷酸序列已知的产物。产物能够基于长度大小分离，在每个片段的最后碱基的荧光上就可以知道是什么碱基。

- Next-generation sequencing technologies have reduced costs of sequencing further through miniaturization and parallelization.

- 下一代测序技术可以通过微型化和平行化来节约测序成本。

- Physical maps are ordered sets of clones containing overlapping pieces of DNA, which together represent large pieces of chromosomes.

- 物理图谱是包括彼此重叠部分 DNA 片段的一系列克隆，这些克隆共同代表着大片段染色体。

- Whole genomes may be sequenced using either a clone-by-clone approach, which requires a physical map, or by a shot gun approach, in which small fragments are randomly sequenced.

- 整个基因组测序既可以采用依赖于物理图谱的逐步克隆法，也可以采用通过小片段随机测序的鸟枪法进行。

- Genome analysis does not end after sequence acquisition; various features of the genome including genes (and their introns, exons, etc.) must be identified through a process called annotation.

- 获得序列后基因组分析还没有结束，基因组包括基因（和它们的内含子、外显子等）的各种各样特征还必须通过叫做注释的过程进行鉴定。

- Functional genomics techniques including microarray analysis correlate transcript abundance with particular tissue samples. Genes who transcripts are highly abundant under certain biological conditions may cause or respond to that condition.

- 功能基因组学技术包括与组织样品中转录丰度相关的微阵列分析。在一定生物学条件下转录丰度较高的基因可能源于对条件的反应。

Key Terms

genome 基因组
genomics 基因组学
-omics 组学
proteomics 蛋白质组学
transcriptomics 转录组学
metabolomics 代谢组学
ddNTP 双脱氧核苷酸
terminator nucleotide 终止子核苷酸
next-generation sequencing 下一代测序
Illumina
physical map 物理图谱
map-based cloning 图位克隆
BAC 细菌人工染色体
clone-by-clone sequencing 逐步克隆测序
whole genome shotgun 全基因组鸟枪
genome annotation 基因组注释

capillary electrophoresis 毛细管电泳
chromatogram 色谱
functional genomics 功能基因组学
microarray 微阵列

Study Questions

10.1 What are the advantages of high-throughput -omics techniques compared to studying a single gene or protein at a time? What are the disadvantages?

10.1 和一次只研究单个基因或蛋白质对比，高通量测序技术有什么优势和劣势？

10.2 What would the chromatogram from a capillary sequencer look like if you accidentally added only template, primers, polymerase, and fluorescent terminators to your sequencing reaction?

10.2 如果你故意在测序反应中仅仅加入模板、引物、聚合酶、荧光标记的终止子，毛细管测序仪产生的色谱看起来是什么样的？

10.3 What are the advantages and disadvantages of clone-by clone vs. whole genome shotgun sequencing?

10.3 逐步测序法和全基因组鸟枪法的优缺点各是什么？

10.4 How could you use DNA sequencing to identify new species of marine microorganism?

10.4 你怎样使用 DNA 测序技术鉴定海洋微生物新种？

10.5 Explain how you could use a microarray to identify genes that are affected during drought in wheat.

10.5 试说明你如何运用微阵列技术鉴定小麦在干旱期间受影响的基因？

10.6 A microarray identified 100 genes whose transcripts are highly abundant in tumors, but not in normal tissues. Do any or all of these transcripts cause cancer? Explain your answer.

10.6 一个微阵列鉴定了肿瘤中高水平转录而在正常组织不转录的 100 个基因，所有或者部分的这些转录本导致了癌症吗？解释你的答案。

10.7 How do you ensure that each spot printed on a microarray contains DNA for only one gene?

10.7 你怎样保证在微阵列上每个点仅仅包括一个基因的 DNA？

10.8 What would the spots look like on a microarray after hybridization, if each spot contained a mixture of genes?

10.8 如果微阵列的每个点包括多个基因，在杂交后微阵列上的点看起来是什么样子的？

10.9 What would the spots look like if the hybridization of green and red labeled DNA was done at low stringency?

10.9 如果用绿色和红色标记的 DNA 在低严谨条件下进行杂交，微阵列上的点起来是什么样子的？

Chapter 11

REGULATION OF GENE EXPRESSION
基因表达调控

(彩图)

The stickleback is an example of an organism for which changes in the regulation of gene expression have been shown to confer a selective advantage in some environments

棘鱼是生物体基因表达调控发生改变的一个例子， 这个变化使棘鱼在某些生态环境下具有选择性优势

Within an individual organism, every cell contains essentially identical genomic sequence. How then do cells develop and function differently from each other? The answer lies in the

在一个生物体个体内，每个细胞都含有本质上相同的基因组序列。那么细胞的发育和功能又怎么会各

regulation of **gene expression**. Only certain genes are expressed (i.e. are functionally active) under any particular biological circumstances. Gene expression is regulated at many different stages of the process that converts DNA information into active protein. In the first stage, transcript abundance can be controlled by regulating the rate of initiation of transcription, and the processing and degradation of transcripts. In many cases, higher abundance of a gene's transcripts is correlated with its increased expression. In this chapter, we will focus on **transcriptional regulation**, but be aware that cells also regulate the activity of genes in other ways. For example, by controlling the rate of translation, processing, degradation, and post-translational modification of proteins and protein complexes.

不相同呢？答案就在于**基因表达**的调控。某些基因只有在某一特定的生物环境下表达（即功能上是活跃的）。基因表达可以在DNA信息转化为活性蛋白过程中的不同阶段被调控。在初始阶段，转录丰度可以通过调节转录起始速度、转录本的加工和降解来调控。在很多情况下，基因转录的较高丰度与其增加的表达量相关。在这一章中，我们将集中学习**转录调控**，但也要注意到细胞也以其他方式调控基因的表达。例如，通过控制翻译速度、加工、降解及蛋白质和蛋白质复合体的翻译后修饰等调控表达。

THE LAC OPERON 乳糖操纵子

Early insights into mechanisms of transcriptional regulation came from studies of *E. coli* by researchers Francois Jacob & Jacques Monod. In *E. coli* and many other bacteria, genes for several different proteins may be encoded on a single transcript in a unit called an **operon**. The genes of an operon share the same transcriptional regulation, but are translated individually. With the exception of *C. elegans* and a few other species, eukaryotes generally do not group genes together in operons.

早期对转录调控机制的阐明来自于研究人员 Francois Jacob 和 Jacques Monod 对大肠杆菌的研究。在大肠杆菌和许多其他细菌中，合成几种不同蛋白质的基因可能被在一个单元中单一转录本所编码，这个单元称为**操纵子**。一个操纵子的基因受相同的转录调控，但蛋白质却被各自单独翻译。除了线虫和一些其他的物种外，真核生物通常不将基因集中成操纵子。

E. coli encounters many different sugars in its environment. These sugars, such as **lactose** and **glucose**, require different enzymes for their metabolism. Three of the enzymes for lactose metabolism are grouped in the ***lac* operon**: ***lacZ***, ***lacY***, and ***lacA*** (Figure 11.1). *LacZ* encodes an enzyme called **β-galactosidase**, which digests lactose into its two constituent sugars: glucose and galactose. *lacY* is a **permease** that helps to transfer lactose into the cell. Finally, *lacA* is a

大肠杆菌在其周围的环境中会遇到许多不同的糖类，如**乳糖**和**葡萄糖**，这些糖类的代谢需要不同的酶。乳糖代谢酶的3种酶组合成**乳糖操纵子**：***lacZ***、***lacY*** 和 ***lacA***（图11.1）。*LacZ* 编码的一种称为**β-半乳糖苷酶**的酶，它将乳糖分解为乳糖的两种组成糖分——葡萄糖和

trans-acetylase; the relevance of which in lactose metabolism is not entirely clear. *E. coli* activates transcription of the *lac* operon only when lactose is available for it to digest. Presumably, this avoids wasting energy in the synthesis of enzymes for which no substrate is present.

半乳糖。*lacY* 编码一种**透性酶**，它能够帮助乳糖转移到细胞内。最后，*lacA* 编码一种**转乙酰酶**，它与乳糖代谢的关系还不完全清楚。大肠杆菌只有当乳糖存在可用于消化时才能激活乳糖操纵子的转录。推测可能是在无底物存在时，避免酶的合成而浪费能量。

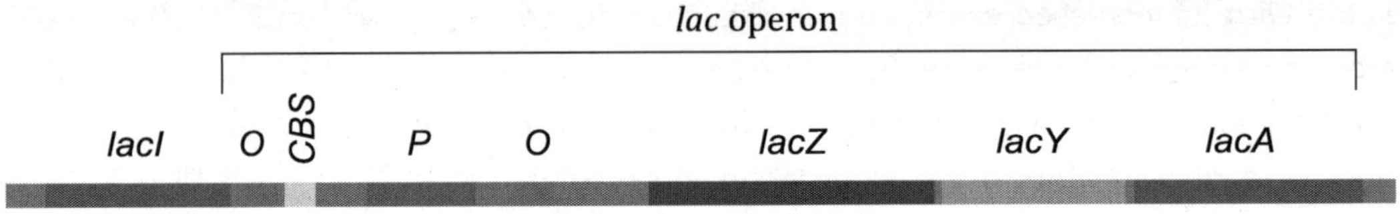

Figure 11.1 Diagram of a segment of an *E. coli* chromosome containing the *lac* operon, as well as the *lacI* coding region. The various genes and *cis*-elements are not drawn to scale

图 11.1 一段包含乳糖操纵子的大肠杆菌染色体片段及 *lacI* 编码区示意图。各基因和顺式元件不是按比例绘制的

In addition to the three protein-coding genes, the *lac* operon contains short DNA sequences that do not encode proteins, but are instead binding sites for proteins involved in transcriptional regulation of the operon. In the *lac* operon, these sequences are called **P (promoter)**, **O (operator)**, and **CBS (CAP-binding site)**. Collectively, sequence elements such as these are called ***cis*-elements** because they must be located on the same piece of DNA as the genes they regulate. On the other hand, the proteins that bind to these *cis*-elements are called ***trans*-regulators** because (as diffusible molecules) they do not necessarily need to be encoded on the same piece of DNA as the genes they regulate.

除了 3 种编码蛋白的基因，乳糖操纵子还含有不能编码蛋白质的短的 DNA 序列，即涉及操纵子转录调控的蛋白结合位点。在乳糖操纵子中，这些序列被称为 **P**（**启动子**）、**O**（**操纵基因**）和 **CBS**（**帽子结合位点**）。诸如此类序列元件共同被称为顺式元件，因为它们必须位于它们调控基因的同一段 DNA 上。另外，与这些顺式元件结合的蛋白质称为**反式调节蛋白**，因为它们（作为可扩散的分子）未必需要在它们调控基因的同一段 DNA 上被编码。

lacI is an allosterically regulated repressor

lacI 是一种变构的调控阻遏蛋白

One of the major *trans*-regulators of the *lac* operon is encoded by ***lacI***. Four identical molecules of *lacI* proteins assemble together to form a **homotetramer** called a **repressor** (Figure 11.2). This repressor binds to two operator sequences

乳糖操纵子的一种重要的反式调节蛋白是由 ***lacI*** 编码的。4 个相同的 lacI 蛋白分子组装到一起形成一个**四聚体**，称为**阻遏蛋白**（图

adjacent to the promoter of the *lac* operon. Binding of the repressor prevents RNA polymerase from binding to the promoter (Figure 11.3). Therefore, the operon cannot be transcribed when the operator is occupied by a repressor.

11.2)。这个阻遏蛋白结合到靠近乳糖操纵子启动子的两个操纵基因序列上。阻遏蛋白的结合阻止了RNA 聚合酶结合到启动子上（图11.3)。因此，当阻遏蛋白结合了操纵基因时操纵子不能被转录。

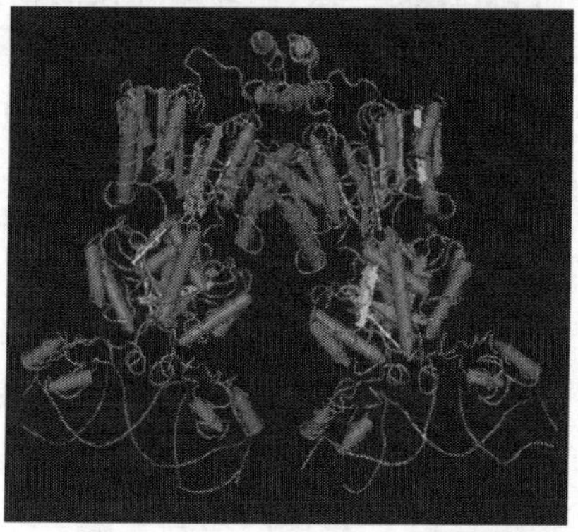

（彩图）

Figure 11.2 Structure of lacI homotetramer bound to DNA

图 11.2 结合在 DNA 上的 lacI 同源四聚体结构

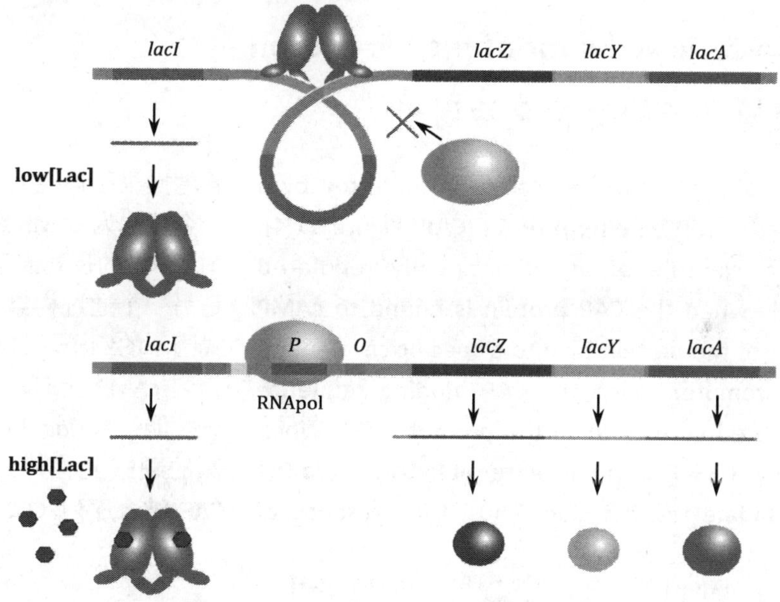

Figure 11.3 When the concentration of lactose [Lac] is low, lacI tetramers bind to operator sequences (O), thereby blocking binding of RNApol to the promoter (P). Alternatively, when [Lac] is high, lactose binds to lacI, preventing the repressor from attaching to O, and allowing transcription by RNApol (see the color figure)

图 11.3 当乳糖 [Lac] 浓度低时，lacI 四聚体与操纵基因（O）结合，从而阻碍了 RNA 聚合酶（绿色）与启动子（P）的结合。此外，当乳糖浓度高时，乳糖与 lacI 结合，阻止阻遏蛋白与操纵基因结合，并允许 RNA 聚合酶进行转录（见彩版）

Besides its ability to bind to specific DNA sequences at the operator, another important property of the lacI protein is its

lacI 蛋白除了具有结合到操纵基因的特殊 DNA 序列的功能外，另

ability to bind to lactose. When lactose is bound to lacI, the shape of the protein changes in a way that prevents it from binding to the operator. Therefore, in the presence of lactose, RNA polymerase is able to bind to the promoter and transcribe the *lac* operon, leading to a moderate level of expression of the *lacZ*, *lacY*, and *lacA* genes. Proteins such as lacI that change their shape and functional properties after binding to a ligand are said to be regulated through an **allosteric** mechanism. The role of lacI in regulating the *lac* operon is summarized in Figure 11.3.

外一个重要的特性就是其结合乳糖的能力。当乳糖结合到 lacI 上，lacI 蛋白的形状发生了改变，从而阻止了其与操纵基因的结合。因此，在乳糖存在的条件下，RNA 聚合酶就能够结合到启动子上并转录乳糖操纵子，从而使 *lacZ*、*lacY* 和 *lacA* 基因在中等的水平上得以表达。像 lacI 蛋白这样在结合了一个配体后改变了形状和功能属性的蛋白质是通过一种变构机制来进行调节的。 图 11.3 总结概括了 lacI 蛋白在调控乳糖操纵子中所扮演的角色。

CAP is an allosteric activator of the lac operon

CAP 是乳糖操纵子的变构激活因子

A second aspect of *lac* operon regulation is conferred by a *trans*-factor called **cAMP binding protein** (**CAP**, Figure 11.4). CAP is another example of an allosterically regulated *trans*-factor. Only when the CAP protein is bound to cAMP can another part of the protein bind to a specific *cis*-element within the *lac* promoter called the **CAP binding sequence (CBS)**. CBS is located very close to the promoter (P). When CAP is bound to at CBS, RNA pol is better able to bind to the promoter and initiate transcription. Thus, the presence of

乳糖操纵子调控的另一方面是通过一个被称为 **cAMP 结合蛋白**（**CAP**，图 11.4）的反式因子来进行的。CAP 是另一个通过构象改变来调控的反式因子的例子。只有当 CAP 蛋白结合到 cAMP 上时，蛋白质的另一部分才能结合 *lac* 启动子上的一个特殊的顺式元件，这个元件被称为 **CAP 结合序列**（**CBS**）。CBS 与启动

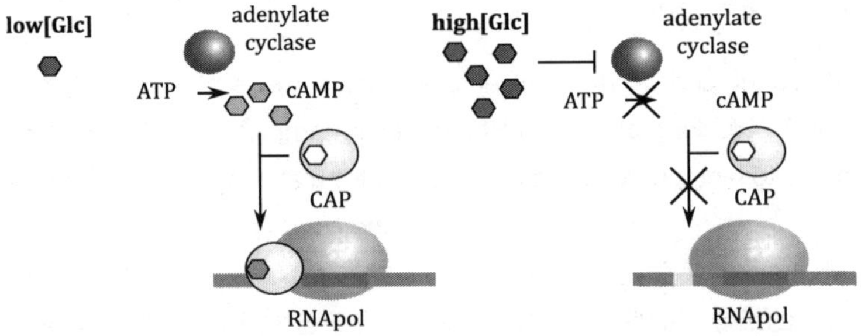

Figure 11.4 CAP, when bound to cAMP, helps RNApol to bind to the *lac* operon. cAMP is produced only when glucose [Glc] is low

图 11.4 当 CAP 与 cAMP 结合，能帮助 RNA 聚合酶与乳糖操纵子结合。cAMP 只有在葡萄糖[Glc]浓度低时才能产生

cAMP ultimately leads to a further increase in *lac* operon transcription.

子（P）位置非常接近。当 CAP 结合到 CBS 上时， RNA 聚合酶就能够更好地结合到启动子上并起始转录。因此，cAMP 的存在最终促使了乳糖操纵子转录的进一步增强。

The physiological significance of regulation by cAMP becomes more obvious in the context of the following information. The concentration of cAMP is inversely proportional to the abundance of glucose: when glucose concentrations are low, an enzyme called **adenylate cyclase** is able to produce cAMP from ATP. Evidently, *E. coli* prefers glucose over lactose, and so expresses the *lac* operon at high levels only when glucose is absent and lactose is present. This provides another layer of logical control of *lac* operon expression: only in the presence of lactose, and in the absence of glucose is the operon expressed at its highest levels.

cAMP 调控的生理意义在下面的内容中将会更加清晰。cAMP 的浓度与葡萄糖的总量成反比：葡萄糖浓度低时，**腺苷酸环化酶**起作用能够使 ATP 产生 cAMP。显然，与乳糖相比，大肠杆菌更加喜欢葡萄糖，所以只有当葡萄糖不存在而乳糖存在时才能够高水平地表达乳糖操纵子。这是乳糖操纵子表达合理控制的另一个层面：只有在乳糖存在而葡萄糖不存在的情况下，操纵子才在最高的水平表达。

MUTANTS OF THE LAC OPERON 乳糖操纵子的突变体

The *lac* operon and its regulators were first characterized by studying mutants of *E. coli* that exhibited various abnormalities in lactose metabolism. Some mutants expressed the *lac* operon genes constitutively, meaning the operon was expressed whether lactose was present in the medium or not. One example of a **constitutive** mutant is O^c (Figure 11.5), in which a mutation in an operator sequence prevents *lacI* from recognizing and binding to the operator. Thus, in O^c mutants, *lacZ*, *lacY*, and *lacA* are expressed whether lactose is present or not. A mutant allele of *lacI* (e.g. I^-) that prevents it from binding to DNA is also a constitutive expresser of the *lac* operon. On the other hand, a mutant of *lacI* called I^s prevents it from binding lactose, so that the mutant represses the *lac* operon whether lactose is present or not.

通过研究在乳糖代谢过程中呈现各种异常的大肠杆菌突变体，首次鉴定了乳糖操纵子及其调控因子。一些突变体组成性地表达乳糖操纵子基因，即在培养基中无论乳糖是否存在操纵子均表达。O^c 是**组成型**突变体的一个例子（图 11.5），其操纵子序列的突变阻止了 *lacI* 识别及结合操纵基因。因此，在 O^c 突变体中，无论乳糖存在与否，*lacZ*、*lacY* 和 *lacA* 均表达。阻止 lacI 结合 DNA 的 *lacI* 等位基因突变体(如 I^-)也会导致乳糖操纵子组成性表达。另外，称为 I^s 的 *lacI* 突变体阻止其结合乳糖，以至于无论乳糖存在与否，突变体均抑制乳糖操纵子表达。

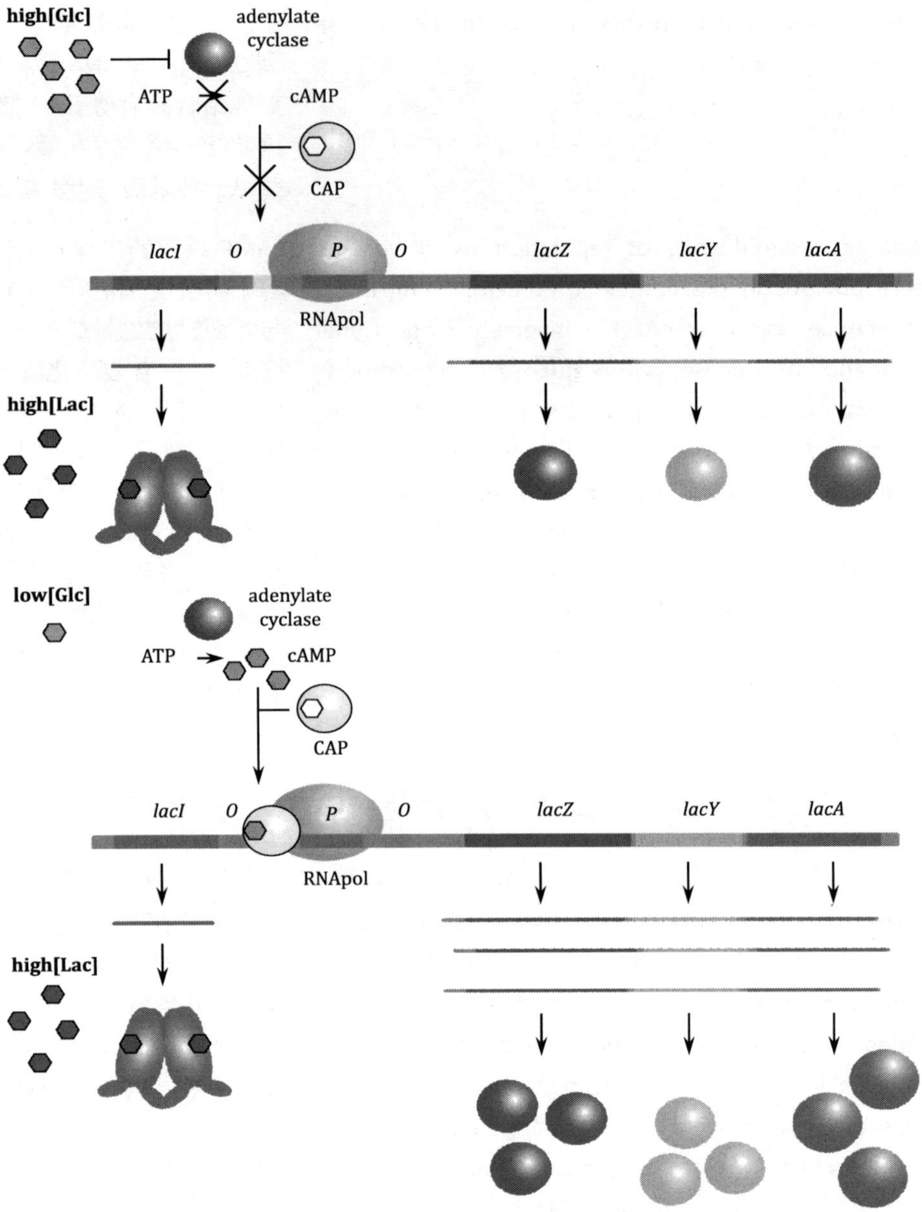

Figure 11.5 When glucose [Glc] and lactose [Lac] are both high, the *lac* operon is transcribed at a moderate level, because CAP (in the absence of cAMP) is unable to bind to its corresponding *cis*-element (yellow) and therefore cannot help to stabilize binding of RNApol at the promoter. Alternatively, when [Glc] is low, and [Lac] is high, CAP and cAMP can bind near the promoter and increase further the transcription of the *lac* operon (see the color figure)

图 11.5 当葡萄糖 [Glc]和乳糖 [Lac]浓度均较高时，乳糖操纵子在中等水平上被转录，因为 CAP（在缺少 cAMP 情况下）不能与其相应的顺式元件（黄色）结合，因此不能帮助稳定 RNA 聚合酶在启动子上的结合。此外，当葡萄糖[Glc]浓度低，乳糖[Lac]浓度高时，CAP 和 cAMP 能在启动子附近结合，并且进一步增强了乳糖操纵子的转录（见彩版）

EUKARYOTIC GENE REGULATION 真核生物基因调控

As we have seen in prokaryotes, transcriptional regulation in eukaryotes involves both *cis*-elements and *trans*-factors. A typical eukaryotic gene, including several types of *cis*-elements, is shown in Figure 11.6. RNA polymerase binds to the gene at its promoter. In eukaryotes, RNApol is part of a large protein complex that includes additional proteins that bind to one or more specific *cis*-elements near the promoter, including **GC boxes, CAAT boxes, and TATA boxes**. High levels of transcription require both the presence of this protein complex at the promoter, as well as their interaction with other *trans*-factors described below. The approximate position of these elements relative to the **transcription start site** (+1) is shown in Figure 11.6, but it should be emphasized that the distance between any of these elements and the transcription start site can vary.

正如我们在原核生物中所知道的那样，真核生物的转录调控也涉及了顺式元件和反式因子。一个典型的包括几种不同类型顺式元件的真核基因如图 11.6 所示。RNA 聚合酶与基因的启动子相结合。在真核生物中，RNA 聚合酶是一个大蛋白质复合体的一部分，这个蛋白质复合体包括了结合启动子附近的一个或更多个特殊顺式元件的其他蛋白，特殊顺式元件包括 **GC 盒**、**CAAT 盒**和 **TATA 盒**等。高水平的转录既要求启动子中这个蛋白质复合体的存在，又要与下面描述的其他反式因子相互作用。这些元件相对于转录起始位点（+1）的大概位置如图 11.6 所示，但是强调一点，任何这些元件和转录起始位点之间的距离是变化的。

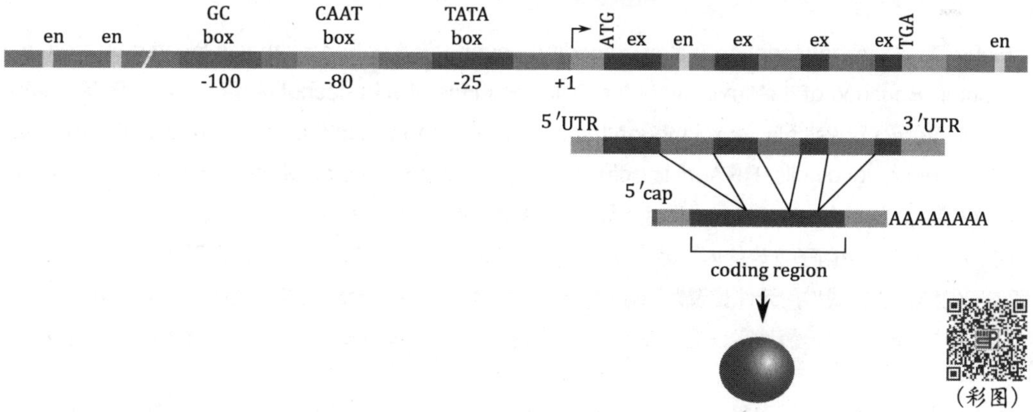

Figure 11.6 Structure of a typical eukaryotic gene. RNA polymerase binding may involve one or more *cis*-elements within the region of a promoter. Enhancers (en) may be located any distance upstream or downstream of the promoter

图 11.6 典型的真核基因结构。启动子区域内，RNA 聚合酶结合可以包括一种或更多的顺式元件。增强子（en）可能位于启动子的上游或下游的任意位置

Even more variation is observed in the position and orientation of the second major type of *cis*-regulatory element in eukaryotes, which are called **enhancers**. Regulatory *trans*-factor proteins called **transcription factors** bind to enhancers, then while still bound to DNA, these proteins interact with RNApol and other proteins at the promoter to activate transcription. Specific transcription factors recognize the DNA sequence of specific enhancers to activate gene expression in specific circumstances. Because DNA is a flexible molecule, enhancers can be located near or far, and either upstream or downstream, from the promoter (Figure 11.7).

真核生物中还存在被称为**增强子**的第二种主要顺式调控元件，在该种元件的位置和方向上可以观察到更多的变化。称为**转录因子**、进行调控的反式因子与增强子结合，当这些蛋白质与 DNA 结合时，其与 RNA 聚合酶及启动子上的其他蛋白相互作用进而激活转录。在特定条件下，特定的转录因子识别特定增强子的 DNA 序列以激活基因表达。因为 DNA 是一个柔性分子，增强子可以位于启动子附近或远处，上游或下游（图 11.7）。

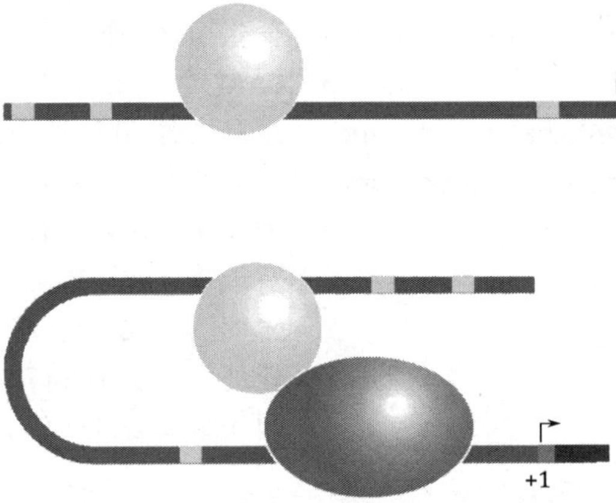

Figure 11.7 A transcription factor (rotundity) bound to an enhancer that is located far from a promoter. Because of the flexibility of the DNA molecule, the transcription factor and RNApol are able to interact physically, even though the *cis*-elements to which they are bound are located far apart. In eukaryotic cells, RNApol is actually part of a large complex of proteins (not shown here) that assembles at the promoter

图 11.7 一个转录因子（球状体）结合在距离启动子较远的一个增强子上。由于 DNA 分子的柔韧性，即使它们结合的顺式作用元件位置距离较远，转录因子和 RNA 聚合酶也能够实体上相互作用。在真核细胞中，RNA 聚合酶其实是组装在启动子上面的一个大蛋白质复合体（此处未给出）的一部分

The *yellow* gene of *Drosophila* demonstrates the modular nature of enhancers. This gene is part of a pathway that produces a black pigment (recall that genes are sometimes named after their mutant phenotypes). Each tissue in *Drosophila* that makes the black pigment produces a specific transcription factor that binds to a corresponding enhancer

果蝇的 *yellow* 基因证明了增强子的组合属性。这个基因是产生黑色素途径中的一个基因（回忆基因有时候是以它们的突变体表现型而命名的）。产生黑色素的果蝇的每个组织都会产生一个特殊的转录

in *yellow* to activate its transcription (Figure 11.8). Thus, specific combinations of *cis*-elements and *trans*-factors control the tissue-specific expression of genes. This is typical of the transcriptional activation of almost any eukaryotic gene: specific transcription factors activate (or in some cases repress) the transcription of target genes under specific conditions.

因子，这个转录因子结合到一个 *yellow* 基因相应的增强子上以激活其转录（图 11.8）。因此，顺式元件和反式因子的特异结合调控了基因的组织特异性表达。这是几乎任何真核基因的转录激活的特点：在特殊的条件下特殊的转录因子激活（或在某些情况下抑制）目标基因的转录。

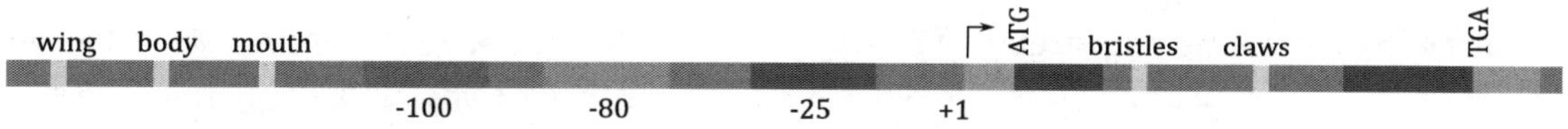

Figure 11.8 Tissue-specific *cis*-regulatory elements within a simplified representation of the *yellow* gene of *Drosophila*

图 11.8 果蝇 *yellow* 基因简图中的组织特异顺式调控元件

REGULATORY ELEMENTS IN EVOLUTION 进化中的调控元件

Mutations can occur in both *cis*-elements and *trans*-factors, resulting in altered patterns of gene expression. If these altered patterns of gene expression produce a selective advantage (or at least do not produce a major disadvantage), they may be maintained and even contribute to evolution of new species.

突变在顺式元件和反式因子中均能发生，结果改变了基因表达的模式。如果这些改变了的基因表达模式产生了一个选择性的优势（或者至少不会产生一个主要的劣势），它们就可能会被保留下来，并且甚至会促成新物种的进化。

The three-spined **stickleback** (Figure 11.9) provides an example of natural selection of a mutation in a *cis*-regulatory element. This fish occurs in two forms: populations that naturally inhabit deep, open water have a spiny pelvic fin that deters larger predator fish from feeding on the stickleback. However, populations of stickleback from shallow water environments lack this spiny pelvic fin. In shallow water, it appears that a long, spiny pelvic fin would be a disadvantage because it frequently contacts the sediment at the bottom of the pond and allows parasitic insects in the sediment to invade the stickleback. Researchers compared genomic DNA fragments of individuals from both deep and shallow water

棘鱼（图 11.9）提供了一个顺式调控元件变异的自然选择的范例。这种鱼以两种形式存在，深栖在开阔水域的种群有一种带刺腹鳍，可以阻止以棘鱼为食的大型捕食性鱼类的捕食。然而，浅水域的棘鱼种群缺乏这种带刺的腹鳍。在浅水区域内，一个带刺的长的腹鳍可能是个劣势，因为它频繁的接触池塘底部的沉积物会使沉积物中的寄生虫入侵棘鱼。如图 11.9 所示，研究人员对比了深、浅水域的棘鱼

environments as shown in Figure 11.9. They observed that in embryos from the deep-water population, a gene called *Pitx* was expressed in several groups of cells, including those that developed into the pelvic fin. Embryos from the shallow-water population expressed *Pitx* in the same groups of cells as the other population, with an important exception: *Pitx* was not expressed in the pelvic fin **primordium** in the shallow-water population. Further analysis showed that the absence of *Pitx* gene expression from the developing pelvic fin of shallow-water stickleback was due to the absence of a particular enhancer element upstream of *Pitx*.

个体的基因组 DNA 片段。他们观察到深水种群的胚胎中，一个称为 *Pitx* 的基因在几个细胞群中表达，包括那些发展成为腹鳍的细胞。像深水种群一样，浅水种群的胚胎在相同的细胞群中表达 *Pitx* 基因，但有一个重要的不同：浅水种群中 *Pitx* 基因不在腹鳍**原基**中表达。进一步分析显示，来自于浅水棘鱼的发育中的腹鳍缺乏 *Pitx* 基因的表达，是由 *Pitx* 基因上游一个特定增强子元件缺失引起的。

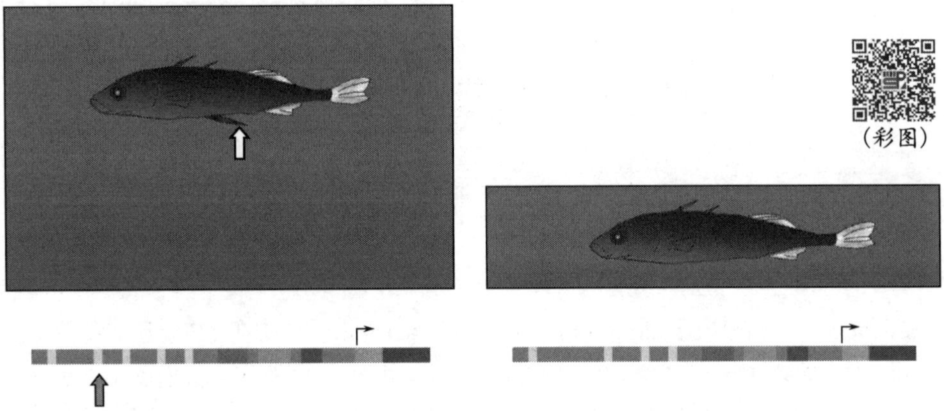

（彩图）

Figure 11.9 Development of a large, spiny pelvic fin in stickleback depends on the presence of a particular enhancer element upstream of a gene called *Pitx*. Mutants lacking this element (and therefore the large pelvic fin) have been selected for in shallow-water environments

图 11.9 棘鱼大的带刺腹鳍的发育取决于 *Pitx* 基因上游一个特殊增强子的存在。缺少这种元件的突变体（因此没有大的带刺腹鳍）在浅水生态环境系下生活

OTHER REGULATORS OF TRANSCRIPTION 其他转录调控因子

Despite the simplified way in which we often represent DNA in figures such as those in this chapter, DNA is almost never entirely separated from chromatin proteins during interphase, and histones remain associated with the DNA at many positions along the molecule even during transcription. The rate of transcription is therefore also controlled by the accessibility of DNA to RNApol and regulatory proteins. If the

尽管我们经常像在本章中的图片那样将 DNA 以简化形式表示出来，但 DNA 在细胞间期几乎从未彻底地从染色质蛋白中分离出来，而且甚至在转录期间，组蛋白仍然沿着分子的许多位置与 DNA 结合。因此转录速率也受 DNA 分子与 RNA

chromatin that contains a particular gene is highly compacted, it is unlikely that the gene will be transcribed, even if all of the necessary *cis*- and *trans*- factors are present. Cells regulate the local structure of chromatin through the action of proteins called **chromatin remodeling** proteins. These include enzymes that add or remove chemical tags such as methyl or acetyl groups. **Acetylated** histones, for example, tend to be associated with actively transcribed genes, whereas deacetylation can causes associated genes to be silenced. Methylation of DNA itself also regulates transcription. Cytosine bases, particularly when followed by a guanine (**CpG sites**) are important targets for methylation. Methylated cytosine within clusters of CpG sites is often associated with transcriptionally inactive DNA. Reversible histone modification and DNA methylation are thus another layer by which eukaryotic cells control the transcription of specific genes.

聚合酶和调控蛋白的结合程度所控制。如果包含一个特定基因的染色质是高度紧缩的，即使所有必需的顺式和反式因子都存在，那这个基因也不可能被转录。细胞通过称为**染色质重构**蛋白的作用调节染色质的自身结构。这个过程包括增加和移除化学标签（如甲基或乙酰基）的酶。例如，**乙酰化**的组蛋白倾向于与活跃转录的基因结合在一起，然而，脱乙酰作用能够导致与组蛋白相结合的基因沉默。DNA 甲基化也调控转录。胞嘧啶碱基，尤其后面是鸟嘌呤（CpG 位点）的时候，这是甲基化的重要靶点。在 CpG 位点簇中甲基化的胞嘧啶经常与转录不活跃的 DNA 联系在一起。因此，可逆的组蛋白修饰和 DNA 甲基化是真核细胞调控特定基因转录的另一个方面。

Interestingly, some apparent changes in gene expression are heritable. For example, the grandchildren of famine victims are known to have lower birth weight than children without a family history of famine. The heritability of altered states of gene expression is surprising, since gene regulation does not usually involve changes in the sequence of DNA. The term **epigenetics** describes any heritable change in phenotype that is associated with a change in something other than chromosomal DNA sequence. Some epigenetic information is inherited transgenerationally, while in other cases, the epigenetic state is inherited following mitotic divisions, but not following meiosis. The basis of at least some types of epigenetic inheritance appears to be the replication of patterns of histone modifications and DNA methylation in parallel with the replication of the primary DNA sequence. It is becoming clear that epigenetics is an important part of biology, and can serve as a type of cellular memory, sometimes within an individual, or sometimes across a few generations.

有趣的是，基因表达中有些明显的改变是可遗传的。例如，众所周知，饥民的孙辈比无饥荒史家族的孩子出生体重轻。基因表达得以改变的遗传力是令人惊奇的，因为基因调控通常不涉及DNA序列的改变。**表观遗传学**这一术语描述了任何表现型的可遗传改变，这些表现型与染色体 DNA 序列改变无关，而与其他某些方面的变化有关系。一些表观遗传信息是隔代遗传的，而在一些其他情况中，表观遗传状态是随着有丝分裂而不是随着减数分裂而遗传的。至少有些类型的表观遗传的基础显示是组蛋白修饰和 DNA 甲基化模式下进行的 DNA 复制，这些复制与基本 DNA 序列复制平行进行。很明显表观遗传学成为了生物学的一个重要部分，并且能够作为一种细胞记忆，有时表观遗传在一个个体内，有时可以贯穿几代。

A winter wheat crop (green) in early spring in the English countryside (see the cover)
英国乡村早春的冬小麦作物（绿色部分）（见封面）

VERNALIZATION IS AN EXAMPLE OF EPIGENETIC CELLULAR MEMORY
春化是表观遗传细胞记忆的一个例子

Many plant species in temperate regions are **winter annuals**, meaning that their seeds germinate in the late summer, and grow vegetatively through early fall before entering a dormant phase during the winter, often under a cover of snow. In the spring, the plant resumes growth and is able to produce seeds before other species that germinated in the spring. In order for this life strategy to work, the winter annual must not resume growth or start flower production until winter has ended. **Vernalization** is the name given to the requirement to experience a long period of cold temperatures prior to flowering.

温带地区许多植物物种是**冬季一年生**植物，也就意味着其种子在夏季晚期发芽，秋季早期迅速营养生长，然后在冬季进入休眠期，通常被积雪覆盖。在次年春季，在其他物种春季发芽之前冬季一年生植物能够恢复生长并结籽。为了使这种生活方式得以实现，冬季一年生植物必须在冬季结束之后恢复生长或开花。**春化作用**是指需要在开花之前经历一段长时间的低温。

How does a plant sense that winter has passed? The signal for resuming growth cannot simply be warm air temperature, since occasional warm days, followed by long periods of freezing, are common in temperate climates. Researchers have discovered that winter annuals use epigenetic mechanisms to sense and "remember" that winter has occurred.

植物是如何感受到冬天已经过去了呢？恢复生长的信号不单纯是温暖的气温，因为在温带气候，偶尔的暖流之后出现长期冰冻的天气是很普遍的现象。研究人员已经发现冬季一年生植物利用表观遗传机制感受并“记忆”冬天已经过去。

Fortunately for the researchers who were interested in vernalization, some varieties of *Arabidopsis* are winter annuals. Through mutational analysis of *Arabidopsis*, researchers found that a gene called *FLC* (*FLOWERING LOCUS C*) is a repressor of the transcription of several of the genes involved in early stages of flowering (Figure 11.10). In the fall and under other warm conditions, the histones associated with *FLC* are acetylated and so *FLC* is transcribed at high levels; expression of flowering genes is therefore entirely repressed. However, in response to cold temperatures, enzymes gradually deacetylate the histones associated with *FLC*. The longer the cold temperatures persist, the more acetyl groups are removed from the *FLC*-associated histones, until finally the

幸运的是，对于那些对春化感兴趣的科研人员来说，有些拟南芥品种是冬季一年生植物。通过拟南芥突变分析，研究人员发现了一个称为*FLC*(*FLOWERING LOCUS C*)的基因，它是在开花初期时几个基因转录的阻遏因子（图 11.10）。在秋天和其他温暖的条件下，与 FLC 结合的组蛋白被乙酰化，故 *FLC* 被高水平转录，因此开花基因的表达被完全抑制。然而，作为对低温的响应，酶逐渐地对 *FLC* 结合的组蛋白脱去乙酰基。低温持续的时间越长，从

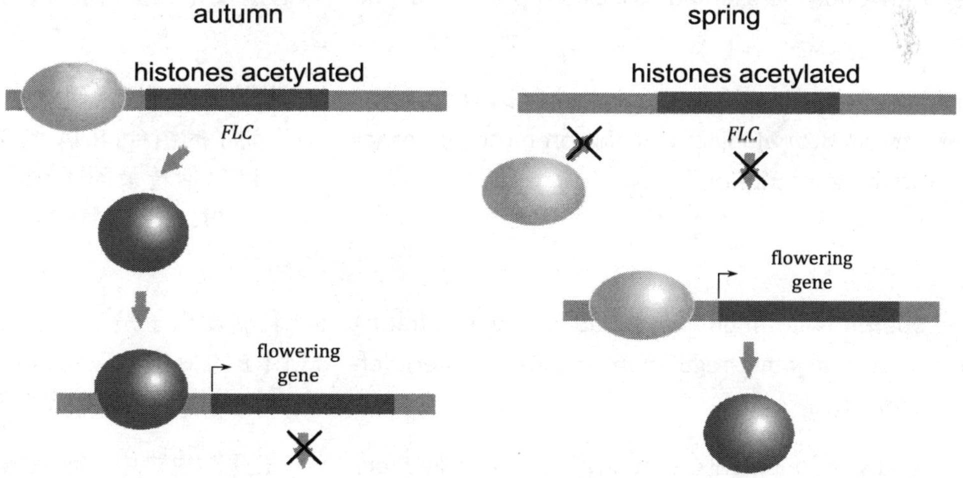

Figure 11.10 In the autumn, histones associated with FLC are acetylated, allowing this repressor of flowering genes to be expressed. During winter, enzymes progressive deacetylate FLC, preventing it from being expressed, and therefore allowing flowering genes to respond to other signals that induce flowering

图 11.10 在秋季，与 FLC 结合的组蛋白乙酰化，允许了这个开花基因阻遏因子的表达。在冬季，酶逐渐对 FLC 脱去乙酰化阻止其表达，因而允许开花基因响应其他诱导开花的信号

FLC locus is no longer transcribed and the flowering genes are free to respond to other environmental and hormonal signals that induce flowering later in the spring. Because the deacetylated state of *FLC* is inherited as cells divide and the plant grows in the early spring, this is an example of a type of cellular memory mediated by an epigenetic mechanism.

FLC 结合的组蛋白上被去除的乙酰基就越多，直到最后 *FLC* 位点不再被转录，开花基因被释放表达，去响应其他在春季晚期诱导开花的环境和激素信号。因为 *FLC* 脱去乙酰基的情况是可以随着早春植物细胞分裂和生长而遗传的，所以这是一个通过表观遗传机制介导细胞记忆的一个实例。

Summary

- Regulation of gene expression is essential to the normal development and efficient functioning of cells.

- 基因表达调控对细胞正常的生长发育和高效功能是必不可少的。

- Gene expression may be regulated by many mechanisms, including those affecting transcript abundance, protein abundance, and post-translational modifications.

- 基因表达可能由许多机制进行调控，包括影响转录本丰度、蛋白质丰度和翻译后修饰等。

- Regulation of transcript abundance may involve controlling the rate of initiation and elongation of transcription, as well as transcript splicing, stability, and turnover.

- 转录本丰度的调控可能包含控制转录起始和延伸速率，以及转录拼接、稳定性和逆转等。

- The rate of initiation of transcription is related to the presence of RNA polymerase and associated proteins at the promoter.

- 转录起始速率与启动子上 RNA 聚合酶及相关蛋白的存在有关。

- RNApol may be blocked from the promoter by repressors, or may be recruited or stabilized at the promoter by other proteins including transcription factors.

- 阻遏蛋白可以阻碍 RNA 聚合酶与启动子的结合，RNA 聚合酶也可能通过包括转录因子在内的其他蛋白使 RNA 聚合酶恢复或稳定在启动子上。

- The *lac* operon is an important paradigm demonstrating both positive and negative regulation through allosteric effects on *trans*-factors.

- 乳糖操纵子是一个证实通过反式因子的变构效应可以正向或反向调控基因表达的重要范例。

- In eukaryotes, *cis*-elements that are usually called enhancers bind to specific *trans*-factors to regulate transcriptional initiation.

- 在真核生物中，通常被称为增强子的顺式元件结合特定的反式因子进而调控转录起始。

- Enhancers may be modular, with each enhancer and its transcription factor regulating a distinct component of a

- 增强子可能是组合作用的，就像在 *yellow* 基因上一样，每一个增

gene's expression pattern, as in the *yellow* gene.

强子及其转录因子共同调控一个基因表达模式中的特定元件。

• Sticklebacks provide examples of recent evolutionary events in which mutation of an enhancer produced a change in morphology and a selective advantage.

• 棘鱼提供了一个通过增强子突变产生形态和选择性优势变化的近期进化事件的例子。

• Chromatin structure, including reversible modifications such as acetylation of histones, and DNA methylation CpG sites also regulates the initiation of transcription.

• 染色质结构，包括像组蛋白乙酰化和 DNA 甲基化 CpG 位点那样的可逆修饰，也能调控转录起始。

• Chromatin modifications or DNA methylation of some genes are heritable over many mitotic, and sometimes even meiotic divisions.

• 一些基因的染色质修饰或者 DNA 甲基化是在进行许多有丝分裂，甚至减数分裂时产生的，是可以遗传的。

• Heritable changes in phenotype that do not result from a change in DNA sequence are called epigenetic. Many epigenetic phenomena involve regulation of gene expression by chromatin modification and/or DNA methylation.

• 由非 DNA 序列改变引起的可遗传的表现型变化称为表观遗传。许多表观遗传现象包括通过染色质修饰和（或）DNA 甲基化以实现基因表达的调控。

Key Terms

gene expression 基因表达
transcriptional regulation 转录调控
operon 操纵子
lactose 乳糖
glucose 葡萄糖
lac operon 乳糖操纵子
lacZ
lacY
lacA
galactosidase 半乳糖苷酶
permease 透性酶
trans-acetylase 转乙酰酶
promoter 启动子
operator 操纵基因
CBS CAP 结合序列
CAP-binding site CAP 结合位点
cis-elements 顺式元件
trans-regulators 反式因子
CAP binding sequence CAP 结合序列
adenylate cyclase 腺苷酸环化酶
constitutive 组成性的
O^c
I^-
I^s
GC boxes GC 盒
CAAT boxes CAAT 盒
TATA boxes TATA 盒
transcription start site 转录起始位点
enhancers 增强子
transcription factors 转录因子
stickleback 棘鱼
primordium 原基
chromatin remodeling 染色质重构
acetylation 乙酰化作用
deacetylation 脱乙酰作用
methylation 甲基化

lacI
homotetramer 同源四聚体
repressor 阻遏蛋白
allosteric 变构
cAMP binding protein cAMP 结合蛋白
CAP cAMP 结合蛋白
CpG
epigenetics 表观遗传学
winter annual 冬季一年生植物
vernalization 春化
FLC

Study Questions

11.1 List all the mechanisms that can be used to regulate gene expression in eukaryotes.

11.1 列出所有能够用来调控真核生物基因表达的机制。

11.2 With respect to the expression of β-galactosidase, what would be the phenotype of each of the following strains of *E. coli*?

a) I^+, O^+, Z^+, Y^+ (no glucose, no lactose)
b) I^+, O^+, Z^+, Y^+ (no glucose, high lactose)
c) I^+, O^+, Z^+, Y^+ (high glucose, no lactose)
d) I^+, O^+, Z^+, Y^+ (high glucose, high lactose)
e) I^+, O^+, Z^-, Y^+ (no glucose, no lactose)
f) I^+, O^+, Z^-, Y^+ (high glucose, high lactose)
g) I^+, O^+, Z^+, Y^- (high glucose, high lactose)
h) I^+, O^c, Z^+, Y^+ (no glucose, no lactose)
i) I^+, O^c, Z^+, Y^+ (no glucose, high lactose)
j) I^+, O^c, Z^+, Y^+ (high glucose, no lactose)
k) I^+, O^c, Z^+, Y^+ (high glucose, high lactose)
l) I^-, O^+, Z^+, Y^+ (no glucose, no lactose)
m) I^-, O^+, Z^+, Y^+ (no glucose, high lactose)
n) I^-, O^+, Z^+, Y^+ (high glucose, no lactose)
o) I^-, O^+, Z^+, Y^+ (high glucose, high lactose)
p) I^s, O^+, Z^+, Y^+ (no glucose, no lactose)
q) I^s, O^+, Z^+, Y^+ (no glucose, high lactose)
r) I^s, O^+, Z^+, Y^+ (high glucose, no lactose)
s) I^s, O^+, Z^+, Y^+ (high glucose, high lactose)

11.2 关于β-半乳糖苷酶的表达，以下每一个大肠杆菌菌株的表现型是什么？

a）I^+, O^+, Z^+, Y^+ (无葡萄糖，无乳糖)
b）I^+, O^+, Z^+, Y^+ (无葡萄糖，高乳糖)
c）I^+, O^+, Z^+, Y^+ (高葡萄糖，无乳糖)
d）I^+, O^+, Z^+, Y^+ (高葡萄糖，高乳糖)
e）I^+, O^+, Z^-, Y^+ (无葡萄糖，无乳糖)
f）I^+, O^+, Z^-, Y^+ (高葡萄糖，高乳糖)
g）I^+, O^+, Z^+, Y^- (高葡萄糖，高乳糖)
h）I^+, O^c, Z^+, Y^+ (无葡萄糖，无乳糖)
i）I^+, O^c, Z^+, Y^+ (无葡萄糖，高乳糖)
j）I^+, O^c, Z^+, Y^+ (高葡萄糖，无乳糖)
k）I^+, O^c, Z^+, Y^+ (高葡萄糖，高乳糖)
l）I^-, O^+, Z^+, Y^+ (无葡萄糖，无乳糖)
m）I^-, O^+, Z^+, Y^+ (无葡萄糖，高乳糖)
n）I^-, O^+, Z^+, Y^+ (高葡萄糖，无乳糖)
o）I^-, O^+, Z^+, Y^+ (高葡萄糖，高乳糖)
p）I^s, O^+, Z^+, Y^+ (无葡萄糖，无乳糖)
q）I^s, O^+, Z^+, Y^+ (无葡萄糖，高乳糖)
r）I^s, O^+, Z^+, Y^+ (高葡萄糖，无乳糖)
s）I^s, O^+, Z^+, Y^+ (高葡萄糖，高乳糖)

11.3 In the *E.coli* strains listed below, some genes are present on both the chromosome, and the extrachromosomal F-factor episome. The genotypes of the chromosome and episome are separated by a slash. What will be the β-galactosidase phenotype of these strains? All of the strains are grown in media that lacks glucose.

11.3 在以下列出的大肠杆菌的菌株中，有些基因既存在于染色体中，也存在于染色体外的 F 因子附加体中。染色体和附加体的表现型是用斜线分开的。这些菌株的β-半乳糖苷酶表现型将会是什么？所有的菌株均生长在缺少葡萄糖的培养基中。

a) $I^+, O^+, Z^+, Y^+ / O^-, Z^-, Y^-$ (high lactose)
b) $I^+, O^+, Z^+, Y^+ / O^-, Z^-, Y^-$ (no lactose)
c) $I^+, O^+, Z^-, Y^+ / O^-, Z^+ Y^+$ (high lactose)
d) $I^+, O^+, Z^-, Y^+ / O^-, Z^+, Y^+$ (no lactose)
e) $I^+, O^+, Z^-, Y^+ / I^-, O^+, Z^+, Y^+$ (high lactose)
f) $I^+, O^+, Z^-, Y^+ / I^-, O^+, Z^+, Y^+$ (no lactose)
g) $I^-, O^+, Z^+, Y^+ / I^+, O^+, Z^-, Y^+$ (high lactose)
h) $I^-, O^+, Z^+, Y^+ / I^+, O^+, Z^-, Y^+$ (no lactose)
i) $I^+, O^c, Z^+, Y^+ / I^+, O^+, Z^-, Y^+$ (high lactose)
j) $I^+, O^c, Z^+, Y^+ / I^+, O^+, Z$-, Y^+ (no lactose)
k) $I^+, O^+, Z^-, Y^+ / I^+, O^c, Z^+, Y^+$ (high lactose)
l) $I^+, O^+, Z^-, Y^+ / I^+, O^c, Z^+, Y^+$ (no lactose)
m) $I^+, O^+, Z^-, Y^+ / I^s, O^+, Z^+, Y^+$ (high lactose)
n) $I^+, O^+, Z^-, Y^+ / I^s, O^+, Z^+, Y^+$ (no lactose)
o) $I^s, O^+, Z^+, Y^+ / I^+, O^+, Z^-, Y^+$ (high lactose)
p) $I^s, O^+, Z^+, Y^+ / I^+, O^+, Z^-, Y^+$ (no lactose)

a) $I^+, O^+, Z^+, Y^+ / O^-, Z^-, Y^-$ (高乳糖)
b) $I^+, O^+, Z^+, Y^+ / O^-, Z^-, Y^-$ (无乳糖)
c) $I^+, O^+, Z^-, Y^+ / O^-, Z^+, Y^+$ (高乳糖)
d) $I^+, O^+, Z^-, Y^+ / O^-, Z^+, Y^+$ (无乳糖)
e) $I^+, O^+, Z^-, Y^+ / I^-, O^+, Z^+, Y^+$ (高乳糖)
f) $I^+, O^+ Z^-, Y^+ / I^-, O^+, Z^+, Y^+$ (无乳糖)
g) $I^-, O^+, Z^+, Y^+ / I^+, O^+, Z^-, Y^+$ (高乳糖)
h) $I^-, O^+, Z^+, Y^+ / I^+, O^+, Z^-, Y^+$ (无乳糖)
i) $I^+, O^c, Z^+, Y^+ / I^+, O^+ Z^-, Y^+$ (高乳糖)
j) $I^+, O^c, Z^+, Y^+ / I^+, O^+, Z^-, Y^+$ (无乳糖)
k) $I^+, O^+, Z^-, Y^+ / I^+, O^c, Z^+, Y^+$ (高乳糖)
l) $I^+, O^+, Z^-, Y^+ / I^+, O^c, Z^+, Y^+$ (无乳糖)
m) $I^+, O^+, Z^-, Y^+ / I^s, O^+, Z^+, Y^+$(高乳糖)
n) $I^+, O^+, Z^-, Y^+ / I^s, O^+, Z^+, Y^+$ (无乳糖)
o) $I^s, O^+, Z^+, Y^+ / I^+, O^+, Z^-, Y^+$ (高乳糖)
p) $I^s, O^+, Z^+, Y^+ / I^+, O^+, Z^-, Y^+$ (无乳糖)

11.4 What genotypes of *E. coli* would be most useful in demonstrating that the *lacO* operator is a cis-acting regulatory factor?

11.4 什么基因型的大肠杆菌在论证乳糖操纵基因（*lacO*）是顺式作用调控因子时是最有用的？

11.5 What genotypes of *E.coli* would be useful in demonstrating that the *lacI* repressor is a *trans*-acting regulatory factor?

11.5 什么基因型的大肠杆菌在论证 *lacI* 阻遏蛋白是一个反式作用调控因子上是最有用的？

11.6 What would be the effect of the following loss-of-function mutations on the expression of the *lac* operon?
a) loss-of-function of adenylate cyclase
b) loss of DNA binding ability of CAP
c) loss of cAMP binding ability of CAP
d) mutation of CAP binding site (CBS) cis-element so that CAP could not bind

11.6 以下功能丧失的突变对乳糖操纵子的表达会有什么影响？
a）腺苷环化酶的功能丧失
b）CAP 的 DNA 结合能力丧失
c）CAP 的 cAMP 结合能力丧失
d）CAP 结合位点（CBS）顺式元件的突变结果使 CAP 不能够结合

11.7 How are eukaryotic and prokaryotic gene regulation systems similar? How are they different?

11.7 真核生物和原核生物的基因调控系统有何相似之处？它们又有何不同？

11.8 Deep-water sticklebacks that are heterozygous for a loss-of-function mutation in the coding region of *Pitx* look just like homozygous wild-type fish from the same popula-

11.8 *Pitx* 编码区功能缺失的深水域棘鱼突变杂合体看起来与来自相同种群的纯合的野生型一样。如果

tion. What phenotype or phenotypes would be observed if a wild-type fish from a deep-water population mated with a wild-type fish from a shallow-water population?

来自深水种群的野生型鱼与浅水域种群的野生型鱼交配，那么会观察到什么表现型呢？

11.9 Some varieties of *Arabidopsis*, including those adopted for lab use, do not require vernalization before flowering. How might these varieties have evolved?

11.9 有些种类的拟南芥，包括那些实验室所采用的，不要求开花前春化，这些种类可能是如何进化的？

11.10 Histone deacetylase (HDAC) is an enzyme involved in gene regulation. What might be the phenotype of a winter annual plant that lacked HDAC function?

11.10 组蛋白脱乙酰酶（HDAC）是一种涉及基因调控的酶。缺少 HDAC 功能的冬季一年生植物的表现型可能是什么？

Chapter 12

CANCER GENETICS 癌症遗传学

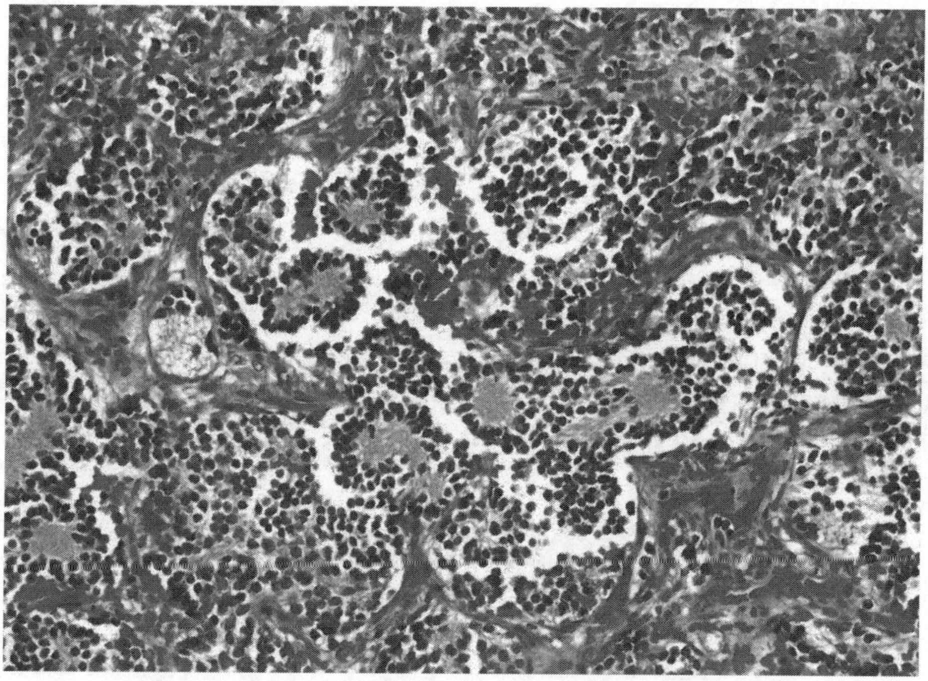

Stained histological section of a neuroblastoma in an adrenal gland (see the cover)
肾上腺成神经细胞瘤的染色组织切片（见封面）

Cancer is any one of a group of diseases that exhibit uncontrolled growth, invasion of adjacent tissues, and sometimes **metastasis** (the movement of cancer cells through the blood or lymph). In cancer cells, the regulatory mechanisms that control cell division and limit abnormal growth have been disrupted, usually by the accumulation of several mutations. Cancer is therefore essentially a genetic disease. Although

癌症是无限制增长，能够侵染邻近组织并且有时候发生**转移**（癌细胞通过血液和淋巴液移动）的一种疾病。癌细胞中，控制细胞分裂并且限制异常增长的调控机制通常已经被数个突变积累所破坏。因此，本质上癌症是遗传性疾病，尽管一

some cancer-related mutations may be heritable, most cancers are sporadic, meaning they arise from new mutations that occur in the individual who has the disease. In this chapter we will examine the connection between cancer and genes.

些与癌症相关的突变可能是遗传的，但大多数癌症是散发性的，也就意味着它们是由患病个体上发生的新突变引起的。在本章中，我们将探讨癌症与基因之间的联系。

CANCER CELL BIOLOGY 癌症细胞生物学

Cancer is a progressive disease that usually begins with increased frequency of cell division (Figure 12.1). Under the microscope, this may be detectable as increased cellular and nuclear size, and an increased proportion of cells undergoing mitosis. As the disease progresses, cells typically lose their normal shape and tissue organization. Tissues with increased cell division and abnormal tissue organization exhibit **dysplasia**. Eventually a tumor develops, which can grow rapidly and expand into adjacent tissues. As cellular damage accumulates and additional control mechanisms are lost, some cells may break free of the primary tumor, pass into the blood or lymph system, and be transported to another organ, where they develop into new tumors (Figure 12.2). The early detection of tumors is important so that they can be treated or

癌症是一种进行性疾病，通常以细胞分裂的频率增加开始（图 12.1）。在显微镜下，癌症可能随着细胞数量、细胞核大小和处于有丝分裂的细胞增长比例而被检测出来。随着疾病进一步发展，细胞通常会失去它们原有的形状和组织结构。携带分裂频率增加的细胞和异常结构的组织会表现出**发育异常**。最后，肿瘤进一步发育，它会迅速增长并扩散到邻近组织当中。随着细胞损伤的积累和其他调控机制被破坏，一些细胞可能脱离原发肿瘤并释放出来，进入到血液或淋巴系统

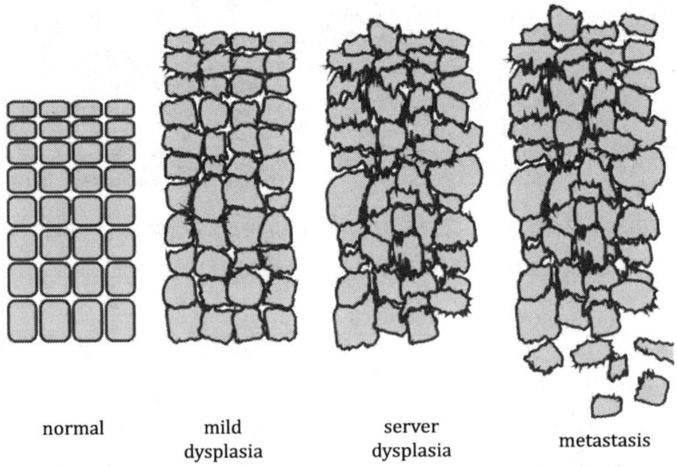

Figure 12.1 Progressive increases in cell division and abnormal cell morphology associated with cancer

图 12.1 与癌症有关的细胞分裂进行性增长和异常的细胞形态

removed before the onset of metastasis.

中，并且运输到另一个器官形成新的肿瘤（图 12.2）。肿瘤的早期检测是很重要的，因为在癌细胞转移扩散前是可以被治愈或切除的。

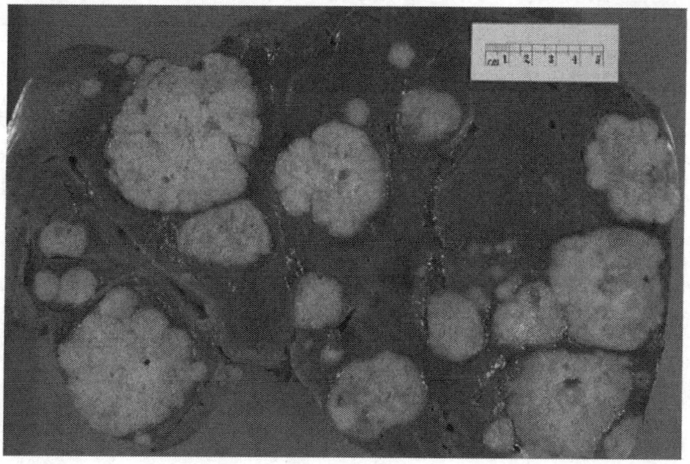

（彩图）

Figure 12.2 Secondary tumors (white) develop in the liver from cells of a metastatic pancreatic cancer

图 12.2 来源于转移性胰腺癌细胞的继发性肿瘤（白色）在肝脏中生长

MUTAGENS AND CARCINOGENS 诱变剂与致癌物

A **carcinogen** is any agent that directly increases the incidence of cancer. Most, but not all carcinogens are mutagens. Carcinogens that do not directly damage DNA include substances that accelerate cell division, thereby leaving less opportunity for cell to repair induced mutations, or errors in replication. Carcinogens that act as mutagens may be biological, physical, or chemical in nature, although the term is most often used in relation to chemical substances.

致癌物是直接增加癌变发生率的任何物质。大多数但并不是所有的致癌物都是诱变剂。不直接损伤 DNA 的致癌物包括加速细胞分裂的物质，这类致癌物使细胞很少有机会去修复突变或复制中的错误。尽管“致癌物”这一术语经常与化学物质有关，但充当诱变剂的致癌物在本质上则可能是生物、物理或化学物质。

Human papilloma virus (**HPV**, Figure 12.3) is an example of a biological carcinogen. Almost all cervical cancers begin with infection by HPV, which contains genes that disrupt the normal pattern of cell division within the host cell. Any gene that

人乳头状瘤病毒（**HPV**，图 12.3）是生物致癌物的例子。几乎所有的宫颈癌都开始于人乳头状瘤病毒的感染，该病毒含有在宿主细胞中

leads to an uncontrolled increase in cell division is called an **oncogene**. The HPV E6 and E7 genes are considered oncogenes because they inhibit the host cell's natural tumor suppressing proteins (include p53, described below). The product of the E5 gene mimics the host's own signals for cell division, and these and other viral gene products may contribute to dysplasia, which is detected during a Pap smear (Figure 12.4). Detection of abnormal cell morphology in a Pap smear is not necessarily evidence of cancer. It must be emphasized again that cells have many regulatory mechanisms to limit division and growth, and for cancer to occur, each of these mechanisms must be disrupted. This is one reason why only a minority of individuals with HPV infections ultimately develop cancer. Although most HPV-related cancers are cervical, HPV infection can also lead to cancer in other tissues, in both women and men.

破坏细胞分裂正常模式的基因。任何引起细胞分裂无限增长的基因都被称作**致癌基因**。人乳头状瘤病毒 E6 和 E7 基因被认为是致癌基因，因为它们可以抑制宿主细胞原有的肿瘤抑制蛋白（包括 p53，下述）。E5 基因的产物模拟宿主细胞进行细胞分裂的信号，并且这些基因和其他病毒基因产物可能导致发育异常，这些病毒基因产物在子宫颈抹片中可以被检测到（图 12.4）。在子宫颈抹片检查中发现异常细胞形态不一定是患有癌症的证据。必须再次强调一下，细胞有许多调控机制限制分裂和增长，因此癌症若想发生，必须每个机制都被破坏。这就是为什么最终仅仅少数感染 HPV 的个体患癌症。尽管大多数与 HPV 相关的癌症是宫颈癌，但 HPV 感染也能导致女性或男性其他组织产生癌症。

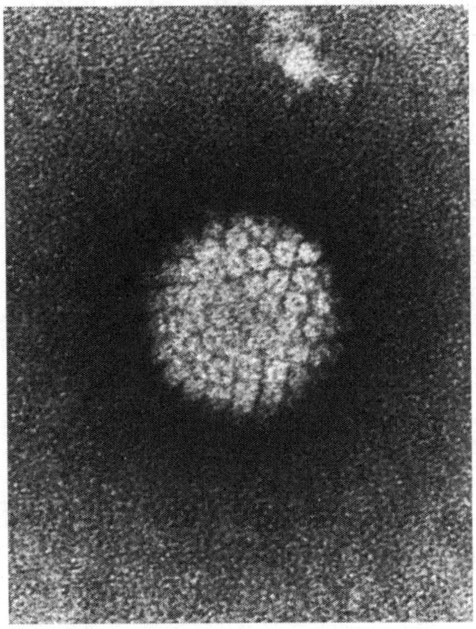

Figure 12.3 Electron micrograph of HPV

图 12.3 人乳头状瘤病毒的电子显微照片

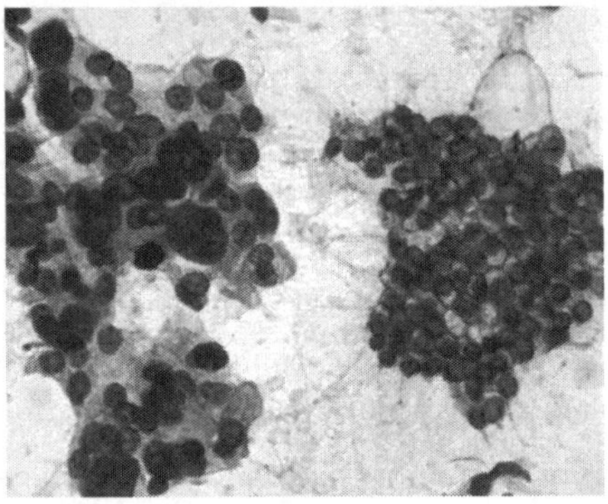

Figure 12.4 Dysplastic (left) and normal (right) cells from a Pap smea

图 12.4 子宫颈抹片检查中发育异常（左）和正常的（右）细胞

Radiation is a well-known physical carcinogen, because of its potential to induce DNA damage within the body. The most damaging type of radiation is **ionizing**, meaning waves or particles with sufficient energy to strip electrons from the

辐射是众所周知的物理致癌剂，因为它具有诱导身体内部 DNA 损伤的潜在危险。最具破坏性的辐射类型是**电离辐射**，即具有充足能量的

molecules they encounter, including DNA or molecules that can subsequently react with DNA. Ionizing radiation, which includes X-rays, gamma rays, and some wavelengths of ultraviolet rays, is distinct from the non-ionizing radiation of microwave ovens, cell phones, and radios. As with other carcinogens, mutation of multiple, independent genes that normally regulate cell division is required before cancer develops.

波或粒子剥离了它们遇到的分子中的电子，其中包括 DNA 分子或之后与 DNA 反应的分子。电离辐射包括 X 射线、γ 射线和一些波长的紫外线，明显不同于微波炉、手机和收音机的非电离辐射。正如其他致癌物那样，癌症发展前需要正常调控细胞分裂的多个独立基因的突变。

Chemical carcinogens (Table 12.1) can be either natural or synthetic compounds that, based on animal feeding trials or **epidemiological** (i.e. human population) studies, increase the incidence of cancer. The definition of a chemical as a carcinogen is problematic for several reasons. Some chemicals become carcinogenic only after they are metabolized into another compound in the body; not all species or individuals may metabolize chemicals in the same way. Also, the carcinogenic properties of a compound are usually dependent on its dose. It can be difficult to define a relevant dose for both lab animals and humans. Nevertheless, when a correlation between cancer incidence and chemical exposure is observed, it is usually possible to find ways to reduce exposure to that chemical.

化学致癌物（表 12.1）可以是天然的，也可以是基于动物饲养试验或**流行病学**（即人类群体）研究能够增加癌症发生率的人工合成的化合物。由于几种原因作为致癌物的化学药品是很难下确切定义的。一些化学物质只有当它们在身体中代谢为其他化合物时才是致癌的，但并不是所有的物种或个体都能通过相同的方式代谢该化学物质。一种化合物的致癌性通常也取决于它的剂量，但是很难为实验室动物和人类规定一个确切的剂量。尽管如此，当观察到癌症发生率和接触化学药品之间的相关性时，通常可以发现一些方法去减少对这种化学药品的接触。

Table 12.1 Known human carcinogens [International Agency for Research on Cancer "Carcinogenic to humans" (Group 1)]. (Source: American Cancer Society)

表 12.1 已知的人类致癌物[国际癌症研究机构 1 类“人类致癌物”]（来源：美国癌症协会）

Exposure circumstances	暴露环境
* Aluminum production	* 铝生产
* Arsenic in drinking-water	* 饮用水中的砷
* Auramine production	* 碱性嫩黄的生产
* Boot and shoe manufacture and repair	* 靴子和鞋的生产及修理
* Chimney sweeping	* 烟囱打扫
* Coal gasification , Coal-tar distillation, Coke production	* 煤的气化，煤焦油分馏，焦炭生产
* Furniture and cabinet making	* 家具及橱柜制造

Continues	续表
Exposure circumstances	**暴露环境**
* Hematite mining (underground) with exposure to radon	* 接触氡气的赤铁矿业（地下）
* Involuntary smoking (exposure to secondhand or 'environmental' tobacco smoke)	* 被动吸烟（暴露在二手烟或周围的吸烟环境中）
* Iron and steel founding	* 钢铁铸造
* Isopropyl alcohol manufacture (strong-acid process)	* 异丙醇制造（强酸法）
* Magenta production	* 品红染料生产
* Painter (occupational exposure as a)	* 油漆匠（职业性接触）
* Paving and roofing with coal-tar pitch	* 用焦油沥青铺装和铺盖屋顶
* Rubber industry	* 橡胶产业
* Strong-inorganic-acid mists containing sulfuric acid (occupational exposure to)	* 含硫酸的无机强酸雾（职业性接触）
* Tobacco smoking and tobacco smoke	* 烟草烟雾和吸烟
Mixtures	**混合物**
* Aflatoxins (naturally occurring mixtures of)	* 黄曲霉毒素（自然发生的混合物）
* Alcoholic beverages	* 酒精饮料
* Areca nut	* 槟榔果
* Betel quid	* 槟榔嚼块
* Coal-tar pitches	* 煤沥青
* Coal-tars	* 煤焦油
* Herbal remedies containing plant species of the genus *Aristolochia*	* 含有马兜铃属植物种类的草药
* Household combustion of coal, indoor emissions from	* 家庭燃烧煤（室内燃烧）
* Mineral oils, untreated and mildly treated	* 未经处理或粗糙处理的矿物油
* Phenacetin, analgesic mixtures containing	* 含有非那西汀的镇痛剂
* Salted fish (Chinese-style)	* 中国式咸鱼
* Shale-oils	* 页岩油
* Soots	* 煤烟
* Tobacco, smokeless	* 无烟的烟草制品（如嚼烟）
* Wood dust	* 木粉尘
Agents and groups of agents	**媒介物和一组媒介混合物**
* 4-Aminobiphenyl	* 4 -氨基联苯
* Arsenic and arsenic compounds (Note: This applies to the group of compounds as a whole)	* 砷及砷的化合物（注：本评价适用于一组化合物作为一个整体）
* Asbestos	* 石棉
* Azathioprine	* 硫唑嘌呤
* Benzene	* 苯
* Benzidine	* 联苯胺
* Benzo[a]pyrene	* 苯并[a]芘
* Beryllium and beryllium compounds	* 铍及铍的化合物

Continues 续表

Agents and groups of agents	媒介物和一组媒介混合物
* *N,N*-Bis(2-chloroethyl)-2-naphthylamine (Chlornaphazine)	* *N,N*-二（2-氯乙基）-2-萘胺（萘氮芥）
* Bis(chloromethyl)ether and chloromethyl methyl ether (technical-grade)	* 二（氯甲基）醚和氯甲基甲醚（工业级）
* 1,3-Butadiene	* 1,3-丁二烯
* 1,4-Butanediol dimethanesulfonate (Busulphan; Myleran)	* 1,4-丁二醇二甲烷磺酸酯（又名白消安、马利兰）
* Cadmium and cadmium compounds	* 镉及镉的化合物
* Chlorambucil	* 苯丁酸氮芥
* 1-(2-Chloroethyl)-3-(4-methylcyclohexyl)-1-nitrosourea (Methyl-CCNU; Semustine)	* 1-(2-氯乙基)-3-(4-甲基)-1-亚硝基脲（甲基亚硝脲，司莫司汀）
* Chromium[Ⅵ]	* 铬化合物（六价）
* Ciclosporin	* 环霉素
* Cyclophosphamide	* 环磷酰胺
* Diethylstilbestrol	* 己烯雌酚
* Dyes metabolized to benzidine	* 基于连苯胺的染料
* Epstein-Barr virus	* EB 病毒
* Erionite	* 毛沸石
* Estrogen-progestogen menopausal therapy (combined)	* 绝经期雌孕激素联合疗法
* Estrogen-progestogen oral contraceptives (combined) (Note: There is also convincing evidence in humans that these agents confer a protective effect against cancer in the endometrium and ovary)	* 雌孕激素类口服避孕药（注：有可靠证据显示这类药物也有对子宫内膜癌与卵巢癌的抵抗作用）
* Estrogen therapy, postmenopausal	* 绝经后的雌激素替代疗法
* Ethanol in alcoholic beverages	* 酒精饮料中的乙醇
* Ethylene oxide	* 环氧乙烷
* Etoposide in combination with cisplatin and bleomycin	* 依托泊苷与顺铂和博莱霉素合用
* Formaldehyde	* 甲醛
* Gallium arsenide	* 砷化镓
* Helicobacter pylori (infection with)	* 幽门螺杆菌（感染）
* Hepatitis B virus (chronic infection with)	* 乙型肝炎病毒（慢性感染）
* Hepatitis C virus (chronic infection with)	* 丙型肝炎病毒（慢性感染）
* Human immunodeficiency virus type 1 (infection with)	* 人类免疫缺陷病毒 1 型，即艾滋病（感染）
* Human papillomavirus types 16, 18, 31, 33, 35, 39, 45, 51, 52, 56, 58, 59 and 66	* 人体乳头状瘤病毒 16、18、31、33、35、39、45、51、52、56、58、59 和 66 型
* Human T-cell lymphotropic virus type Ⅰ	* 人类 T 细胞淋巴病毒Ⅰ型（HTLV-1）
* Melphalan	* 左旋苯丙氨酸氮芥（米尔法兰）
* 8-Methoxypsoralen (Methoxsalen) plus ultraviolet A radiation	* 8-甲氧补骨脂素（甲氧沙林），加上紫外线的辐射

Agents and groups of agents	媒介物和一组媒介混合物
* Methylenebis(chloroaniline) (MOCA)	* 亚甲基双（氯胺苯）（二苯基甲烷）
* MOPP and other combined chemotherapy including alkylating agents	* NOPP（氮芥、长春新碱、丙卡巴肼、强的松）及其他包括烷化剂的联合化疗
* Mustard gas (Sulfur mustard)	* 芥子气（硫芥）
* 2-Naphthylamine	* 2-萘胺
* Neutrons	* 中子辐射
* Nickel compounds	* 镍化合物
* *N*'-nitrosonornicotine (NNN) and 4-(*N*-nitrosomethylamino)-1-(3-pyridyl)-1-butanone (NNK)	* *N*'-亚硝基降烟碱（NNN）与 4-(*N*-亚硝基甲氨基)-1-(3-吡啶基)-1-丁酮（NNK）
* *Opisthorchis* viverrini (infection with)	* 后睾吸虫（感染）
* Oral contraceptives, combined estrogen-progestogen	* 口服避孕药，结合雌性激素-孕激素
* Oral contraceptives, sequential	* 口服避孕药，连续
* Phosphorus-32, as phosphate	* 磷-32，作为磷酸盐
* Plutonium-239 and its decay products (may contain plutonium-240 and other isotopes),	* 钚-239 和其衰变产物（可能含有钚 240 和其他同位素）
*Radioiodines, short-lived isotopes, including iodine-131	* 含碘-131 的短期同位素放射性碘
* Radionuclides, a-particle-emitting, internally deposited	* 体内沉积的释放 α 粒子的放射性同位素
* Radionuclides, b-particle-emitting, internally deposited	* 体内沉积的释放 β 粒子的放射性同位素
* Radium-224, Radium-226, Radium-228, Radium-222 and their decay products	* 镭-224，镭-226，镭-228，镭-222 及其衰变产物
* *Schistosoma* haematobium (infection with)	* 埃及血吸虫（感染）
* Silica, crystalline (inhaled in the form of quartz or cristobalite from occupational sources)	* 二氧化硅晶体（来自职业资源的以石英或方石英的形态吸入）
* Solar radiation	* 太阳辐射
* Talc containing asbestiform fibres	* 滑石含石棉状纤维
* Tamoxifen (Note: tamoxifen reduces the risk of contralateral breast cancer)	* 他莫西芬，三苯氧胺（注：有确凿的证据证明他莫西芬也能够减少乳腺癌患者发生对侧乳腺癌的风险）
* 2,3,7,8-Tetrachlorodibenzo-para-dioxin	* 2,3,7,8-四氯二苯并二噁英（TCDD）
* Thiotepa	* 噻替哌（1,1',1"-三乙撑硫代磷酰胺）
* Thorium-232 and its decay productsortho-Toluidine	* 钍-232 及其衰变产物
* Treosulfan	* 苏消安（丁四醇磺酯）
* Vinyl chloride	* 氯乙烯
* X- and Gamma (g)-radiation	* X 射线和 γ 射线

Continues　续表

ONCOGENES 致癌基因

The control of cell division involves many different genes. Some of these genes act as signaling molecules to activate normal progression through the cell cycle. One of the pre-requisites for cancer occurs when one or more of these activators of cell division become mutated.

细胞分裂的调控与许多不同的基因有关。其中一些基因作为信号分子通过细胞周期去激活正常生长过程。癌症发生的首要条件之一是一个或多个上述细胞分裂的活化因子发生突变。

The mutation may involve a change in the coding sequence of the protein, so that it is more active than normal, or a change in the regulation of its expression, so that it is produced at higher levels than normal, or persists in the cell longer than normal. Genes that are a part of the normal regulation of cell division, but which after mutation contribute to cancer, are called **proto-oncogenes**. Once a proto-oncogene has been abnormally activated by mutation, it is called an oncogene. More than 100 genes have been defined as proto-oncogenes. These include genes at almost every step of the signaling pathways that normally induce cell to divide, including growth factors, **receptors**, **signal transducers**, and transcription factors.

突变可能包括蛋白质编码序列的改变，以至于它比正常基因更加活跃，或由于其表达调控的变化，因此它会比正常基因表达水平更高或表达持续时间更长。正常调控细胞分裂的一部分基因突变后会引发癌症，这些基因被称为**原癌基因**。一旦原癌基因由于突变异常地激活，它便被称为致癌基因。已经有超过 100 个基因被定义为原癌基因。这些原癌基因包括正常诱导细胞分裂的信号转导通路的几乎每个步骤中的基因，包括生长因子、**受体**、**信号转导分子**和转录因子。

ras is an example of a proto-oncogene(Figure 12.5). ras acts as a switch within signal transduction pathways, including the regulation of cell division. When a receptor protein receives a signal for cell division, the receptor activates *ras*, which in turn activates other signaling components, ultimately leading to activation of genes involved in cell division. Certain mutations of the *ras* sequence causes it to be in a permanently active form, which can lead to constitutive activation of the cell cycle. This mutation is dominant as are most oncogenes.

ras 是一个原癌基因的例子（图 12.5）。ras 充当信号转导通路中的开关，包括细胞分裂的调控。当受体蛋白接收到细胞分裂的信号时，受体蛋白就激活 *ras*，ras 进而依次激活其他的信号组分，最后导致参与细胞分裂的基因活化。*ras* 基因序列的某些突变会使它处于持续的激活状态，这能导致细胞周期组成性激活。正如大多数致癌基因那样，这个突变是显性突变。

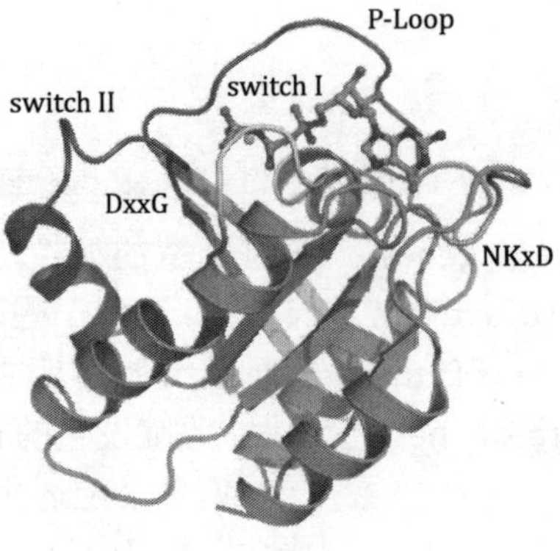

Figure 12.5 Structure of the ras protein (see the color figure)

图 12.5 ras 蛋白结构（见彩版）

TUMOR SUPPRESSOR GENES 肿瘤抑制基因

More than 30 genes are classified as **tumor suppressors**. The normal functions of these genes include repair of DNA, induction of programmed cell death (**apoptosis**) and prevention of abnormal cell division. In contrast to proto-oncogenes, in tumor suppressors it is loss-of-function mutations that contribute to the progression of cancer. This means that tumor suppressor mutations tend to be recessive, and thus both alleles must be mutated in order to allow abnormal growth to proceed. It is perhaps not surprising that mutations in tumor suppressor genes, are more likely than oncogenes to be inherited. An example is the tumor suppressor gene, ***BRCA1***, which is involved in DNA-repair. Inherited mutations in *BRCA1* increase a woman's lifetime risk of breast cancer by up to seven times, although these heritable mutations account for only about 10% of breast cancer. Thus, sporadic rather than inherited mutations are the most common sources of both oncogenes and disabled tumor suppressor genes.

30 多个基因被归类为**肿瘤抑制基因**。这些基因的正常功能包括 DNA 修复、诱导程序性细胞死亡（**细胞凋亡**）和阻止细胞异常分裂。与原癌基因相比，肿瘤抑制基因的功能性缺失突变促进了癌症发展。这就意味着肿瘤抑制基因突变倾向于隐性，因此只有两个等位基因都产生了突变才导致细胞异常生长。因而肿瘤抑制基因的突变比致癌基因更容易被遗传或许就不足为奇了。肿瘤抑制基因的一个例子是乳腺癌易感基因（***BRCA1***），它参与 DNA 的修复。尽管 *BRCA1* 基因的遗传突变导致的乳腺癌大约只占了乳腺癌总数的 10%，但它使女性一生当中患乳腺癌的风险增加了 7 倍。因此，不是遗传突变，而是散发性突变才是致癌基因和无效的肿瘤抑制基因的最普遍来源。

An important tumor suppressor gene is a transcription factor named **p53** (Figure 12.6). Other proteins in the cell sense DNA damage, or abnormalities in the cell cycle and activate p53 through several mechanisms including **phosphorylation** (attachment of phosphate to specific site on the protein) and transport into the nucleus. In its active form, p53 induces the transcription of genes with several different types of tumor

一个重要的肿瘤抑制基因是名为 **p53** 的转录因子（图 12.6）。细胞中的其他蛋白感受到 DNA 损伤或细胞周期中的异常情况，且通过包括**磷酸化**（磷酸基团结合到蛋白质的特定位置上）在内的几种机制激活 p53 并将其运输到细胞核

suppressing functions, including DNA repair, cell cycle arrest, and apoptosis. Over 50% of human tumors contain mutations in p53. People who inherit only one function copy of p53 have a greatly increased incidence of early onset cancer. However, as with the other cancer related genes we have discussed, most mutations in p53 are sporadic, rather than inherited.

中。在其活化状态下，p53 诱导几种具有不同类型的肿瘤抑制功能的基因转录，其中包括 DNA 修复、细胞周期阻滞和细胞凋亡等相关的基因。超过 50%的人类肿瘤中含有 p53 基因突变。只遗传了 p53 的一个功能拷贝的人有很高的早发性癌症发生率。然而，正如我们讨论过的其他与基因相关的癌症一样，大多数 p53 基因突变是散发性的，而不是遗传的。

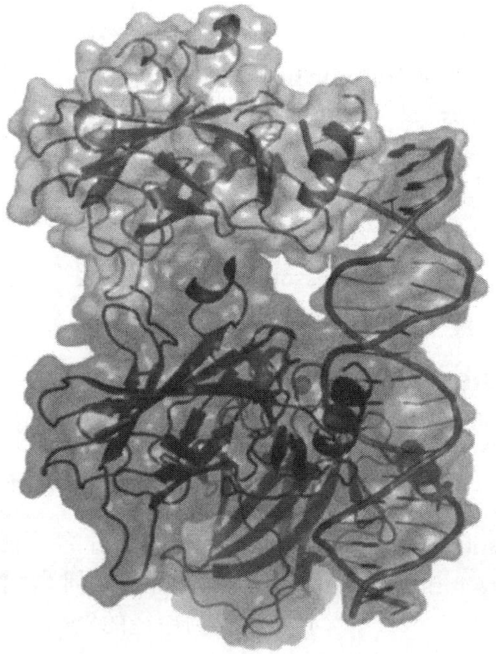

Figure 12.6 p53 bound to its target site on a DNA molecule (see the color figure)

图 12.6 p53 结合到 DNA 分子的靶点上（见彩版）

Summary

- Cancer is the name given to a class of different diseases that share common properties.

• 癌症是一类具有共同特征的疾病的代名词。

- Most cancers require accumulation of mutations in several different genes.

• 大多数癌症的产生需要在几个不同基因上产生突变积累。

- Most cancer causing mutations are sporadic, rather than inherited, and most are caused by environmental carcinogens, including virus, radiation, and certain chemicals.

• 引起突变的大部分癌症是散发的，而不是遗传的，并且大多数是由环境致癌物引起的，其中包括病毒、辐射和某些化学药品。

- Oncogenes are hyperactivated regulators of cell division, and are often derived from gain-of-function mutations in

• 致癌基因是高度活化的细胞分裂的调控因子，并且经常来源于原

proto-oncogenes.

• Tumor suppressor genes normal help to repair DNA damage, arrest cell division, or to kill over proliferating cells. Loss-of-function of these genes contributes to the progression of cancer.

癌基因的功能获得性突变。

• 正常的肿瘤抑制基因帮助修复DNA损伤、阻滞细胞分裂或杀死过度增生细胞。这些基因的功能性缺失促进了癌症的发展。

Key Terms

metastasis 转移
dysplasia 发育不良
carcinogen 致癌物
HPV 人乳头状瘤病毒
oncogene 致癌基因
ionizing 电离
epidemiology 流行病学
proto-oncogene 原癌基因
receptor 受体
signal transduction 信号转导
ras
apoptosis 细胞凋亡
BRC1A
p53
tumor suppressor 肿瘤抑制基因
phosphorylation 磷酸化

Study Questions

12.1 Why do oncogenes tend to be dominant, but mutations in tumor suppressors tend to be recessive?

12.1 为什么致癌基因倾向于显性，但抑癌基因却倾向于隐性？

12.2 What tumor suppressing functions are controlled by p53? How can a single gene affect so many different biological pathways?

12.2 p53 基因的肿瘤抑制功能是什么？单基因是如何影响那么多不同的生物途径的？

12.3 Are all carcinogens mutagens? Are all mutagens carcinogens? Explain why or why not.

12.3 所有的致癌物都是诱变剂吗？所有的诱变剂都是致癌物吗？解释一下为什么是或为什么不是？

12.4 Imagine that a laboratory reports that feeding a chocolate to laboratory rats increases the incidence of cancer. What other details would you want to know before you stopped eating chocolate?

12.4 设想有一份用巧克力饲养实验小鼠来提高癌症发生率的实验报告。在你停止喂食巧克力之前你还想知道哪些其他的细节？

12.5 Do all women with HPV get cancer? Why or why not? Do all women with mutations in *BRCA1* get cancer? Why or why not?

12.5 所有携带人乳头状瘤病毒的女性都会得癌症吗？为什么会或为什么不会？所有携带乳腺癌易感基因突变的女性都会得癌症吗？为什么会或为什么不会？

主要参考文献（Main References）

本杰明·卢因. 2005. 基因Ⅷ. 余龙，江松敏，赵寿元译. 北京：科学出版社

戴灼华，王亚馥，粟翼玟. 2008. 遗传学. 2 版. 北京：高等教育出版社

李学宝，董妍玲. 2011. 遗传学教程. 北京：科学出版社

刘庆昌. 2007. 遗传学. 北京：科学出版社

赵寿元，乔守怡. 2001. 现代遗传学. 北京：高等教育出版社

Anthony J F G, Susan W, Sean B C, et al. 2012. Introduction to Genetic Analysis. 10th ed. USA, New York: W. H. Freeman

Daniel L H, Elizabeth W J. 1998. Genetics: Principles and Analysis. 4th ed. USA, MA, Sudbury:Jones and Bartlett Publishers

Hugh F, Ivor H, Paul W. 2010. 遗传学. 3 版. 张博等译. 北京：科学出版社

John R. 2004. Fundamental Genetics. UK, Cambrige:Cambrige University Press

Leland H H, Leroy H, Michael L G, et al. 2011. Genetics: From Genes to Genomes. 4th ed. USA,IL, Burr Ridge: McGraw-Hill Higher Education

Snustad D P, Michael J S. 2008. Principles of Genetics. 5th ed. USA, NJ, Hoboken: John Wiley & Sons, Inc.

William S K, Michael R C, Charlotte A S, et al. 2009. Essentials of Genetics. 7th ed. USA，CA, San Francisco:Benjamin Cummings